Ann Oakley

is Professor of Sociology and
University and Director of the S
at the Institute of Education.

Her previous books include *The Sociology of Housework*,
which helped to establish housework as a legitimate area of
study; *From Here to Maternity*, which charts women's
expreience of first-time motherhood; *The Captured Womb*, a
history of medical care for pregnant women; *Taking It Like a
Woman*, an autobiography; and five novels, the bestselling
The Men's Room (adapted into a major BBC TV drama
series), *Matilda's Mistake*, *The Secret Lives of Eleanor
Jenkinson*, *Scenes Originating in the Garden of Eden* and *A
Proper Holiday*. Her most recent books are *Social Support
and Motherhood* and *Essays on Women, Medicine and Health*.

Ann Oakley is the mother of three adult children, and a
grandmother. She lives in London.

BY THE SAME AUTHOR

Fiction
The Men's Room
Matilda's Mistake
The Secret Lives of Eleanor Jenkinson
Scenes Originating in the Garden of Eden
A Proper Holiday

Non-fiction
Sex, Gender and Society
The Sociology of Housework
Housewife
Becoming a Mother
Women Confined
Subject Women
The Captured Womb
Taking it Like a Woman
Social Support and Motherhood
Essays on Women, Medicine and Health

ANN OAKLEY

Man and Wife

Richard and Kay Titmuss:
My Parents' Early Years

Flamingo
An Imprint of HarperCollins*Publishers*

Flamingo
An Imprint of HarperCollins*Publishers*
77–85 Fulham Palace Road,
Hammersmith, London W6 8JB

Published by Flamingo 1997
9 8 7 6 5 4 3 2 1

First published in Great Britain by
HarperCollins*Publishers* 1996

Author photograph by Caroline Forbes

ISBN 0 00 655013 4

Set in Linotron Galliard by
Rowland Phototypesetting Ltd,
Bury St Edmunds, Suffolk

Printed and bound in Great Britain by
Caledonian International Book Manufacturing Ltd, Glasgow

For Richard and Kay Titmuss's grandchildren
Adam, Emily and Laura

'Do not allow public issues as they are officially formulated or troubles as they are privately felt, to determine the problems that you take up for study ... Know that many personal troubles ... must be understood in terms of public issues – and in terms of the problems of history-making. Know that the human meaning of public issues must be revealed by relating them to personal troubles – and to the problems of the individual life.'

C. Wright Mills,
The Sociological Imagination, p. 226

'Gender is a social system that divides power. It is therefore a political system.'

C. A. MacKinnon,
Towards a Feminist Theory of the State, p. 160

CONTENTS

ACKNOWLEDGEMENTS

To write this book with help was difficult enough; writing it without help would have been impossible. There are many people I want to thank. For his unflagging detective work and thoughtful analysis of all sorts of loose ends I must thank James Thomas, who spent a considerable amount of time in libraries on my behalf. My daughter Emily transcribed many of the letters on which the book draws, and also undertook much heroic classification of other material. Without the rigorous historical perspective of Jay Winter, I would have been lost, and the final framework of the book (which went through many drafts) owes much to his insights. Others who provided invaluable comments were: Karen Dunnell, Sally Hunt, Juliet Mitchell, Robin Oakley, Hilary Rose and Susan Williams. I am grateful to Berry Mayall who went through the book with the magnifying glass of an ex-English teacher. Two people who were intimately associated with my parents' history, Jerry and Galia Morris, performed a task of great symbolic, as well as practical, importance in reading it from the perspective of people who were there at the time. Brian Abel-Smith allowed it to distract him from more urgent work, and the conversations I had with him about my parents have been informative in a way that no-one else's could be. A different perspective was provided by Frank Honigsbaum, who worked with my father on the history of British medicine; and by conversations with Dennis Kavanagh on the topic of political biography. Finally, and as always, I thank Sandra Stone for the 'people work' involved in providing a finished manuscript, and my colleagues in the Social Science Research Unit at the University of London Institute of Education for many stimulating discussions.

As the saying goes, none of these people is responsible for the final product.

Note on the transcription of letters

Three chapters of this book consist largely of letters, and others are quoted in different chapters. The following devices have been used in reproducing these: [...] indicates material that has been omitted (usually in order to aid readability, rather than for any other reason), [?] a word whose meaning is obscure, and * an illegible word or words. The superscript 'e' by the date at the top of the letter signals an estimated date (judged from the content of letters with dates missing). Otherwise, the letters are printed as in the original – with abbreviations, ampersands and other conventions used by their authors, though usually without the greetings inscribed at the beginning and the end.

ONE

Opening the Suitcase

No facts 'speak for themselves', but it is from the 'facts' that we must start. When she died, my mother left me a brown leather suitcase full of papers about her and my father's lives: 'That's for you, one day,' she used to say, pointing to the suitcase, which had place of honour on the floor opposite her bed in the ground-floor room she lived in, because she was partially disabled, in the last years of her life. I had no idea what was in the brown suitcase, and little curiosity about it either, until one day several weeks after her death, when I snapped open its rusty latches. Inside the lid I saw what I had once written as a child, in the neat italic handwriting taught at my very proper girls' school: my address, in that long-drawn-out child's way which begins with one's full name and expands over many lines to end with 'the Solar System, Space'. I had also prophetically added, 'If this case dares to roam, box its ears and send it home (please).' The suitcase was a carefully garnered storeroom of the past. Everything in it had been 'pruned', in my mother's gardening metaphor, though she left no clue as to what had been cut out and why. One thing was clear: what was in that suitcase was intended for me. It was meant to tell me something my mother thought I needed to know; and it was for me to make use of it however I thought best.

This book is the result. Its theme is one which underlies many twentieth-century dilemmas: the relationship between the public world of 'work', and the private world of the home and personal relationships. The phrase 'man and wife' which I have used as the book's title sums up the traditional arrangement; the two spheres of home and work have historically been identified with men and women, and in marriage the unequal separation is most clearly recognized. Many imputed biological and social differences between the

1

sexes have accompanied the rhetoric and the practice of men dominating the public sphere and women occupying the private world of the home. Many of the tasks of twentieth-century social policy in Europe and North America have involved these issues of the division between the public and the private and between men and women. Where does, or should, the role of the state begin and end? What do we do about women, whose bearing and caring resolutely continue the tradition of 'the family' in a world of modern institutions based on a different set of values? If women are not 'people' because of this, then what can be said about men, who often seem not to care for people at all?

Being based on personal papers, the narrative of the book is in one sense a deeply personal one. But the papers also tell a significant public story. My father, Richard Titmuss, was one of the 'founders' of Britain's welfare state. His work from the late 1930s onwards played a role in the development of British post-war social policy. By the end of his life, he was well known in certain academic, political and social circles and possessed an international reputation based on a lifetime's work analysing health, social and fiscal inequalities and welfarism and human rights. During the latter part of the period with which this book deals – the early 1940s – Britain seemed to be hovering on the edge of one of the most radical social policy shifts of all time. The National Health Service and the welfare state arose like a phoenix out of the ashes of the Second World War. Although the pathway to state intervention had been laid much earlier,[1] the post-war period *was* a brave new world to many. It was one with which Richard Titmuss was intimately associated. He influenced the manner in which the welfare state evolved and was understood, not only in Britain, but as a model to be emulated and improved on by other countries. The Labour Party in the 1950s, '60s, and '70s, particularly its social security and pension plans, would not have been the same without him.

As a measure of Richard Titmuss's success in the public world, over a thousand people attended the memorial service which was held after his death in 1973 in the church of St Martin-in-the-Fields in central London. Memorial speeches were made by the Right Reverend Trevor Huddleston, and by two politicians from either side of the Atlantic: ex-Secretary of State for Social Services Richard Crossman, and his North American counterpart, Wilbur Cohen, former

Secretary of the United States Department of Health, Education and Welfare. Letters of condolence to Richard's widow came from far and wide, including from Sir Keith Joseph, MPs Shirley Williams and Michael Meacher, Queen Margrethe of Denmark, the Prime Minister of Mauritius and President Julius Nyerere of Tanzania. The obituaries which appeared in the newspapers recorded Richard's achievements in glowing terms: 'Richard Titmuss: a great socialist';[2] 'Professor R. Titmuss: an outstanding social administrator';[3] 'Richard Titmuss – social pioneer';[4] 'Titmuss – teacher and thinker'.[5] He was described as 'the most original and most sensitive of post-war socialist thinkers',[6] as 'the unchallenged leader of socialist thinking on welfare in this country',[7] and as 'a teacher revered by an extraordinary range of politicians, academics and students, and a thinker whose ideas, far ahead of their time, have progressively become part of the conventional wisdom'.[8] Many commentators mentioned the inseparability of his achievements from his wife's 'loving support' ('like all great men');[9] and his 'unaffected enjoyment of ordinary English life – his happy home'.[10] Indeed, such a rooting in simple family values *itself* appeared to give him the life-style of 'a great and good man'.[11] Alongside this panoply of achievement, my mother Kathleen ('Kay')[12] Titmuss's own claim to fame was that she could be considered part of it: she was the helpmate wife – intellectual and social companion, co-traveller to international conferences and Buckingham Palace garden parties, domestic and social organizer, carer of Richard's body, clothes, house and daughter. When she met Richard she was active as a social worker in a movement to help the unemployed, and as a founder member of a professional social work organization. But the story of their relationship is also the story of her retirement from this public activity. 'There's only one thing I regret,' she said to me after Richard died, 'that I wasn't Lady Titmuss.' She was referring here to the offer of a life peerage made by PM Harold Wilson, which Richard declined. In the pages of this book, there is a somewhat different story. Kay Titmuss did once have a life of her own. This meant a considerable amount to her, and continued to do so through the years of marriage. It's one reason I wanted to write the book: to show what my mother did and how she lived, to dignify not only what she might have been, but what she, 'in fact', was, to turn into words on the printed page all those declarations that she really must write a book about it all one day.

Richard Titmuss's work represented radicalism, of a kind. It was informed by a passionate belief that human beings could only fulfil their potential in a society which offered equality of opportunity for all. Underpinning his vision was a profound moral sense that an equal society would also be one based on caring and altruism; a 'good' society could not be a self-serving one, in which everyone looked after their own interests and ignored those of others. But in his analyses of the ways in which social institutions such as the education, health care and tax systems supported hierarchies of unequal power, Richard signally failed to notice the deep fissure in the vision of an equal society created by men's and women's different social experiences. It was as though for him the social divisions between men and women were different from all other social divisions. They were not about power. They were about taken-for-granted aspects of our lives which lay beyond the realm of political discourse, and which it would be almost blasphemous to mention in the same breath. Women's very importance rendered them sacred, and what was sacred could not be part of the political state. Ideas about equality were primarily ideas about men defined in traditional occupational-class terms. The welfare state was about reducing class inequality. What it might or should do about women's unequal chances compared to men's was marginal to the main agenda, if, indeed, it was there at all.

The idea that only the public sphere is the substance of 'politics' is part of the way people commonly think about the division between public and private.[13] It was the second wave of the feminist movement – from about 1968 to about 1982 – which highlighted the difference gender makes here. Much of the difficulty women have felt themselves to be in comes from their being equated with the undervalued domestic sphere, while men have the world as their oyster. But the very dichotomy of public and private is itself based on a masculinist world view. Personal relationships have no political significance only to those who deny the importance of private lives in shaping identity and moral values. The home doesn't matter much, except as a retreat from the public world, only to those who aren't responsible for it. They can turn a blind eye to the myriad ways in which homes and families teach class – that is, define for all of us our place in the social world.[14]

There's now a huge literature on the division between the public and the private. Much of this is deeply theoretical and rather unconvincing on the level of everyday experience. The starting point is the myth of the two Adams: two accounts of the social division of labour, one based in the Garden of Eden, and the other with economist Adam Smith, whose concern was production and the social control of workers rather than the temptations of Eve.[15] While the patterning of gender roles is traditionally seen as something different from the rise of various economic classes, history tells us that changes in the public world of work have in practice been associated with changes in the world of gender. For example, it is uncomfortably clear that the growth of central government and of state intervention has been accompanied in many places by the exclusion of women from public life. This hasn't been a policy – there's no simple conspiracy to blame – but more a patchwork of practices reflecting the dominance of private views about women. These remain unchallenged because they *are* private.

What women do in private is human service or 'people work', which lacks the economic and social status of paid labour. They also do the bulk of the world's caring, and in this sense modern health and welfare services rest on women's much more fundamental work in the home.[16] The domestic domain not only shapes the personal experience of people work, but provides the setting for state policies. The welfare state may lack an explicit family policy,[17] but it rests on implicit assumptions about the family being the basic social unit. Middle-class ideology may have it that in the new family men and women create themselves equal (largely by men becoming 'new' themselves), but there is very little evidence that this is happening, and plenty that in most households divisions of labour, responsibility and resources continue to put women in a position where they make up a class of their own.[18] As a class, women perform people work with all its intangible products, while men as a class expropriate women's labour.[19] Women are exploited. Because the state assumes the existence of this pattern, its own actions are essentially exploitative and patriarchal – that is, more often in men's interests than women's.

The denseness of these feminist arguments hides a simple point about how things are seen. Far from being beyond political and economic analysis, personal relationships are the very stuff of these. Nothing exists in neat compartments – policies and legislation aren't made according to a rational process by a democratically elected and representative group of citizens, while men and women and children love each other in apolitical harmony behind the closed doors of the home. There's no safe world outside politics. Everything is political – about power. The representatives who speak in parliament are mostly men, and the processes of 'democratic' selection are patterned in a systematic way against women. In the home, differences in power straddle, infuse and ignite people's bonds with one another.

The personal significance of the papers drawn on for this book thus overlaps with a more public narrative about the representation of the personal in social policy. The political failure – the undermining of the radicalism of socialist/liberal-democratic politics by a blinkered adherence to a model of unequal gender roles and relations – is also illustrated in the private sphere. How people like Richard and Kathleen Titmuss lived their lives says something about 'their' politics. It helps to explain one of the central political puzzles of our time: how and why the socially transformatory vision with which many European nations emerged from their civil war in 1945 has fizzled out to become a damp squib of post-modern post-welfarism – a story of increasing misery, acquisitiveness and social inequality. Of course there are many other factors here, but the failure of the liberal-socialist imagination to deliver what it promised is linked to the lack of any basic shift in the social fissure gender imposes; nothing much has happened because nothing much has happened to women, and vice versa. The present backlash against feminism is the latest in a tide of assaults. All of this may be because there is an unsolvable divergence between the liberation of women and the preservation of 'the' family. None the less, the refusal of liberal political thought to confront the continuing *danse macabre* of the public-private split, and the associated repetitive *pas de deux* of men and women, leaves us all gasping for air, bereft of the possibility of social transformation.

The papers in the suitcase my mother left me included family correspondence and press cuttings from my mother's childhood, a few letters from my father's early life and some from his early adulthood; memorabilia from their early life together; notebook diaries kept by my mother, and pocket diaries used by both my parents from 1939 to 1987; notebooks kept by both my parents containing thoughts, quotations, and details of money and health; a file of papers relating to my father's activities before he met my mother, and one for the social welfare work she did in the 1930s and '40s; a few documents and letters from my own childhood; notes for the lecture series my father gave when he first took up a university post; Ministry of Food ration books for 1953–4, passports and family birth, death and marriage certificates; records of my father's honorary degrees; his CBE and other medals; notebooks with the menus of meals my mother served to visitors in 1967–74; miscellaneous personal news cuttings; and invitations to a Buckingham Palace garden party and to two dinners at 10 Downing Street from Harold Wilson and Edward Heath. But the most substantial documentation in the suitcase is for the period between 1934 and 1944, the first decade of my parents' life together. There is a diary my mother kept intermittently between September 1939 and July 1948, and there are four series of letters dated between 1933 and 1946. Two of these are between my mother and her friends. Remarkably – and this says something about my mother as a historian – both sides of the correspondence are there, because she kept carbon copies of the ones she wrote.[20] The other two series of letters were written by my parents to each other – one at the beginning of the war, between September 1939 and June 1940, and the second from July to October 1944.

This book draws on the papers left in the brown suitcase, particularly the letters.[21] It tells a story, and proposes an argument about public visions and private matters. The story is a personal one about the developing relationship between Richard and Kay Titmuss and the evolution of their/her/his work in the years leading up to and during the Second World War. The argument is a general one about the framing of a liberal-democratic philosophy and political agenda against a backdrop of massive, hidden inequalities of birth and power; it uses the exemplar of Richard and Kay Titmuss's lives and work to tease out the way in which the public philosophy could, and did, ignore the private inequality, and was thus ultimately driven to failure. At the same time, the narrative of this book also shows just how, on a very simple level, there can be no abstract theory or set of values unmediated by the concrete living of everyday life.[22] In this respect, the lives of Richard and Kay Titmuss are interesting primarily for their ordinariness; along with millions of other men and women they met, and fell in love, and made their livings, and a home together, and survived, though not unscarred, the long years of the war. Their diaries and letters resemble those kept by both the rich[23] and the poor,[24] recording the everyday tribulations and triumphs of being alive then. In their living out of the public and the private, Kay and Richard Titmuss were also only one couple among many; millions of men were freed for full participation in the world outside the home through the unpaid services of women within it. He could have been any ordinary labourer, she any ordinary housewife.

But it wasn't as an ordinary housewife that my mother primarily wished to be remembered in the leavings of the brown suitcase. She did go to a garden party at Buckingham Palace once, in 1970. On that grey June day, someone took a photograph of the two of them leaving the house [Plate 1]. The neat, economical figure of Richard blazoning the red tie (emblem of socialism) subdued by the dark suit stands to one side of the pale yellow door of the house, and Kay, in front of the door, is a little fuzzy in a white suit and a navy straw hat awkwardly positioned on her head. She wore hats only on special occasions, like meeting the Queen or the PM or attending parents' days at school. The handbag in the picture is very like the one she used the day she died. Her handbags were always dark, soft leather, with a single strap and a single clasp and very little in them. The gloves were specially for the Queen. And so they stand together there, in the neatly paved front garden, which used to be grassed over and home to a variety of shrubs, but with time Kay had pruned all this to make it the kind of tidy place she felt comfortable in.

My mother treasured this day, just as she treasured all Richard's claims to fame. One of the most poignant insignia of this is the envelope in the brown suitcase which she kept because it found its way to the house in Acton despite its being addressed only to 'Professor Richard Titmuss, British expert on the welfare state, c/o Lord Mayor's Office, London'. His fame was her fame. They were one being, united in his effort to make the world a better place. The file she kept of, and about, my childhood contains none of those childish drawings and scraps of creative writing many parents save. There are only a few letters and cards. On the front of the one I made for their twenty-first wedding anniversary in 1958 was a verse from a poem, 'The Armenian Lady' by William Wordsworth:

> Wedded love with loyal Christians,
> Lady, is a mystery rare;
> Body, heart, and soul in union,
> Make one being of a pair.

Humble love in me would look for no return,
Soft as a guiding star that cheers but cannot burn.

Inside I wished them a happy anniversary and signed myself 'the product of their marriage'.

There's no doubt that this is how I thought of myself when young. I've written something about this in a sort of autobiography I published in 1984,[25] before I inherited the brown suitcase. But *this* book is not an autobiography. It is not primarily an attempt to write about myself; it is not me I am interested in: it is them, and the broad political questions their lives were shaped by and helped to shape. Of course, this is not to say that in writing the book I haven't come to a kind of understanding I lacked before: I have, and it would be extraordinary if this were not so. This understanding is the subject of a later chapter. I have chosen to discuss it only *after* telling the story that springs out of the brown suitcase. The next chapter begins with the family origins of Kathleen Miller and Richard Titmuss and their meeting in 1934. Chapters 3 and 4 describe their early work – hers in the social welfare world, his in the insurance industry, with an intensive part-time pursuit of social statistics. Chapter 5 draws on the first series of letters exchanged between Richard and Kay Titmuss, at the outbreak of the Second World War in 1939. In Chapter 6, we see the development of his work in the field of population and social medicine, and the move from insurance to a government office in Whitehall to write the social history of the war, with her role as supportive wife and secretary taking definite shape. In Chapter 8, Ann, originally Adrian, is conceived and born. In Chapters 9 and 10 the Titmusses are separated again following Ann's birth and write to each other daily about momentous world events and important personal happenings. The final chapter of the book is a comment on the presence/absence of the authorial 'I' throughout the narrative, and a summing up of what the story tells us about the broader political canvas of public policy and gender politics.

Having said that this book isn't an autobiography, I have to say it isn't strictly a biography either. It isn't a book about my father's life and work, nor is it one about my mother's. In disclaiming its biographical intentions, I use the word 'biography' in the sense Virginia Woolf meant when she described the subjects of Victorian political biographies as always 'noble, upright, chaste, severe'.[26] Such biographies are hagiographies, reciting a creed about how selves are created and what they mean which may have very little to do with the texture of either the public or the private experience. I could have written a biography of my father – some relatively straightforward account, like, for example, Joan Fisher Box's meticulously drawn portrait of her scientist father, R. A. Fisher,[27] which begins with the disclaimer that being a daughter doesn't necessarily disqualify one from being one's father's biographer; nor does it, but distancing may not be the proper object. I could have written the kind of biography wives write about their husbands, such as the relatively lifeless *Bernard Bosanquet: A short account of his life* by his widow, Helen,[28] or the considerably franker life of socialist historian G. D. H. Cole by Margaret Cole.[29] Margaret had a public life of her own, which Helen did not, and this may have something to do with it. But a biography of my father by me would have meant omitting my mother, except in a subsidiary role; and this, in turn, would have signalled my acceptance of that very *problematic* of the public and the private which is the argument of this book.

The book is about my parents' *relationship*. A relationship involves the cultural synchronicity of both living *and* working. It includes activities, thoughts, feelings, and in spheres usually thought of as both private *and* public. But for this reason, the chapters that follow do include a relatively comprehensive account of Richard Titmuss's own intellectual and social development in the decade up to the end of the Second World War. His work was done in the context of their relationship, as was hers. The relationship informed the work, and the work affected the relationship. Their lives were lived in parallel, which means a gap as well as a similarity in the two sets of experiences. During the period the book covers, it's no accident that Kay Titmuss disappears as a public figure. She wasn't alone in this, either. Women's disappearance within marriage reflects the uncomfortable fact that marriage is a primary political experience. Like all relationships but more than some, it's about power. The vision that triumphs within marriage is the one with most power, and power is most easily derived from an accessible source such as a widely held paradigm about the way men and women ought to be with one another.[30]

Kathleen Caston Titmuss, née Miller, died in 1987, and Richard Morris Titmuss, né the same, died in 1973. No one has attempted a biography of either Kathleen Miller or Kay Titmuss, but there have been several versions of the framework of Richard Titmuss's life.[31] All of these draw on the intelligent but brief memoir by Margaret Gowing, commissioned by the British Academy.[32] Margaret Gowing worked with Richard on the history of the Second World War whose origin is described later in this book; her memoir of Richard used some of the private papers that came into my possession when my parents died, as well as being directly informed by conversations with my mother. The Gowing memoir describes Richard's early life as culturally, financially and educationally impoverished, and outlines his apparently meteoric rise to a position of some social and political influence, aided by his alliance with my mother, though impeded by his own, who, following her premature widowhood, depended on Richard for financial and emotional support. The story is of Richard's emergence from poor farmer's son and uneducated insurance clerk to innovative social historian, liberal thinker, pioneer professor (the first in Britain to have become one with no formal academic qualifications at all), and ideologue of Britain's welfare state. Richard is the active one – the energized emerger from obscure unhelpful origins to flights of international fame and fancy – and Kay Titmuss's role is that of devoted helper and dutiful wife. It was a perfect division of labour – exactly what families exist for. The narrative of the story is its rhetoric; whether it's true or not is less important than the ideological meaning it transmits.

This is how the economist and peer John Vaizey described getting to know Kay and Richard Titmuss in the 1950s:

> Brian Abel-Smith[33] and I usually went to Acton together, first to coffee, then to supper, then to dinner. We got to know the family: a small daughter, later an attractive girl, to whom Richard was devoted; Mrs Titmuss, at first rather stern but later amusing and amused; the rather tiresome figure of the older Mrs Titmuss. Richard sat characteristically in a low chair, smoking heavily, the floor covered with piles of papers [. . .] his shoulders hunched, his long legs curled under him, his eyes behind their glasses, deep-brown, almost hypnotic, and his carefully enunciating voice [. . .]
>
> It isn't possible to consider Richard Titmuss's influence without putting his extreme courtesy and charm, and his personal happiness at the centre of the picture. When I talk

11

of the Titmuss myth, it was built on this personal charm, this personal achievement.[34]

Vaizey's own rendition is critical of Richard Titmuss's real influence, of the underlying originality and veracity of some of his ideas. My mother carefully annotated Vaizey's critical portrait in pencil in the margins: 'rubbish!', 'no!' or just '!'. As Margaret Gowing said, 'Looking after Richard was her life work.'[35] Whether Richard was alive or dead made little difference. Almost the whole of her energy and passion was brought to bear on the task of supporting the idea of her husband as a great man. On the view he held of her as a woman, the documentary records are mostly silent.

While this book is *not* autobiography, part of getting older is wanting to know more about where one came from. Little children are renowned for asking whether they will become babies again. The linearity of growth is a concept that has to be learnt. As one grows up, so also can one grow down. Children may have it right; the old can be like babies – incontinent, incoherent, dribbling from both ends; dependent, living in a present which cannot be organized by a clearly remembered past and so tends to be disorganized by a chaotically remembered one. We need the past to make sense of the present. Or, rather, a present which is made sense of by the past is a different kind of present from any other.

Ageing affects the relationships between past, present and future. When you're a child, the past and the condition of being parented feel the same. To become one's own person an understanding must be developed of living in a different time zone from one's parents. The future can't be limited by the past, or even by the present with all its fun and wrongdoings. This is one reason why young people sometimes engage in deleterious habits, such as smoking and drug-taking. The deleteriousness of the habits is chiefly confined to the future, which isn't meaningfully related to the present.[36] What adults say, like what the eye can't see, the heart has no business grieving over.

And then – and then one is an adult. In the old phrase, one 'comes of age'. But what is the age one comes into or becomes part of? My mother used to read me a poem by Walter de la Mare, which carried some dark message about children getting stuck in the past:

Do diddle di do,
Poor Jim Jay
Got stuck fast
In Yesterday.
Squinting he was,
On cross-legs bent,
Never heeding
The wind was spent [. . .][37]

I had a mental image of a young man crying in a vortex of wind and lashing rain, strapped to the mast of a boat which sailed on a timeless sea with no land in sight against a timeless, featureless sky. It was very frightening. Part of it was that Jim Jay himself was crying, and I knew even then that for a young man to cry was a true mark of danger, of the cultural order of hard masculinity and soft femininity itself breaking down. But most terrifying of all was the possibility that as a becoming-adult, an idea I had then begun to grasp, one might be caught like Jim Jay inexorably between past and future in a horrible present where the forces of both lash one to the masthead of an incurable distress. Distress about what? In his record of his own English country childhood, Ronald Fraser talks, not of how one must examine and exorcise painful memories, but of the need to reach a 'fundamental understanding' which gives meaning to all memories, whether painful or not. Without such meaning, one is condemned to navigate on 'flatlands like a ship on a fog-bound sea'.[38]

Adults negotiate an identity for themselves between the forces of past and future, and that is what Poor Jim Jay couldn't do. There is the past – the world's past, and the past of one's childhood – and there is a future towards which one strives. In Marcel Proust's famous *petites madeleines* scene, when his mother gives him hot tea and little cakes to revive him from a cold adult tiredness, the most striking thing is not the way the tea-soaked cake brings childhood memories flooding back – of the taste of Aunt Leonie's own tea-dipped *madeleines* on Sunday mornings in Combray as a child – but the coalescence of those memories with the sense of firm, non-contingent personal identity now: 'this essence was not in me, it *was* me'.[39] When being oneself seems to flow from an 'unremembered state',[40] the dependence of the present on the future and the past is sharply underlined.

Thinking about identity and personal history involves questions of

13

gender again. The first problem is that men and women think about their mothers and fathers differently. It's a well-known fact about women who make it in a man's world that they're likely to have been closer to their fathers than their mothers. This emerges in research studies, but also in the way women speak and write of their parents: detective writer Agatha Christie's attribution of her happy childhood largely to her father;[41] or writer Marya Mannes's claim that she grew up without any sense of fixed gender roles – a claim which nestles uneasily alongside her poignant account of how she and her mother and cat would sit day after day at the corner window of their New York apartment watching for her father's emergence from the subway.[42] When Germaine Greer set out to find her father, she didn't begin by asking her mother about him: 'Suffice it to say that for Mother language is a weapon rather than a means of communication.'[43] In any case, she wanted to find her own father rather than her mother's husband. Then, having discovered suave ex-choral scholar and soldier Reg Greer to be in reality Robert King, the illegitimate son of a farm-labouring family with no education or soldiering experience to speak of, the saddest scene of all in Germaine's book is when she resists her mother's pleas not to publish the true story on the grounds that she's had a large publishing advance to check out her father's phoney story.

Many biographies by daughters about mothers aren't flattering. The most straightforwardly damning are those of the Hollywood variety – daughter of superstar tells the truth at last. The adopted daughter of Joan Crawford tells spine-chilling tales about how she and her brother were beaten, tied down and otherwise abused during their mother's enormous rages.[44] It seems to be particularly hard for daughters when their mothers have been the unconventional ones. Kim Chernin's mother, Rose, emigrated to America in 1941 from a small Jewish settlement in Russia, joined the American Communist Party, worked tirelessly for the Party during her daughter's childhood, and then spent six months in jail during the McCarthy era. To the daughter, the mother who came out of jail wasn't the mother who went in, but the mother who went in never would have done so if she'd been a good mother in the first place.[45]

Identity is a masculine concept. The idea that we have clear, separate, knowable personal identities is embedded in the mythology we inherit, part of the cultural code learnt by children, a cause of the fear of growing up which many children feel - the dreadful anticipation of having eventually to get by without one's parents and *be* a separate person knowledgeable about, and responsible for, one's own identity. Studies of how women think and feel show that on the whole their thinking and feeling are characterized by different patterns from those of men.[46] First of all, the logic of the division between subjective and objective tends to elude them: there is no objectivity that isn't someone else's subjectivity. Secondly, women's thinking is mediated by everyday living rather than by abstract principles. I cannot know who I am by thinking about it – Descartes' *cogito ergo sum*, Thoreau looking into his pond or Proust in bed in his sound-proof room, except that Proust relived rather than just thought about the sources of his own arguably feminine self (and in this remembering experienced both the timelessness of living in the present and the fluidity of the boundaries of the self). Men's and women's different voices mean that men often speak 'as if they were not living in relation with others – as if they were autonomous or self-governing, free to speak and move as they please', while women tend to speak of themselves 'as living in connection with others'.[47] Nothing exists apart from the way it is experienced through living a real, everyday life which consists of these connections. But the *idea* of masculinity sets up an opposition to daily life, through which identity is achieved, as some kind of supra-domestic transcendence:

> Masculinity must be attained by means of opposition to the concrete world of daily life, by escaping from contact with the female world of the household into the masculine world of public life. This experience of two worlds, one valuable, if abstract and deeply unattainable, the other useless and demeaning, if concrete and necessary, lies at the heart of a series of dualisms – abstract/concrete, mind/body, culture/nature, ideal/real, stasis/change.[48]

Women are also hoisted on the petard of men's worship of the concept of personal identity: their experience tells them they cannot give up their sensitivity to other people's needs in order to find out what their own are, but the quest for liberation has made this identification of the personal the quintessence of what freedom means, as though being free is only to be an atom spinning round and round on itself in the black thrashing vortex of Poor Jim Jay's yesterday. If freedom is gendered, so are bodies and one's relationship to them, and thus to time itself. Women's bodies arbitrate a different notion of time from the 'clock-time' of capitalist labour. To bleed cyclically, to give birth, to give nourishment with one's body in rhythms not determined by the clock or by the social relations of publicly organized and approved labour, is to relate differently both to artificial and to natural time. Women aren't timeless, but the time(s) of women's lives are simply different from those of men.[49]

And all of this is particular to the 'dominant' culture. For example, studies of young people growing up in Europe today show that separation from the family into some wonderfully autonomous sense of self is not the way teenagers and adults from 'other', 'minority' cultures think about the whole business. Growing up, one is still part of the same family, one's identity continues to be held there like the free movement of the fly with its wings forever caught in the warm colour of the amber: safe because contained; enclosed and therefore whole.[50] But even more fundamentally, human thinking about time is cast in a particular mould of linearity and cause-and-effect relationships that doesn't capture the behaviour of matter in the real, i.e. natural world. Matter, particles of matter, are involved in dynamic patterns of activity. 'They can, in fact, only be observed in terms of their patterned energy interconnectedness. At this level of reality there are no things, signals or causal connections. There are no dancers, only the dance.'[51]

Even people who don't think families are important may get more interested in them as they grow older. This is partly a function of the changing relationships between past, present and future. The moment when one realizes that *most* of one's life is over is a significant one. The problem is that we live in and through time but want to be timeless. The more we live in the present, and thereby give ourselves up to the joyful experience of being alive, the more painful the knowledge becomes that we are only part of the unstoppable march of time, which will swallow us all in its big black hole or strap us to its straining mast like the lachrymose young man of Walter de la Mare's poem.

There's another poem by Walter de la Mare I remember my mother reading to me. The poem, called 'Miss T', which is what I was then, was a joke, for this reason. It suggested that whatever Miss T ate turned into Miss T, including porridge and apples, mince, muffins and mutton, and all sorts of other not very delicious things.[52] I interpreted the poem the wrong way round. I believed that I should have to be careful what I ate in case I turned into it. When I grew older, 'Miss T' seemed more threateningly symbolic: it provided a metaphor for the socialization of children by parents, for my own learning to be an adult in my mother and father's house. For I would become what they told me to be; and what they told me to be would be some kind of extension of themselves. I would be a sponge, soaking it all up, only to go off somewhere and drip on other sponges in turn.

There's no such thing as 'the truth'. 'The truth', like 'the family', is a convenient myth, a misleading assumption, a false trail leading nowhere and everywhere at the same time. Had I had brothers or sisters, their truth would have been different from mine. But there are certain events which did happen. My parents did meet, they did marry, they did love one another; my father did get the CBE, they did go to Buckingham Palace, they did live in the house with the pale yellow door, they did write a lot of letters to each other. All of these statements can be proved by the icon of documentary evidence: photographs, papers, certificates, lumps of metal cradled in white velvet- and satin-lined boxes. It really is pointless to dispute them. It's what was not recorded, those experiences that exist only as auto-biography, and not in any other material form, that are disputable. And it is also the relationship between the archives and the memories – the question of interpretation: what does it all mean?

To list the contents of the brown suitcase my mother left me is to identify the absences as well as the presences – the things that aren't there, as well as those that are. My mother was a most parsi-monious person. As people get more like themselves with age, so she practised the art of reduction – 'pruning' – with increasing vigour as she got older. She'd always had a preference for uncluttered rooms – for rooms with white pictureless walls, plain carpets, muted tones, plain, white-painted or polished furniture, no mess anywhere. It was the same in the garden: lawns marked by weeds were anathema, her favourite plants had neatly rounded shapes patterned on the spherical tidyness of hydrangeas – their colours bleached by the fumes of the traffic that sped down the busy West London road where we lived – and she could be horribly ruthless with the secateurs in every season. Inside the house, she had the doors boarded over and painted white so there were no crevices for the dust to collect in, and she had the Edwardian mahogany banisters going up the stairs boarded in too, and painted white, with a black-painted hand-rail, so that the passing of hands over it wouldn't show. On the top floor of the house there was an attic which was entered by a door, an ordinary door, placed two metres up the wall, so you needed a ladder to get in, and she even had this flat-fronted and painted to match the white walls around it. As my father earned more money, so more and more boarding and covering up seemed to go on. Whether this was to my father's taste, I don't know. Did they discuss how to treat the stairs, or the doors, or what type of net curtain (plain white, of course) to hang at the windows? They may have done, but I think my mother's sanitization was part of the division of labour between them. The house was her domain, a place where he entered, put his slippers on, and sat down to an already laid table, with its seersucker cloth and plain white plates, to tell his stories of the outside world and have them listened to, as I listened to the stars beaming down like a stimulant to keep me on edge and awake. Because most men who live with women don't organize their own domestic spaces, it's impossible to know how they would choose to live on their own. If you can tell a lot about a man from the woman he lives with, it's the physical artefacts and arrangements of the home that are the clue to her character.

But what is most striking at first are not the absences in the leavings of the brown suitcase, but the puzzle of what the presences themselves mean. What is the meaning of the photograph of the young man, signed 'Yours sincerely, Bill'? Why the notes of meals given to visitors? While some things – postcards sent to my mother as a young child by her father on his business travels, for instance – are probably almost a random sample of the total that once existed, other items – such as the two letters from my father's mother to him – have clearly been preserved using some other criterion of selection. The presences are related to the absences. How can one judge the meaning of what was saved for the suitcase without knowing what wasn't? Sometimes there are clues. There was a paper shortage during the war, and some of my mother's letters to my father were written on the backs of other letters written to her which she chose not to preserve. But there's almost nothing from my mother's own childhood there; no note, even, of the formal schooling she received. I know she did a secretarial course later, because she told me. Without this, the letters and the papers wouldn't be nearly as readable as they are (though her shorthand comments on some of them needed some deciphering). There's a copy of my father's school magazine, but not one of hers. There's little indication, apart from letters written to my father when he was abroad or to me, of what she had been doing aside from the work of home-making after the end of the war. Some of these silences may be real, others not. My mother didn't have a paid job outside the home after 1940, but there must have been hundreds of letters she destroyed, and some of these may tell different stories from the ones she kept.

In the suitcase is a little brown leather notebook, soft like my mother's handbags. It measure some six by eight centimetres, and has a tiny leather strap still hanging on by a few threads. The notebook is seventy-four years old: she started it in January 1920, when she was aged seventeen. The first entry is a poem by William Blake about a piper in a valley who, when asked to lay down his pipe and write a book instead, simply vanished. The last dated entry is a quotation from a book review in the *New Statesman* for 22 October 1938. The book was *The Maturing Mind* by T. H. Pear, and the reviewer noted approvingly that it addressed an important question: 'Why bother to learn after you are 25 years old?' (The answer is that you won't become mature unless you go on learning.) The notebook's jottings show my mother to be mystically and nationalistically inclined: Blake features several times, along with G. K. Chesterton, Kipling, Carlyle and Archdeacon Wilberforce Burns, and there are many references to God. For a seventeen-year-old, the choice of extracts is sophisticated and eclectic, and includes several quotations in Latin. It's hard to judge exactly what her interests and philosophy were, but some extracts seem particularly telling in the light of her life to come. For example, this verse (author not given):

> Do what you can, being what you are
> Shine like a glow-worm if you cannot like a star
> Work like a pulley, if you cannot be a crane;
> Be a wheel greaser, if you cannot drive a train.

Or Blake again, a poem entitled 'Freedom and Captivity':

> Love to faults is always blind
> Always to joy inclined

Lawless, winged, unconfined,
And breaks all chains from every mind.

She was searching for something, or someone, to believe in. Like many teenage girls, she was anticipating the salvation, release and safe confines of love. There are signs of incipient concern with social injustice and inequality (though an interest in eugenics, too: Kipling's 1923 verse, 'There is one lesson at all Times and Places – /One changeless Truth on all things changing writ,/For boys and girls, men, women, nations, races – /Be fit – be fit!') The quest for answers is interrupted by a few moments of hesitation – Carlyle: 'If there is a black spot in our sunshine it is very often the shadow of ourselves.' But it's also broken by humour:

> I'm very sorry for
> A cow
> Its clothes seem fashioned
> Anyhow
> They never look as if they fit
> I wonder what is wrong with it.
> And if a cow should need
> A patch
> It never chooses one
> To match
> But makes the oddest pieces
> Do
> I think it's rather sad
> Don't you?

This ditty came from the September 1928 issue of *Punch*, a magazine regularly taken in the household in which my mother grew up.

Half of the notebook is empty. After the last entry, made a year following her marriage, there is nothing. Does it matter that there is nothing? Could the half-empty (half-full) notebook merely mark the passing of Miss Kathleen Miller's life into its next phase as Mrs Richard Titmuss? Was not this next phase everything that Miss Miller had dreamed of in the half-empty, half-full notebook's pages: love, work, a purpose, bettering the welfare of others? What could possibly have been better than what actually happened to her?

TWO

——❊——

'K' and 'Dick'

They're all dead now, the people who could answer questions about who Kathleen Miller and Richard Titmuss were in the beginning. Kay's father died in 1951, her mother in 1956, her only sibling, Donald, in 1988, and Donald's wife, Constance Muriel, in 1992. Donald and Muriel's only child, Andrew, my cousin, died in 1993, early, from cancer; Andrew was the kin-keeper in the family, and a few months before he died he sent me two computer disks containing his (Kay's) side of the family history, using a specialist software programme for recording such things called 'Brother's Keeper'. The other human kin-keeper is Robin Oakley, the father of my own children, Kathleen and Richard's son-in-law, who bought a dark red stiff-sided notebook in 1966 and started to write down the family history using those little circles and triangles beloved of anthropologists. On Richard's side, the deaths go like this: his father 1926, his mother 1972, little sister Barbara (aged three) in 1917, sister Gwendoline 1971, brother Harold 1980, Harold's wife 'Aunt Blue' in 1993. Richard's birth on 16 October 1907 was recorded in Luton. Kay's on 20 January 1903 happened at home, 65 Bradgate Road, Catford, in South London. Her mother's name was given as Katie Louise Miller, formerly Caston. Kathleen was called Kathleen Caston Miller after Katie.

That's where it all starts: in Luton and Lewisham. The Titmusses were a Luton farming family, with the name derived from that small bird, the Titmouse. According to the local telephone directory, there are still Titmusses farming there: G. J. W. Titmuss, corn-merchants in Wheathampstead; J. W. Titmus at a farm in St Ippolyts. Walter Titmuss from Almshoebury, a cousin of Richard's, died in 1979 leaving nearly half a million pounds. Richard Titmuss's own father,

21

Morris, was born in Stevenage, and worked Lane Farm in Stopsley, Bedfordshire until 1918, when the farm was broken up under Lloyd George's scheme for giving land to soldiers returning from the war. Little is known about Morris Titmuss, save for his parents' names – Herbert, a corn-dealer and farmer, and a woman called Mary Ann Campkin – and the dates of his birth and early death at fifty-three, which was said to be due to the disappointment of being deprived of farming and his subsequent incapacities as a small businessman. In 1918, the family moved to Hendon in North London, where Morris started a haulage business which rapidly went bankrupt. He is also said to have been an enthusiastic drinker. It must have been a hard time for the family, with the loss of the farm superimposed on little Barbara's death in 1917 (from maternal neglect, my father used to say).

Richard's mother, Maude Louise Farr, also came from a farming family. Her father, Robert ('Hoppy') Farr, was a farmer of property. When Hoppy died in 1914, his coffin was conveyed by ploughmen on a waggon decorated with evergreens across the countryside from the family farm at Mangrove Hall to the church at Lilley, followed by many carriages full of farm workers, friends and relatives.[1] The Farrs have been traced back to a marriage between 'Willhelmi' Farr and Tryphaine Newman in 1590 at Stevenage; most of them were either farmers or millers, but the esssayist Charles Lamb appears on the left-hand side of the family tree as a relative of 'Hoppy' Farr's ancestors, and another branch of the family, the Brutons, is mentioned in Charles Lamb's *The Essays of Elia*. 'Elia' was Lamb's pseudonym for a series of contributions he wrote for *The London Magazine* beginning in 1820. One, called 'Mackery End, in Hertfordshire', describes a visit to 'that fine corn country' with its 'yeoman' farming families, including the Brutons, 'a comely brood [. . .] Six of them, females, were noted the handsomest young women in the county.'[2] Maude Farr was one of eight surviving children, four girls and four boys. Robert Farr was an autocratic father – his wife, Margaret Lines, came from another long-established farming family – who brought his girls up to be dutiful daughters and idle ladies. The plan didn't really work: Ella married Bert Halliday, who became manager of the Palladium theatre – Bert had many mistresses and the marriage was unhappy; Edith was impregnated in a haystack by a farm worker called Swannell and subsequently dispatched in disgrace to Brighton, where she kept herself and her daughter by working in dingy hotels; Irene, the youngest, became a high-class playgirl, had several abortions and was in and out of mental hospitals – she managed to get hold of most of the Farr capital by looking after her mother, an alcoholic, whom she housed in Cricklewood, and finished by marrying her solicitor and moving to Worthing. My father used to call her 'the Duchess'. Maude herself was said to be an intensely impractical and nervous woman – one senses that she and probably her three sisters as well would have been described as 'neurasthenic' in the medical language of the time.[3] Robert and Margaret Farr had a bad time with their boys, too, though their destiny as more solid citizens than the girls may be partly due to the fact that their father bought or rented farms for them. Charles drank and gambled, but eventually married a Norfolk barmaid called Dorothy and settled down to farming a smallholding there. For Hugh, Robert bought Parsonage Farm, Cockernhoe, and there Hugh lived with Mary, an agoraphobic who was reputed to have never left the house and to have kept her false teeth on top of the coal-scuttle. Tom and Fred (Robert Frederick) did somewhat better, becoming farmers of property, like their father. Tom farmed in Dedham with Meg, the daughter of a Scottish farmer, although unhappily their two children died in infancy. Fred married Lilian, the daughter of a veterinary surgeon, and herself the millinery buyer for a big dress shop in Westbourne Grove, London. Fred and Lilian had one son, whom they named Robert in the family tradition. Unfortunately Fred was a victim of the 1918 influenza epidemic and died aged thirty when his son was only a few months old. Despite at least two offers of marriage, Lilian managed their farm, Barton Hill, near Luton in Bedfordshire, on her own until her son was able to take it over. Barton Hill is the place from which Kay's first series of letters to Richard were exchanged in 1939–40.

Richard Titmuss's ancestry doesn't, then, seem very fortunate, studded as it is with premature male death and dissipated female lives. One wonders especially about the women, consigned to a role as idle ladies which took no account of their individual longings and abilities to be more than this. Margaret Gowing's memoir of Richard paints a picture of culturally and materially impoverished early years: 'The children lived an isolated life [. . .] he was largely self-educated.'[4] In his childhood photographs, Richard stands apart from the other children, sad and watching, though none of the children are poorly dressed and the style of their clothes and the room furnishings suggests no obvious poverty [Plate 2]. At fourteen, he was sent to a commercial college for a six-month course in book-keeping, and thereafter became an office boy in Standard Telephones, helping his father in the evenings with the business accounts. When the business collapsed and his father died leaving substantial debts, Mrs Titmuss wrote to a contact she had in the County Fire Insurance Office soliciting a proper job for her son. He was taken on as a clerk in 1926, and worked there until 1942 when released to move to the cabinet offices in Whitehall and write the social history of the Second World War.

The Gowing memoir speaks of Richard's patience with his 'poor, neurotic mother'; of how, out breadwinning for his mother and younger brother and sister, he had to come in at night and listen to his mother's daily tales of woe; of how her emotional and financial dependence on him was a problem for Richard and Kay's own developing relationship. This is my mother speaking here, for there was no love lost between the two women, both of whom wished to regard Richard as their own. On the back of the pictures of Maude Farr in the family photograph album are the words, 'The Evil One', in my mother's handwriting; the photograph reproduced as Plate 3 has written on the back, 'Before he got away'. There are two letters in the brown suitcase from Maude Titmuss to her son. The first, written in 1918 when 'Dick' was eleven and he and his younger brother Harold had been sent on a visit to relatives, is an ordinary letter from a mother to her small children urging good behaviour and reassuring them that all is well at home. The second letter was written the day Richard married in February 1937: he was twenty-nine, his mother fifty-four. In its cloying sadness, it confirms the characterization of the Gowing memoir:

My darling Richard,

It hardly seems true that you are leaving me – and none of my dreams (or our dreams) to come true. Still dearie, I realize everyone naturally wants their own home – and I trust it will be best for you. As you know I wish for nothing but your happiness – I wish it had all been different, and not so much trouble and worry involved – but it can't be altered now. Don't dearie in your new life let any ambitions or influences make you hard, remember some people in life are not so fitted as others to bear trouble and fight life's battles – it is much harder for the highly strung person to face life than the stronger ones. I should have liked Daddy to have lived – don't quite forget him. I shall think of you so much and pray for you – and hope you will for me – in all these hard days. Well darling there is more I can say – I shall miss you beyond words – especially now Gwen is not here. I hope you will still keep good friends with Harold – he has such a bad job.

My best love and every good wish for your happiness sweetheart and a big hug. Always your loving Mother, Maude L. Titmuss.[5]

You can almost hear her crying as she wrote it. She was alone in the world; she didn't want Richard to go. Perhaps she sensed she was losing him not only to another woman but to a different kind of life. Her own had given her few resources to cope as a widow on her own. All around her the storm clouds of war were gathering, and this was enough to make even the most equable person highly strung. Maude certainly regarded herself as such, and acted the part with conviction for many years after leaving the Hendon house and living with her daughter, Gwen, in nearby Mill Hill, and then in a nursing home near her darling Richard in Ealing, West London, after Gwen's death from heart disease, and until her own in 1972 at the age of eighty-nine from broncho-pneumonia and senility.

So Richard fought to escape from the constrictive clutches of his neurotic mother and then make good as a self- or Kay-made man. Kathleen Miller's family was much more conventional. Her mother, Katie Louise Caston, was the daughter of a wheelwright from Cley in Norfolk, John Randall Caston. Like the Farrs' farming tradition, the family trade was a long-established one in those parts. John Randall Caston's parents were William and Susan Caston, and William was a carpenter. A hand-carved oak chest made by a John Caston in 1663 has been handed down the family; when I was a child it stood in the hall of the house with the pale yellow door and was used as a telephone table. The telephone, black and squat, was always banished to the hall by my mother, who objected to its intrusion into domestic life. The darkness of the hall and the chest mingle with the temperature in my memory to make the whole Caston family rather a cold, unwelcoming lot. Whether this was true or not, I don't know, as the only other member I knew apart from my mother was her mother, Katie – a woman small-boned like a sparrow who only ever gave away a few breadcrumbs of emotion. But this may have been one of those generational reactions that mark family life, as Katie's mother, Katherine Mary Webb, was an Irishwoman, described as 'having a fiery temper'. Kate Webb and John Randall Caston married in Sheffield, and John earned their living by making and painting delivery wagons for a brewery. They are recorded as bearing two other children apart from Katie Louise – a son, who died aged three, and Nora. Katie and Nora were beautiful young women, with penetrating dark eyes, tiny waists, and backs as straight as boards. A photograph taken in 1910 of Katie as a young married woman shows her in a fancy high-necked brocade gown and an enormous hat with an array of gauze on top. Kay annotated the photograph thus: 'She wore this hat for a weekend in Eastbourne, and had to turn sideways to get through the door of the railway carriage.' While Katie moved to London on her marriage, her sister Nora stayed in the north. Nora's husband, Bert Buckland, was an electrical surveyor working in the coalmines. Nora and Bert lived in Wakefield, and their house is the setting for the second series of letters exchanged by my parents in the latter part of the war.

On her paternal side, Kathleen Miller was of Scottish descent. Her father, Thomas Miller, was the son of James Miller, a Scotsman who moved to Sheffield and worked in the import/export trade, despite being more interested in art than business. He took a degree at Edinburgh University and spoke French, German and Spanish fluently, using these languages as he travelled on the continent in the course of business, and taking his seven children with him, one at a time. His wife, Louisa Ward, was the daughter of a Scottish sea-captain, born on the island of Rhum and trained on the mainland as a schoolteacher.

Thomas Miller, Kathleen's father, was the eldest of James and Louisa's seven children. He became a commercial traveller for a Sheffield-based cutlery firm, touring southern England in an ambassadorial capacity, staying in the best hotels. Like his father, he spoke several languages, and had cultural interests beyond the trade at which he made his living. Unlike Richard Titmuss's aunts and uncles, Kathleen's seemed to have made something of their lives. Of Thomas's three brothers, one became a scientific inventor, writing a history of the development of Sheffield through water mills, one became an architect and emigrated to Australia, and the third was a chemist who went to South Africa just before the First World War and set up his own business there. Two of Thomas's three sisters also had professions of their own. Mary was one of the first welfare workers running the welfare department of Pilkington's steel factory in Sheffield. Louisa ran a creche for women munition factory workers during the First World War. The baby of the family, Jessie, went to live in the Peak District and became an amateur philanthropist.

You don't need to speculate much about the significance of genetic factors to see that these different family histories gave 'K' Miller and 'Dick' Titmuss – the names they used when they met – quite different sets of cultural baggage to bring to their relationship. On his side, there was a record of downward social mobility, and of failed masculinity and nervous femininity, combined with a deep attachment to the landscape of rural life – particularly the lanes and fields of Bedfordshire from which the family were driven to North London in 1918 and to which Richard insistently returned throughout the 1930s and '40s and '50s, but especially when he secreted Kay there during the war. Was Richard to be like his father or, even worse, like his mother? How could he recover the lost opportunities of his youth, pitched abruptly out of school and into earning a wage for himself at the young age of fourteen, and then later for his whole family, becoming the sole supporter of his mother from 1926 when his father died until 1972, when she did? What room was there in all of this for the development of talent, and how might it be fostered? By contrast, Kathleen Miller came from a family where the habit of individual achievement was ingrained. Even women were allowed to lead a non-domestic existence – although the traditional fields of welfare and education were preferred. It was a history of discipline, of hard work and committed productivity, of living well by the skills you plied, though not entirely without the flashes of temper and vision (the Rhum theme, and the fiery Irishwoman), nor without the traces of frustration, the many-tongued James Miller touring the continent in the 1880s and Thomas, his son, the hostelries of southern England in the early 1900s. Kathleen's mother never worked outside the home, although she toiled servantless within it for many years, and had been brought to marriage with a myth of asexual reproduction, learning the alternative, truer version from her gentle-mannered husband on their wedding night. Katie Miller's maturely careful femininity shows up in the photographs taken with her children, when her daughter, Kathleen, was fifteen [Plate 4]. Kathleen Miller and her generation were caught between the flighty flapper girls of the First World War and beyond, and the surer independence of second-wave feminism, allowed to do their own thing but only if it was the right one, and only if they lived at home and kept their consorting to the demure kind until setting up new married homes for themselves.

There's a pile of documents in the brown suitcase relating to Richard's youth, including a copy of his school magazine, the *Gregorian*, for December 1920, fronted by a photograph of the school, St Gregory's, a pleasant-looking large Victorian building surrounded by green fields – perhaps not such a bad place after all. Kay destroyed some of Richard's early diaries, and the note she left about this showed that she had searched them not only for 'serious' interests but for evidence of Richard's in her. 'His 1932–3 Diary was London Insurance Officers' Football Association' she noted; it 'contained nothing but entries on some days "chess" and "St Bride's"; 1934–5 was the same only less entries. 24/11/34 said "Bidabble". That was our weekend away but no entry on my birthday. 1935–6 was the same but fewer chess entries and on my birthday "K".' Another note she left simply said: 'Thoroughness of everything he did and the ruthlessness with himself. Sport – Football – Cricket – Chess – Music. All abandoned – Interest in football retained to end – importance of results on Sat [. . .] in five years 1934–9 Liberal Summer School. Recognition and respect. How come? I diverted drives and awakened new interests.' What is she trying to prove? That she had early on won the battle with both chess and Maude Louise?

There are exercise books filled with details of home and away matches played by Luton football team between 1921 and 1924, detailed records of Richard's chess match results from 1928 to 1938, and extracts from Mason's *Art of Chess*. There are his membership cards for the Alliance Sports Club 1931–8, and menus for two sports dinners: the Ninth Annual Dinner and Presentation of Medals and Trophies of the Hendon and District Football League and Challenge Cup Competitions on 10 May 1930 at the Old Welsh Harp Hotel in the Edgware Road, and the London Insurance Officers' Football Association Annual Dinner on 3 May 1934. At the first, they ate St Julien Soup, Fried Fillets of Plaice and Chips, Roast Lamb and Mint Sauce, Trifle or Queen Pudding and Cheddar Cheese, accompanied by a medley of songs including 'Nobody Noticed Me' and 'I Think of You', and at the second, a more up-market affair, at Gatti's restaurant in the Strand, the menu consisted of Hors d'Oeuvres Variés, Grape Fruit, Consommé Celestine, Crème Solferino, Sole Colbert, Volaille de Surrey à la Broche, Haricots Verts Provençale, Pommes Noisette, Glace Napolitaine, Gaufrette and Café, all washed down by Miss Olive Tyson, Soprano, singing 'Bird Songs of Eventide' by E. Coates and 'Garden of Happiness' by D. Wood.

Dick Titmuss compiled a collection of quotations in a hard-backed green leather notebook with an alphabetical index: E for 'economics', 'education', 'ends and means', F for 'food', P for 'poverty'. The notebook included Cyril Connolly, '[. . .] the human race is not yet old enough to manage firearms'; Plato, 'The penalty that good men pay for indifference to public affairs is to be ruled by evil men'; 'The price of liberty is eternal committees', 'Woman's place is on the sofa' (both unattributed); R. H. Tawney, '[. . .] our democracy struggles for breath in an atmosphere more sodden with a servile respect for money and position than exists in any other country in Western Europe'; a parody by 'I.F. Parry' of the well-known lullaby, 'Rock a bye baby,/On the Means Test./How the wind blows/Through your cotton vest!/Till the dole ends/The cradle's in pawn./Newspaper round you/Since you were born'; and, significantly, in view of Richard's later role in the British eugenics movement, John Stuart Mill: 'Of all the vulgar modes of escaping from the consideration of the effect of social and moral influences on the human mind, the most vulgar is that of attributing the diversities of conduct and character to inherent natural differences.' There is also a scrupulously written account of the meetings of something called 'Group Four' to which Kay appended a note during her pruning activities after Richard died: 'An attempt on the part of four friends at the County Fire Office [. . .] to add interest to the dullness and hopefully to make additional income by acting as agents for a firm of insurance brokers. Suspiciously irregular but it came to nothing.'

Kathleen Miller's childhood is represented by a series of postcards written to her by her father in 1907–9 when she was from four to six years old. They show ponies, horses, a group of toys looking at a golliwog, and a stately rural mansion, Haddon Hall, in the Wye Valley. 'My dear Kathleen, Best Love from Daddy. Kiss T. D. ["tiny Donald", her brother] for me.' 'My Dear Daughter. Just a po. as promised. Hope you are a good girl and like school again. Best love Daddy.' Thomas Miller also sent postcards to Kathleen's mother, and Kathleen kept one of these: 'My Dear Wife. I shall try to be home for tea tomorrow but am afraid it will not come off. Today the weather has been delightful. Best love I remain Tom.' After that, there's nothing apart from the little leather notebook, until a collection of typed extracts and quotations dating from the 1930s. In here are quotations from Vera Brittain's book on her visit to America, *Thrice a Stranger*, and from her *Testament of Friendship*; extracts from *My Part in a Changing World* by Mrs Pethick Lawrence, Laura Krey's *And Tell of Time*, Joanna Field/Marian Milner's *A Life of One's Own*, Sir John Simon's *English Sanitary Institutions* and R. Llewellyn's *How Green Was My Valley*; a copy of an article by Harry Roberts on 'Love, Marriage and Jealousy' in the *New Statesman* for 26 June 1937; a parody of Gray's 'Elegy in a Country Churchyard'; and a poem written by Lucy Masterman to her husband C. F. G. Masterman, which Kay has marked 'wore himself out in the Civil Service – forget his job'.[6]

This motley collection of texts must have represented something of Kay's philosophy of life as a young woman. The philosophy emanating from the texts isn't centrally about either God or politics, but one in which the *ideas* of self-sacrificial public service and of monogamous marriage are core values, existing, as it were, side by side like identical twins. From Llewellyn's sentimental story about Welsh family life, Kay took this vignette of the way a man and a woman experience life together.

My mother was watching them both, in quiet, pale, with brightness in the eyes, but not of smiles. 'Well' my father said to her, and looked at her. 'Well' my mother said to him and looked at him. In that quietness they were speaking their own language, with their eyes, and the way they stood, with what they put into the air about them, each knowing what the other was saying, and having strength one from the other, for they had been learning through forty years of being together, and their minds were one. 'Good-bye now' said my father. My mother nodded and he went.[7]

Even more telling is the quotation from Mrs Pethick Lawrence's *My Part in a Changing World*:

> Our intimate personal relationship, growing deeper every year, does not belong to the story told in this book; but during those summer months we found that identity of thought, feeling and purpose which has continued to the present day. His outstanding qualities of intellect, balanced judgement and practical administration in business and finance became the rock upon which I have built since then, the structure of my life. Even in those early days I came to realize that my work was as important to him as his own. Our engagement was the first to take place amongst those of us who for five years had carried on social work together, and now that he had come into the circle it meant a new security for that work, and a new foothold from which new developments were to arise in the future.[8]

It's the relationship between men and women which is mystical, serving as a religion of a kind. The Welsh marriage, and the Pethick Lawrences', represented an ideal the young Kathleen Miller strived after, or the one she thought she'd found with Dick Titmuss. The man is the rock, but on the rock there are also the two of them, hand in hand, doing equal work. Men take their leave of women, silently or not, and women are taken leave of.

Kathleen Miller was thirty-one when she met Dick Titmuss in the summer of 1934, and he was twenty-seven. 'I took a fortnight's holiday in August,' she wrote to her friend and 'patron' Helen Johnston,[9] 'and went on an International Tramping Tour of North Wales. It was great fun but I think the twelve other people I was with rather interfered with my impression of the beauties of North Wales. They were all strangers when we met at Chester to start the tour and I found them all so interesting that I never really got into tune with the atmosphere of the country.'[10]

And there are some of Kay's co-walkers in the photograph [Plate 5]

– four lads and five lasses lined up against a Welsh crag, Kathleen looking like a dark-eyed gypsy at the back with the low-slung bosom of the time, and Dick looking vaguely into the distance with his hands in his pockets and a cigarette hanging out of his mouth. One or other of them recorded this holiday on two typed sheets of foolscap paper. The list of characters includes: 'Dick. Publichouse Enemy No. 1', and 'K: Enigmatical. Has a facility for taking people by surprise, rather so when in drinking haunts. A determined smoker whilst swimming and in the rain. The only member fortunate enough to pack an evening dress in a mug.' The level of conversation among the group was noted to be 'good', 'ranging from Psychology to the Corporate State [. . .] it is gratifying to know that at least some of the youth of the country is thinking.'

Today people in their late twenties and early thirties would prob-ably not be described as 'youth'. Kay appears to have gone on this walking tour on her own, which must have been quite enterprising for a single woman sixty years ago. Richard wrote his first letter to Kay on 27 August that year: 'Dear "K", I rang Fulham 2736 to-day to inquire if you would like to accompany me "with a pure heart" etc to the Proms [BBC Promenade Concerts] on Thursday. A most charming voice seemed however a little uncertain as to your activities [. . .] Sincerely, Dick.'[11]

When they met, Kathleen Miller was doing social welfare work for the unemployed in West London, and Dick Titmuss was working for the County Fire Office in central London as an insurance agent. They both still lived at home – she with her parents in South London and he with his mother in North London. There's no record of the development of their relationship between his first letter in August 1934 and over a year later when Kathleen writes to her friend Helen Johnston in terms which indicate that the two of them are by now clearly understood to be a couple, though not a couple without problems:

> I am not too happy about things with Dick just now, but I expect we shall be able to adjust them [. . .] Although I am not really interested in politics, to please him and to hear him speak I attended a meeting the other night. When asked for my opinion afterwards I told him quite frankly that I loathe the bickering and back-biting that goes on in the

political world and I feel that people who are concerned in such a vital thing as the Government of a country should keep themselves above and beyond that sort of thing. I further said that I thought that if they could have the Christian Gospel in the background as an ideal and work towards that ideal a number of the present difficulties in this country and in fact the world would be more easily solved. Unfortunately, my statement seems to have upset his equilibrium altogether, and I was very concerned when he came to me after a week's deliberation and said that he felt he could not go on with his political work unless he felt he had me behind him and in sympathy with it! It's a bit of a blow to me, because although I know it is usual for a man to put the woman he loves on a sort of pedestal I had hoped that I had successfully avoided it in our case. I've tried to make him see that he should not depend on me and that it is what he thinks is right that counts in his life and activities but I'm dashed if I know really what to do about it. What do you think about it? Can't you see a shadow of that 'cramping' which you and I so deplore between men and women beginning to enter in? Do please let me have your independent opinion.[12]

Helen didn't – at least not by any letter that Kay chose to preserve. By the following March, Kay writes to Helen that she and Richard haven't yet fixed the date for their wedding, 'but we have said to ourselves that we will manage it this summer'. She was worried about money; how would they have enough to furnish even a small flat? They were both very busy – she with her welfare work, and he with the political and writing activities which had sustained him through the boredom of eleven years in insurance, and to which Kathleen, at this stage, had a distinctly sceptical attitude. Her religious beliefs clashed with his political ones: 'He is organising a meeting at Hendon which he calls a Youth protest against Rearmament, a notice of which will probably appear in *The New Statesman*,' she wrote, somewhat critically, to Helen. 'In addition he is writing a pamphlet which he hopes Victor Gollancz will publish – he had the typewriter out on Sunday and we spent the afternoon together on his "public works".'[13]

In the house in Forest Hill, South London, Kay had a small back bedroom where she kept her ebony Olivetti typewriter. She used to tell me how she and my father before their marriage would shut themselves in there and work together when her parents suspected them of doing other, more (or less?) reprehensible things. She would chuckle as she said it. But they were Richard's works, not hers. She hammered out his early political treatises on the fat little Olivetti, and his letters, and then his first book and then his second and then his third, which became 'their' book, and his fourth as well. But she was no mere factotum: she told me how, in those Forest Hill days, she taught the young Dick to write. His education and background had given him less literacy than hers. To the gauche, long-legged Dick Titmuss, fumbling to find his true place in the world from his unfortunate, though hardly menial, origins and with his lowly, boring white-collar job, it must have seemed that 'K' Miller had everything: she was, in the photographs that survive, striking in appearance, with a strong face and assertive posture, dark somewhat Chinese-looking eyes, and a regard that appeared to say I know what I'm doing, and I'm going to get what I want. In her social work job, his nascent desire to improve the common lot was being translated daily into real acts of middle-class charity. She had a solid family behind her, with two parents who evidently loved each other, and a younger brother, Donald, the apple of his mother's, if not his sister's, eye. She had considerable cultural resources, whereas he was desperately trying to piece together his own life from a small bundle of these so he could proceed on his way like his namesake Dick Whittington to make his future in a place where the streets might genuinely be paved with gold. No wonder he put her on a pedestal. But the problem for women is as much what happens when they fall off pedestals as why they're put there in the first place.

THREE

Her work and his

She was in the world he wanted to get into, and he was still at its margins. The relative positions of 'K' Miller and Dick Titmuss, when they met, are wonderfully summed up in the still life of a photograph of the Duke of Kent's visit to the centre for the unemployed in West London which Kay Miller helped to run in the 1930s [Plate 6]. There's His Royal Highness, at the centre of the photograph, hands folded and head inclined in the royal visiting pose; next to him is the strong, clear figure of Kay, with her neat rounded face and glowing eyes, wearing a dark striped suit, silk shirt and hat at a rakish angle; and then there is one of the unemployed themselves wearing a slightly less cheerful expression and also a suit, though under his regulation white apron which marks him out as one of the labourers, and he's holding a hammer and mending a shoe, or pretending to, just so there can be no mistake about it. Behind the Duke is some local dignitary in his chains, and right at the back of the photograph trying to get a look in is Dick Titmuss, taller than the others and craning his neck sideways so as to see what's going on.

Kay Miller was one of many thousands of women who from the early nineteenth century onwards added social welfare work to women's traditional caring roles. In the mid nineteenth century the main forms of help were material – money, clothes and food – but 'friendly visiting' and various community-based activities came gradually to be as important. While some of the early women welfare workers espoused high ideals of social and political reform for women, others definitely did not. Social work was regarded as par-ticularly useful for unmarried women or women without children.[1] Its pervasive association with middle- and upper-class female idleness was no incentive to develop its scientific basis. Teaching social science students in the 1920s, Barbara Wootton recalled the arrival of students 'in their cars and their pearls and their elegant clothes' with the motive of acquiring some understanding of the lives of the poor in order more successfully to set them to rights.[2] Most social workers, like Kay Miller herself, were untaught and untrained. The significance of Kay Miller-Titmuss's career as an untrained social worker was that it was the only career she ever had – that is, apart from that of Richard Titmuss's wife.

Judging from the memorabilia in the brown suitcase, Kay Miller thought about herself and her situation quite a lot as a teenager and a young woman. According to the quotation from Laura Krey's *And Tell of Time*, she found growing up and becoming independent quite a fearful thing, involving 'the hard and painful truth that every human being, facing his own destiny, has no choice except to find his own way out of grief and fear'.[3] Yet it was just this sort of thinking which inhibited happiness. When Marion Milner[4] carried out her experiment in living to find out how to be happy, she encountered many obstacles. But 'the root cause of them all was fear [. . .] there was a perpetual self-centred chatter which came between me and my surroundings, and me and myself, and till I had learnt how to silence it I was liable to live in a world of distorted make believe, cut off from any vital contact between my real need and my real circumstances'.[5] The role of fear and grief and longing and 'perpetual self-centred chatter' struck resonances in Kay Miller's life, poised as she was on the edge of getting something or rather someone – Dick Titmuss – she believed to be an essential part of her adult vision of herself.

On the back of a crookedly cut out photograph of a man who looked remarkably like the man she married, my mother wrote 'Rev. Robert Birch: The other really vital man in my life in the 1930s' [Plate 7]. The Reverend Dr Birch was the moving force behind a series of charitable ventures for the unemployed in London. He was minister of the Congregational Church in London's West Kensington, and in the early 1930s he opened his church premises to unemployed men,[6] to offer them somewhere to go and activities to keep them busy and help to protect them from the morale-lowering effects of being out of work: 'In the country a man could do some gardening or poaching, and keep himself fit in various ways; but in the towns, in spite of the efforts of various voluntary and governmental services to provide re-training or recreation, there was all too often little alternative to sheer street-corner idleness, month in and month out – often year in and year out.'[7] Kay was the Organizing Secretary of the Reverend Birch's Fulham Fellowship for the Unemployed, and afterwards its Honorary Secretary and Treasurer from 1932 until it closed down in 1940. She often talked of those years of her life as particularly significant ones. As she got older, they became more vivid, and she regretted the fact that she had never put together a record of her life during that period.

The brown suitcase contained a thick wadge of papers relating to the Fulham work, including the Minute Book of the Fellowship from 1937 to 1940, but there's no record of when Kay Miller first met Dr Birch. Indeed, there's no record of any work she did before this in the ten years since she left school, or of any other significant personal relationship. Kay must have been an attractive young woman enjoying a certain amount of freedom, chafing at the reins of middle-class life in Forest Hill and wanting to make longer journeys than the early morning 'printers' train' from central London back to her parents' home. She kept a few books from her pre-Richard life, mostly volumes of poetry and a few classic novels, on a little oak bookcase that shared a style with the two wardrobes, the chest of drawers and the dressing table which stood in all my parents' bedrooms in turn – bought, one imagines, from the scraped savings of 1937 and never replaced, being perfectly serviceable, and in themselves – in the stern solidity of their presence – intoning the very theme of marriage itself as an irrefutably joint project.

One of the books Kay kept was a volume by the Reverend Birch called *Psychology and the Individual*. She bought it originally in 1931, when she was twenty-eight, and it was probably around this time that she and Birch first met. His book drew on the principles of 'psycho-analytic' psychology in order to give guidance 'to those whose vocation brings them into intimate contact with individuals'. The book stated with simplicity some of the principles underlying the newly established 'science' of psychology, including the indivisi-bility of body and mind: 'Take away body or mind and you have no experience.'[8] Robert Sproat Birch was born in Glasgow in 1883, ordained in 1910, took two degrees at a Scottish university, spent twelve years at a pastorate in London and died there suddenly and early in 1947.[9] During his time in London, Dr Birch was an amateur counsellor, and some of Kay's work in Fulham was due to his occupation in private counselling activities.

The history of Kay's work with the unemployed captures a culture in transition between the two views of poverty, as personal fecklessness and as structural malignancy – the product of a class-ridden 'diswelfare' society. During the years of her Fulham work and her early knowledge of Dick Titmuss, Kay's own thinking moves from seeing social welfare as a form of voluntary philanthropy in which the state has no proper role, to a vision in which *only* the state must provide. In December 1930, there were two and a half million unemployed in Britain;[10] in Fulham, the site of the Reverend Birch's church, the unemployed numbered some four to five thousand.[11] Not only the level of unemployment, but the question of how the state should provide financial help, particularly for the long-term unemployed, were major public issues. In 1932, following a meeting called by the Mayor of Fulham in the town hall, Birch's work became part of the local government initiative for helping the unemployed, and the Fulham Unemployment Scheme was formally launched with £1,055 raised locally.[12] There were many private subscriptions, and local businesses were generous: the British Vacuum Cleaner Company, the Direct Supply Aerated Water Company and the Bluebell Polish Company all contributed. When the Reverend Birch's work was amalgamated with the Borough scheme, it became known as the Fulham Fellowship for the Unemployed, and was lodged in a house, 522 Fulham Road, provided free by the London County Council. A local business, the Gas Light and Coke Company (later the North Thames Gas Board), guaranteed the running expenses, and the Mayor's scheme provided a level of support of £400–£700 a year. Other funds came from the London Council for Voluntary Occupation during Unemployment (the London branch of the National Council for Social Service, set up to co-ordinate the work of voluntary bodies running centres), the Winter Distress League, the Agricultural Camps Committee, and the Personal Service League, and later on from membership fees charged at the centres themselves. The constitution of the Fellowship specified that the men would learn bootrepairing, carpentry and handicrafts, while women were offered handicrafts, cooking and sewing. Later on, discussion groups and sports were added. Membership was limited to men and women of Fulham without regular employment, and members paid threepence a week, to cover the provision of refreshments during the classes and social evenings. By September 1933, the Fulham Fellowship had grown to four centres, including a clothing centre, one for the uninsured 'blackcoated' unemployed which offered classes in Spanish, French, German, shorthand and dramatic art,[13] and one for women which had not been so successful as 'it was found extremely difficult to keep the women together as an active social group'.[14] At the end of the 1930s, it was estimated that some 1,500 such clubs existed nationally.[15]

The largest window on Kay's welfare work in Fulham is provided by a series of letters she exchanged between early 1934 and 1939 with a wealthy Scottish philanthropist. Helen Johnston was the daughter of Sir William Campbell Johnston and Lady Johnston of Edinburgh; Sir William was a solicitor, an agent of the Scottish Episcopal Church, and holder of an important local office, that of Deputy Keeper of the Signet. The Signet was the private seal of the early Scottish kings, and Writers to the Signet were those authorized to supervise its use. The formal office of Deputy Keeper and eighteen others were created in 1594. Today the main function of the Writers to the Signet Society is that of representing the legal profession and maintaining a prestigious law library in Edinburgh.[16] Helen was one of three daughters. She was unmarried, lived alone with a maid for most of her life, and occupied herself with philanthropic works and visits to London or abroad. As with Dr Birch, my mother left no record of how she met Helen Johnston, but the two would seem to have first encountered each other in late 1933 or early 1934. They kept in touch until Helen died in November 1974. Helen's letters, in neat handwriting on thick blue notepaper, are pinned to carbons of the letters Kay wrote to her. Helen's last letter was dictated to her sister shortly after Richard died in 1973; it expressed great sympathy for Kay's loss and said she would be sending a donation to War on Want in memory of Richard. Throughout my childhood Helen made regular visits to my parents' house, and I remember her as a very beautiful woman, with a straight back, sharp blue eyes, and silver hair drawn tightly back from her face in a hairstyle like my mother's, though rather neater. She spoke with a precise but lyrical Scottish accent, her manners and bearing were upright and proper, and she was always kind to me, making me a present of an unusual green mohair rug when I got married, which is still in active service more than thirty years later.

The correspondence between the two women is polite and formal at first – they call each other 'Miss Miller' and 'Miss Johnston' – but as the months and years pass, evidence of a real friendship develops. Kay goes to stay with Helen in her Edinburgh flat, and Helen with Kay in her family home in Forest Hill. It is not quite an equal friendship, however, as it is Helen Johnston who eventually agrees to pay Kay Miller's salary, and this makes Kay's continued involvement with the Fulham work possible – so when Helen's form of address has changed to 'Dear Kathleen', Kay's remains 'Miss Johnston' for a while. In their letters they exchange gardening, domestic and literary news, and discuss films they've seen and the welfare of their families, as well as homing in on the real business at hand – the welfare work in Fulham. Kay's letters are more interesting than Helen's, for, on her own admission, Helen did little and had little to write about. Because her family had money, she had no need to 'work', and she was evidently not needed to keep anyone company at home. Helen fulfilled a real role as Kay's confidante in her early troubles trying to pin Richard Titmuss down to marriage, yet at the same time she seemed to keep her distance, as if the whole business of marriage was really too much for her.

In her first letter to Kay in April 1934,[17] Helen sends foxglove roots for the Forest Hill garden, and she also forwards 'a small photograph of Rhum which I think you said was your grandmother's home'. When Kay writes to thank Helen for the foxglove roots, she describes having recently read Vera Brittain's *Testament of Youth*, which she found both vivid and courageous in its portrayal of intimacy.[18] By October, the foxgloves have rooted and bloomed well, and Kay writes to report at some length on the development of the Fulham work, including the obstructive role of the local 'labourites':

> . . . the case for the Centres we are running at Fulham grows stronger day by day [. . .] we have no difficulty in enrolling members, but we have the very present difficulty of finding money to keep the Centres open. As I think you know, funds were raised in the borough in 1932 which have kept us going up to the present time, but now we are faced with an election and the possibility of a Labour Council which will mean almost certainly that we get no support officially. The Labourites do not countenance voluntary help for those in

distress amongst them. They consider it is the function of the State to provide the necessities of life and to look after the welfare of its people, and, even if they realise that the State is not doing all it should according to their ideas they will do nothing to help. In anticipation of being cut off I have been busy making independent arrangements and have been successful in getting the employees of one of the large firms[19] to adopt one of the Centres. This means that they will all voluntarily contribute a regular weekly sum of a few pence and will hand over the money to Dr Birch and me so that we can buy the things needed by the Occupational Classes and keep the Centre cleaned, lighted and warmed. They are also arranging to send down groups of their men in the evenings to mix with the men who are out of work and we hope that by this means the unemployed will be helped to overcome the dreadful 'outcast' feeling which sooner or later gets each man down.

Another of Kay's schemes involves co-operating with a group called the Agricultural Camps Committee to send unemployed men away to the country for the summer. Some of the men get jobs there, but all of them benefit from time spent in the open air. There is a serious point to this letter of Kay's, which she leads into rather ingenuously: 'The funny part – or perhaps I should say the tragic part – is that although I know I can manage to raise enough money to keep the Centres going I can't very well ask anyone to give me money for my own salary. There is just enough in the original fund to keep me going until about November but after that Dr Birch and I don't quite know what we are going to do.'[20] The future of the unemployment scheme was threatened when the Borough funds raised in 1932 ran out. The national unemployment figures had gone down, and, although the Mayor supported a continuation of the work, sending out an appeal to 'The Citizens of Fulham' which showed that attendance at the centres was running at 480 a week, the local Labour Party was implacably opposed. They suggested that the centres had been done up with cheap labour,[21] but there were also critical issues of principle involved. These Kay mentions in her next letter to Helen, in which she reports on a meeting of the Borough Council she and Dr Birch have attended:

.... some of the new Councillors seem to be 'reds' who
want to tear down every constitution there is in England.
After a very stormy meeting at the Town Hall Dr Birch and
I were forced to the conclusion that a number of them do
not want our work to continue because we are helping to
alleviate the distress among the unemployed and make them
less discontented with their lot. They want them to be discontented so that they will soak up wild ideas and be more easily
headed for revolution. It is a ghastly state of affairs but there
it is.[22]

Kay's opposition to the left-wing line on state support for the
unemployed is a fascinating contrast to the position on the welfare
state she and Richard Titmuss later adopted as part of their 'life's
work' together. But like everything else it must be read in the context
of its time: the widespread suspicion of anything that reeked of communism; the radicalism of the Labour Party faced with the apparent
collapse of capitalism in the Depression years. Richard Titmuss himself was no Labour supporter when she met him.

New hope for the future of the Fulham work comes from the
Mayor, a 'very sympathetic' woman. The Mayor is Alice Gilliatt, an
ex-suffragette, who according to Kay's later marginal note on the
letter 'always suffered from digestive troubles as a consequence of
forced feeding in prison'.[23] Helen Johnston agrees to pay Kay's salary,
but she isn't over-generous in her response, insisting that Kay and
Dr Birch try to match her donation with local support. The LCC
have already decided to let the fellowship use the flat at the top of
522 Fulham Road for a caretaker, and the Winter Distress League
have said they will provide a salary for a man called Clarke with a
wife and four children, who later turns out to be a disaster, earning
money from other places and not declaring it, and 'borrowing' from
the petty cash. Because the Winter Distress League only pay for three
months of Clarke at a time, Kay is continually hassling them for more
support. She argues that even when the centre is closed in August,
'Parcels of clothing are continually being delivered to the house and
Mr Clarke [...] has in his charge the Collecting Boxes which are
distributed throughout the district and will require his continued
attention.'[24]

She must have become very skilled at writing begging letters. Her

letters to Helen Johnston are infused with the device of reciting
illustrative case-stories which prove the value of the work that is
being done (and which Helen is paying for): 'Did I tell you that the
woman whose letter I showed you decided to take a cookery course
instead of the weaving? She will be about three months on the Course
and then she will stand a very good chance of getting a job as a sort
of housekeeper through the Y.W.C.A. where she is training. Anyhow
the new interest has made a tremendous difference to her.' Kay has
been talking to the manageress of the local Labour Exchange about
the plight of women who are 'too old' to follow their usual occupations. 'The over 30 Association' has recently been formed in connection with the National Council for Social Service with the aim of
providing cheap accommodation and courses 'other than cookery'
to help the women find jobs.[25]

In January 1935, a Mayor's meeting is called to review the position
of the Fulham Fellowship work. In March, Kay writes to Helen of
the reluctance she and Dr Birch feel about having to co-operate with
a Labour council.[26] Kay is unwell, and is facing an operation on her
tonsils. This will mean that Dr Birch will have to take over some
of her work, but he is being 'very good' about this, despite the
fact that Kay's illness has coincided with a difficult time for him
personally:

> Did I tell you Mrs Birch has been very ill. Dr Birch took her
> up to Scotland [...] to recuperate and she is now well on
> the way to recovery but they have had a very anxious time.
> Nearly all his psychological work had to stand by for a time
> but he is now in full swing again and I have a hard job to
> keep his appointments straight. I don't think he could ever
> learn to look after them properly himself, but I feel that he
> should really not have to bother about details like that when
> his mind is occupied with bigger things and I am glad I am
> able to help him.
>
> The Mayor has managed to raise about £200 for the
> Unemployed – a little less than half of what we need [...]
> She is really getting rather tired and worn and I know she
> will not resume office next November when her year is up.
>
> Poor soul, she has had a difficult time and in the circum-
> stances I think she has done quite well.[27]

The tired Mayor had sent out another appeal to the citizens of Fulham in April: 'There are still nearly 3000 unemployed persons in the Borough and my Committee are anxious that the facilities now in existence shall continue. To make this possible I must appeal again to your generosity.' Three centres are still open: 522 Fulham Road ('Boot repairing; classes in carpentry; games and recreation; reception and distribution of boots and clothing'); the Congregational Church hall in Challenor Street ('Handicrafts, Rug and Basket Making, Musical pipe making. Classes in physical training. Sports and indoor games'); and the clerical workers' centre at Bishop Creighton House, 378 Lillie Road ('Classes in languages; shorthand and drama; practice in typewriting, etc').[28] A tear-off slip at the bottom of the letter invited people to send in their contributions.

The Fulham work has other troubles: the Winter Distress League won't pay for Clarke any more, and the LCC declines to accept any liability for a ceiling on the first floor which is falling down. It's Kay's job to sort out all these problems, as well as being Dr Birch's factotum and appointment-keeper.

In Kay's mid-June letter,[29] she tells Helen Johnston (perhaps partly in response to Helen's accounts of her own recent travels on the Orient Line to Palestine) that she feels it's time she herself visited another country. She plans to spend the first fortnight of August in Germany, walking in the Black Forest. The holiday is to be arranged by International Youth Tramps, the organization which had been responsible for Kay and Richard's first meeting in North Wales. Its object was to bring 'into contact small groups of different nationalities and provide unique facilities for combining a delightful holiday with the opportunity of exchanging ideas, thus leading towards that mutual understanding desired by all'.[30] Holidays in Germany were particularly popular. International Youth Tramps' 1936 brochure contained many seductive pictures, including of the Rhine Gorge, the Bavarian alps, and one of four young ladies in extraordinary costume bearing the legend 'German Village Maidens'. One photograph from the previous year's adventure showed a tall young man reading a map and a woman with a straw hat and a rucksack – 'photo of us from 1935 Black Forest Tour', noted my mother on the front. The two photographs that survive in the family collection show Richard by the Rhine, wonderfully relaxed with a walking stick and rumpled socks [Plate 8], and a group of Hitler's 'boys' assembled on the steps of Cologne Cathedral.

A further crisis in the Fulham work occurs in September. It concerns just who is in charge: Miss Miller or the Mayor? There's a dispute about arrangements for some of the men's classes and the organization of the clothing work. Dr Birch's letter to the Mayor about Miss Miller's unsatisfactory role, especially in relation to the Clothing Centre, gets no reply, and on 30 September he writes to the Mayor to say: 'I am sorry that I have to ask you to accept my resignation from the Executive Committee and the withdrawal of Miss Miller's services to the Scheme.' The Mayor's reply[31] expresses great regret that Dr Birch should have felt it necessary to take this step, and, 'With regard to Miss Miller's services, they have been invaluable, and I know that we shall miss her able assistance very much.' It appears that the Mayor patches this squabble up, and Dr Birch and Kay withdraw their resignations. Kay immediately launches into a major re-organization of the Clothing Centre, which has got into 'a horrible mess'. Not one to miss any opportunity for soliciting help, she says to Helen:

I suppose your friends and relations in Edinburgh have already a way of disposing of boots and shoes with which they have finished, but, if not, we would be very grateful if you could arrange for them to be sent along to us. We are just coming on to the time when the 'feet' question is going to be a very difficult one [because of the approaching winter], as to meet the demand we should have to allocate to the Clothing Centre far more than its fair share of the funds. Anything that is at all mendable is very welcome as the men repair them in the Boot repairing shop at the Centre you know.[32]

A measure of the extent of Kay's other activities at this time was her attendance once a week at Professor Joad's lectures on modern thought. Dr Suttie, the author of the well-known *Origins of Love and Hate*, whose lectures she had also heard, had died quite suddenly: 'It is a great blow to us and Dr Birch has been very upset about it. He was only 45.'

As Kay had predicted, the helpful but tired Alice Gilliatt is replaced by a new Mayor, Mr S. Vanderhook. The tone of his letters to Miss Miller after the fracas of the previous autumn is conciliatory. In

January, they have an exchange about providing a table-tennis table for the sports activities, and the need for a supply of plimsolls for the men, who currently have to perform in socks. He would consider this a legitimate use of the fund: what does Miss Miller think? Miss Miller is bristly:

> So far as the plimsolls are concerned, it seems to me that the best way out of the difficulty would be to have plimsolls available at the Centres which could be loaned to men when they were going to do P.T.[...] I have a number of pairs left from our P.T. classes last winter which are still in good condition and are available for the men now. That is the matter so far as I see it. We have no jurisdiction whatever in relation to the classes [...] and for that reason I cannot see how we are to have any financial relationship for financial relationship implies executive control.[33]

Kay has to keep detailed records of how each contribution to the work of the fellowship is spent. In February 1936, she sent the LCVO a record of what had happened to their grant for £50: £33 17s 5d had been spent on three months' salary for the supervisor of 522 Fulham Road, £3 on redecoration, £4 10s 8d on wiring and plugs for electric radiators, £6 8s 9d on new chairs, 11s 11d on curtains and £1 10s. on textbooks. Fortunately, her own salary continues to be paid by Helen Johnston, who sends a further cheque in March 1936. Kay responds with gratitude and further news about the work, including Richard's own involvement in it:

> I don't know what we would do without you. It is such a comfort to know that you are interested, for in this district it is becoming increasingly difficult to keep up people's enthusiasm for the work. The men who have been associating with the members of the Centres during the social evenings have dropped off one by one until the group is almost non-existent. However, Dick has come to the rescue and has persuaded some of his friends to come along. He, himself, is very popular with the men and they are constantly asking me 'Is Mr Titmuss coming tonight?' Of course, he can't come very often.[34]

46

The Clerical Workers' Centre is thriving, and some of its activities are particularly interesting in view of the march of world events. Lectures on the Soviet Union take place and there is one from 'a young German Lady Doctor [. . .] an ardent follower of Hitler' who is intensively questioned about events in Germany. Kay starts German classes, but there are too many interruptions. She is not short of energy for other things: 'Dick and I went to Prof. Catlin's [Vera Brittain's husband] meeting which was advertised in the New Statesman a short time ago. The place in Lupus Street in which it was held is a queer little gas lit room and there were some very strange people there. We found him very interesting but he did not keep to his subject. To my mind he is rather inclined to "lay down the law". Dick says he is sure Vera Brittain doesn't allow him to behave like that when in her company!' Was Richard referring to his own relationship with Kay? They must have been groping their way towards a mutually acceptable definition of their roles in and outside the relationship. Workwise, Kay is in great demand: she takes on the honorary secretaryship of the North West Section of the Federation of Unemployed Clubs formed by the London branch of the National Council for Social Service. She's given a voluntary worker to do the clerical work, and the Gestetner Duplicator Company makes a welcome present of a duplicating machine. 'The men' are very pleased because they want to start a magazine which Kay will now be able to type and duplicate at very little expense.

It's in this letter that Kay begins to discuss with Helen the pro-crastinations over her and Richard's wedding. There seems by now no doubt that they will marry, the question is when, and how. Kay concentrates on what was probably not the main issue – the difficulty of getting money and furniture together:

> We are both trying hard to save a little but we feel it is right that we should carry on all our various activities and without cutting out something it is very difficult. We have thought about going round the secondhand shops and trying to buy things cheaply but that of course would take a good deal of time and we cannot embark on anything of that kind until my slack time in the summer. Dick's holiday dates are not yet settled. When they are we shall no doubt try to make more definite plans. We are simply longing for a home of

our own not only on our own account but so that our friends
may have a meeting place for the many and varied discussions
that at the present time have to take place in restaurants in
London as not one of us can afford a club subscription – if
we could find a suitable Club to house us![35]

On 8 April 1936, Kay sends Helen a copy of the mazagine the
men have produced with the aid of the duplicating machine. The
Clerical Centre membership is enlarging, and at the Heckfield Place
Centre, the window boxes the men made are full of daffodils in
bloom. She's finding her work for the Federation of Unemployed
Clubs interesting, though it has obviously come in for some criticism:
'There is a definite feeling here in London that we should as far as
possible begin to drop the word "unemployed" from the work on
account of the segregation it implies, and to encourage employed
men – or men from the Clubs who have got work – to join with the
unemployed in evening activities, so that the whole movement can
be looked upon as having for its basis the constructive use of leisure
[. . .] Of course,' she goes on rather condescendingly, 'as far as Dr
Birch and I are concerned we have always encouraged the men to
keep in touch with us when they were in work and, as you know,
we have always kept open two evenings a week and encouraged
visitors to our Centres, but I find that to some folks this is a new idea.'
As to private matters, things with Richard are no nearer resolution.
Moreover, Kay voices some scepticism about Richard's extra-
curricular activities: 'We haven't fixed our holiday dates yet. Richard
is very busy with the pamphlet he is writing.[36] I wonder if it will ever
be published. I do hope so because he has spent a tremendous
amount of time on its preparation which has involved quite a lot of
research.'[37]

In June, Kay writes to Helen at unusual length. There's a lot she
wants to discuss, both about the Fulham work and her and Richard's
plans. First, there's another of her success stories to recite: a woman
who had been living on the Unemployment Assistance Board allowance of 15s a week in a flat near the Church – 'one of those sad
cases of a girl being thrust out into the world to earn her own
living without training after having been brought up in luxury'. Kay
suggested that she might like to train as a chiropodist, and fixed her
up through the Over Thirty Association with a training scholarship

funded by the Ministry of Labour: 'The Local Labour Exchange knew nothing about it and when she went along to tell them they gasped in amazement and asked her how it had been arranged.'

As to Richard's plans, the problem is his inability to make any:

> We discussed the possibility of getting married at the end of August a few weeks ago but Dick has come to no decision. Some months ago we worked out what we thought was the minimum we required for furnishing a flat and a holiday together. Not only are we short of that estimate but Dick has not yet cleared up all the debts left him by his Father at his death. There is only about £27 to be paid so I have suggested that we pay it and be done with them. Then as soon as we have saved up the £27 and about another £30 I think we might manage it. However, speaking quite candidly, I am not at all sure that if he were willing I would not be prepared to cut down our estimate for holiday and furniture and make the plunge, but I have to be tactful and try and work things so that the suggestion comes from him. We have both been looking forward to going abroad again this year, and although I would very much like to go there are other things nearer my heart and I have told Dick that I feel I cannot spend money on a holiday – at least more than is absolutely necessary for a change of air – when we need it so much for other things. He hasn't yet come to the same conclusion. Anyway, I have decided in my own mind that if we are not getting married I will take my holiday without him. I don't know whether you can understand this but I feel it would be for the best.
>
> What a lot of courage one needs in this life! Do you realise my dear that if I do marry Dick unless something miraculous occurs we shall be dependent on my earning nearly as much as you are allowing me now on account of our liability with regard to his mother. I sometimes wonder if I can face it but if I am going to I would rather do it quickly and get on with it.

Was it 'I' or 'we'? Kay reminds herself that she wants it to be 'we', though she remains unsure about the young Richard's promise:

In all our estimates and discussions of ways and means we are ignoring Dick's book which is perhaps not quite fair. I do believe it is good and that it will have a chance of publication. It is now ready for a final typing and I must admit that I am rather appalled at the thought of more precious Sunday afternoons being spent on it. We have already spent so many up here in my room with the typewriter and stacks of papers and notes. Nevertheless it must be done or all our previous work will be wasted. I am sure I shall feel quite thrilled if it is accepted. We went away for four days at Whitsun and the manuscript went into the country with us! It hasn't meant only the time spent in writing but also the time spent in reading books and reports for the necessary information. I am afraid it is not at all complimentary to Mr Baldwin and the British Government.[38]

Kay seemed to be surrounded by men who wanted to write books and needed her help or forbearance in order to do so: 'Dr Birch is as busy as ever. He hopes to start a new book in the Autumn, but I seem to have heard this book mentioned before. I think he ought to write it and perhaps I can persuade him to settle down to it if I try very hard.'[39]

While the men entertain their great intellectual plans, the women get on with the practical work. Kay had the same slightly sceptical attitude to another aspect of men's dreams to which both Dr Birch and Richard introduce her – the peace movement. For Dr Birch, there is the 'Peace and Reconstruction' policy which is being taken up by the Nonconformist churches, with a view to putting up candidates for the next parliamentary election. For Richard, the promotion of peace is part of the uncomplimentary opposition to the British government's foreign policy he keeps writing into tracts that might or might not get published. But Kay does join Richard in a journey to Geneva in the summer of 1936 to attend the World Youth Congress and the International Peace Conference. Richard is a delegate to both. As Kay explains to Helen, he 'is arranging for me to have an observer's ticket so that I can attend any of the meetings if I wish to do so. It will be a bit of a busman's holiday but I do feel that with the world in the state it is we ought to do our utmost to make an effort to do something to get things sorted out and this seems to be one way. Dick will have his expenses paid by the organisations he is representing so we shall only have to pay for me, and we shall manage to have four days' holiday at the end of the meetings.'[40]

The Geneva Congress was held in the Palais de la Société des Nations. Its aim was to 'provide an opportunity for youth in all countries to exchange ideas on international affairs and to reach agreement upon a common plan of international cooperation for the prevention of war'.[41] In the photograph of Richard and Kay outside it [Plate 9], Richard is now occupying the centre of the stage with his cigarette, and Kay is standing slightly behind him, looking quite pleased with herself. Some 750 young people, including Conservatives, Communists, Quakers and Catholics, attended from 36 countries.[42] Great Britain sent 47 delegates – Mr Titmuss was one of the 31 men in this group, representing the National League of Young Liberals and Youth House, Camden – and 52 observers, of which Miss Miller was one of 28 women, representing the NCVO.

The other major issue which was preoccupying Kay at home was the change in the organization of social welfare for the unemployed. The intention of Neville Chamberlain's Unemployment Act of 1934 had been to take unemployment 'out of politics' by removing its relief from the control of the Ministry of Labour and the public assistance committees. 'Benefit', renamed 'assistance', had been transferred to an Unemployment Assistance Board of six non-party-political members, with offices and full-time staff throughout the country. This meant that the financial level at which assistance was paid was set nationally, rather than locally, as before. The new rates fixed by the national board were in many cases lower than those set by the old local committees, leading to public demonstrations and renewed hunger marches.[43] 'You will have read about the new regulations for the U.A.B. which are to come into force in November,' writes Kay to Helen, 'and you have probably seen that Advisory Committees are being set up in the various areas. Dr Birch has been asked to join the one for the Fulham district and he has accepted. It will probably mean a good deal of his time being spent on the work during the first few months at any rate but it is impossible to tell quite what it will mean until the work starts.'[44] Several months later, the future is still very uncertain: discussions are taking place with the National Council of Social Service and the London Council for Voluntary Occupation during Unemployment and nothing

definite has been settled, except that the Unemployed Centres ought
to be kept going through the winter as there's no immediate prospect
of the government taking over their proper responsibility for the
welfare of the unemployed.

In October, Kay and Richard attend another youth peace conference, in Birmingham, where they meet many of their friends from
Geneva. Because of all this peace work, Richard is busy with a great
deal of public speaking. Together, Richard and Kay have started the
first Youth Peace Group in Poplar, and Richard is helping with a
group in Camden. But on the personal front, there's still an impasse:

> Again I have to say we have not fixed the date of our wedding.
> When we do we shall allow ourselves six weeks to get the flat
> and make it habitable. The only thing that is really holding us
> up is that the house at Hendon is not yet sold, and even if
> it stands in his Mother's name he feels committed. I don't
> really know what to advise him to do about it. It seems a
> pity to let it fall into the hands of the mortgagees as they
> would lose so much but on the other hand it might remain
> on sale for months and I don't think we should wait indefi-
> nitely. Dick is still hoping we shall get married in January
> and he says the final date is March but as I see it we might
> be in exactly the same position with the house unsold in
> March.

While marriage seems uncertain, the possibilities for Kay's own
career continue to open up. She feels she doesn't know what to do
about this, and wants Helen's advice:

> I have had a letter from my friend at the National Institute
> of Industrial Psychology, Dr Bevington, telling me that the
> secretaryship of the Nursery School Association is falling vac-
> ant and asking if I would care to apply. I did so about two
> years ago I think and failed to get the job because the com-
> mittee thought I was too young! I don't know whether to
> apply or not. I did discuss the question of another job where
> the folks could afford to pay my salary with the secretary of
> the L.C.V.O. last week and he seemed quite alarmed at the
> thought that I might be thinking of giving up all the work

I am doing now. When I was in the running for the Nursery School Association work before I felt quite keen on it but now I don't think I am at all anxious to take it on.[45]

Significantly, it is an aspect of Kay's work that provides the necessary prod for the finalization of the wedding plans: 'We have decided to get married as soon as we can find a flat and make it fit for habitation,' Kay tells Helen triumphantly in her next letter:

> The house at Hendon is still unsold but a number of things have happened which have brought us to this decision.
>
> I did not put in an application for the Nursery School post as we felt it was not the right thing for me to do. I simply could not abandon the unemployed and the Over Thirty Association: it did not seem right somehow. However, shortly after we had come to that decision I was approached by another organisation – the British Association for Physical Training – who wanted an Hon. Secretary to carry on their work in her own time and in her own home. To please the Chairman, who is working with me as Chairman for the Federation of Unemployed Clubs I sent an application and attended a meeting of the Council of the Association last Thursday to discuss the job. To my surprise the job was offered to me with an honorarium which really makes it a consideration and they offered also to pay for a telephone. The conditions were, however, that I decided before I took it on on January 1st what would be my address and whether I would keep my own name or take my husband's. As Father won't have a telephone at home and as the Association would not like me to change my address after a few months I had to decide either to turn the job down or take it and get on with things at once, and I have decided to take it.

This decision entailed a good deal of thinking and planning on both their parts. Kay's mother immediately started to agitate about the wedding: 'I knew she would. I expect in the end we shall be married quietly by Dr Birch at West Kensington but I am sure Mother won't feel we are properly married if the ceremony is not performed here in the Parish Church! I don't suppose you will want to come will you? As we have to go through this tiresome business I would rather like you to be present. I shall probably be horribly nervous and feel I am being sort of on show.'

There doesn't appear to have been any discussion of the name-changing issue – or, if there was, it went unrecorded. The financial calculations were complicated. While the British Association work would pay an honorarium, this would not provide the addition to Richard's income they would need to keep themselves and help Richard's family. For Kay to go on with the unemployment work would therefore mean continued financial support from Helen. What did Helen feel about helping next year? Before Helen makes her decision, Kay wants her to know that she and Dr Birch have decided that the bureaucracy of the Fulham Unemployment Scheme is now too much. They want to work independently, as they had at the beginning, unobstructed by the Mayor and an 'apathetic' committee. It doesn't help that the new Mayor is 'an insignificant little man with 15 children' who 'showers "h"'s and bad grammar all over the place when he speaks' and who shows no interest in their work at all.[46]

Helen declines to attend the wedding, without giving a reason, but agrees to pay Kay's salary. By the spring of 1937, the clerical workers' centre isn't doing well, probably due to an increase in employment in this group. Paradoxically, of course, the better things get economically, the worse the future looks for the welfare work. Kay anticipates the imminent closure of the centre. But there is still a need for a main one at 522 Fulham Road, and she and Dr Birch intend to struggle on.

Kay and Richard found a pleasant flat in the Pimlico area of Victoria. It had elegant tiled fireplaces, and they bought a modicum of dark furniture for it. In the surviving photographs, the comfortable chairs, the solid square table and the twin beds covered with heavy embroidered bedspreads are flooded by light from the flat's long windows and several strategically placed soft white lamps. On 6 February, Kay Miller became Kay Titmuss at the parish church on Perry Hill in Lewisham. Her father and Richard's mother acted as witnesses. On the last day of that year, the Mayor of Fulham's Unemployment Scheme came to a formal end. Funds were low and the Mayor considered that the creation of the new Unemployment Assistance Board relieved the Borough from the need to provide help for able-bodied unemployed men.[47] It must all have been something of a relief to Kay and Dr Birch, as they had disliked officialdom so much. At the end of 1937, they reverted to their old freestanding church status as the Fulham Fellowship for the Unemployed with a committee of five, including three members of the staff of the Gas Light and Coke Company, the Area Officer of the UAB and a representative of the local labour exchange; as before, Kay acts as Honorary Secretary and Treasurer. It's agreed that a room at the main centre should be set aside for a women's group affiliated through Kay to the Over Thirty Association.

Although released from the bureaucracy of Borough control, and the unpleasantness of interviews with the new Mayor, Kay and Dr Birch experienced heightened financial difficulties in 1938. In the spring, Fellowship House had a total membership of 31 men and 14 women, of whom 22 and 10 were regular attenders. Boot-repairing classes and social evenings were held twice weekly, and carpentry classes once a week. Recreations provided included books, darts, dominoes, a piano and 'There is also a wireless set which has been reconstructed recently by the men.' The canteen was open twice daily for tea and cakes, sandwiches, bread, cheese and fruit. The women's group met once a week – mostly single women and widows over fifty. They spent their time 'preparing and cooking food – a gas cooker is at their disposal – in knitting and handicrafts (mostly soft toys)'.[48]

Kay pens many fund-raising letters to local businesses – Shell Mex and BP Ltd, the Sunlight Laundry Ltd, Convoys Ltd, and a second branch of the Gas Light and Coke Company, who decline to help on the grounds that their staff consist mainly of 'workmen and trade boys' who don't earn enough to afford any contributions to charity. None of the letters brings any useful response. Kay also writes to the two local MPs, Dr Edith Summerskill and the Hon. W. W. Astor, to try to interest them in the 'great social ministry' of the Fulham work. Her letters stress her and Dr Birch's disagreement with the view that the UAB renders their work unnecessary: '. . . this is social work with which we can all help and the results are greater than we know. It is not assistance work, it is social and personal and has for its aim the bringing of men and women together in a way that is of very real benefit.'[49]

The main event in early 1939 was the Duke of Kent's visit [Plate 6]. The Duke toured in his role as vice patron of the National Council for Social Service, nine clubs and voluntary institutions in the London area. After Fulham, he went on to see a settlement in Notting Hill, the Kentish Town Men's Institute, Toynbee Hall in Whitechapel, a settlement in Bethnal Green and the pioneer Peckham Health Centre. It was Kay who made all the arrangements; under duress from Mr Haynes, the Deputy Secretary of the National Council for Social Service who was organizing the visit, she wrote to the objectionable Mayor telling him that, although the visit was a private one, he might like to be present; she also wrote to the LCC instructor about arrangements for the classes the Duke would see in progress (although boot repairing was the usual one for that day she wanted some of the men to be seen doing leather work and woodwork as well). She planned to have the women preparing lunch for themselves and the men (hot veal and ham pie, boiled rice and jam tart). The women who wouldn't be cooking would be knitting or making soft toys. The logistics of the visit were all a bit of a nightmare, as the passages of the house were narrow and there was a very small entrance hall; also the Duke's visit was timed to last only fifteen minutes.

The Duke arrived in a heavy snowstorm wearing a dark overcoat and carrying a bowler hat, and stayed half an hour. He was received by the Mayor and Mayoress, a local councillor and his wife, Dr Birch and Mrs Titmuss. Others presented to the Duke included Mr Clarke, the caretaker, two representatives of the all-important Gas Light and Coke Company, the district and area officers of the UAB, and Mr Titmuss. When he saw the women preparing dinner, the Duke 'remarked that it was rather dull work preparing food'.[50] Upstairs, at the leather-working class, he coveted a blue handbag and asked if it was for sale, but was told firmly it was the men's own property.

Asked for her impressions of the Duke's visit, Mrs Titmuss told a *Gazette* representative: 'He was very nice. He asked a lot of questions and wanted to know how long they had been here, about their wives and families, how long they had been out of work. He seemed to show that he had a good knowledge of unemployment questions. When I pointed out that some of the men were no better off when they were working, he seemed to show a knowledge of that aspect, and agreed that it was very sad.'[51]

Although Dr Birch used the publicity of the royal visit to appeal for money, the situation of the fellowship got no better. In May, the LCVO cut its support. In June, Clarke resigned, and Fellowship

House was closed for two months. Kay complained to Helen that she had to harden her heart to Mr Clarke and his family's fate:

> Goodness knows I have had enough trouble clearing out the mess he left in the house to help me to do so. It was a horrible business. Every cupboard full of rubbish and in the attic umpteen empty milk bottles.
>
> We have had to have the workmen to do the ceilings of the top floor and the walls and I am going to try to do the paintwork next week. It was in such a dreadfully dirty state that we couldn't even ask a new supervisor to look at the accommodation we have to offer him. In addition we have had to have four new chimneys and about 75 new slates on the roof and we shall have to find about £25 to pay the bill.[52]

There was considerable dissatisfaction with the impact of the new administrative arrangements on social work, and Dr Birch and others felt that social workers should be appointed to individual area offices to co-ordinate the work of the board with that of the Ministry of Labour and the voluntary organizations. Nobody quite knew who was responsible for what, and in this state of confusion it was those who needed help who were suffering. Dr Birch, said Kay, had written to the UAB expressing these views, but the board had not replied. In the meantime, Kay herself wrote that she was

> trying to show by the handling of a few concrete cases, on which I am spending considerable care, just how the social workers would help. For instance the Board suggest training a clerical worker of 38 as a machinist. I find her health is so bad partly due to malnutrition and through bad teeth that the training would be useless. Through the Charity Organisation Society it is possible to arrange for the teeth to be attended to, the Board with a certificate from the panel doctor are usually able to give an allowance for additional nourishment and eventually when the girl does start training there will be a very much better chance of her staying the course and eventually being fixed up with work. If the Board had their own social workers they would be able to deal with many more cases in this way. After all I can only handle the people

who come along to Fellowship House and there must be
many more on whom it would be well worth spending personal attention.

Dr Birch was planning to consult Richard about a pamphlet on
unemployment to be published in connection with the Congregational churches. Either in response to Kay's letters, or prompted
by the Duke's visit, both the local MPs had been along to take a
look. The Hon. William Astor seemed 'very young and not very au
fait with things. He stayed a long time and talked with all the men
and women and he certainly knows all about us now, but unless he
changes his policy I don't feel he can be of very much help.'[53] Dr
Edith Summerskill arrived a few days later, but neither of the visits
made any difference to the future of the Fulham work.

The last few exchanges of letters between Kay and Helen cover
the period leading up to the outbreak of war in September 1939.
Kay reports a delightful Easter at the farm in Bedfordshire – so
'peaceful and remote', with a non-functioning wireless set and
nobody feeling disposed to read the papers. Cousin Bob, the young
farmer, was fighting the possibility of conscription in the interests of
his cattle and crops. When she writes to Helen of work, she has only
failures to report in hers (the Winter Distress League won't help any
more, and many of their staunch Gas Light and Coke Company
supporters are moving out of the district). This is the point at which
her work has really started to become *theirs*, which means *his*.
Richard's name is beginning to appear in print, as some of the many
letters he fires off to the newspapers strike home:

There was one in the Spectator last week and about a fortnight ago the Times actually published a letter on the same
subject which brought us some amusing correspondence.
The Editor of the Eugenics Review has asked for one for
their next issue and has asked for an editorial note on the
letter also [...] Richard looks as though he would go on
working out figures indefinitely so I must put the typewriter
away and show him the way to bed. Last night I came home
about midnight to find all the lights on in the flat and the
wireless on and Richard fast asleep in bed with a book in

58

his hand. It seemed most odd. Much love from us both,
Kathleen.[54]

The Fulham Fellowship soldiered on until April 1940, when Dr
Birch resigned, and the committee agreed to wind things up for the
time being. The tenancy of 522 Fulham Road was surrendered in
January – in any case, the house couldn't be used as a club because
its condition was unsafe and there was no air-raid shelter. Kay was
left to tidy up the ends: returning the key to County Hall, sorting
out with the LCC whose responsibility the 'dirty condition' of the
house was – though for this she needed the intervention of Dr Birch,
who persuaded the LCC to take a 'sane' view of the matter.[55] There
was a protracted dispute about the Gestetner duplicating machine.
Although everyone agreed it really belonged to the Gestetner Company, they didn't want it back, and it was the view of Dr Birch's
replacement at the West Kensington Congregational Church that as
it had been lent originally to Dr Birch, it was properly 'domiciled'
at the church. The machine itself would have had an interesting
story to tell. Until mid-1940, it was used by Kay, and probably in
connection with Richard Titmuss's own work, and then it did some
service with the Forward March movement in Gower Street,[56] ending
up with the British Federation of Social Workers in Victoria, 'a struggling organisation with very little money [. . .] doing valuable work
which is thought well of by many people including the National
Council of Social Service'.[57] Politician and social reformer Eleanor
Rathbone had lent the social workers a machine, but she'd taken it
back, just as they most needed it to help with organizing their first
conference.

In the 1940s correspondence Kay clearly held out some hope
that the Fulham work would resume at the end of the war. She
even asked the LCC for a fresh tenancy should this transpire. But
by the end of the Gestetner duplicating-machine saga in 1943
she's taking a different view: 'As far as I can see the old Fulham
Fellowship Committee will never meet again or function in any way
[. . .] it is most unlikely that I shall come back to run Clubs in
Fulham.'[58]

It was the end of an era. The distressing pre-welfare state social
conditions of the 1930s had called forth the sympathetic energy of
many charitable men and women, and amongst these was Kay Miller/

Titmuss. Countless women found a useful role in this voluntary work – either by paying for it, like Helen Johnston, or by subsidizing it through accepting a low salary, like Kay Miller. What the people at the receiving end of these charitable endeavours really thought about them is unknown. Even if not exploited as cheap labourers doing up buildings, as the Labourites of Fulham feared, they are likely to have noticed the 'us and them' attitude evident in some of Kay Miller and Helen Johnston's letters. Kay and Dr Birch knew what the unemployed needed, but it was hardly fashionable to ask the unemployed themselves. Later on, social workers' notions about needs would be underpinned by a wealth of local and state regulations justifying their moral intrusion into people's lives, but at the time welfare was an individual thing, a case of benevolent hand-outs from one person (or from one class) to another. The men seem to have got a good deal more attention than the women, so what did the women think? There are many unanswered questions.

The sense of Kay Miller/Titmuss's creative energy leaps out of the documents in the brown suitcase. She was no ordinary woman. The young Dick Titmuss's 'public works' were a dubious and fragile enterprise compared to the solidity of her own. And then there was his constant, irritating elusion of her plans for marriage, the faltering quality of his commitment to that model of marriage she so much admired. But it all changed; she got him, and he got her. If Kay Titmuss believed the fable of her helpmate role in Richard Titmuss's ascent from obscurity, those years in Fulham with Dr Birch – the endless busyness of it all, the exhilarating scratching around for money, the dreaming up of new activities, like sending men to the country to give them a good dose of rural air, the distribution of clothes and boots and advice, the sense of doing something practical at the centre where it counted – retained a very special quality. They were for her a golden period. 'Husband Led to New Work' says the carefully preserved byline in the page from the *Vancouver Sun* dated 21 June 1966. Even the heading is ambiguous – was the husband led or did he lead instead? The Titmusses were in Vancouver in 1966 because he was speaking at a social welfare conference. The interview with Kay shares the social page with accounts of golden wedding anniversaries, epilepsy support groups, bingo parties for hospital patients, 'strawberry chatter' teas, and advertisements for slimming lessons and chiffon dresses for ladies who want to glide through evenings of dining and dancing. The 'Husband Led to New Work' piece goes on:

> Hamelin is not the only city that had a Pied Piper. London had one too.
>
> It was Mrs Richard M. Titmuss, wife of the Professor of Social Administration at the University of London. She led her husband to a career that was to be their life work [. . .]
>
> When they first met in 1934, Mrs Titmuss was working in the social welfare area [. . .] That's when the Pied Piper business started.
>
> Her enthusiasm was so contagious that Professor Titmuss gradually developed an interest in social welfare and decided that something should be done about providing social security for those in need.

Mrs Titmuss talked to the *Vancouver Sun* reporter about her husband's lack of formal education and his three honorary degrees. She mentioned her daughter, who had carried on her own enthusiasm, and was now married and working with her husband[59] and raising a family at the same time: 'Mrs Titmuss is no longer active in social work,' the interview concluded: 'She is now her husband's right hand. She travels with him, helps him in his writing, does some research[60] and generally directs his busy life. She played her pipe well . . .'

FOUR

---━━﹡━━---

His work and hers

In the early years of his career, Richard Titmuss was described as 'gangling' and 'dark-haired', and as claiming that a decline of one and a half million children since the Boer War had been matched by the acquisition of one and a half million more pet dogs.[1] He had 'something of a young Wellsian hero' about him, 'with his youth hostelling, his talking and arguing', despite which he always looked so unfit and unhealthy – but this probably served him well, as it gave him an abiding and profitable interest in the problem of social rejects,[2] and also suggested he had been spared active service during the war, so he could go on thinking, arguing and writing about population and social issues and generally being the 'nuisance' he would not have been if he'd been forced into soldiering instead.[3] He wrote five books while working in the insurance industry, all 'at snatched moments during the day or in the evenings',[4] rose to minor prominence in the powerful circles of those who were interested, as many were in those days, in questions of eugenics, became a spokesman for 'young' liberals who wanted peace, helped to orchestrate the Forward March political movement which argued that the common ownership of all property and a new set of moral values would be the only enduring solution to the problem of war, volunteered for the role of adviser on German vital statistics for the Ministry of Economic Warfare, pioneered the practical study of social medicine, and wrote the best known and most controversial history of the government's management of domestic aspects of the Second World War. In other words, he succeeded in making a name for himself in the public world of social policy and political activity, and by the end of the war his academic career was well and truly launched.

The beginning of the beginning is one of those silences, which, despite Richard Titmuss's wife's careful record-keeping, can only be interrogated across the chasm of known and unknown history sixty years on. In 1939, Kay wrote a brief biography of Richard, presumably in response to a request from someone. Her account highlights her own role in leading the fledgling Richard Titmuss out of obscurity:

> R.M.T. was the son of a farmer & it was not until his adolescent years that he had any contact with town life. Sudden and unforeseen family circumstances thrust him as a very young man into an unfamiliar environment. The work he took up, while providing 'bread and butter' offered no outlet for his rapidly growing mental capacity. Voracious, though unguided reading, led to the development of a social conscience which has been ever since the driving power behind his constant questioning into the causes & results of poverty. He soon discovered an innate aptitude for vital statistics [. . .] Side by side with the findings in this field & *in contact with men and women engaged on research into social problems & social workers* his interest in the question of population has developed. [italics added]

It reads more like a teacher's report on an able student or a job reference than a wife's comment on her husband. But it was an important part of Kay Titmuss's private vision that Richard was *her* discovery. Her work produced him. The possibility that his then elided her was masked by a deeply held conviction that she remained essential to it in more than an ordinary housewifely, 'people work' role.

Richard's own curriculum vitae, composed in 1948, was confined to the public appointments:

> *Work*: 1921, Office boy, Standard Telephones & Cables Ltd; 1926, Insurance official, County Fire Office Ltd. Appointed inspector for London at age 32. 1939, Awarded Leverhulme Research Grant (two years) for analysis of vital statistics during spare-time [. . .] 1942, Historian: offices of the Cabinet. Responsible for volumes of official war history on the social services (covering Ministry of Health, Home Office, Assistance Board, General Register Office, Scottish Department of

Health, Local Authorities, Voluntary organisations, and part of Ministry of Education).

When the *Post Magazine & Insurance Monitor* asked for his biography in 1943, Richard added his many articles in '*The Times, The Spectator, The Lancet, The Eugenics Review, The New Statesman and Nation*, and many other journals'; membership of the Population Investigation Committee and of the Council of the Eugenics Society, and the fellowship of the Royal Statistical Society; and for relaxation there was still, despite Kay's influence, chess, and, thanks to the war, the new hobby of allotment-digging. He described his occupation as that of 'Writer and Statistician'.[5] The biography supplied to the *Post Magazine* was for an editorial alerting the journal's readers to Richard Titmuss's true identity: 'Probably few readers know that the Richard M. Titmuss who has been in the news recently for his research work in connection with various aspects of vital statistics is an insurance man.'[6]

When the bereaved Maude Titmuss wrote to her friend in the County Fire Office in June 1926 to solicit a better job for her bread-winning son, she was told there was a long waiting list. But the friend must have been a good one, for the County Fire Office took Richard on as a probationary clerk in July, and then the following January gave him a permanent job. What he did for the County Fire Office was clearly not as important to him as what he was able to accomplish in snatched moments away from it, but he must have been very conscientious or they would not have made him an inspector at such a young age, nor would they have so resisted his leaving in 1942 for the infinitely more interesting reaches of Whitehall. His first publications on vital statistics – statistics of birth and death – were all written for the insurance press. Indeed, he contributed to the 'Records and Reflections' section of the *Insurance Record* until October 1943, when he told the editor regretfully that this task was no longer worth the time it took him.[7]

It was the football and the chess that kept him going – and the politics. By the early 1930s, Richard had become passionately involved in Liberal politics and in the peace and anti-rearmament movements. Kept in one of the brown suitcase's files is the notice of a meeting on peace and world disarmament organized by the Women's International League which Richard attended in February

1932, on the eve of the World Disarmament Conference. By 1936, when he and Kay went to the Geneva Peace Congress together, he had found his own public voice: 'Must we be Cannon Fodder?' asked a notice advertising a meeting in Hendon on 20 March: 'Come and Hear Youth's Views on Re-armament & Foreign Policy. Chairman: Mr D. M. Smith (League of Nations' Youth Group) Speakers: Mr Basil E. Goldstone (Liberal Candidate, Hendon 1935), Mr R. Titmuss (and others).'

Just as Kay had introduced Richard to the practical realities of social work among the unemployed, it was he who led her into the wider political world of what it all meant in terms of theories and policy. We know that Kay Miller was not over-fond of 'Labourites'.[8] The first record of *his* political interest dates from 1932, when he applied for membership of the Hendon Young Liberals. Its Honorary Secretary, a J. M. Henderson, wrote to express great enthusiasm at the prospect, 'as liberals are few and far between in Hendon', and to charge Richard the annual subscription of one shilling.[9] Politics was not part of the family tradition, though in eugenist circles Richard would later find it a useful ploy to claim an inherited interest in health and population questions, traceable via the comely Misses Bruton of Lamb's *Essays* to William Farr, statistician to Britain's first Registrar-General, and beyond him to Samuel Farr, propagandist of the Hippocratic oath.[10] Privately, Richard also believed he had Southern European blood in him, as he always tanned easily, and liked Spanish dancing as exhibited in London by 'Antonio' in the 1950s – but Spanish dancing hardly provided the right kind of passport to the world he wished to enter.

Why did he become a Young Liberal? His boredom with the insurance industry is one reason for the political involvement, but why liberalism? In a letter written in 1935 to his local newspaper, the *Hendon and Finchley Times*, in support of the new Liberal MP, Richard provided something of an explanation. Since 1918, liberalism had been fighting the totalitarianism of both Right and Left. Although many people would now be unable to remember a Liberal government, he wrote, the party itself persisted because 'it represents the English mind at its best'. The country did not want socialism, 'embracing as it does the means of Production, Distribution, and Exchange', and the only way of avoiding this would be to retain a 'Liberal or Centre Party'. Socialism was Marxism, and liberalism was really a socialism of the centre. It demanded an integrated mixed economy with that balance between state and local control which would ensure the solution of the Twin Problem – preventing war and relieving poverty.[11]

A wide range of reformist positions sheltered under the Liberal umbrella in the 1930s. Some of these offered the kind of apparently radical critique of the capitalist status quo that Richard Titmuss himself came to espouse. Identification with liberalism rather than socialism was partly a matter of class interest. An aspiring intellectual was likely to find the 'false consciousness of the radical bourgeoisie'[12] a more congenial and helpful place than the Marxist or unionist branches of socialism. There is no hint in the personal papers that Richard Titmuss's choice of Liberal politics was the result of any particular personal contact. The person who was introduced to me in the 1950s as 'your father's previous girlfriend' was an unassuming apolitical woman who became secretary to a women's college in North America, dying in Miami in 1979. The man she married, Nicolas Sandor, was a scientist who worked for a film company; he invented a special sort of searchlight which lit up the sky with artificial lightning flashes secured by firing a series of small explosive shells from a machine gun. The point of these flashes was that they provided a means of clearly illuminating enemy bombers without the usual dazzle and cloud reflection. Sandor's invention was patented after the heavy loss of life in the autumn 1940 bombing raids, but he was unable to get very far in his efforts to persuade the Ministry of Aircraft Production to pay for the necessary development work. As he was pleased to do for other friends and family, Richard took on Sandor's case. 'I have staked what little reputation I have on helping him,' Richard wrote to a friend in early 1941; 'in the last ten days by sheer aggressiveness (demanding to see people like Beaverbrook, etc) I have seen the heads of the Services. When it is all over I shall have an incredible story to tell of stupidity and obscurantism in higher places.'[13] Richard was convinced that Sandor had found the answer to the raids. He arranged an interview with an MP and one about finance with Laurence Cadbury (of Cadbury brothers, the chocolate firm, and Managing Director of the *News Chronicle*), and also enlisted the help of Julian Huxley, brother of Aldous. Half a century later my mother considered the whole saga sufficiently important to preserve the correspondence on it, noting that Sir Henry Tizard, to whom responsibility for developing the idea had eventually been handed, had assured Richard 'that if there was anything helpful in the invention it would be made use of'.[14] Tizard was Rector of the Imperial College of Science and Technology and a member of the Aircraft Production Ministry; a man with a 'mischievous, provocative, sarcastic, and gamin-like' sense of humour, grizzled red hair and a pince-nez,[15] he went on to chair the important government Advisory Council on Scientific Policy and Defence Research.

But the seachlight invention that illuminated the sky provides no clue to the politicization of Richard Titmuss. Questions of life expectancy and the factors affecting this were important in the insurance industry, and it was essential to get sums right, so that what was predicted to happen was in fact likely to do so. This meant a knowledge both of 'politico-economic events' and of demographic factors.[16] People of Richard's age could remember the First World War, and many would have lost relatives in it. The impetus for an active political involvement which might forestall the possibility of a second war was a personal one. Beyond that, Richard's capacity to be involved in public affairs must have stemmed from intrinsic interest or from ambition – or both. Whatever it was, it increased exponentially after he met Kay Miller. She showed him the way to promote his own work through personal contacts – to exploit any lead, however tenuous, to the well-known and powerful – and she gave him the language and the techniques with which to do this. One imagines them sitting together in the evenings and at weekends, at first in the small back bedroom in Forest Hill with the typewriter which kept Mother and Father awake, and then, later, in their first flat together, in Pimlico, cooking up schemes for getting Richard into print, and putting new political and social initiatives on their feet – all as well as grappling in the daytime with the tedious computations of insurance claims (him), and how to raise money for the unemployed and cope with the ups and downs of the Reverend Birch's health (her).

Until 1934, the main outlet for Richard's political interests was a body called the Fleet Street Parliament, which met every Monday evening in the St Bride's Institute in Fleet Street. The Fleet Street Parliament offered a forum for young people to practise public speaking by debating burning questions of the day using the procedural framework of party politics. It took on a wide range of issues – the incompatibility of socialism 'with the needs of a progressive nation';

the physical deterioration of the population and consequent need to extend poor relief; the government of India; the nationalization of the coal, iron and steel industries; the liberalization of the divorce laws.

Attached to a page of the *Brideian* for December 1935 is a small photograph of Richard with ill-fitting dentures and an overtight white collar. 'Leader of the Liberal party' is inscribed on it in my mother's 'pruning' handwriting. Richard's call to action as the leading Fleet Street Liberal in the September issue of the *Brideian* was transparently influenced by her concerns, though not yet by the improvements she would succeed in making to his writing style, which was much spattered at the time with exclamation marks, verbless sentences and clichéd adjectives:

> 2,000,000 unemployed! That is tragic enough; but has the Government at Westminster, and the nation as a whole, forgotten the destitute army of over 1,500,000 driven to Poor Law Relief? An increase of over 700,000 since the present National Government took office. And still steadily mounting. Thus, 3,500,000 without work – with their dependants over 8,500,000. One-fifth of the nation! Out of the 12,000,000 insured workers, two in five suffer unemployment. Their experience – two months out, three in. One's conscience cannot ignore indefinitely this pitiable army [. . .] It is our intention to thrust this tragedy of wasted lives into the forefront of political debate. Action is imperative![17]

The main problem Richard identified was the government's handling of foreign policy. Consequently, the Young Liberals under his leadership planned to work for a more realistic policy based on collective security and economic sanctions through the League of Nations.[18]

In 1935, the Fleet Street Liberals endorsed the programme of the newly formed Council of Action for Peace and Reconstruction, in which key figures were Elizabeth Cadbury (mother of Laurence),[19] Cambridge economist H. A. L. Fisher, politician David Lloyd George, and Eleanor Rathbone, political campaigner and tireless advocate of family allowances for mothers.[20] The council's programme called for the British people, irrespective of party, to work together in demanding a stop to the fatalistic drift towards war. It argued for support to be given at the next election only to those candidates committed to disarmament through the League of Nations. Unemployment was considered to be the main domestic issue.

The inter-war period was a fertile time for the breeding of British peace organizations. There was a widespread belief that the 'great' war had ushered in a new international morality.[21] What had been minority opinion in the 1920s became orthodox fashion in the 1930s. Historian A. J. P. Taylor has pointed out that most of the well-known books on the First World War were published at the end of the 1920s; they all preached the same lesson – the futility of war, the incompetence of politicians, and the resultant sufferings of ordinary people.[22] Canon Dick Sheppard's Peace Pledge Union ('I renounce War and I will never support or sanction another'; sponsors Aldous Huxley, Storm Jameson, George Lansbury, Rose Macaulay, Siegfried Sassoon, Donald Soper, Ellen Wilkinson and others) had a hundred thousand members, and in the summer of 1935, a 'peace ballot' conducted by supporters of the League of Nations allowed eleven and a half million Britons to record a 10 to 1 majority in favour of disarmament and collective security through the League.[23] The shift to pacifism was confirmed by the October election results in East Fulham, close to where Kay Miller was working with the unemployed; a Conservative advocate of rearmament was defeated by an out-and-out pacifist, and a Conservative majority of 14,521 became a Labour one of 4,840.[24]

A second world war was simply unthinkable. It was unthinkable that the collective movement for world peace represented by the democratic organ of the League of Nations would not overcome the selfish resistances of individual countries. It was difficult for some to believe in Nazism as the appallingly destructive force it would turn out to be. To those on the right, Hitler's regime appeared to offer a strong alternative to communism. Moreover, rearmament would be expensive, and the economic agenda at home was dominated by the need to solve the urgent problems of mass unemployment and poverty. In these circumstances, politicians of all parties aligned themselves with the disarmament movement, though many were, at the same time, practically involved in preparations for war. The result was a dreadful schizophrenia: a 'story of steadily accelerating prep- arations for an inevitable war' conjoined with 'groping attempts' to prevent it.[25] No wonder many young people, including Richard Titmuss, felt moved to speak and write angrily against their elders, but not betters, who were so evidently making a mess of everything.

After Richard and Kay attended the Youth Peace Congress in Geneva in 1936, he wrote, and she typed, various reports of the congress which captured in his lurid prose the atmosphere of youthful passion and international struggle:

> From Australia, U.S.A., Canada, Russia, India and every corner of the world young men and women came to discuss the problems that will have to be solved unless civilisation is to crash in a welter of blood and misery [...] China was led by a girl from the Heroic Chinese Student Movement, the Spanish delegation of 15 from Madrid came straight from the front in their blue overalls, one of the delegates – a girl – still with shrapnel in her arm, the result of helping to defend her village against the rebels and Moors.[26]

By now a British Youth Peace Assembly had been formed, with the aim of enabling 'Youth organisations of Great Britain to take common action on questions relating to Peace'.[27] The great challenge was to override the domestic divisions of party politics, and translate all this enthusiasm into constructive action. But the BYPA was also concerned with the general economic and social status of youth, regarding such issues as part and parcel of equipping young people properly to serve their country. A visionary Twelve Point Charter was drawn up in 1937 which anticipated fundamental aspects of the British post-war education and health services. Its twelve points ran from a forty-hour working week for young people, 'safety classes, adequate supervision of machine work and regular medical examinations in employer's time', to the abolition of the household means test and adequate unemployment benefit for young people in their own right. It included raising the school leaving age to sixteen, demanded equal educational opportunity and health care for all, and highlighted the importance of leisure facilities and improving the social and cultural amenities available to young people in rural areas.[28] Richard was asked to write some publicity for the 1937 conference at which the Youth Charter was to be discussed. His text, arguing that youth throughout Europe was in chains, 'condemned to silence,

70

unable to voice its hopes and beliefs, prevented from thinking, and denied the right to determine its inheritance', was appended to a photograph of German youth being drilled, and set in a map of Europe surrounded by the said chains.[29]

Richard, however, quickly grew disillusioned with the inward-looking state of the organization. He refused to contribute to a voluntary levy of committee members proposed as a solution to its financial problems. Aside from his increasing disapproval of all the time and energy wasted on 'hypothetical problems of policy and constitution', Richard referred to his recent marriage and the fact that he and his wife were trying to keep two Occupational Employment Centres going in London.[30] In the midst of *his* work, he was also willing to claim *hers*. But this was presumably a project of which Kay herself approved.

The offices of the BYPA were initially housed in those of another organization with which Richard had been closely involved since the late 1920s, Youth House, in Camden, North London. Youth House offered lectures and social evenings once a week; study, language and drama classes; discussions, rambles, camps, dances, table tennis and swimming; an international summer hostel; a restaurant; and general work for the peace movement through the local peace council and the BYPA. It was also supposed to be an experiment in communal living, with residence open to any person under the age of thirty who could afford 17s 6d a week and was willing to abide by the house rules, which included doing two hours a week communal housework, attending monthly house meetings, making no noise after 10.30 p.m. and paying one penny per week for every 10 watts electricity used in excess of the 60 watt lamp (100 watt for couples) provided in the bedrooms. 'This was an international hostel founded by idealistic vegetarians,' noted my mother dismissively in a note composed during her 'pruning' activities. 'I remember attending a vegetarian Christmas Dinner & seem to recollect that those residents from other than Gt. Britain were mainly refugees from Hitler.' She kept a letter from one of them, a Helmut Blume, who wrote to Richard asking for help in getting free board and lodging at Youth House or another hostel in return for giving his services as a pianist and composer and linguist.[31] Youth House offered Helmut Blume participation in their Wednesday evening band, but regretted they weren't in a position to exchange food for art.[32]

71

Richard lived at Youth House himself briefly in the 1930s but left no record of the quality of the experience. He became one of its directors in 1937. This was the substance of a claim he later entered on his form for the Central Register of professional people held by the Ministry of Labour during the war to be 'Director of [a] Community Centre in London'. He bought a £5 share in Youth House, which he kept until the building was sold in 1971, when he realized £100. During his period of active involvement, he sorted out (unsurprisingly) Youth House's fire insurance premiums, helped them to set up the local St Pancras Peace Council, and hassled the London County Council, St Pancras Town Hall and the National Fitness Council for grants under the 1937 Physical Training and Recreation Act to build an extension for a new gymnasium and other recreational facilities.

It was becoming a life of unrelenting and diverse activity. The manuscript which Kay had so toiled over and so complained about to Helen Johnston was completed in 1936. *Crime and Tragedy* (alternative titles 'Government by Betrayal' or 'Creation of Anarchy') began with a quote from Baldwin inciting the young not to blame the old when the next war wiped out European civilization, as it undoubtedly would: 'Let them remember that they, they principally, or they alone, are responsible for the terrors that have fallen upon the earth.'[33] This seemed rather unfair, but it was a challenge to which Richard wanted young people everywhere to rise, echoing Baldwin's words with his own: 'Let youth turn back the pages [...] Upon their conscience [...] may rest the responsibility for imperilling our civilisation.'[34] The theme of youth having to take on, single-handedly, the task of fighting war and building peace was a common one at the time. Writer J. B. Priestley penned a similar clarion call to the youth of Great Britain before the 1936 Youth Peace Congress in Geneva:

> Youth, with its life before it, has more to lose through War than any other section of the community. We see clearly now that elderly statesmen do not know how to prevent War; probably because unconsciously they believe that international conflict is always inevitable. It is more than likely that the only people who can save the Western World from self-destruction are the young, whose minds are not fixed in mutual distrust and hate, who still have generosity and an

idealistic vision, who have a natural sympathy with young men and women of their own age everywhere, and who realise that it is our business now to combat the world-wide evils of poverty, ignorance, waste, stupidity, and prejudice, and not to engage ourselves all over again in futile mass murder . . .[35]

The adjective 'futile' must have been more heavily used in the 1930s than in any other decade of British history.

Richard's *Crime and Tragedy* charted the errors made by the British government in foreign policy since 1931, and particularly its actions at the 1932 world disarmament conference, when Germany's need to be treated fairly after the unfair Treaty of Versailles was not honoured; instead of allowing armaments up to the level of other countries, the proper response to Germany's position should have been equal disarmament all round. Richard wasn't willing to let other countries off the hook, but he firmly believed that Britain should have played a leading role in the League of Nations – not just speaking the *language* of support but matching this with *action* – of the kind that 'she' would have played in defending 'her' Empire. Patriotism, he emphasized, need not be 'synonymous with the state of a country's armaments and defence forces. I am no less a patriot than any General of the Army.' He was prepared to lay down his life for the collective approach to world peace, and for the 'passionate conviction in the power of the British Empire to lead the Nations towards the banishment of anarchy from the earth'.[36]

What the manuscript lacked in style, it made up for in verve and passion, and a kind of tongue-in-cheek sarcasm that didn't quite come off. In one of the last chapters, Richard pondered on the inborn leadership qualities underlying Britain's responsibility to ensure world peace. He identified as critical 'the altruistic activities of that expanding organism the British Armament Industry',[37] controlling, as it did, 'one third of the world trade in weapons of destruction, disembowelment and death'. According to the statistics in *Crime and Tragedy*, the industry was providing forty-four countries with munitions, and selling aircraft to Germany and at least fifteen other countries, all of which evidenced a quite outstanding devotion to 'fratricidal passions'.[38] Another section of the manuscript ridiculed the British government's strategy for protecting the populace against

73

gas and chemical warfare. The peace movement gave these inadequate plans a good deal of publicity. An anti-government leaflet produced by the St Pancras Peace Council in 1935 and preserved in the brown suitcase was headed 'GAS???', and went on: 'ST PANCRAS CITIZENS! Will Gas Masks protect you HOUSEHOLDERS! Is your house proof against Gas Attack? FATHERS! Do you know how to put sand on a Thermite Bomb? MOTHERS! Can you make your babies Gas Proof? Hear The Facts About These Defence (?) Plans.'[39] *Crime and Tragedy* warned of the 'criminal' delusions behind the proselytization of gas masks as a satisfactory answer to the dangers of a war which would be waged on the basis of the vast improvements in 'the technique of mass murder'[40] achieved since 1918, including incendiary bombs and 'over 1,000 different types of inhuman and revolting gases'.[41] Richard's arguments here drew on the labours of a group of Cambridge scientists, who in 1932 had formed an anti-war group to provide technical advice to the peace movement. They carried out many practical experiments on government instructions for gas-proofing homes and people, and showed that these would be either fatal, useless or only effective against certain gases and for healthy adults who possessed a good pair of lungs in the first place.[42] As Richard put it, not so tongue-in-cheek, 'Unemployment may not be soluble but poison gas producers know no obstacle.'[43] There was mustard gas, which choked but unfortunately didn't kill, and the arsenic-based so-called (after its smell) 'geranium' gas, which would enable two planes to get rid of London. Then there were the weapons of bacteriological warfare: the germs of bubonic plague, anthrax or rabies; the pollution of drinking water by typhus or cholera. Even the government's calculations for a conventional war were wrong, as the falling birthrate – a 70 per cent decline since 1911 – would mean inadequate 'cannon fodder'.[44]

Crime and Tragedy is Richard's first major statement of that theme linking the public and the private which most preoccupied him during the first phase of his life beyond the County Fire Office. Wars and other disasters had implications for people's sexual behaviour. For a nation to be sustained, more deaths required more births. Without enough people, no nation could be a great power. But the moral lesson hardly jumped out of the statistics; it had to be put there in phrases such as 'the British race'[45] and 'the unity of the Empire'.[46]

. Most of Richard's vital statistics might have been soundly based, but the purpleness of his prose and the unoriginality of some of his sentiments were sufficient to prevent anyone publishing the book. Kay's typed letters in 1936–7 accompanied the manuscript to Secker and Warburg, Victor Gollancz, the *News Chronicle*, the Union of Democratic Control, and Sheppard's Peace Pledge Union. In his letter to the Peace Pledge Union,[47] Richard mentioned that he'd been speaking on the same platform as Canon Morris of Birmingham at Watford last month (one can almost hear Kay inciting him to add this), and offered to make any adaptations the union might want. But they didn't want, though they were sure he had worked hard on it, and neither did Arthur Cummings of the *News Chronicle*, whose opinion was that the book too much resembled other recently published tomes on world affairs.[48] Richard had also met Dorothy Woodman of the Union of Democratic Control at Watford, and he offered to add a chapter on Spain for them, but they had unfortunately published a number of pamphlets covering the same ground.[49] By November 1936, he was getting desperate to see the results of his clandestine labours in the light of day. He dispatched *Crime and Tragedy* to ex-suffragette Sylvia Pankhurst, suggesting a serialization of the chapter on Abyssinia in *New Times and Ethiopia News* – or, indeed, any other means of getting the material into print she could think of. He didn't hear from her until the end of the following May, by which time she still hadn't read the manuscript, and numerous further promptings typed by Kay were required to get it back. Finally, Richard wrote to tell Sylvia duplicitously that an offer of publication had been made, at which point she wrote back to say she liked it, and might do as he had suggested originally and serialize part of it in her newspaper. When Richard replied enthusiastically, he made the mistake of asking for money – £2 for as much of the manuscript as she wanted.[50] Sylvia was outraged at the suggestion that she should pay,[51] so that was the end of that particular saga. As a literary agent to whom Richard also passed the manuscript kindly put it: 'It is quite well done but [. . .] such books only get accepted when they are by well-known writers on politics and economics.'[52]

Richard's task was therefore clear: to get himself well known. *Crime and Tragedy* was written under the pseudonym of Richard Caston 'for business reasons'.[53] He feared the wrath of the County Fire Office, should they discover what he was up to. He was now leading a definite double life. Writing to an office colleague in April 1939, enclosing an autographed copy of the first book he did succeed in getting published, *Poverty and Population*, he admitted:

> It was with some misgiving that I ordered a copy of my book for you [. . .] It is unnecessary for me to explain why it has failed to penetrate the County Fire Office but perhaps my second book which deals more particularly with Food and Defence problems[54] may find its way to the stomachs of the hierarchy.
>
> I was sorry to hear that your brother was not at his best in the Troc, I and four others went there too but perhaps we were too interested in the strip-tease display to notice such things. I hope you were not in the crowd that got caught in a police raid in some low night club.
>
> I must now write some reports on Loss of Profits otherwise I might lose sight of the next step on the 'County' ladder.[55]

The 'all-chaps-together' careerist tone of this letter is at odds with the seriousness of the letters Richard was writing in the other half of his life. And the reference to the insurance career ladder was inserted as an alibi, as he was by now actively seeking other jobs. For example, at the beginning of February 1939, he had written to the Clerk of the Grocers' Company about three scholarships which had recently been advertised for 'enquiring into the causation of prevalent diseases or into means of prevention of premature death'.[56]

From 1936 on, an increasing stream of Titmuss writings designed to bring him the reputation advised by his agent issues forth from the Forest Hill typewriter. Richard keeps a meticulous list of the coverage and rates of different journals and magazines: 'British Empire Review – 1,200 £2 2s'; 'Everybody's Weekly – Outspoken – Informative £3 3s per 1200'; 'Cornhill Magazine – Educated. £1 1s per page'. He positively pesters magazine and newspaper editors with his wares. For example, his letter to the editor of *Picture Post* followed a series of illustrated articles on 'depressed areas'. Richard said it had occurred to him that some of the facts in his book, *Poverty and Population*, might be good material, and was enclosing copies of reviews from the *Daily Herald* and the *Listener*: 'it seems to me that some of the statistics it would be useful to quote might well be illustrated by something on the following lines, namely: 1. Family at meal in slum house. 2. Doctor visiting slum house. 3. Ambulance scenes in slum district. 4. Long queues of relations and friends at Hospital. 5. Funeral scenes in slum district. 6. Orphans (illustrating excessive maternal mortality). 7. Physical examination of malnourished school children. 8. Physical examination and rejection of Army recruits.'[57] Not only is Richard Titmuss trying to make a name for himself here, he's also trying to make some money as well, caught as he is between the need to support his mother in the unsold Hendon house and Kay's computations of what it costs for the two of them to be married and fund a home of their own.

Poverty and Population, Richard's first published book, appeared in 1938.[58] Its focus was the importance and incidence of preventable death associated with poor diet and other negative environmental factors. Richard showed that both preventable death and poor environment were strongly differentiated across the North–South regional divide. His estimate was that some 50,000 British men, women and children were dying unnecessarily every year. The disappearance of 'one-quarter of our population every generation' was plugged in the publisher's promotion of the book as evidence of 'the presence of intense poverty' hitherto ignored because of the refusal of public opinion to recognize that such conditions were possible 'in the heart of the British Empire'.[59]

Poverty and Population started out as a pamphlet, but Richard had the same trouble getting it published as he had with *Crime and Tragedy*. The Liberal Publications Department turned him down, and an appeal to historian G. D. H. Cole led to a contact with the New Fabian Research Bureau, who suggested a book instead. Meanwhile, a friend had shown the outline to Macmillan; Harold Macmillan, who was then active in the family publishing house, agreed to take it on. Demographer David Glass[60] suggested that Lord Horder,[61] President of the Eugenics Society and physician to the royal family, might be willing to write a preface. Horder penned a short complimentary note from his private clinic in Welbeck Street, and sent Richard some possible proof corrections from a liner en route to Gothenburg in Sweden. Horder's preface amounted to Eugenics Society sponsorship for the book, which received a good deal of media coverage. 'Social Waste – State Must Intervene' said the *Chester Chronicle*;[62] 'Two Nations: the North and the South' noted the *Yorkshire Observer* appropriately;[63] while the *Daily Herald*[64] quoted the 50,000 who were condemned to die of poverty and the *Sheffield Telegraph* concluded that the consequence of all this was 'Britain's Peril of Extinction – Serious Threats to Our Racial Stock'.[65] The *Newcastle Journal* repeated Richard's vivid sentiments about maternal mortality,[66] which in his somewhat unkind view was more likely to be cured 'by a herd of cows than a herd of specialists'. The *Medical Press*[67] picked up *Poverty and Population* rather late in the day, but enthused about it, deeming it 'an outstanding book' which should be read by 'every medical and every educated man'. 'Go on!' it urged. 'Buy it and talk it over with your wife!'

In addition to all the administrative and writing work, Richard was by now increasingly in demand as a public speaker. In 1936, his engagements included a speech on 'the general outlook of youth and the question of peace' to the Watford and District Peace Council in November,[68] participation in a Youth House lecture series ('Music and the Twenty-first century, Mr M. Tippett', 'Mr R. Titmuss on the Geneva Youth Congress', 'Mr P. Ridgeway, Youth and the Theatre') at Youth House,[69] and a meeting at the City of London Debating Society, which wanted him to talk to the motion 'That the Declining Birth-Rate is a Menace to White Civilization'.[70] Richard himself preferred the term 'Race Suicide'.[71]

His life was not all work and no play: there were some pleasant interludes. One of these occurred in the summer of 1939, just before the outbreak of war, when Richard took Kay to Cambridge for a few days for a meeting of the Nineteenth Liberal Summer School at the University Arms Hotel. The advance programme anticipated that, by the time August came, world events might have already answered some of the questions the meeting would address, but hoped that even in 'this year of dark foreboding' people would be able to enjoy the mental stimulus of the lectures and discussions provided in the pleasant atmosphere of Cambridge: 'vigorous tennis', 'lazy afternoons in a punt', 'expeditions to Colleges and to the charming East Anglian countryside'.[72]

Richard spoke on 'Contemporary Poverty: Its Regional Distribution and Social Consequences' at the morning session on 9 August. The session was chaired by Lucy Masterman, Liberal candidate and poet, whose elegy to her husband Kay was later preserved in the brown suitcase.[73] Richard's talk was followed by one from Laurence

Cadbury on 'A Population Policy and Family Allowances'. At the suggestion of C. P. Blacker,[74] who shared the administration of the Population Investigation Committee[75] with Cadbury as Treasurer, Cadbury and Titmuss exchanged notes on their talks in advance so as to avoid duplication. More copies of the *Poverty and Population* reviews went to Cadbury, and Richard noted that he planned to restrict himself 'to an examination of indices of poverty, such as mortality statistics, unemployment, poor relief, overcrowding, etc. I thought of extending this,' he went on chattily:

> to cover an international comparison with conditions in such countries as U.S.A., parts of the Dominions and Scandinavia (i.e. the Oslo experiment where the Infant Mortality rate has been reduced to below 30 per 1000) to show that in some respects we are falling behind (to take one example, Buenos Aires (56) and Tokyo (90) have now reduced their Infant Mortality rates to below that for Glasgow, where one in ten die before reaching the age of one).
>
> I also thought of illustrating the regional incidence of poverty in the U.K. to show that the continued growth of an unsound distribution of population and wealth demands inter alia, regional government and national economic planning.

Richard intended to impress Cadbury with his erudition. He also thought he knew what Cadbury would be saying: 'These are problems in terms of communities, whilst you I take it will be more concerned with individuals in dealing with Family Allowances. As neither of us will be there to advocate larger families but to emphasize the need for (a) the elimination of social waste, and (b) the creation of conditions in which people will wish to bear children, it seems that I should begin and leave you with the problem of being constructive . . .'[76]

Richard's presentation at the Liberal Summer School flagged the direction his intellectual interests were now taking: health, and the relationship with social conditions; the deleterious health effects of unemployment; the development of adequate measures of health; the importance of good nutrition. The links between these issues derived both from his statistical computations and his reading, and from personal observation. In 1938, he and Kay travelled for both his work and hers to one of the depressed areas in the North. She left no record of her visit – a silence which seems to symbolize the progressive transformation of her professional identity from public social worker to personal assistant: Richard's helpmate and his right-hand woman. The short (unpublished) essay Richard wrote about their visit to the North delineates the human reality which for him always prompted the academic study. It must have supported Kay's conviction that without her introduction of social reality into his dry statistics, the man who helped to make the welfare state might himself never have made it:

As the car bumped along on the uneven ground and slowly came to a standstill the four men turned and looked at us. They evinced no surprise as they sat there on the bench at the back of the lavatory wall on that dull September afternoon. The stone wall ran along to the end of the row of slums as the stony ground sloped down to the Solway Firth. To the left of the men sprawled the communal drying ground. It was a Monday and the tawdry bits of finery, the one-and-eleven penny blouse, the cheap woollen pants, the darned and mended underclothes, and all the emblems of unfreedom stirred slightly in the breeze [...] Between the pants and an over-patched shirt could be faintly seen the coast of Scotland.

In front of the men the ground was dusted with the worn out playthings of a derelict industry. Mangled tins and bits of twisted, tarnished iron competed with sprouting weeds for a place in the watery sun. Ahead ranged the grey, menacing dome of a cold, immobile slag heap. Towards this the men sat and stared without expression. They were middle-aged with lined, greying faces [...] Collectively and individually these victims of a grey mechanomorphic civilisation had nothing to decide. Even their biological needs were satisfied by a fish-and-chip culture. Protein was obtained from the fish, the potatoes and fat supplied the vitamins and minerals whilst the newspaper provided the roughage.

We turned and went into the Unemployed Club alongside the bench. There were about twenty men inside [...] One of us offered to play table-tennis. The game went on in silence until the ball was hit against the ceiling and some of us laughed. The man who was playing smiled for the first time. Smiled as though it hurt [. . .] Society had denied to him the right to work for ten years. The broad civilising sweep of a just and humane democracy had by-passed West Cumberland.[77]

It was the relationship between people and their social environment that fascinated him. What accounts for the fact that some people live a long time, while others don't, and some people are more susceptible to some diseases than others? How important are the relative inputs of biology and social differences? In 1937, Richard began a lifelong membership of the Eugenics Society,[78] whose central concern lay in precisely these kinds of questions. During the war, he was to become very involved in the business of the Eugenics Society, as his concern with social aspects of health fed neatly into the Eugenics Society's need to disentangle itself from the more biologically determinist definition of eugenics which smacked of Nazism, and the contacts the society offered Richard proved he was making a distinctly smart career move.

As a result of his visit to the depressed areas, Richard wrote to Bill le Gros Clark of the Committee Against Malnutrition to suggest that they might collaborate on a social survey of such areas, particularly those where the unemployment rate was above 50 per cent.[79] Clark, a writer on social and industrial problems (and also of two novels and many short stories), was the prime mover behind the Committee Against Malnutrition. He'd served in the First World War, and had lost his right eye and hand on the last day of the war, becoming completely blind because of damage to his other eye. Many people remembered him for his extraordinary ability to find his way unaided round houses that he'd visited only once or twice before.[80] The survey Richard proposed to carry out with him would be funded by the Friends' Committee. This contact resulted, not in a social survey, but in a joint book, *Our Food Problem*, which was published as a Penguin Special in 1939. Richard contributed material to the book's second half, 'Stamina of the British People'. *Our Food Problem* argued the need for a planned food policy, whereby Government-subsidized schemes would ensure the proper distribution of food to those most in need, especially children, young people and childbearing women. Richard and le Gros Clark declared their political bias by noting calmly that, 'It is perhaps difficult for one interested in human diets not to be a democrat.'[81]

Richard's growing interest in eugenics, his nutrition and his Leverhulme work all produced a flood of national and international correspondence – more work for Kay's typewriter. One strategy for becoming well known was to be a nuisance. He'd actually practised being a nuisance in the County Fire Office, by spearheading a campaign for higher salaries and getting 90 per cent of those in his own salary range to sign a statement objecting to the low salaries they earned compared to those of other insurance office employees.[82] Less domestically, and spurred on by the paucity of good statistics, Richard took on the Registrar-General, writing in January 1938 to complain that while cows, eggs, pigs and potatoes could be graded, human mothers couldn't, as birth registration forms had no space for the ages of women when they reproduced.[83] During the war he took the Registrar-General to task again for failing to publish the usual annual medical statistics.[84] But it was genuinely the case that the work Richard wanted to do could not be done without social-statistical data. The following month he wrote (enclosing yet another pamphlet advertising *Poverty and Population*), to the editors of the Population Index of the School of Public Affairs in Princeton, New Jersey. He'd been through their valuable index at the London School of Economics for statistical data on mortality, but had been unable to find what he needed – mortality trends from 1900 to 1938 for Germany, Sweden, Holland, Denmark, the UK and New Zealand, with details (preferably for urban and rural populations separately) of all-cause death rates, the rates of death from tuberculosis, cancer and other main killing diseases, and infant and maternal mortality rates. Did they know of any 'authoritative studies' analysing the trend in mortality for the countries in question, with particular reference to the social and economic causes influencing the decline in the past twenty to thirty years? Did they have any knowledge of 'attempts in any country to correlate variations in mortality rates with variations in unemployment'?[85] The Secretary of the League of Nations in Geneva received a very similar letter.[86]

Yet sometimes the contacts Richard made had more of a social than a statistical purpose. After hearing the Quaker penal reformer (and relative of the chocolate Cadburys), Margery Fry,[87] speak at a Liberal meeting in London, he wrote to her in January 1939 about the links she'd mentioned between poverty and crime, telling her that he himself wanted to investigate the possible relationship between regional morbidity and mortality rates and the incidence of juvenile delinquency and crime.[88] His work had led him to think about the influence of environment on the propensity to crime. So he wanted to know the incidence of crime by sex and age for different regions of the country. Margery Fry directed him to Dr Herman Mannheim, part-time lecturer in criminology at the London School of Economics.[89] Similarly, in February 1939, Richard contacted the Right Honourable Sir Montague Barlow of the Royal Commission on the Geographical Distribution of the Industrial Population. The minutes of the discussion the Commission had had with officials in the Registrar-General's Office, and with the Ministry of Health, on the subject of the effects of unemployment and economic status on mortality rates, had, he said, made extremely interesting reading. Apparently, the Commission had asked the relevant government departments to undertake further investigation. Had any such investigation been done, and, if so, what were the results? He noticed that his book *Poverty and Population* was referred to in the minutes, and he thought that the Commission would like to know that he was now carrying out further statistical research.[90]

Some of these contacts led to a sustained and wide-ranging exchange of ideas which show how Richard was managing to infiltrate with his population and health work an international community of scholars and social policy analysts. One example is the protracted correspondence he had with Professor Leonard Marsh, Director of Social Research at McGill University in Canada. Richard first wrote to Marsh in 1938 to compliment him on his book on health and unemployment: 'My book *Poverty and Population* (concerning which I enclose a leaflet) was written about the same time and has just been published. Lord Horder who writes the Foreword was, you know, the late King George's Physician.' Richard went on to summarize the contents of his book at length because he thought Marsh would be interested in his findings, but also because, as usual, he wanted some help getting further data, specifically: the death rate from all causes and from tuberculosis for the 15–24 and 25–34 age groups for Canada as a whole, and preferably for one or more large Canadian city. Did Marsh know any book like *Poverty and Population* for North America? 'Or, for instance, are there any publications, official or otherwise, showing the death rates by age groups of the populations according to their geographical distribution?'[91]

Marsh replied to say he'd ordered Richard's book, and would get the information he wanted for him. In January 1939, Richard wrote to Marsh again about nutrition and family health. He was concerned with the 'man-value' scale of Cathcart and Murray which was widely used as a way of measuring nutritional standards. This scale took the adult man as a unit and expressed women and children as fractions of a 'man'; thus a child of 12 to 14 years was considered 0.9 of a man. The Cathcart and Murray coefficients were based on sex and age energy requirements which had recently been recognized to be inaccurate. They could not be applied in the same way to proteins, minerals and vitamins; thus, for example, a 12–14-year-old needed 90 gm of protein per day, and a man only 70 gm. 'I think you will agree that this factor is of fundamental importance in any survey of family needs.'[92] Marsh did, and wrote, enclosing the data Richard wanted, to say he planned to pass on the information in Richard's letter to the Dominion Bureau of Statistics, who were currently carrying out a survey of Canadian family budgets.[93] In May, Richard thanked Marsh, and at the same time sent him the results of two further studies of family nutrition – one carried out in Bristol, and one of 5,000 families by Sir William Crawford, which showed that 52 per cent of the British population lived in homes where the per capita weekly expenditure on food fell below the diet prescribed by the League of Nations.[94]

But if Richard was interested in the health of all populations, he was especially interested, because of the war, in German health. Between 1939 and 1942 he worked on German vital and medical statistics, acting as adviser on this subject to the Ministry of Economic Warfare from 1941. It was extremely difficult to get adequate information about what was happening to the health of the German people. In January 1939, Richard called at the Anglo-German Academic Bureau in 45 Russell Square to see what they could offer. But they weren't very useful, and at the end of the month he wrote a long letter to the Ministry of Health asking for help.[95] February saw another demanding letter, this time to a 'Professor Dr N. W. Posthumus' of the International Institute for Social History in

Amsterdam. Richard had noticed a mention of his book *Poverty and Population* in the Institute's bulletin no. 3 for 1938, and would welcome some help with gathering international statistics. He would like the German death rates in all age groups for all causes and specific diseases according to sex, with a breakdown for large towns, rural areas and different administrative districts; infant and maternal mortality rates, similarly disaggregated by area; and any information bearing on the relationship between death rates and economic status or sex.[96]

It was important for propaganda reasons that the Nazis should not be seen to be succeeding in their social policy. At the end of 1941, Richard hired a German-speaking research assistant, Marie Meinhardt, who helped by translating from the German what figures were available. Marie later worked with Richard on his social medicine projects. She was herself a refugee from the Nazis, and the many weeks she worked without pay because Richard and the Ministry couldn't sort themselves out became a minor detail in the context of Richard's overall kindness to her, and his later support for her naturalization as a British citizen.[97] Richard was interested in many indices of German health, including the birth rate, which the National government had been trying to boost by a variety of means. He found these wanting in their success. He also found it difficult to get his material published. A general piece called 'Health under the Nazis'[98] was eventually accepted in the journal *Truth* in 1940. In it Richard argued that the direct effect of Nazism in Germany over the six years from 1933 to 1939 had been to increase death rates. For example, the infant mortality rate in Munich was now 100 per cent higher than that in Chicago; although German scientists had given the world the anti-diphtheria toxin, four times as many children were now dying of diphtheria in Germany than in the United States. In 1942, the *Lancet* took a piece on 'Recent German vital statistics'[99] and the *Spectator* an earlier one on 'Hitler's man-power problem'.[100]

The health of British army recruits was also of concern to Richard. The tradition of using the health of army recruits as a measure of national fitness had been established in the nineteenth century.[101] Because recruits to armies were so exhaustively weighed and measured, this provided a ready means of accessing general standards of population health.[102] Indeed, in *Poverty and Population*, Richard was able to show that regional differences in mortality and health were paralleled by different rates of rejection of army recruits: rejection rates in the North were 50–80 per cent higher than in the South. But, again, he needed more data. His letter to the Director-General of the War Office's Medical Division asked for information for each of the years 1903 to 1913 and 1928 to 1938 on the total number of applicants to the army, the numbers rejected for physical or medical reasons, and the numbers accepted for each of the War Office regional divisions.[103] The reply he got[104] was that these data were all available already. This response was evidently inadequate, as Richard pursued the answers he wanted by the device of getting a question asked in the House of Commons. His long-suffering contact there was the Liberal MP Sir Richard Acland.[105] Richard Titmuss first wrote to Richard Acland in August 1938, introducing himself again by means of *Poverty and Population*, which he had noticed 'was quoted by Mr Cartland in the House last Monday'. Richard wanted Acland to put down the following question and let him know the result: 'To ask the Secretary of State for War (a) The percentage of recruits for the Army rejected on medical examination during 1937 for each of the separate War Office Areas in England, Wales and Scotland. (b) What percentage of the total applicants were unemployed? (c) Whether the present standard of acceptance differs to any material extent from that in use during the period of 1901–1913 inclusive.'[106]

Acland undertook to pursue these questions on Richard's behalf, but the War Office made it plain that they would rather communicate the information by private letter than publicly in the house. A total of 30.3 per cent of applicants in the year before September 1937 were unemployed; there had been no material changes in the physical standards applied – the required height was never lower than 5 ft 2 in, but the necessary chest measurement had been reduced by half an inch in 1931. Spectacles and dentures were now supplied at public expense to men whose eyes or teeth would previously have caused them to be rejected, and those with minor physical disabilities were now accepted provided they agreed to have the necessary treatment.[107]

Richard contacted Acland again in connection with a debate on encouraging the younger unemployed to enter the defence forces, and to send him the fruits of his labours which might be of use in the debate. He'd discovered that the total rejection rate for England

and Wales in 1936 was 48.2 per cent; for the Home Counties it was 32 per cent. If the lower rejection rate of the Home Counties had obtained over the whole of the country, 5,993 more recruits would have joined the army during the year; if the rates had been the same for the previous ten years, the additional recruits would have numbered some 50,000 – half the strength of the total army in 1935.[108] Richard's comparison of the rejection figures with pre-war rates showed the latter to be lower, which was disquieting. Acland promised to make the data available to anyone who was going to speak in the debate, but the Liberal who did do so refused to include them because his speech was already written.[109]

Richard was also trying to get his material on the health of the army accepted for publication. The magazine *Reynolds News* was offered an article on army rejection figures.[110] A longer piece had been sent to *The Times*, but they had refused it, as Richard had expected they would. *Reynolds News* didn't take the piece, but they did use some of Richard's figures in an editorial called 'Arms and the Men'.[111] Richard thought all this non-publication of his vital data was of some political interest in itself. In April, he wrote to the King's physician, Lord Horder, to tell him about *The Times*'s refusal to publish his revelations about the state of the British army: 'To what extent it was not accepted on grounds of national interest I do not know.' Did Lord Horder realize that, of the last million men who applied to the regular army, 650,000 had been rejected as unfit? One of the conclusions to be drawn from this was that more detailed data on the economic status of applicants were needed; could Lord Horder insert a request for this in the debate about the Military Training Bill next Thursday?[112]

But all this letter-writing, statistic-getting and library work was liable to leave Richard without the kind of day-to-day contact with those very experiences of poverty and ill-health about which he was writing. How did he know what was really going on? And who was he to speak on behalf of other people? One somewhat critical letter, signed, 'a Mother & Grandmother – a born lover of children' reached him in August 1939:

> I see in *The News Chronicle* to-day that you are devoting your life to an investigation of poverty & I write to wish you God speed in this noble undertaking.

You also say that 'It is not surprising that parents do not desire to bring children into an overcrowded underfed community.'

Also I say it is not surprising that parents are reluctant to bring children into this war ridden world. It is the height of cruelty to thus provide more cannon fodder. Children do not ask to be born.

When war is abolished, the best parents will have children naturally without wanting to be paid for having them! I see no references to the *Mothers* in the discussions at the Liberal Summer School – Surely Mothers should be the first to be consulted. They have all the suffering connected with childbearing, childbirth & childrearing. It ill becomes *men* to urge it upon them.

Men should exercise self control, & then there would be no need for birth control or contraceptives etc. It is appalling that now after war has been proved to be worse than futile, the Nations should be rushing into another mass slaughter – slaughter of the innocents chiefly. These boys of 20–21 have 'done nothing worthy of death' & they are caught in the war machine & deliberately taught the most cruel methods of mass murder. Do please take your stand against it all & especially on behalf of all the men women and children who will be the first victims. I know only too well what I am writing about & I beseech you to do all you can to prevent such a catastrophe.[113]

This was not to be the only complaint Richard received about his failure to take the experiences of women seriously. But the fault lay in the underlying conceptualization of women and society; the public and the private. The language of 'parents' which hid the different interests and behaviour of mothers and fathers was merely a symptom of it.

When Richard eventually got his paper on the health of the army published, a Major-General Alexander of Beaulieu wrote to point out that it wasn't only poverty that made unfit soldiers. After thirty-five years in the army, he knew that some of the toughest soldiers were 'East End cockneys' who lacked good food when young, and some of the best soldiers came from poor Irish peasant stock with a diet of potatoes. Was this a question of the survival of the fittest, perhaps?[114] Richard's careful reply pointed out the beneficial effect of proper feeding *in* the army on a man's health. He doubted whether the inclusion of meat in the diet was necessary 'always providing that protein is obtained through the medium of cheese, eggs and certain vegetables'. Further, the Irish peasant, though poor in a financial sense, may have been better off in terms of nutrition than many inhabitants of our over-industrialized cities. 'For example, the infant mortality rate in certain parts of Ireland in the nineteenth century was lower than it is in Glasgow today.'[115]

One wonders whether the Major-General took this in, and what he made of it if he did. Richard Titmuss was obviously a most persistent young man. He was capable of extraordinary single-mindedness in the pursuit of the questions he wanted to answer, and there were many of them. He had made up his mind that he would not be working in the County Fire Office for ever, but as he had no education to speak of, his only alternative was to try to make his work known by pestering the powerful. It was fortunate for him that these were times in which anyone with 'any remote claim' to be a statistician was likely to be 'gobbled up [. . .] by some government office'[116] – as, indeed, Richard eventually was. When he applied to become a fellow of the Royal Statistical Society in 1940, they were amazed to hear he was not already one.[117] Richard didn't tell them that his main reason for joining was that he needed the services of their library, as those of the LSE which he normally used had been rendered inaccessible with the school's wartime evacuation to Cambridge.

In all this furthering of his career, Richard was substantially helped in both motive and activity by Kay, who must have seen in Richard's gangling, dark-haired frame an intellectual and emotional passion just looking for a home. The home would not be her – or, rather, it would, but she wouldn't be enough for it. The upwards direction of Richard Titmuss's career to higher peaks than the Hendon Young Liberals, or the management of Youth House's electricity arrangements, was *her* work as much, or as well, as *his*. Or was it?

FIVE

What love can do

'Everything had changed, yet nothing was different,'[1] wrote Vera Brittain, of *Testament of Youth* fame, about the moment on the morning of 3 September 1939 when Prime Minister Neville Chamberlain announced to the British people that the Second World War had begun. Vera Brittain was in the New Forest with her children when she heard the news. After listening to Chamberlain's BBC broadcast, she went for a walk. The countryside in the autumn sunshine was incongruously peaceful and beautiful; yellow sunflowers opened their hearts to butterflies beneath cloudless skies. Kay and Richard Titmuss were also in the English countryside, in Bedfordshire, at the farm belonging to Richard's Aunt Lilian. 'Sept. 3. 1939. War 11.00 a.m.,' wrote Richard on a scrap of paper preserved in the brown suitcase:

> The first casualty: truth, At 11.20 Neville Chamberlain said over B.B.C. 'Our conscience is clear.' Outside at Barton Hill the sun was pouring down. I wondered if it would continue to do so when this War – the end to which no man could see – ended. Was Europe – was mankind – doomed? Yet it might not have been had we in this country followed a moral foreign policy from 1931. 8 years of stupidity [. . .] The only thing Kay and I find solace in – we have no children. And what will happen to the birth rate in G.B., France and Germany? Will it drop like it did in 1914 never to recover?[2]
>
> All our efforts and work towards improving social conditions ruined in a minute. Our one object now appears to be but animal preservation.

Every possible resonance of that much-used word 'futile' must have echoed in many people's heads as they heard the news that day. Kay and Richard Titmuss had pinned their own hopes for peace on an international movement of young and like-minded people, who would shake governments out of selfish militaristic foreign policies. Now all that effort was wasted.

At the farm in Bedfordshire, nothing was different, although everything had changed. The farm acquired a new significance for Kay and Richard as a retreat for him and a home for her; it was the setting of a series of letters she preserved in the brown suitcase, and which are quoted in this chapter, many of them as they were written. The letters tell their own story, and through them the dry-boned account of how Richard Titmuss's public career was made and Kay Titmuss's unmade acquires the flesh that is the detail of everyday life. In the act of understanding how people go about their daily lives, they become human to us. But the story of the letters is really many stories. There is the story of his role and hers: that of the split between public and private worlds; and the division between dangerous metropolis and safe rural haven which involved much complicated bridging, with tales of unpredictable, over-full trains and rusty bicycles. There is the private story of the war itself, the form its impacts and dislocations took in the lives of ordinary people. Then there is the public story of the war, and the impact it had on the social services and on social policy in Britain. But while both *his* letters and *hers* narrate the everyday events, only Richard was to chart the broader social context in the work he began in 1942 as official war historian, when he moved from the County Fire Office to Whitehall to begin the business of sifting through thousands of official and unofficial files in order to record the backroom domestic story of the war. In this hiatus between the public and the private, the narrative of the letters is ineluctably and increasingly gendered. The tension introduced into Richard and Kay's partnership by their separation positions them differently; an inequality of both experience and sentiment follows. During the early months of the war their lives fell into an archetypal gender pattern: man in the public sphere, woman in the private. The move to the country replaced for Kay the energetic activity of social work in Fulham with the different rhythm of private welfare work on the farm. And her country refuge identified her with the 'rural idyll' of Victorian mythology[3]: the safe, green place where domestic life could flourish uninterrupted by the strains of the commercial world.

Ever since Richard's family moved to London in 1918, he had been used to spending time at Barton Hill Farm forty miles north-west of London – the farm his grandfather, Hoppy Farr, had bought for his mother's brother Fred, and Fred's wife, Aunt Lilian. Fred's early death in 1918 had left Lilian in charge of the farm; Bob, their son, was twenty years old when the Second World War broke out. Today, Barton Hill Farm is still there, red-bricked and prosperous, and backed by acres of chemically aided peas and beans grown for frozen food companies [Plate 10]. When the farm was first let to Hoppy Farr, it was described in estate agent-ese as a 'good light land Farm [. . .] including 45 Acres Pasture' with a 'Modern Residence' 'suitable for a Gentleman Farmer's occupation'. The large area in front of the farmhouse accommodated stables, a cow house, horse boxes, an engine house, a large barn with a cement floor, a fowl house and miscellaneous other useful outbuildings.[4] A public footpath running down beside the farmhouse grounds leads to the beautiful chalk grasslands of a deep valley carved by the last ice age [Plate 11]. Rare butterflies and wildflowers flourish on what has now been turned into a nature reserve, but was in those days just undisturbed woodland, where couples like Kay and Richard could happily wander, look for blackberries or discuss matters of war and peace. The sepia photographs in the family album show Richard in the 1920s and '30s as an awkward young man in an open-necked shirt and with a mouth full of badly fitting dentures helping with farm tasks: making hay, feeding chickens. In one photograph, which looks like something out of the nineteenth century [Plate 12], Richard is fetching water with a pony and cart from the pond at the front of the farmhouse for the chickens at the back.

The nearest town to Barton Hill Farm is Luton, famous since the seventeenth century for its straw-hat industry.[5] In the 1930s and '40s, the area round Luton was free from smoke and industrial pollution and from the 'fringe' developments that would later put it within attractive commuting distance of London. The outbreak of war turned Luton and the country round it into an evacuation area. The government's plans for the administration of the war on the home front centred on the need to defend the population against air attack. Estimates as to what this might mean in terms of daily bombardment and casualties had been made from the early 1920s on, based on the out-of-date evidence of the damage wrought by eighteen German air raids in 1917–18, and otherwise poorly inspired guesses. Britain was divided into evacuation, reception and neutral areas. No local authority wanted to be categorized as a reception area, and 200 of those so defined pleaded to be regarded as neutral.[6] Eventually, over 14 million people were classified as living in evacuation areas, but only certain 'vulnerable' groups were considered actually to merit evacuation: schoolchildren, younger children, pregnant women and the adult disabled. The official evacuation exodus started on 31 August, before war was declared; the next day the first of the four million mothers and children classified as evacuable were moved out of the vulnerable areas. It was a massive operation. Thousands of buildings were requisitioned, patients summarily discharged from hospital, and offenders from prison: working out the railway timetables alone was a major headache. In three days 1.5 million people were transferred from the cities to safer places, all without a single accident or casualty, though not without discomfort, particularly for young children, many of whom had to make long journeys on trains without corridors or lavatories.[7]

The Luton area received 8,000 evacuees in three days of that first week of war.[8] Most of these were London schoolchildren. Medical inspection of the evacuees allayed local concerns about health problems, revealing an incidence of infestation which was no greater than the level already prevailing locally; only 133 evacuees had to pass through the local cleansing station.[9] But throughout Britain, town and country greeted each other in a critical mood. The country didn't want the town to come, there were many deserved and undeserved complaints about the dirty state and rude behaviour of evacuees, and the system whereby country householders could take their pick of those who would be billeted on them was described as 'a cross between an early Roman slave market and Selfridge's bargain basement'.[10] Catholic mothers with several children were especially unpopular. There was a shortage of essential resources, including medical equipment, maternity beds, furniture, crockery, blackout material and blankets. Amongst the things the war did prove good for was the health of the textile trade, which experienced its greatest boom for many years when the government suddenly ordered millions of blankets. The other vital statistic augmented by the start of the war, and noted by Richard Titmuss's keen statistical eyes,[11] was the marriage rate; August and September 1939 saw more British marriages per month than ever previously recorded.

The months from September 1939 to April 1940 acquired a name coined by the Americans: the 'phoney' war.[12] The blackout came down; cinemas and theatres hastily closed. Everyone waited for the bombs to fall. Before September, few people had believed war to be inevitable, and when its declaration was followed by so little apart from endless preparation the atmosphere of uncertainty was heightened: what really was going on? But although the war was deemed 'phoney', on a psychological level it was real. People's lives were already changed.

The figure for official evacuees was more than matched by two million unofficial evacuees, many of whom could not be categorized as belonging to a vulnerable group, but left the cities either to be safe themselves or to work on the land or help with the work of receiving the evacuees. Kay Titmuss was one of these. 'I stayed at Barton Hill to help with evacuees at the outbreak of war,' reads a note in my mother's handwriting in the brown suitcase. 'We had 4 boys in the house & additional catering for land girls. Cooking facilities limited to a 3 burner Florence Oil stove.' Kay's attic bedroom, with a view over the front of the farmhouse, was large enough to house Richard when he visited, and much later in the war, baby Ann. It was a working farm; the first sounds you heard in the morning, particularly high up through the window of that attic room, were those of the pigs being fed in the stalls at the front of the farmhouse. On the back of a photograph of three women posed by the front door, Kay wrote, by way of explanation, 'me, the maid and the landgirl' [Plate 13]. The maid sports a maid's uniform, the land girl looks aggressively free on a bicycle, and my mother wears her gypsy look, scarf tied sideways over her dark hair. Her own diary for 3 September, matching Richard's own, noted: 'The fateful day has arrived. Keynote of despondency. An awful feeling of hopelessness. Lunch had to be prepared for 12 people. Altho' anticipated the blow fell heavily. The country looked so lovely. Cycled with R to Luton & round Lilley & Lane Farm. Tea [. . .] in the pub garden at Lilley. R and I later to the Raven for a drink. Resolved to spend the night happily & in peace & succeeded.' The next day Richard went back to London, the first part of his journey accomplished on the local milk lorry, and Kay helped to prepare the farmhouse for war: 'Main job of the day window screening. With German girl fed [...] chickens. Glorious hot day. Hard to realize we are at war, but R is already separated from me. Temporarily I hope. Torpedoeing of British liner with 160 Americans on board announced.'

Richard escaped being called up for war service because his occupation of 'Insurance Inspector and Surveyor' was a 'reserved' one – considered to be of national importance. During the week he continued to work at the County Fire Office in Regent Street, with his spare-time writing and other activities based in their small flat in St George's Drive, Pimlico, taking up the evenings. In September 1939, most of the County Fire Office staff were evacuated to Hindhead in Surrey, where they shared a converted hotel with firewatchers, the Home Guard and Air Raid Precautions, and worked in offices in corrugated iron huts hastily erected in the hotel grounds.[13] Richard himself dealt with war risks insurance, which included inspecting premises to estimate the risk of fire, and the investigation of claims made. The war brought an enormous boom in the insurance business, though that first winter of the phoney war was dominated with the results of burst pipes and frost damage to cars because of the unusually severe weather.[14] As before, however, it is chiefly what Richard did in his spare time which has survived in the records, not the details of his insurance work ('office rubbish', he calls it in one of his letters).

During the early part of the war, it was Richard's insurance salary that supported them, though Kay tried to keep in touch with her welfare work for the unemployed in Fulham, struggling between her sense of duty to help out at the farm, and the discontent she felt at not doing the work she enjoyed. Encouraged by Richard, she tried to explore setting up welfare centres near the farm, but co-ordinating interests and turning latent enthusiasm into a practicable venture proved difficult, especially since evacuated mothers and children rapidly started returning to the towns. There were also many domestic matters to attend to: arrangements concerning Richard's mother and other relatives, and Kay's own parents in Forest Hill.

They wrote to each other almost every day. To talk on the telephone was a rare treat: letters were the vehicle not only for confiding the events of the day, feelings about the war and each other, and news of family and friends, but for making practical arrangements to meet. The confidence (well-placed) they had in the letters arriving promptly seems extraordinary today, but there are many examples of letters being relied on to set meeting times and places, or transmit other urgently needed information. Thirty-six letters dated between September 1939 and June 1940 – the period of the phoney war – survive in the brown suitcase. Some are typewritten, on the famous Olivetti, which found itself relocated to Bedfordshire, and some are handwritten on thin plain paper or on official County Fire Office notepaper with a picture of Boadicea and a flowing-maned lion in the corner above the inscription 'R. M. Titmuss District Representative'. Apart from when Kay and Richard met and had no need to write to each other, there are some gaps in the correspondence – not everything has been preserved. Kay obviously kept Richard's letters to her, and she must have added hers to him when he died, carrying out any pruning perceived as necessary then.

All the issues Kay and Richard discuss in their letters – the condition of the evacuees, the food shortages, the price rises, the unanticipated effects of government health and social policy – turn up either in Richard's official account of the war, or elsewhere in his versatile, prolific writings and enquiries. Together *they* make history, but only *he* writes it down. Richard Titmuss's methodological, scientific gaze reaches everywhere. Whereas everything Miss T ate in the poem by Walter de la Mare turned into Miss T, everything Mr T experienced turned into an investigation, or a letter to *The Times*, or an article, or a book. Even the peaceful countryside round Barton Hill and the sleepy town of Luton later became the topic of a study conducted by Richard and the local Medical Officer of Health, Dr Fred Grundy. Grundy and Titmuss's study of Luton was published in 1945 under the title *Report on Luton*.[15] The book was a comprehensive record of the borough's population, housing, education, health services, industry and finance, and was based on a meticulous survey of one in ten households conducted in May 1945 by fifty dutiful members of the Women's Voluntary Service. As was the case with many of those with whom Richard worked in these years, Fred Grundy was no ordinary representative of his profession; he was a barrister as well, and later wrote a much-used text on social medicine.[16] After leaving his Luton post in 1949, Grundy became professor of preventive medicine in Cardiff, and then in 1960 one of four assistant director-generals of the World Health Organization with responsibility for public health services and health promotion.[17]

As well as the letters, there is also a diary kept intermittently by Kay. This was sometimes privy to a depth of feeling with which she clearly felt it would be unfair to burden Richard. She lived for their communications and their meetings, and so did he, but she was a woman and he was a man and so her existence depended more on him than his did on her. This psychological truth was reflected in the physical texture of their lives; he did more and had more to report than she did. But this was also because her function and his had different values attached to them: 'Husband lunches at the [. . .] Club, wife does "charring",' as she put it in one of her letters to him. Who, in those unenlightened days, could regard the menial repetitive round of housework with the same wide-eyed stare as the meetings of politicians and social pundits, the calculation of the statistics of war and peace, or the veritable writing of history even as it was lived? Within the narrative of the letters, the shift which started early in their marriage intensified, as Kay took on the task of helping Richard with his logarithms ('I've solved the mystery of the points [. . .] You can take a large number from a smaller'), or cycled to fetch the manuscript of 'our' book, *Crime and Tragedy*, just to remind herself what 'they' had said; and *her* unemployment work became *his* as well ('*We* are re-opening the unemployment centres,' said he).[18] While he laid claim to *her* territory, her claim over *his* was qualitatively different. She gloried in his triumphs, feeling them to be her own; but the concept of her own started at the same time to become merely an idea – a memory. Once her independent life began to slide into the past, Kay started to think she ought to write a 'serious' book about it one day. But the sound of planes overhead disturbed her concentration. There was also the problem of how to avoid writing something too personal, something of the sort their friend François Lafitte's stepfather, Havelock Ellis, shocked the 'drawing room standard of good taste'[19] by publishing in 1940, with its intimate and unnecessary tales of the dark alleys of human sexuality.

So Kay goes to Barton Hill, and no sooner is Richard back in London than he starts plotting the ending of this separation. Perhaps he can relocate to Bedford? Perhaps Kay can open an unemployment centre in Luton? Richard acts as a go-between for conversations between Kay and the Reverend Birch on this matter. There are other more pressing family matters to attend to:

4 September 1939, RMT to KCT at Barton Hill
'Yesterday's Heaven'
Darling,

Chaos at the [County Fire] Office. Have spent some time at
the B. of Trade this morning over War Risks. Whole Office
is being evacuated to Hindhead. I expect I shall be in residence there very soon. One good thing may emerge from
my coming back. Cockman at Bedford has been called up
so I have to-day applied for Bedford Office. In which case
you would have to teach me to drive or at any rate drive me
round.[20] But don't bank on it too much yet my dear.

Chaos and indecision at Hendon. So I have made up their
minds. Have a few hours in the morning so am packing
M[other]. up and shall deposit her on the 2.19 train from
Hendon. I shall load her up with some of the things you
want in cases that are here and perhaps the typewriter for it
seems that most of our stuff will eventually have to be either
at Barton Hill or Bedford. So it might as well start on the
journey. There is no room for Wives at Hindhead I learn.
Will you therefore please meet the parent (the train gets in
at 3.10 p.m. at Luton) be on the platform and help her get
the luggage out of train etc. Perhaps you could get either
Ida or Uncle Hugh to have a car there and take her to
Cockernhoe [the nearby farm belonging to Richard's uncle,
Hugh Farr] and you (plus luggage) to B.H. [Barton Hill]

As for myself dear I'm all right but very lonely and feel
just like one of those beastly balloons that has lost its moorings. Yes I have temporarily lost my moorings. The Laffittes
[François and Eileen Lafitte: François was deputy secretary
of Political and Economic Planning, and Eileen worked with
Kay in the unemployment centre in Fulham] are in a very
bad state – still at Dulwich but likely to be without any
income at all. The tenants have fled and F.'s job seems to
have finished. I am going down there this evening to stay with
them for the night. Then back to the Flat in the morning, the
Office and then Hendon plus luggage. Keep this from the
parent as I did not want to go to Hendon. She will be at
Rene's [Irene, another of Richard's aunts] and thinks that I
shall be at Hindhead.

I enclose a letter from Helen [Johnston]. I expect you will be writing her. Tell her about possibility of Luton job. If it gets going perhaps Eileen could come down and help [...]

Must catch the post as I want you to have this letter ...

Kay got the letter the next day and she must have replied instantly:

5 September, KCT to RMT in London
Darlingest,
Your letter from 'Yesterday's Heaven' this morning fair made me ache but it was marvellous to have news from you. Mother wrote too. They don't know where Don [Donald, Kay's brother] is. She finished by saying Heaven knows when we shall meet again but we must try to keep in touch with letters.

The parent arrived in order with luggage. Hugh met her with me on my bike [...] Where is Helen's letter? It was not in the envelope.

I brought the typewriter with me and left the case for Hugh to bring over later, as he is busy in the fields. Strangely this little machine makes it seem much more like home and will be such a help in writing to my beloved. Thank you very much for sending it.

Not much time to write now as the German girl [?] is just going home and will take this to post. I can see that reading and letter writing will be difficult here but I suppose we shall settle down to some sort of routine. I pray that the Bedford job may materialise but will not bank on it.

It's a heavenly day. I longed to lay in the fields with you but without you I have no desire to do so. I am better occupied and there is a hell of a lot to be done here. Lena [the maid] and David are getting married on Saturday. I shall have to cook at the weekend because Auntie and I feel we just must let them have a weekend.

Some of the evacuees are already returning to London with their babies. They are fed up with the country. Two School teachers called at the farm to-day and asked the way over the hills. One has a home in St George's Square. Her husband is at Guildford. Is there no end to this separation?

I'm quite well thank you. Take care of yourself my love.
Ever your Kay

Richard was trying to sort out the business of their flat in St George's
Drive: could they afford to keep it?

6 September, RMT to KCT at Barton Hill
I am starting this to-night but I don't suppose that I shall
finish it as it is now after eleven. I am in OUR flat but it
seems unreal and all wrong without you.

One of our bedspreads is over part of the window and
faces me whilst the other side is decorated with [the] bed-
spread. My football shorts enfold the reading lamp and my
scarf is over and around the centre light. In all, an effectual
blackout [. . .]

In any event it seems that our Flat must go for the time
being however sentimental I get over it. I have to-night had
a long talk with the Olivers [their landlords]. They are awfully
nice and want to feed me. I have told them frankly about
our position (including the parent) and should I have to
leave the flat (as seems probable – either to Bedford or Hindhead, etc.) they allow us to leave our things here and merely
charge us a nominal storage fee (amount not stated) until
things are clearer [. . .]

Continuation Wed. morning. All clear signal has just gone.
Mr. O. woke me up at 7 o'clock and we all descended to
the basement. I therefore met Mrs. Walker [?] for the first
time – in my dressing gown. We had two hours there sitting
in chairs alongside the centre wall. Tea was served at 7.45.
Family portraits were passed round by Mrs. W. at 8.5. My
dear Husband, Beatrice in adolescence, etc., etc. Even at 14
she was conspicuous[ly] on the port side. Mrs. Mason has a
very good hair net. I must make note to ask her where she
got it as my hair was all over the place. When it was all over
at 9 Mrs. O. insisted on bringing down to me a tray with
tea and four slices of thickly buttered toast. It was damned
good. I think that Mrs. W. has fallen for Mr. O. Beatrice of
course was at her post. Good girl Beatrice.

Just got your letter dear. It made me feel all bitter again

that our lives have been disrupted. So I went and washed up. There was a smell when I first got here – we had left a cabbage – do you remember – on the side – and rigor something had set in.

To keep herself going, Kay cycled to Cockernhoe and brought back the manuscript of Richard's unpublished *Crime and Tragedy*. She wanted to read it again, now that Richard's worst predictions about the failure of government foreign policy had come true. Life in Bedfordshire was hardly intellectually stimulating. She couldn't even rely on the *News Chronicle* being delivered with any regularity. Richard visited Barton Hill at the weekend and told Kay he thought the war would last five years. But ever practical, he pursued their plans for welfare work in Luton: did Kay realize that local authorities had the power to pay helpers to organize local clubs? Why didn't she contact the local council? And the local newspaper for publicity? What about caretaker Clarke – he of the delicate Winter Distress League negotiations – perhaps he'd like a spell in the country? Perhaps Helen Johnston would come up with the funds? 'Damn and blast the warmongers' wrote Kay disconsolately in her 12 September letter:

> *12 September, KCT to RMT in London*
> Just a line so that you hear from me. Nothing to report. The common round of menial tasks continues. Am feeling rather tired. At Barton this morning the Postmaster was slow in his calculations. I drew the money for two weeks for the boys. Auntie thinks I should keep their money for extra housekeeping in addition to the Co-op orders. Not a bad idea I think. The old bike conked out on the back tyre just as I was leaving the village. Slit about 4 inches long right through the cover. The whole thing had perished with standing so many years. Luckily the man at the garage had a new tyre so bang went 7/-. I expected it to happen before long. I got him to see to the back brake also so we should be O.K. with the steed for a bit.

After their mid-September weekend together, Kay confided to her diary that although they both hated the separation, she knew it was the wisest thing to do. But knowing it was sensible didn't stop her feeling depressed. When she wrote in her diary on 17 September she noted that Richard was disturbed by the news of Russia's invasion of Poland: 'He says we are like the flies on the paper we have just put up in this room.' There was little hope of starting any social work in the villages as the evacuated mothers and children had nearly all gone home. Back in London, Richard was determined to keep her interested:

18 September, RMT to KCT at Barton Hill
Here am I writing you tonight and I only left you this morning. It's as absurd as it's true. Nevertheless I shall continue to be ridiculous as long as 'they' keep us apart. So I am going to talk to you here and now and tell you the events of the day. Two very large office posts when I arrived – I had to stand all the way from Luton – I notice with interest that the L.M.S. [London, Midland and Scottish railway] have quite forgotten their share of the Square Deal. I remembered it this morning. So did François. He used to manage on a 6½d cheap day. It's now doubled. Only Hitler could explain – and then it would not be the right answer. But to return to the Office. It (the post) kept me busy for the rest of the morning and the afternoon and I've been on reports this evening. I was even sent some damn silly little case and asked to collect 1/- additional premium (90/- case) and then managed to collect the Builders Insurance on the new Kensington Library – over £43,000. So I hied to Lyons and had steak pudding and cabbage. The latter was interesting. It was pale green in colour, limpid in character, sired in a watery bed and must have been still-born in the cabbage world.

I rang Gwen [Richard's sister]. She got the sack on Saturday. I told her to tell Mother to look out for a job in the Luton News. James [Gwen's husband, a doctor] is still at the same Hospital. Evidently the authorities have not decided where he ought to go for the better prosecution of the War.

[. . .] Also I had a somewhat delicate tete-a-tete (I know it's wrong but then we are living in a world of violent change) with Mrs O. Rent. What about it. Well what do you suggest Mr T.? I don't really know (swivelling on one toe – the new one). Well, what can you afford line etc. Awfully nice about it too. Wanted to help you know. In the end I suggested 22/6. She seemed very happy about it and thought George would love it. It's better than losing me altogether isn't it?

Eileen was glad to have your letter and wants to come and work with you [...] François tells me that Glass [David Glass, the demographer] is also looking for a job. All his other work has come to an end. F. doesn't know yet but he is hopeful.

I have turned out something for Askes [Stephen Aske, Richard's literary agent] and did a spare copy for you to look at. It's only a rough synopsis.

Bedtime story. Ex three week old N.S.&N. [*New Statesman and Nation*] Period about 1850. 'My mother says that at Dursley in Gloucestershire, when ladies and gentlemen used to go out to dinner together on dark nights, the gentlemen pulled out the tail of their shirts and walked before to show the way and light the ladies.' Why not take a tail out of the past?

In the country, Kay had too much time to think. Their next two letters must have crossed in the post:

19 September, KCT to RMT in London
7.15 p.m. Am feeling desperately tired and somewhat depressed. I have only been pottering about all day but I suppose it is fairly energetic pottering. This afternoon I wandered up to the wood with a stick and basket for blackberries and I just ached as I visited the various posts where you and I have lazed in the sun. It was a glorious afternoon – very peaceful – except for the wind, but on the field side of the wood the wind was still and it was perfect. I lay down just near the spot where you and I had a rest one afternoon in the spring and pretended you were with me, but it just didn't work. I got a burr stuck in my hair and I wanted you to take it out for me.

Have just cut two of the boys' hair. Difficult for them to get it done as the barber at Barton only works after 7 in the evening.

I think I shall get in to bed really early with a hot water bottle. I was cold last night, and the old bull [period?] wakened me up in the middle of the night [. . .]

We will go back berrying at the weekend. Pray for fine weather. It will be a grand excuse to get away and laze.

You went without your list of things to bring. Here are a few. None is urgent.

A folder.

Kaross.

Pair of shoe trees.

1 suit hanger.

1 embroidered sheet.

1 small towel.

Thick green jersey.

Yours full of longing (and it's not half time yet), Kay.

19 September, RMT to KCT at Barton Hill

A most depressing individual is talking on the wireless to evacuated Mothers – STAY WHERE YOU ARE STAY WHERE YOU ARE STAY WHERE YOU ARE. But, says Mrs Smith, for 3 years? It is the lull before the storm, THE STORM. Wait – for another month. Then we shall see, so STAY WHERE YOU ARE.

I feel in my bones that things are going to happen in the next 14 days. What, I don't know except that much mud is going down many sewers. What now are our war aims? I, and nobody else I have spoken to, knows. The map of Europe will never again appear as it did on Sept. 2. If the last war was stupid this one is the War of the Morons. François now says that he will have to purge his Library of Stalin & Co.

I have given the Laffittes a résumé of the Barton position. Dr Birch (with whom I had a talk yesterday) is writing to you. He has asked to open a C.A. [Citizens' Advice] Bureau and Community Centre at Fulham. He is suggesting that you might come up one day and talk things over with him [. . .] The Adjutant General of the U.S.A. Army has written me a long letter with lots of information and books. One cause of rejection is 'Ugliness'. No one is taken in the Army unless he has at least 6 perfect teeth top and bottom.

Had lunch with François at P.E.P. to-day, Julian Huxley and Mallon [Warden of Toynbee Hall: adviser to the government on the provision of food in London's air-raid shelters] were at same table [. . .]

Please send me list which I forgot. Bike is at the Parking place as Shop was not open.

On 20 September, Kay noted in her diary that she felt it might be better to abandon Bedfordshire and go back to Fulham and Birch. But what would life be like in town, especially if the air raids started? Richard reported talking to 'Miss Skinner' who had taught some of the Fulham classes, and was 'holding herself open' for resuming these. His brother Harold had applied for enlistment in the RAF and was expecting the sack from his job imminently. Richard himself was already enjoying counting some of the effects of the war:

20 September, RMT to KCT at Barton Hill
From various reports I have had the longest queues in London are those outside the Exchanges. One estimate that has been made (not by the Gov. or newspaper) is that 750,000 people have been thrown out of work in 14 days. The Ministry of Labour announces that no more unemployment figures are to be published (the M.L.G. [*Ministry of Labour Gazette*] stops publication). The compilation of accidents figures has broken down completely and no more building plans statistics are to be published, etc. etc. 'One by One the Lights are going out' as Grewy said in 1914 [. . .] I wrote to Kuczynski[21] for the German figures during the last War. Then I worked out the loss of potential citizens by the decline in the birth rate assuming extrapolation of 1913 trends. Anyway I arrived at a loss of 2,140,000. Then I rang François to tell him and he had in the meantime unearthed a rough calculation by the Registrar-General giving 2,100,000 . . .

Kay spent a week in London at the end of September – she just had to go to Fulham and talk to Birch. While Richard had a great deal to occupy himself with – not only his job, but talking to

105

population experts such as Glass and Kuczynski about the fate of the birth rate and other interesting matters – the activities available to Kay were much more limited. Their letters start to refer to Jerry and Galia/Galya (both spellings are used: her full name is Galina) Morris, a couple who became close friends during this period and were to remain so for the rest of the Titmusses' lives. Jerry is a doctor whose interest in social aspects of health combined with Richard's to fuel an unusually vital working partnership; Jerry first contacted Richard after he'd read *Poverty and Population*, which was published the year before the war. The two would write several key papers in the emerging field of social medicine together, and after the war would set up the country's first social medicine research unit. Like Kay, Galia Morris did social work. After the war, she took an economic history degree at LSE, and then a social work training.

On 4 October, Kay wrote in her diary:

> Spent last week in town & felt very helpless. So many people hanging about with nothing to do. Gladly returned to the farm where to a large extent I can forget there is a war on. Busy making pickles & crab apple jelly.
>
> R has 'Hitler makes war on the German people' accepted by the Spectator.
>
> How bad will things get before they are better. There is a lot of talk about Peace negotiations led by Mussolini but I have a feeling that with the Hitler regime still unbroken nothing will come of Peace talks now. It is all very depressing.

It's hard to tell whether Richard wasn't as depressed by the war as Kay, or whether the lighter tone of his letters simply reflects his determination to cheer her up by holding up the prospect of a job in the country, giving her little things to do, and trying to involve her in the political ruminations which occupied him and his friends in town. Kay turns to thoughts of using her experiences for a different project – one that Richard hasn't imagined for her: fiction.

10 October, RMT to KCT at Barton Hill
My dearest,
I missed your arms round me last night. And it's so strange waking up in the morning and asking myself where you are. Everything comes back with a bang. What a lot Mr Chamber-

lain is responsible for [. . .] Then – one of your old habits
I proceeded to mend the connection in the bedside whatnot.
I knew that I had no one's feet to warm and no one to warm
mine [. . .] Birch has [. . .] promised to get E. [Eileen] on
U.A.B. [Unemployment Assistance Board] enquiries. Any-
how she is starting to-day to get the Centre open, cleaning
etc., and getting in touch with your friends. Shall we want
Miss Skinner? [. . .]

If you have any time at all would you attempt to guess a
revised business of doing our accounts. I don't like this
business of handing out £1s every now and then. I.e. H. K.
[housekeeping] for me and an allowance for you.

To-morrow I go to Banstead [where the Morrises lived].
Incidentally I had a letter from G. [Galia] to-day. I enclose
it. We haven't got the book here have we?

I am still playing at the statistics – but they like this unique
war still puzzle me. If only we had a dynamic government
in power anything might happen now. By the way François
has now come round to my point of view that, in all the
circumstances, we should now 'call it a day' and leave Adolf,
where he belongs, in the hands of Joe.

Devotedly for ever, R.

11 October,[c] *KCT to RMT in London*
Some amusing episodes on the farm today. Must tell you
about them at the weekend. Lil & Bob are taking more
definite shape in my mind for the book I mean to write one
day. The elevator broke down – as it is wont to do – this
morning. Bert & Son [?] stalked the house looking for something as they are wont to do. Their walk took them to cellar
& Bob followed by parent returned triumphant with an old
ironing board. Apparently it was just the thing needed to
put matters right [. . .]

Can you tell me why Auntie searched the veg patch this
morning for a bit of missing belting? She didn't find it there
but she was so pleased to discover 2 or 3 lettuces. Everyone
was under suspicion until the yd of belting was found in a
box in the egg room. I'm so glad they found it or we
shouldn't have been able to thrash at all.

It's been lovely again today & I went out for an hour this afternoon ostensibly to gather blackberries . . .

They spent the weekend before Richard's birthday together:

16 October, KCT to RMT in London
Did you forget too that you had a birthday this morning? It wasn't till I was standing in my wellingtons washing in the dairy that I remembered, but I wasn't upset about it cos I mentioned it in bed last night. I've finished the washing and Auntie has insisted on my taking a rest this afternoon so here I am sitting in the sun in our room. It's turned out a glorious autumn day but there is no wind to dry the clothes. Everything would be lovely if you were here. Somehow I am missing you badly to-day; it's been an extra specially good weekend with you. I'm feeling at bursting point.

Probably there will be nothing more to add to this although the postman will not take it until tomorrow morning. Lena is still in bed and I expect I shall be busy. There's more jelly to be made and the ironing to do.

16 October, RMT to KCT at Barton Hill
Well, I suppose you've seen the N.C.[22] I am not quite sure whether Oliver Twist was appropriate – but I imagine it was the work of one of their bright boys. 6 guineas – so the Valor is a present from the N.C. and it will help during Nov [. . .] I had a talk with Birch this morning – I had not mentioned it but he suddenly said congratulations. Curious that Edinburgh should get an air raid before London. Have you heard from H. [Helen]? Birch is writing you. Several of the men have been asking for the Centre to open. About 10 Eileen says. Birch [. . .] suggests that if we can collect about £1 per week we could continue on a limited basis [. . .]

Lots more queries but to Eileen and Birch I have said that you may be coming on Thursday or early next week when we can go into the lot [. . .]

The official figures are just out re Cost of Living. Have you seen them in N.C.? A 10 per cent rise to many of our friends in Fulham means far more in terms of existence than 7/6 income tax rate.

François is still at home with his cold – he can't shake it off, but he tells me that he and Eileen have fallen in love again. I had two telephone calls last night I could have done without. One [. . .] [from] the Duchess [Richard's aunt Irene]. Birthday greetings you know. Inquisitive old b . . . I was coldly distant. Went to hear Moiseiwitsch play Chopin at 1 today. The place was crammed – people sitting on the floor. An hour's peace during which my mind went wandering . . . I wanted you beside me dear [. . .]

    R

Cauliflower au gratin went wrong last night.

These were hardly good conditions for the husbandly learning of culinary skills. But London was at least peaceful. The anticipated 'hammer blow' was still a 'mass of itches'.[23] The main itch was the blackout, which was total and immediate, and brought a 100 per cent increase in the accident figures, as people fell down steps and off railway platforms and couldn't see the pavement for the streets. But as the itches continued, cinemas and theatres reopened, and by December the dance halls were packed again. Ration books had been ready since 1938, but bacon and butter rationing was delayed until after Christmas. The evacuees streamed back to the towns, and by January 1940 only 14 per cent of the expected refugees remained in their allotted places of safety.[24]

In September, Richard wrote to *The Times* about the failure of the government's evacuation scheme. His personal acquaintance with the situation in Bedfordshire became, for the purposes of the *Times* letter, ' a recent investigation in reception areas'. This revealed why things hadn't gone according to plan, and what needed to be done to put things right:

The solution lies in bringing pressure upon the reception authorities (in many cases lethargic rural councils only too glad to be rid of the evacuees) either to erect hutments or take empty buildings as community centres. These should be equipped and provided if possible with plots of land for use as vegetable gardens. Communal meals should be provided at

the centre which should also act not only as a Citizens' Advice
Bureau but as a social club in the best sense of the word. In
time the centres could radiate all forms of useful and educational activity including no doubt some types of war work.

The expense of such a scheme, declared Richard confidently, would
soon be balanced by its beneficial effect on the mental and physical
health of the evacuees, 'to say nothing of their hosts who would be
relieved of their guests for the major part of the day'. Naturally, such
centres would need to be run by trained social workers, 'particularly
those versed in handling the London mother'. Richard himself knew
of several such social workers who would be prepared to tackle the
problem immediately.[25]

Whether or not this veiled plea for Kay's re-employment produced
any effect went unrecorded. The appeal to the importance of training
was a little disingenuous, as Kay herself wasn't trained. But not to
be deterred by any lack of response, Richard sent another letter to
The Times in October[26] about a different aspect of the evacuation
problem: whose responsibility were the evacuated children? Richard
reported an anomaly whereby unemployed households whose children had been evacuated had their child allowance of 3s per child
per week stopped by the Unemployment Assistance Board. So who
was supposed to clothe their children and provide other necessities?

Richard's statistical and other musings about the meaning of evacuation would later become an important part of the narrative of his
war history. He wrote to his friend Bill le Gros Clark (with whom
he co-authored *Our Food Problem*) about an earlier experience of
evacuation. When the Persians invaded Greece in 480 BC, the population of Athens was evacuated to the Peloponnesian city of Troezen,
on the far side of the Saronic Gulf. North's translation of Plutarch's
description of this ran: 'The most part of them (the Athenians) did
convey their aged Fathers and Mothers, their wives and little children,
into the city of Troezen, where the Troezenians received them very
lovingly and gently. For they gave order that they should be entertained of the common charge, allowing them apiece, two oboloes of
their money a day [. . .] and furthermore did hire schoolmasters at
the charge of the commonwealth, to bring them up at school.'[27]
Richard wondered if there had been any comments about vermin.
He and Bill were trying (unsuccessfully) to get hold of the height

and weight records of evacuated London schoolchildren in order to find out whether the move to the country improved their health. One problem, though, was that it seemed to be disproportionately the children of the lowest income groups who were going back to the towns.

Evacuation was a 'natural' experiment, the results of which were of considerable interest to keen social analysts like Richard Titmuss. It formed part of a general pattern of resource-redistribution brought about by the war, which resulted in a narrowing of the traditional gap between the life-chances of different social groups. Richard was also interested in 'unnatural' experiments – deliberate social interventions aimed at changing social conditions. In his book *Poverty and Population*, published the previous year, he had mentioned an important experiment in the field of nutrition – the dietary supplementation programme for pregnant women provided by the pioneering National Birthday Trust Fund in the 'depressed' areas.[28] In October 1939, he wrote to Lady Juliet Rhys Williams, the moving force behind this experiment, to voice the hope that the NBTF's valuable work would not be impeded by the war, and to pass on a reprint of his recently published paper on 'Puerperal Mortality'. This looked at the rate of deaths in, and due to, childbearing in England and Wales over the period from 1929 to 1937. Whereas infant mortality (the deaths of children under one year) had fallen dramatically, maternal deaths had actually risen until 1934, when they started to decline. Richard's concern, as always, was with the North–South divide. He showed that mothers were more likely to die in Lancashire, Durham and Glamorgan than in the south-east of the country, and that this differential had been increasing.[29] Lady Williams approved of Richard's work: 'It brings out the point which I have tried throughout my experiments to prove, namely, that there is a clear association between maternal and neo-natal mortality and poverty.'[30] Unfortunately, the NBTF's feeding scheme had come to an end through lack of money and because of questions about the way in which the scheme was being evaluated.[31]

He was very busy, and one wonders how he fitted it all in. Was some of his industry due to Kay's absence, or in spite of it? Richard's central concern, with the social effects of the war, resembled a wheel with many spokes to it. His 'cauliflower au gratin' letter referred to another of these: the rise in the cost of living. Even the government's official figures, which underestimated the extent of the increase, showed that food prices had risen by a seventh and the price of clothes by a quarter in the first five months of the war.[32] Richard ventured his own opinion on this to Seebohm Rowntree, author of the famous poverty survey of York, whom he thanked for the nice review of *Poverty and Population* in the *Listener*: was there not a 'supreme need' which was being ignored by the government, asked Richard, to control inflation? Did Rowntree understand that one significant contributing cause of inflation was the introduction of compulsory insurance against war risks for sellers of goods? The result of this could be as much as a 6 per cent rise in the price of goods to the consumer.[33] This was the insurance man speaking.

Richard's speculations on the German birth rate, for which he had so struggled to find data, were published in the *Spectator*, as Kay noted in her 4 October letter. The article appeared on 20 October under the title 'Hitler's man-power problem'.[34] Its focus was the demographic riddle that war, which required more births to replace the excess deaths taking place, seemed to have the opposite effect. People did not have children, either because they chose not to, or for other reasons. Under these circumstances, herculean efforts were required to reverse the trend. Such efforts did not include government bureaucracy, whose rules and regulations, by penalizing large families through the child allowance system, made it resemble 'a birth-control clinic'. Richard had some fun with the nonsense of these rules, which were not the same for active soldiers, for those disabled by war, and for the unemployed. 'Why should the fourth child of a soldier qualify for 3s a week,' he enquired, in another article called 'The penalisation of parenthood' and published in the magazine *Truth* the following month, 'when its father is fighting and for nothing when he is totally disabled? Why should an unemployed man, rejected for the Army on physical or mental grounds, receive at least 12s a week for four children, while the same four children would qualify for only 5s 10d if their father had lost the use of one leg in fighting to defend democracy?'[35]

A stay of a few weeks in London during October enabled Kay to slip temporarily back into her former life. She wrote to the Hon. Mrs Ursula Grant-Duff about the financial difficulties of the Fulham unemployment work. Mrs Grant-Duff features in many of the

Titmusses' letters to one another, mainly through her role in the Eugenics Society, which she joined in 1921, and for which she acted as Honorary Secretary before becoming a member of Council from 1933 until her death in 1959. She was, as she noted in one of her letters to Kay, old enough to be her mother.[36] Uninterested in such frivolities as 'dress, food and gracious living' and mean to herself in everything 'except guilty outbursts of book-buying',[37] Mrs Grant-Duff had interests ranging from women's rights to the need for more trees. She was especially interested in events in Germany, had friends in Berlin, and spoke fluent German. Many powerful administrators and doctors grew used to her small figure appearing in front of them with indignant questions about the quality of their mercy in relation to some topic or other. My mother referred in a note on the back of a letter to a reason for Mrs Grant-Duff's tenacity: 'lost husband in 1914–18 war & only son in 2nd. We spent his last night in England with them both.'

Mrs Grant-Duff responded to Kay's request by sending a cheque, but it was Richard who wrote to thank her on his wife's behalf, because Kay was feeling 'rather tired'. They had also received £50 from an anonymous donor. In November, Kay sent Dr Birch an estimate arrived at by herself and Richard of what it would cost to restart the Fellowship in the Congregational Church Hall (assuming this could be effectively blacked out). Dr Birch seemed to understand Kay's feelings about being in Bedfordshire. He was glad to hear through Richard that she was 'Alive and Kicking' against her inability 'to find some real constructive and helpful work'.[38]

In mid-November Kay reluctantly went back to Barton Hill. She was still not well (with a cold and an infection in her foot), and after nearly a month together it was hard to be parted again. But the cloud of her absence at least gave Richard the silver lining of more reading time. The book he was reading was one by the Swedish couple Alva and Gunnar Myrdal, whom Richard and Kay would later get to know. Like the Titmusses, the Myrdals were professionally interested in problems of population and family life. But unlike Kay Titmuss, Alva maintained her professional career through the mothering of three children. That cold night in November 1939, Richard must either have been reading Gunnar Myrdal's *Population – A problem for democracy*[39] or the Myrdals' joint product, *Crisis in the Population Question*, which had been published in 1934.[40] He wrote of this and of his concern about her, and of the duplicity they shared in relation to the ever-present problem of his mother:

14 November, RMT to KCT at Barton Hill
Darling,
First of all I want to know how you are. How is the foot? Are you behaving yourself and resting? If you are not careful you will see Mrs T. coming out in me. I just can't get used to this separation but I keep on saying well it's only for a week and what would you do if this bloody Gov. wanted you to hold a rifle by the wrong end [. . .]

Was cold last night. It took me longer to go to sleep so I read Myrdal on Family Allowances in Sweden. Have been snowed up two days with office rubbish. It's C.F.O. all the way. François wanted me to go to Dulwich to-night but I felt too tired and said no.

I have managed however to act as Stock Exchange adviser to your M. Bought her 50 London tin shares at 4/- each. A better investment for £10 than British Tin. Have written her to-night.

Had a letter on Monday from Lady Layton [Sir Walter Layton was editor of the *News Chronicle*]. She says that she has been very busy on family matters but that she and Walter are taking a small flat near us in December and hopes that we will come and see them.

There was a letter from H. [Helen Johnston] this morning so I opened it. You will see what she says. I don't suppose you will want her at B.H. Anyway I will leave you to write her and do what you think best. Let me know if you are coming back as we don't want to cross in the train. If you do return will you ring up the parent (unpleasant task) and tell her that I shan't be coming. Perhaps it would be wise to say that I have far too much Office work to come down this week-end (perfectly true at the moment). You know how touchy she is. I shall be writing her to-morrow but perhaps it would be as well to put the blow off until Friday [. . .]

I am sure the enclosed re Rabbits will be of interest. So now you know what happens to skins or don't you.

It was a lovely morning on Monday as I rode down the

cutting. The sky was just perfect – all grey and orange, and I thought what a fool I was leaving it all – and the most perfect Wife – just for Inefficiency Limited.

After another short interlude in London, Kay wrote in her diary on 25 November:

> The weeks have slipped by. Part of my time has been spent at the farm & part at the flat. At the flat I was ill with a cold & a secondary ringworm foot for nearly a fortnight & I have yet to regain my strength, which in these trying times it is difficult to do. R's aptitude for finding humorous situations helps us along [...] I sometimes wonder if I am right in leaving him at all, since we may be parted entirely before this war is over. Before this war is over!! Would that I knew what will happen to us. Air activity increases. How shall we carry on when it becomes intense? I have no happiness without Richard. To leave him & the flat this morning was very hard.
>
> Mother & Muriel [her brother Donald's wife] have disagreed & Mother & Father have returned to Marler Rd [in Forest Hill, London]. Perhaps I should be helping her with her blackout but I feel this is a more useful home for me.
>
> Helen is in town & I have seen much of her during the past week. Our link with her strengthens since we have a common bond in the fight against poverty & distress.
>
> I want to write but how to set about it is difficult. I think I must plan a serious book & attempt fiction also. Too many ideas are wandering around at once.
>
> Fulham is unsatisfactory but I have no heart to do the detailed work & no strength. I must leave it to Eileen & Birch for the time being.
>
> And so to bed with Francis Hackett's 'Anne Boleyn'.

The story of Richard's adventures getting back to London by bicycle and train after his last weekend at the farm proved that very aptitude for humour Kay so relied on:

28 November, RMT to KCT to Barton Hill
. . . I was drenched to the marrow. It ran up my arms and down my leg. Every time I nodded to the landscape I let

loose a small cascade part of which I sucked up. What I looked like when I got to the garage I can't imagine. Both my handkerchiefs had absorbed moisture up to 101% and all I had left was the tail of my shirt which I had been sitting on to keep dry. In the train four men were playing rummy on the N.C. (What sacrilege!) Uncomfortably I sat in the corner and slowly formed a little river on the floor. When we had got as far as St Albans one of the men looked down and said, 'Good God, did you fellows know we are sitting in a pond?' Embarrassed beyond measure (were they thinking of amoral social habits?) I buried my face in a damp Times. And I dared not re-cross my legs because I knew I should ring some more out.

Back at the Flat at last I changed everything – even the panties (which have acquired a somewhat colourful hue from the saddle). No harm done. But would you believe it as though I had not had sufficient water for one day I upset the kettle all over the trousers of my grey suit – and changed again.

Mrs Grant Duff very worried to-day. Sheila [her daughter?] was badly hurt in a car crash in the blackout last night. (She was apparently being driven at some speed. Why?) Anyway she spoke to the hospital during the Meeting this morning and it appears that she is not in danger. I gave her Working Class Wives.[41] She has just bought P.&P. [Poverty and Population] and is busy digesting it [...] I have been deputed to attend a P.E.P. [Political and Economic Planning] luncheon to-morrow and report on Valentine Bell's talk on Evacuation. They graciously presented me with 3/- so I shall get a good meal tomorrow. I believe the Laffittes are going.

Other news must be brief as Office have been very trouble-some – got to see a man called something like Botchee-Botchee to-morrow. World Digest want to buy Penalisation of P. [Parenthood]. Usual £1.1 – I suppose. Office scandal re salaries must wait. (Very strong rumours that we are all to expect a 10% cut at Xmas. I believe it to be authentic.) [...]

Very hard last night. Very hard. Didn't know what to do with my arms.

Everyone at the farm enjoyed Richard's description of his journey, and Kay told him he wasn't the only one who had arm trouble at night.

Richard's next letter regaled her with events at the Eugenics Society. The British eugenics movement played an important role in the development of Richard Titmuss's career. Through its patronage by key members of the social and political elite, Richard was able to make the contacts necessary to get his work into print and to be taken seriously in circles from which his lack of education, particularly a public school and a university education, would otherwise have debarred him. His strategic infiltration of the Eugenics Society caught it at a precarious moment, balanced as it was between the eugenics of National Socialism in Germany and the need for some honourable preservation of the basic eugenist creed. 'Eugenics' was a term originally coined by Francis Galton, a cousin of Charles Darwin's, and meant 'the science which deals with all influences that improve the inborn qualities of a race'.[42] Galton's interest in eugenics was provoked by an excursion into dictionaries of biography which showed that distinguished people were often related, and he was considerably aided by a large family inheritance which meant he didn't have to work for his living; he was given throughout his life to an obsessional interest in counting things, even if all he had to count was the number of fidgets in an audience.[43] By the late 1930s, with events in Germany, Galton's definition of eugenics was clearly problematic. Richard Titmuss's attraction for members of the Eugenics Society was not his background, but his sociological bent: his systematic statistical probing of the environment for the ways in which the expression of genetic inheritance might have less to do with genes than with social circumstance. This offered an escape route for British eugenics, which could thereby redefine itself as about inequalities of social opportunity rather than those of biology.

The British Eugenics Society (originally the Eugenics Education Society) was founded in 1907 by Sybil Gotto, a tireless organizer of multiple voluntary initiatives. Then a 21-year-old naval widow, Sybil Gotto's interest in social problems was inflamed further by reading Galton's works. A contact in the Sociological Society introduced her to a lawyer friend of Galton's, Montague Crackanthorpe, and then Galton himself.[44] Together they set up the nucleus of the society, and Sybil was Honorary Secretary until 1920. Another product of her

117

organizing verve was the National Council for Combating Venereal Disease, later the British Social Hygiene Council. Sybil Gotto reappears in the BSHC archives and in many letters to and from Richard under the name of Mrs Neville Rolfe after her second marriage, to another naval officer, in 1917.

Richard himself joined the Eugenics Society in 1937 and resigned seventeen days before his death in 1973. His involvement intensified during the war, when he took over from Maurice Newfield as acting editor of the society's journal, the *Eugenics Review*. Maurice and his wife, Sigrid, became two of the Titmusses' closest friends. Newfield, a 'small dark man, birdlike in his quickness of glance and movement, like a bird in the incredible fragility of his body,'[45] was a doctor who published books on birth control using the pseudonym of Michael Fielding, and had for this reason to be watched over very carefully by some of the more conservative members of the society. He'd served as a major in the First World War, but refused to stay in the army long enough to collect a disability pension (he caught cholera and malaria in the East). He was a tireless campaigner for birth control, a practising doctor, founder of the medical section of the publishing house Hamish Hamilton, and assistant editor of the *British Medical Journal* before turning his editorial hand to the *Eugenics Review*. He contracted TB in 1930 and died of it in 1949. When he died, people remembered him as charming, sensitive, but perhaps above all intensely curious; the poet Robert Graves recalled an evening the Newfields spent with him in Devonshire early in the war when Newfield grilled his next-door neighbour, Agatha Christie, about the drugs that could be used for undetected murder. (She passed his cross-examination.)[46]

The Titmusses and Newfields first got to know one another in the early months of the war. Richard asked to see Maurice in December 1939, and they met in early 1940, when he became concerned about the tendency of the committee of the society to axe everything because of the war. He wasn't very polite about his fellow eugenists, even complaining about Mrs Grant-Duff, who had pushed him into becoming a member of the committee though he really couldn't afford to spend a whole day every month 'listening to irrelevancies'. 'What would you say,' he interrogated Maurice, harking back to one of his favourite topics, 'to one member of the Committee who remarks that he cannot see anything of eugenic value in surveying the results of the medical examination of conscripts and recruits?'[47]

Members of the Eugenics Society came from a variety of both right- and left-wing political backgrounds. Most of them considered themselves to be progressives, whether advocating social reform to reduce class inequality or to increase it by boosting the fertility of the 'better' classes. The tenets of eugenics could be, and were, harnessed to an impressive range of agendas. Reformers like Sidney Webb, for example, exploited as an argument for free state education the eugenist concern that the best genetic stock be encouraged to reproduce by all available means.[48]

Of Richard and Kay's friends, François Lafitte did some work for the society, though not as much as Richard, and what he did do was largely as a consequence of his stepfather Havelock Ellis's friendship with C. P. Blacker.[49] Blacker was a tall, spare man, a psychiatrist by training; 'stern in manner, he married the daughter of a British army major [. . .] and ran five miles before breakfast every morning until the age of 65'.[50] He was secretary of the Eugenics Society from 1931 to 1952, and advocated compulsory family trees so that doctors could advise on the desirability of parenthood. He was also a distinguished soldier, winning the Military Cross in the First World War and the George Medal in the second.[51] Not every eugenist was keen on birth control, but Blacker was of Newfield's own persuasion – indeed so much so that he helped to develop the successful spermicidal contraceptive known as Volpar Gel.[52] It might have been the same qualities that contributed to his successful soldiering which enabled him to take one of these by mouth each day for a month in order to satisfy sceptics of their harmlessness.[53] Alexander Carr-Saunders, who took over from William Beveridge as Director of the London School of Economics in 1937, and was a key player in Richard's own move there in 1950, was another active Eugenics Society member. He played a vital role in an important offshoot of it – the Population Investigation Committee.[54] Other members of the Eugenics Society who featured in the Titmusses' lives and correspondence included Byrom Bramwell, Laurence Cadbury, Clinton Chance, Lord Horder and Julian Huxley. Bramwell, a somewhat secretive man, was a lawyer with a sideline interest in genealogy which led him to the Eugenics Society. He was chair of the society's council from 1932 until 1948.[55] Cadbury, a businessman, ran the chocolate firm Cadbury Brothers, was a director of the Bank of England, and took over the chairmanship of the *News Chronicle* in 1950. Clinton Chance was treasurer of the Eugenics Society from 1933 until 1946, a close friend of the birth control agitator, Margaret Sanger, and a keen advocate of the need for research into social and medical problems. He was responsible for introducing to the society Lord 'Tommy' Horder, a short, stocky man described as the 'enfant terrible' of English medicine. Horder's education in biology had been guided by H. G. Wells, who considered him not his most able pupil. Horder moved on rapidly to a practice in Harley Street, was knighted for his services as a captain in the First World War, and in 1923 became Physician in Ordinary to the royal family. Redeemingly to the democrats, he was also medical adviser to London Transport, and during the Second World War chaired the Shelter Hygiene Committee, on whose behalf he visited shelters during some of the city's worst raids, becoming known as the 'Blitz doctor'.[56]

The topic at that meeting of the Eugenics Society in November 1939 was the axing of the society's war-time activities. This threat had prompted Richard to write to Maurice Newfield to request a meeting:

November (undated), RMT to KCT at Barton Hill
It'll have to be a short note to-night – it's the Eugenics Meeting and Mrs G. D. [Grant-Duff]. My dear, I could write pages but most of it will have to be reserved until the week-end. Horder was there from 1 to 2.30 and then left and Bramwell took over. Then the dog-fight began, Mrs G. D. violently aggressive and practically resigning with Sir Charles. You see Chance, Gunn (the paralysed one) and one or two others want to stop everything and all expenditure for the duration. Chance even wanted to stop François's salary from December and give him notice at once. Then I had to say something. Really it was pitiful. They haggled over £5 and yet have a marvellous lunch of chicken, tongue, salad, soup, drinks, coffee, etc., and cigarettes provided free which must, I calculated, cost £25 a year. Sir Walter Langdon-Brown, Mrs Neville Rolfe and others have already resigned in protest. Remind me to tell you the story of the man who after a life search for a woman who he could love with a pure and idealistic love wants the Society to grant him

and his 'betrothed' marriage certificates of fitness. In a 3 page letter demanding a certificate by the wedding day 23rd Dec. (when he proposes to tell all his guests) he says 'if you fail me I dread breaking the news to my betrothed.'

[. . .] Eileen [Lafitte] says she can do without any money. I spent the evening there last night but felt very tired when I got back at 11.30.

Only allowed ¼ butter at the Dairy. Don't know what I shall do. Must go and buy some Stork and mix it up. I've promised myself that I will do the ironing this evening. What a fuss to make over 6 handkerchiefs.

Kay and Richard's last letters to each other before Christmas were all undated, so the order can only be guessed at. Their subjects are food, events in Denmark, the prospect of a holiday in Mrs Grant-Duff's cottage in Worcestershire, logarithms, the weather, eugenics and 'Inefficiency Limited' (Richard's codename for the County Fire Office), and the evacuees on the farm. Although Kay's letters refer to 'the boys' who had been evacuated to Barton Hill, she never gives any details; perhaps they were more of a burden to her than individual personalities. Like the children who were evacuated to Oxford, and who were the subject of a survey by social workers in 1942–3, the boys whom Kay helped to look after probably missed their parents and families first, and the 'traffic and noises' of London second.[57]

December (undated), KCT to RMT in London
Beloved,
[. . .] Tea is scarce. Could you manage to include ½ lb of yours if possible? Apparently there is more to be had in Luton. Shall you write & complain to the Food Controllers?

[. . .] Bob is 'doing' his Christmas cards. To my amazement he always sends about 40. A letter awaited me from Aunt Meg. I must send her a few lines (no card necessary).

[. . .] Husband lunches at the Bath Club, wife does 'charring'. What a life.

Lena goes on Saturday. What can we give the boys? Perhaps I'll find something in Luton on Friday.

Y.L.W. Kay
P.S. Don't forget the Blue Danish if you haven't eaten it all.

December (undated), RMT to KCT at Barton Hill
My dearest,

It would happen whilst you are at B.H. wouldn't it? So we have dragged in Norway. Isn't it tragic to think of Copenhagen and Elsinore in German hands. I was told last evening that the fleet had moved towards the Baltic but as I did not get back from Acland's until 11 it was too late to phone. I wasn't too early this morning and Carr-Saunders rang me up at 9. Saw him at 10.30 for about 3/4 hour. We discussed quite a lot of things [...] and he was very friendly.

I don't think that the latest developments mean an immediate air Blitzkrieg (although every searchlight in London was at work last night for the first time since Sept.) It does mean of course a great speed-up in conscription for at least 250,000 men will have to go to Norway. It also means – for B.H. consumption – far greater difficulties over feeding stuffs. If I think there are likely to be serious developments within the next week I shall ring you.

Ursula [Grant-Duff] also rang up this morning to tell me that she had got the B.B.C. job – in the country. She asked whether we should be interested to rent a furnished cottage (water laid on, linen, etc.,) on the famous Bredon Hill, 10 miles from Evesham in Worcestershire in the heart of the fruit country. Friends of hers. To rent for about one week only – about £1. Dates confirmed this morning. So we have some choice [...]

Friday seems a long way off to tell you the rest of all the unimportant details but the damn post goes in an hour and I have lots of silly office memos but I love you.

Don't worry sweetheart.

R.

December (undated), KCT to RMT in London
Only Monday evening & here I am unable to restrain myself from writing to you. Of course I feel I have a legitimate call to do so for I set the old brain to work on the logs this afternoon & I've solved the mystery of the points. It's really quite simple. You can take a larger number from a smaller & then the bar business enters in. *I'll show you.*

N.C. very depressing this morning, both special Correspondent re Summer Welles Musso & Adolph & Vernon
Bartlett. Weather doesn't help. It's pouring & blowing but
quite mild. Tempers are a bit frayed [...] The sledge has
broken down & I notice the lavatory chain is missing. Probably requisitioned for repairs.

Wants. A long pencil, & a bit o' india rubber.

In spite of the rain the sky is red with the setting sun
& the trees look grand. If only there were peace in the
world.

[...] Found Jack [farm worker] walking up the road last
night.

December (undated), RMT to KCT at Barton Hill
What a foul day it was. Twice I got soaked. By the time I
got to the flat I was a bit damp and then after about five
calls I collected some more water. Not much waiting for me
except a lot of rubbish from Inefficiency and Eugenics. When
I got back at 5.15 the phone started going – the whole damn
family rang me up. The parent in bed with bronchitis and
nobody there. I said I would go over this evening about
6 p.m. [...]

I woke up at 7 this morning and wanted you – did not
feel at all like getting up and facing things. First I thought
– must be getting old. But no the answer's at B.H.

Doesn't look as though I shall get that report done so I
shall expect you Friday. I am taking some work over to
Hendon to-night but it will have to be the knitting.

[...] Oh how I want to just lay in a field with you and
feel the sun.

[...] Would you believe it – McCleary is in New York.
Won't be back for weeks. He would be.

Richard had written to G. F. McCleary, pioneer of, and author of
several books on, the maternity and child welfare movement,[58] to
enlist his help in gaining access to the books he needed for his work.[59]
He and McCleary had met at the annual Eugenics Society dinner.

Richard and Kay left the farm soon after Christmas, returning
together to a city which, apart from the blackout, still showed few

signs of war. Indeed, when General de Gaulle visited in the summer, he reported 'a look of tranquillity, almost indifference', with people going peacefully about their business, queuing for cinemas, driving smart cars and frequenting clubs and hotels – as though nothing at all warlike was going on.[60] But food rationing had started: sugar in December, bacon and butter in January, meat in March and tea in July. It was a miserable winter, the coldest in forty-five years, and the Thames froze for a good eight miles. The spring which followed was unusually wonderful, but it was the spring of Chamberlain's fateful 'peace in our time' speech. At the end of April a German mine-laying bomber was shot down and crashed in the garden of a house in Clacton, Essex, bringing the first civilian casualties of the war. The first deliberate attack on the mainland of Britain followed in May, and bombs fell near Canterbury. From mid-June there were light raids every night on the Midlands, East Anglia and elsewhere, and on 19 June the first bomb dropped in the vicinity of London. To many people's surprise, the aged Churchill came to power with his coalition government in May, despite his fumbling speech about the Scandinavian campaign in which he got his notes in the wrong order, put the wrong spectacles on and kept saying Sweden when he meant Denmark.[61] Going anywhere became more difficult when in May the removal of signposts joined the blackout as a method of confusing the enemy. Those who tried to holiday by the seaside were frustrated by the requisitioning of hotels, the sprouting of machine guns from piers, and rules forbidding bathing. When J. B. Priestley went to Margate in July, he reported, unlike de Gaulle, few signs of ordinary life.[62]

May saw a renewed attempt to evacuate vulnerable groups away from urban areas. Children sent near the coast in East Anglia, Kent or Sussex were removed to south Wales, and all state schools in the evacuation areas were closed. About 300,000 people moved to the country, some of them for the second time. Yet again there was a drift back: families wanted to be together.

During this period Richard succeeded in persuading the *Spectator* to publish one of his much-circulated pieces, *Can the Poor Save*. This addressed the latest fashion in government announcements of the need to restrict consumption in order to curb spiralling prices. But how could the poor save, demanded Richard, when they already had too little money to feed themselves properly?[63] Good nutrition in large families was particularly a problem. Again, the basic issue was one of inequality: 1 per cent of the people had 15 per cent of the national income, and unequal death rates reflected this. Richard's article received a stern reply from a female doctor in Tunbridge Wells who maintained that poor children were not short of food; it was their mothers who were ignorant and needed training in proper childbearing methods.[64] Richard rebuked her, pointing out that such a view would 'incidentally absolve any Government from attempting to abolish poverty': 'Perhaps Dr Jones would hold that the infant mortality rate in Glasgow (which suffers from high unemployment and poor relief and an overcrowding index of 29 per cent), exceeding as it does the corresponding rate in such cities as Oslo and Stockholm by over 200 per cent, was due to the British mother being hopelessly ignorant and incompetent. I prefer to believe that the art of mother-hood is as high in this country as anywhere in the world.'[65] Richard advised Dr Jones to find out about the modern science of nutrition. He himself was continually fascinated by it. In a memorandum pro-duced in April 1940 for the British Youth Peace Assembly, he drew together statistical evidence on the health of British youth, quoting Robert McCarrison's famous experiments with rats. Two groups of young rats were shut in large cages; one group received a good diet, and the other was fed on a diet in common use by many in Britain: white bread and margarine, tinned meat and jam, tea, sugar and vegetables boiled with soda. The rats fed on the good diet grew well, lived long and seemed happy together. Those on the British diet were ill, had short lives, and were generally unhappy about being with other rats: 'The diseases from which they suffered were of three chief kinds; diseases of the lungs, diseases of the stomach and intes-tines, and diseases of the nerves, diseases from which *one in every three sick persons among the insured classes in England and Wales suffer.* Thus the white rat shows us in miniature what happens when we attempt to by-pass Nature. Also, as a result of the poor diet, the ethical standard of the rat deteriorates and he becomes what we are pleased to call a criminal.'[66]

One of the strategies that was coming to the fore for redressing the inequalities leading to these miserable outcomes was the payment of family allowances to mothers. Richard had already read 'Myrdal on family allowances'. But the name principally associated with the movement for family allowances in Britain was that of Eleanor

Rathbone, daughter of a wealthy philanthropist ship-owning family in Liverpool, first independent MP for the English universities, and tireless campaigner for the plight of working-class mothers, which she felt always tended to be forgotten by middle-class feminists, with their narrow emphasis on the vote and the right of women to enter the professions. In Eleanor Rathbone's thinking, women's responsibilities as mothers were central. Her own apprenticeship was served, not as a mother, but as an Oxford undergraduate in the days when women could attend lectures and take examinations but not get a degree, and then working for the Liverpool Central Relief Society, which introduced her to the notion that social workers could do more harm than good. It was a survey of the economics of working-class family life, published as *The Condition of Widows Under the Poor Law in Liverpool* in 1913, which first led Eleanor to focus on the economics of motherhood and the value to the community of women's unpaid services – just as valuable as those of a dock labourer, or a plumber or a soldier. In 1918 she published with a small committee of like-minded people a pamphlet called *Equal Pay and the Family: A Proposal for the National Endowment of Motherhood*. One member of the committee was William Beveridge. Before he wrote his own famous report, Beveridge established in 1925 a scheme for paying children's allowances to staff at the London School of Economics, of which he was then director. By 1939 a number of avant-garde firms, including the Cadbury brothers', had followed the LSE example.[67]

The case for 'family endowment', as Rathbone called it in 1927,[68] was an argument for paying financial allowances directly to mothers, both to cover the costs of childbearing and to recompense them for their own labour. Sometime in the late 1930s, Eleanor Rathbone wrote to Richard Titmuss to request help putting together a 'little book for the Penguins'.[69] She paid him to do some calculations for her and to go through the text making suggestions for amendments. In February 1940, Richard sent her an eight-page memorandum listing his suggested revisions. This brought to her attention the findings from recent poverty surveys, urged her to consider the unequal distribution of wealth in society as a further justification for family allowances, highlighted the anomaly that it paid men with large families not to work rather than work for low wages, corrected her suppositions about the expectation of life for married women compared with spinsters (higher, he said, not lower), summarized for her much of his own work on the relationship between poverty and mothers' and children's deaths, and repeated the lessons of McCarrison's rat experiment. In April, Rathbone sent him the revised typescript. On the long-awaited holiday, courtesy of Mrs Grant-Duff, in the remote cottage on Bredon Hill, the typewriter went with Kay and Richard on the back of their bicycles.

When Kay went back to the farm, in her diary on 12 March she reflected on the events of the last few months. Again, she tried to channel her discontent, her growing feeling of being on the margin of things, into the more positive goal of writing a book:

> Left the farm on Dec 29th with snow on the ground intending to return a week later. Bronchial influenza. R's flu, coal shortage, more snow & frost etc & setting up Fellowship House have kept me in town until today.
>
> During the interval Prof. Jewkes has approached R re Economic Advisory Cttee work & there was also a possibility of the Board of Trade job.
>
> Martin Secker & Warburg have written direct about a book. They found his address in the Spectator in correspondence following his article 'Can the Poor Save?''
>
> At Sir Richard Acland's request he has seen him today at the H of C. Reason for interview still unknown to me.
>
> Have just spent an hour working out death rates for R. *What* a boring job. What love can & will do. Here it seems easier to do them, as removed from him it is about the only thing I can be doing to help him.
>
> [. . .] Resolve to set about planning the book which is to be written one day.

A couple of days later, she writes to Richard about bicycles, Germany and babies:

14 March 1940ᵉ, KCT to RMT in London
Darling,
I have been in to Luton to-day shopping and among other things I have bought a new bike. The man in Collingdon Street sold it to me when he told me he couldn't do anything about my back brake as the fittings for those old bikes could

no longer be bought. The new one is one of my bargains. Reduced 25/- because it is a bit shop soiled. Price £5 and I hope to make 15/- out of the old one. I was going to consult you first and then I realised I had some money in reserve still in the Bank which would cover the cost and so I decided to buy it myself. And the deed is done. Now I shall go along like wildfire. Cycling back against a headwind on the old one nearly did me in. I shall probably bring the new one to town on Friday. I shall be so proud of it.

[. . .] Liddell Hart was interesting in the N.C. this morning. You will have seen it. Will they be allowed to carry their ore away? And shall we prevent reinforcements and supplies getting through to the men who have been landed? I shouldn't like any relative of mine to be in the German Expeditionary Force. God how I wish it could be disastrous for Germany and bring about her collapse this summer. What about Denmark's cattle too if they can't get feeding stuffs. Will Germany find she has to feed Denmark and get little from her [. . .] No baby for us.

[. . .] Yours for ever and then some, Kay.

Had the solace of *not* having a child, which Richard noted at the beginning of the war, now become a burden? The major non-domestic burden was the war news, which was bad. In April, German forces invaded Denmark and Norway. In May the surrender of Norway was announced. Germany advanced into Holland, Belgium and Luxembourg and began to threaten France. Even the King must have begun to grasp the impact of what was happening when Queen Wilhelmina of Holland phoned him up at 5 a.m. asking him to send aircraft to help her country. The King passed the message on and went back to bed.[70] In Britain, people listened keenly to the accounts of the rescue of troops stranded at Dunkirk during the last days of May and the first of June. In early June, Churchill made his post-Dunkirk 'we shall fight on the beaches . . . in the fields . . . in the streets' speech, with all the rousing oratory of one who had never been on an omnibus.[71] On 10 June, Mussolini declared war on the allies, and a few days later the German army reached Paris. The awfulness of the news contrasted with the weather: a beautiful spring had become an early and lovely summer. This made it hard to believe what many were coming round to – that there *would* be a German invasion. A note of hopelessness, shared with many, enters the Titmuss records, and on 11 June Kay writes in her diary:

For the first time I am making my belated entry without looking back to see what I last wrote. I reproach myself for a desultoriness in writing up reactions under the valuable emotional urges of the past weeks. Hopelessness as a key note to my life is the cause. It seems so little worth doing anything constructive. Acland has said 'I sometimes feel it is written in the Book that Hitler is to dominate Europe'. These words from such an authority I can't forget. I have been careful for that reason to pass them on to very few. It seems well now for people to be kept in a certain ignorance. Discouragement is so easily fostered.

I can't swim with the tide. A re-reading of *our* 1936 book 'Crime and Tragedy' increases my rebelliousness & at the same time my weariness. Oh that the bloodshed might cease & that we could then enter the fight on the true cause of justice. Was Kant right? Is Europe now about to become the great graveyard of the human race? So many men during the 1930s prophesied that another war would see the end of civilisation as we know it. What are they thinking today? Censorship forbids their writing their thoughts so that they can be read by me. I wish I could feel with Helen that what happens to us doesn't matter. Acceptance means sitting down & waiting for the bullet or bomb that will kill, or flinging oneself into the bloody battle in one form or another.

Perhaps Richard & I are fools to endure voluntary separation when our time together may be so short. Perhaps we have been fools in the past to work so hard in the cause of humanity & yet I think we could not have gone against our natures & indulged in frivolity. He is so much a part of me that I find it difficult to function adequately in separation. My mind loses its balance without his near.

'My Life' by Havelock Ellis has shown me the error of a too-personal book. I wish I could find the right medium of expression for my book. I wish I could get it started. What is holding me back? No doubt the sound of the planes constantly passing to & fro & constantly reminding me that any effort may be wasted.

Mussolini entered the war yesterday, & the papers call him bad names. Why did they refrain from doing so when he attacked Abyssinia?

Reluctant tonight to take to my lonely bed [. . .] I will write and write in future. Let me be definite about something.

The same day, Richard's letter to Kay talks of 'midsummer madness':

11 June, RMT to KCT at Barton Hill

[. . .] So one gentleman has broken the other gentleman's agreement. The amount of wish-thinking over the wireless last night, in the papers this morning and at the Office makes me feel tired. Pooh, they say, lot of dirty dagoes, wipe them off the map in a few months. And did you hear our friend Duff-Cooper? 'We know these Italians of old'; then Caporetto (he didn't mention the main reason – vitamin deficiency in the Italian Army ration which was reduced 9 months before the rout) and the childish nonsense about 'ruins for which the Italians are so justly famous.' Yet five years ago we couldn't take the Italians on alone with the help of France and other countries. I have just remembered C's famous words about sanctions – could not think of them this morning – 'midsummer madness'. Now both midsummer and madness have arrived. Our propaganda should surely not be aimed at identifying the Italian people and Government by behaving like a small boy and saying, 'Yah, you can't fight.' We shan't win that way. Our aim should be to drive a wedge between Gov. and people. Tell the Italians that we admire much in their way of life, their music, their literature and painting, etc. We know that they are not to blame – it is their Government, etc.

I must stop this war talk if I am to tell you anything else. François was examined last night and graded 3. Heart I believe. He was told that he will be called in 3 weeks. So there must be a speed-up. The Colonel told him that he intended to put him down for the Ordinance Corps (looking after Stores except food). Saw Acland last night – looks as though he will shortly be in uniform.

It was a very curious day yesterday. Marvellous morning until I got to Harpenden [on the train from Luton] then it came over dark and stormy. No rain however. I went through Mill Hill at 8.10 (I tried a new route) and took 3 hours 5 mins from B.H. to the Flat [. . .] To finish the day I listened in to U.S.A. to hear Roosevelt at 12.15. The most interesting part of it was the almost hysterical enthusiasm shown by his audience.

[. . .] It's a funny thing but whenever I come into the Flat something inside tells me that only half has come through the door. Then I wonder what you are doing. I just can't contemplate life without you if we had to be separated for say 6 months. Well, goodbye darling, and to the most wonderful wife in the world – don't work too hard.

R.

Richard's reference to the need for a speed up in relation to their friend François Lafitte's imminent conscription was to his efforts to prevent François going into the army. Richard wrote to Laurence Cadbury explaining that, 'As he is one of the few good men we have doing research work in this country on such vital questions [as population problems] it does seem to me a tragic waste to allow him to be enrolled into the Army. His calling up will of course prevent him from completing his report on Family Allowances.'[72] Cadbury wasn't terribly sympathetic, reminding Richard that going into the army was a necessary process under the circumstances.[73] Richard next turned to Lord Horder, and Lafitte was spared from conscription. Richard's ploys were less successful with his cousin, Gordon Harman. Gordon was the husband of Joan, the daughter of Richard's mother's unfortunate sister, Edith, who had been dispatched to Brighton in disgrace as an unmarried mother. The problem was Gordon's butcher's shop at Blindley Heath in Surrey, which needed to be maintained while Gordon served in the RAF as a flight mechanic. Richard's letter to Gordon's MP requesting support for an application for compassionate leave was written in Gordon's name but unmistakably on the Titmusses' own Olivetti.[74] Despite the appeal to national economy, Gordon's application was refused, and Joan ran the shop singlehandedly for most of the war.

Kay presumably read Havelock Ellis's book because of the connection with François, whose French mother became Ellis's second wife. Ellis's first wife, the writer Edith Lees, was a bisexual, and their life together was mostly one of affection rather than physical passion. But probably the most shocking thing about Ellis's book was the revelation of Ellis's love of fountains of various kinds, which he traced back to hearing his nurse urinate while he lay in his pram as a baby.[75] This episode was later reinforced by the sound of his mother performing the same act even more sonorously on a gravelled path at the zoo when Havelock was twelve.[76]

Still, it must have been a bit of a change from hearing the news of the war. On 13 June, Kay responded to Richard's 11 June letter about the war news and his new route home:

13 June, KCT to RMT in London
My dearest one,
I had to fight hard not to rush to the phone as soon as I got your letter this morning. I did so want to talk to you but Avril went back to bed sick and would you believe it from 8–11 your wife spent her entire time on breakfast and clearing them up. They get worse here. When I was criticised this morning for making a fresh pot of tea at 8.15 for myself the boys and Avril I felt it was almost the last straw. However, I just pointed out that the last pot was made at 7 a.m. according to information received.

I felt as you did about the papers and Italy. Just made me feel sick. Wrote such a lot in my diary last night. Letting off steam I suppose. I also re-read the major part of 'Crime and Tragedy' last evening. It is a good book you know and should have been published. As a chronicle of events leading up to the war I think it is unique isn't it? Surely Kant's prophecy is about to become true unless we and France succumb to the aggressors, and how can France hold out now? It just seems an impossibility. How are our losses? I see from the MS we lost only 744,000 in the last war by military deaths whereas the Dutch estimated their losses in a couple of weeks at 400,000. Parts of Europe must already be a stinking graveyard. I notice the air raids on Paris are now relegated to a short paragraph. They still tell us they have happened. How

132

much is happening of which we are kept in complete ignorance?

You had a record run to the flat. But you must have been tired [...] I was wondering what you thought about my returning to the flat for a few days. Great excitement here about a mystic sign on a telegraph pole up the lane and a chalk mark on the gate opposite the Dutch barn which we have duly reported to the police.

So F. will have to go. One by one the friends depart. What about Acland – is he volunteering? Just for something to cotton onto I'm looking forward to Bredon in four weeks' time. I'm wondering if I could stick it out here if you had to go in the Army.

Blast. It is now time to get the dinner ready [...] the Aunt has taken herself out in the car.

I'd like to live to experience life in peace but only if I can share the experience with you.

Oh my darling why were we born into a world of fools?

The discontented dishwasher, Kay.

Richard and his 'discontented dishwasher' had the better part of the war still to go. Why Kay wanted to rejoin him in London may be obvious, but why she stayed there once the bombing started is perhaps less so. By August 1940, London was the victim of sporadic air raids, and Londoners were accustomed to the wail of the siren, the 'ping' of anti-aircraft fire and 'the sight of planes streaking across blue skies among bursts of white smoke'.[77] Yet in this Kay – and Richard – were merely behaving as thousands of others did. Richard's own story of the war showed how rarely could human behaviour be explained in any straightforward, rational way. The logic underlying their behaviour had less to do with the calculation of personal safety than with the unwritten rules of the journey they had both set out on in being born man and woman in an unequal world.

——— ✺ ———

Parents Revolt

On the first anniversary of the day war broke out, 3 September, Kay wrote in her diary:

> Heavy still summer days with brilliant hot sunshine that seem to be going on for ever and make us more sad than ever about the war. We long to sit in the sun even in Battersea Park in peace but we know it is useless to go thus far unless prepared for siren interruptions.
>
> Disturbed nights are now our lot with the German planes wasping around dropping bombs at intervals with apparently no discrimination until dawn brings a respite & an opportunity of a quiet sleep.
>
> A visit to parents at Hendon or Forest Hill is now a hazardous adventure not to be undertaken without consideration.
>
> R is now on his way to Elliotts at Lewisham & the siren went five minutes after he left me.
>
> When & how shall we get a break? There is no sign of anything but an intensification of air raids here & in Germany.
>
> Saw Birch for a few minutes last week. He is not happy in Edinburgh.[1] Oh that he would return to Fulham.
>
> My job seems to be developing as the one who sits & waits. I wish I knew R was all right. The planes may be over Lewisham. I'm spending so much more time as a housewife cooking & cleaning as we are tied more to the flat now. What of the writer?

This is one of only nine entries Kay made in her diary between June 1940 and July 1944. Something was holding her back from

the writing she wanted to do. Living with Richard through the
vicissitudes of wartime London, there was no need even for letters.
So the narrative thread of Kay and Richard's correspondence is
broken off in one of those silences which frustrate the historian, and
the movement of their lives has to be constructed from other evidence. Fortunately, there's a good deal of this: a dozen box files of
papers, a mound of Richard's publications and a very large correspondence, some of it challengingly conducted between Richard in England and his friend Jerry Morris in India on army aerograph forms
that have to be read with a magnifying glass. There are also a few
surviving letters to and from Kay's parents, and a series of letters to
and from a childhood friend of hers in Canada. These give a flavour
of what was going on from Kay's point of view, though the style is
rather artificial and reserved, as though she was trying to present her
life with Richard in a certain way.

Life in London was bearable because they escaped to Barton Hill
at weekends. This entailed a hazardous journey, with many devious
cycle routes across London in the blackout and with all the papers
Richard was working on carried on the backs of the bicycles, and
then the eight-mile journey from Luton station to the farm the other
end. But they went on living in London. As Richard was later to
remark in his official social history of the war, fewer people left
London during the nine months of active air attack than either just
before or after the declaration of war.[2] The way in which the pro-
nouncements of the experts were so unpredictably resisted was one
of the major lessons emerging from the war for the peace-time development of the social services. This time the government, unwilling
to repeat the errors of the first exodus, resisted compulsory evacuation, and instead introduced a private scheme whereby 'vulnerable'
people who wanted to leave the evacuation areas were helped with
travel vouchers and lodging allowances. But even in places which
received the worst of the bombing, such as London's East End,
people were reluctant to leave. Despite the hasty erection of many
communal shelters, Londoners preferred the Underground as a place
of safety; at the peak of its use 177,000 people bought platform
tickets and spent their nights there. Dora Russell recalls that, when
the alert sounded in the late evening, she and her family would go
'by tube to St John's Wood, and there share the platforms with other
weary citizens. There was an old empty shop on the corner, where

we kept our sleeping bags and old blankets.[3] There was even an Underground shelter newspaper, run by the intelligentsia users of Swiss Cottage station, who tried to spray everyone's throats with disinfectant to counteract the dreadfully unhygienic conditions that prevailed – if you were lucky people walked a few paces down the line in order to relieve themselves.[4] Matters improved when Lord Horder was put in charge of medical conditions. He did something about the sewage problem, though the fierce winds which blew through the tunnels and sent bedclothes flying weren't so easily cured.[5]

Some enterprising commuters established a refuge in a set of caves in Chislehurst, Kent, to which regular trains were then run every night. But a census in November 1940 showed that 60 per cent of Londoners simply stayed at home when the bombs came. They slept in their own beds, or in basements, or in cupboards under the stairs, or in some other shakily improvised arrangement. Some people, like Vera Brittain and her husband, developed the ability to sleep with a writing table over them through the dropping of a bomb only twenty yards away.[6] Eleanor Rathbone, confined to sleeping in a basement with communal lights that went off at 10.30 every night, triumphed over this inconvenience to go on working with the aid of a bicycle lamp.[7] The middle classes were notably less scrupulous than the working classes at blacking themselves out.[8]

While London was bombed, the Titmusses themselves worked, and wrote, and typed and published; they met their friends and took care of their relatives and went to political meetings and campaigned for what they believed in. All this business-as-usual was what so impressed Winston Churchill, catching glimpses of the lives of ordinary citizens as he emerged periodically from the 'annexe' above the War Room near St James's Park, on the walls of which Mrs Churchill had defiantly hung a few of their favourite paintings to make it seem more homely.[9] Others found their lives utterly changed as they became the unofficial social workers of the war. The story of 'Mrs B' was preserved by Richard for thirty years in an envelope labelled 'personal treasures'. 'Mrs B' was Jane Bixby, a mother of three, otherwise known as the 'angel' of the Angel, Islington. She'd been a beetroot seller for many years. When the raids started she left the first aid post where she was a part-time volunteer, and took charge of a rest centre in Islington which was home every night to between one and three hundred people. She was particularly successful with the babies, finding a supply of milk for them, and bedding them down early with their mothers, and with the aid of 'powders',[10] the secret of which was later revealed: they contained merely a teething remedy. But Mrs B understood the principle of the placebo effect – the belief in the curative power of medicine, whatever its basis in fact. Her bombed-out families bought her a gold watch after the war to express their gratitude. She herself had to wear a steel jacket to protect her spine, which had been injured when a bomb threw her against a wall.[11]

But in general, and apart from the direct effects of bombing, the health of the British people was better during the war than it had ever been. This had much to do with the enforced redistribution from the rich to the poor of food and other resources necessary to health; by the end of the war, government policy had achieved, by accident rather than design, a reduction in those very class inequalities which Richard Titmuss spent his evenings away from insurance work analysing. Although such measures as the introduction (in July 1940) of free or cheap milk to mothers and children, and the immunization against diphtheria of 7 million children between 1940 and 1945,[12] were by-products of war, they also laid the foundations of the post-war welfare state. Living through the war was something of a levelling experience in itself; many, like writer Elizabeth Bowen,[13] observed how life could never be the same again, once you had suffered the dirt and the smells and known what it was like to clean up a house in which every ceiling had come down and every window had been blown in.

While the experts had not anticipated that war would improve health, they had predicted that mental illness would epidemically increase. No such increase was detected; on the contrary, there seemed to be a decline.[14] The explanation probably lay in the social cohesion generated by war, in the stimulation to morale provided by useful work after long years of unemployment, and in the greater meaning to routine existence yielded by the thinning of the wall between the living and the dead.[15]

But the binding camaraderie of war must not be overdone. While many people survived, 43,000 British people were killed and more than a quarter of a million injured. In three years of war the enemy killed more women and children than soldiers.[16] Two out of every seven homes throughout Britain were destroyed or damaged. The bombing of London started on 7 September 1940, and went on for seventy-six consecutive nights, except for 2 November, when the weather was bad. Kay's parents in Forest Hill were in the danger zone. Father still refused to have a telephone installed, so letters were the only means of letting people know they were safe, and of hearing news from them. Kay's mother wrote to her a few days after the bombing started, one of her stilted Victorian letters:

12 September 1940, Katie Miller to KCT
Dear Kathleen,
Just to let you know we are still alright & the house intact, though it really seemed at times during the night as though something must happen, it shook so badly with some of the explosions. We are wondering very much how you fared. The firing was worse than ever last night with hardly an interval.

There is a lot of damage in all directions – St Saviour's Church & Hall there is little left & all the houses along Brockley Rise & the roads leading off have no glass in the windows. Some of the small property near the gas works is down & oh by the way we have no gas today. There was just a glimmer & I managed to boil a kettle for breakfast but since then it has gone altogether & I had to cook our lunch on the kitchen fire – What a life!![. . .]

Sorry not to see you but don't attempt to come until things are quieter. It does not seem safe to get far from home. We only go out to do shopping. Just let us have a line to know how you are getting on – our united love, hoping you may both be kept free from harm.
Father and Mother

Kay and Richard's Pimlico flat received its first damage in October. Kay wrote about this to her childhood friend 'Kasso' – Kathleen Hobday – in Canada. The Hobdays had lived next door to the Millers in Marler Road, when the two Kathleens were children, but had emigrated to Toronto before the war. Kay Titmuss's account of that first bomb attack on their home was included in a narrative about food shortages, the impact of the war on her welfare work, and the general experience of living in London in wartime. It's significant that for her the return to London, though dangerous, allowed her to be active in social work again – this time attached to the Citizens' Advice Bureau in Westminster to help with the bombed and homeless:

10 January 1941, KCT to Kathleen Hobday in Canada
You will have heard of our reduced meat ration and of the shortage of cheese. So far we have not suffered as we have managed to get sufficient protein. To-day Richard saw meat queues in a poor part of London and we felt very sad about it. Shopping takes longer as I find I have to go out each day to see if we can get a pound of oranges or lemons or onions and Richard joins in the search. We don't really mind if we can get a few oranges and with the exception of a fortnight a few weeks ago we have managed to have one between us each day [. . .]

Well, you see I am in London and perhaps you are surprised that we still have a home in Westminster [. . .] We had to close down the Fellowship as the running of a Club became impossible. A great many of our members have lost their homes, some we persuaded to leave for the country so now our only contact with them is a voluminous correspondence. Most of these women are quite uneducated and it is amazing how they write to us. They just don't bother about their spelling or punctuation and we have a grand time deciphering and replying to them. It's very lonely in the new places for most of them. Since the raids on London started I have been busy up here in Westminster attached to the Citizens' Advice Bureau helping to trace missing people [. . .] It is very interesting but very depressing. On the whole the organisation here is very good but I form a sort of link between the various departments of the Ministry of Health, the Billeting Officer, the Borough Surveyor (who removes furniture from damaged houses), the allocator of the Mayor's Distress Fund, L.C.C., etc. etc. I find a bicycle invaluable these days as my area extends to Oxford Street and Soho and the bus services are not what they were and often make very circuitous routes.

[. . .] I don't know whether you want to hear or whether I want to tell you our own bomb stories. This district is pretty badly knocked about you know, and from the outside we look so derelict that some of our letters have not been delivered. There was one particular night in October which we shall never forget. It was Richard's birthday and we did not expect to live through to the morning to celebrate it. As it was we spent the day clearing our flat of soot, broken glass and masonry. One of our biggest discomforts at the moment is draught from broken windows. They are patched with Essex Board but the whole frame is so shattered that the draught just whizzes through and we have to sit in dressing gowns on top of our clothes with a huge fire to try to keep warm. Coal is scarce and in parts of London non-existent [. . .] We sleep in the basement each night we are here. Basements are not considered particularly safe but we are lucky in having a landlord in the flat above us who spent £50 on having the basement rooms sandbagged and strutted so that anyone in the house can sleep down there. He and his wife don't favour the place much and trek out most nights to a caravan in the middle of a field in Hertfordshire. They often ask us to go with them but we think it is even odds between bombs and pneumonia and prefer to stay here as a rule [. . .]

Nothing can be more pathetic than to see elderly women with lined care-worn faces searching among the wreckage of their homes and carrying away on borrowed perambulators some of the oddest things they are able to salvage. Father told me the story of watching a woman at Lower Sydenham with one shoe in her hand searching for the other and of the joy on her face when she found it and had a pair.

The Pimlico flat suffered again in April, when the heavy offensive was resumed. This time it was Richard who described the results in a letter to Maurice Newfield:[17]

To show you that we are still unscathed I am sending you a Review [a piece for the *Eugenics Review*]. We were in the flat on that Wednesday night and it was by far the worst raid we have experienced. The adjoining house received a direct hit at 10 p.m. and trapped a mother and baby in the basement, and at about the same time the gas main outside our front door was set alight so that we had a magnificent jet of flame 40 feet high. Part of our roof fell in and the flat itself became a shambles of glass, debris and soot. We thought it was about time to leave and clutching my precious papers we fled (with intervals for horizontal rest on the glass) to a friend's house in Eccleston Square. At about 1 a.m. we were blitzed out of the room we were in and had to descend to an underground passage. At 5 o'clock we climbed to the top of an 8-storey building which gives a panoramic view of London. In all my life I have never seen such a magnificent colouring; the sky was blood-red and below one could pick out within a radius of a mile at least 30 separate infernos. Of one thing I am certain. The civil defence workers (who all through have been superb – the ambulance, digging squad and the rest were outside the flat within 5 minutes of the bomb falling) deserve something immeasurably better than A. P. Herbert and his friends . . .

Even if a decline in mental health could not be proved, the 'arithmetic of stress' was such that some people's well-being was clearly impaired. Richard's observation[18] that all the official statistics were none the less consistent with some 'harmful psychological effects' having occurred, reflected his own experience: during 1941 and again in 1942, Kay's health broke down; in 1942, he himself was advised to rest.

In May 1941 the Titmusses abandoned their beloved flat in Pimlico and moved to a new one in a purpose-built block in West London where they were to live for the next nine years: number 5, Beaumont Court. The new flat was a few minutes' walk away from the nearest Underground station across an area of open ground called Turnham Green, which during the war was dug up and turned into allotments. Richard himself liked to emphasize the pleasantness of the area, close to the green spaces of Kew Gardens and the ribbon of Georgian houses stretched out by the Thames at Strand-on-the-Green.[19] Kay had many 'forebodings' about the heavy rent they would have to pay: £115 a year including central heating, hot water and porter service. In June, she told Kasso about it, as well as reporting on the food situation – considerably helped now by the purchase of a refrigerator:

12 June 1941, KCT to Kathleen Hobday in Canada
We are now settled in our new home, except for carpets which are still at the cleaners. We were very lucky in being able to salvage most of our things and now they are cleaned and polished up we ourselves are beginning to feel better. For over a month we had no home of our own to live in as we were just patching up from the April 17th blitz when the May 10th packet undid all our work and made things impossible. Luckily for us we were away for the final dose as it was a weekend and we were at the farm [. . .] Our surroundings are very pleasant. We look out on a communal garden with trees and lawns and an open air swimming pool for residents. Mother thinks it is a good thing we have had to move [. . .]

Since my last long letter to you there has been a vast change in the food situation. Catering is an irksome business these days, and no cookery book, even an economical one is the slightest use. It would be easier to tell you the things we can buy rather than those we can't, but, nevertheless, it is still possible to feed adequately. There are times when one longs for a nice fat juicy steak and onions or a sugary bun or a bit of fruit cake but I suppose we shouldn't be human if we didn't. Fruit, apart from rhubarb, has been non-existent for weeks unless one can afford 2/- a piece for a small peach. We eat raw shredded cabbage and carrots, but I rather feel when the war is over I shall banish carrots from my menus with joy. Owing to the weather we are expecting a poor soft fruit crop which is a pity. I only hope the later fruits, apples and plums don't let us down. I have a refrigerator here which is a help I find in keeping things good.

Writing to Kasso again at the end of the year, Kay added a few comments about Richard's work and her own role in relation to it, about which she wasn't completely happy:

14 December 1941, KCT to Kathleen Hobday in Canada
Richard has three books in preparation for publication – two
technical and rather stiff and one for the general reader. He
has a secretary to help him with the editing of a Journal [the
Eugenics Review] which is one of his jobs but apart from that
I have to do all that is needed in that connection and as you
know the preparation of manuscripts for publication is no
light task. In addition, he is supervising some work on German statistics for the Ministry of Economic Warfare and is
collaborating with a doctor friend doing a pretty hefty piece
of research on rheumatism and heart disease. All this in his
spare time, and I have only picked out a few of his activities
[...] The book for the general reader has no satisfactory
title yet but it deals with the fall in population – the revolt
from parenthood [...] Personally, after a weekend on the
MS I'm distinctly fed up with the subject!

Richard's expanding career was taking up more and more of Kay's
time. His work overflowed in tidal waves into the evenings and
weekends, and she was amanuensis, typist, social secretary, librarian,
bibliographer, proof-reader and research assistant, as well as wife and
housewife. 'Have we told you about the private investigation that
Kay is carrying out for me?' asked Richard in a letter to his friend
Jerry Morris, with whom he was undertaking the 'pretty hefty piece'
of social medicine research:[20] 'The birth rate is rising and it is my
impression that we are in for a minor boom [...] Now why? Well,
I have my suspicions and accordingly Kay is sampling 3000 record
cards in the M. & C.W. clinics.' This must have kept Kay busy for
some time. The dividing lines between her roles were thin. When a
Mrs Dobson of Iffley, Oxford, wrote to 'R.T. of the News Chronicle'
in November 1941 about the expense of having babies, it was Kay
who answered on his behalf. Mrs Dobson wanted to have a large
family but life had not been kind to her:

My greatest ambition was to have had a happy family of four
or five children, as my mother did.
    After I had been married seven months, my husband had
a nervous breakdown & lost his position. He was glad to
accept anything and took a post at £3 per wk, plus com-

mission. At the time our rent was £1.2.6. plus rates for a small house in Oxford.

However, we decided to have our first baby.

To provide me with little extras we knew were vital to health my husband went without smokes without new clothes and without food. We went to the pictures only three times in two years.

In spite of it all we had a healthy baby girl. She was born in the Maternity Home Oxford and on the 11th day I was sent home to make room for fresh cases.

The next six months were a night-mare.

After feeding my baby in the evening I went to bed, setting the alarm clock to wake me about 8.30 p.m. to get up and wash etc.

I could never afford more than 1 cwt of coal, plus an occasional bag of slack, to eke it out.

My girlie now is 3½ yrs old. A beautiful healthy child. She does not know what a cold is and she is typically English with large blue eyes & fair hair.

She will be brought up in a really happy Christian home.

[. . .] Many of my friends, like myself, cannot afford to have babies.

My husband is in the RAF now and my allowance is 36/ - for myself and daughter – laughable if it were not so pitiful![21]

Kay answered, in her social work voice:

My husband (R.T. of the News Chronicle) has asked me to thank you for your letter. He is passing on a copy of it to the Family Endowment Society of which Miss Eleanor Rathbone is the Chairman.

We are only too well aware of the difficulties many people like yourself are experiencing in bringing children into the world and bringing them up and are doing all we can to bring about a wiser attitude. As you say your present allowance would be 'laughable if it were not so pitiful'.

I presume you have made sure that is the maximum amount available and that there is no further hardship allowance which could be paid to you. We are, of course, expecting a revision of the scales shortly and I hope you will benefit.

If you find yourself in difficulties, do you know that you can apply to the Soldiers', Sailors' and Airmen's Association? While the allowances remain at so low a figure they are helping countless wives and children with clothing. I don't know where your local office will be but it may be at the same address as the Council of Social Service, 35 Beaumont Street, Oxford. In any case they will be able to tell you where the Association can be found.[22]

Kay was commissioned by the National Council of Social Service to carry out a statistical analysis of the role of voluntary organizations in providing 'material relief'. She earnt £50 for this work (the only record of her earning anything during this period, as the CAB work was unpaid). Two series of cases in the North St Pancras office of the Charity Organization Society and Chesterfield Borough Welfare Committee showed the wide variation in type of case-load by area; in North St Pancras, most applicants were given cash help, whereas most cases in Chesterfield involved boots, repairs and secondhand clothing, and one fifth of the applicants just got Horlicks.[23]

In these difficult and momentous years, not only did the Titmusses move house, but Richard also disentangled himself finally from the clutches of the insurance industry. In December 1941, he told Jerry Morris that the secretary to the Cabinet had offered him the job of writing up 'the history of the Ministry of Health in war-time'. The County Fire Office was refusing to release him, so he intended to resign.[24] He had been seeking a change of occupation for some time. In June 1940, he had written to Magee at the Ministry of Health.

Like so many people I am anxious to do something more useful than the work on which I am at present engaged and it occurred to me that you might be able to advise me. I am 32 and reserved as an Insurance Inspector under the Schedule [. . .] Believing that in my main job as an Insurance Inspector I could contribute nothing to the war effort I applied to the Central Register [of skilled professional workers available for wartime service] months ago and was accepted. I was asked in March whether I would allow my name to go forward for an Assistant Principalship at the Board of Trade but have heard nothing since.

I am not in search of a senior post and am quite prepared to do routine work in any Government Department. Alternatively I am quite willing to do evening work without pay.[25]

Magee's reply noted that the Ministry of Food might be more suitable, and that he was passing Richard's letter on. One other sign of Richard's dissatisfaction with his current work was an inquiry he made in November 1940 about the possibility of doing a doctorate at London University. His letter to the Registrar raised a slight problem: he was not a university graduate.[26] But Richard need not have worried about his future, for by early 1941 the Ministries of Food and Information were fighting for his services: 'Food wants me as Deputy Director of Intelligence and the Ministry of Information as Editor of the War-time Social Survey. To crown it all the Office refuses to release me at the present. All *I* want is to be left alone to get on with my book.'[27]

All Richard's efforts to get himself known, to get his work into print, and to meet the right people, were now paying off. The turning point came when an economic historian, Keith Hancock, was asked in the summer of 1941 to be supervisor of an extremely ambitious project: a series of official civil histories of the war commissioned by the War Cabinet. The origins of these lay in the creation in 1906 of a Historical Section of the Committee for Imperial Defence (which later became the War Cabinet). The small group of men who made up this section were found to be still writing the military history of the First World War when the second one had started. This anomaly was pointed out to the secretary of the War Cabinet, Sir Edward Bridges, who, conscious of the need for historical records, urged all government departments at least to keep a diary of the progress of the new war.[28] Sir Edward might have had more imagination and more contact with progressive thinkers than some civil servants, being the son of the poet Robert Bridges, who had been a close friend of the biologist Julian Huxley during the 1920s.[29] Eventually the idea matured that official civil histories should be commissioned as a project contemporaneous with the war itself. Consultation with the Vice-Chancellor of Cambridge, himself a historian, yielded a list of names of possible 'supervisors', among which one was starred – that of W. K. Hancock of Birmingham University.

Keith Hancock had grown up in Australia, but moved to Birmingham in 1934, where he wrote an impressive two-volume account of British Commonwealth Affairs. He would later return to Australia, diversifying after 'retirement' into a fascinating study of land use in the water-providing region of Monaro in the south-east corner of Australia,[30] and walking hundreds of miles in his seventies in pursuit of his love of history and open air and in order to substantiate his belief that the best historians were those with the strongest boots.[31] The 'brilliant', 'quizzical', 'kindly', energetic pipe-smoking Hancock was to become one of Richard Titmuss's keenest advocates and supporters. But in 1941, it was Hancock's concern with issues of empire that rendered him acceptable for the war history post.[32] This he summarized in one of those limp-fronted orange Penguin specials, *Argument of Empire*, published in 1943: the British Empire represented an 'indispensable contribution of power to the cause of law and freedom'[33] – provided it was used correctly. The empire was merely another word for community, and what the world needed was more of a sense of community, not less.

Hancock was bored with his university post in Birmingham. He thought talent was wasted in administration and committee work, and would later complain that the 'massive yet sensitive study' Richard Titmuss would write of the war was unlikely to be followed by any other good books unless Richard shed some of the committees he took on when he became a professor at the London School of Economics in 1950.[34] In 1941 Hancock heard that Sir Edward Bridges was looking for someone to supervise the history of the war. Hancock went to interrogate Bridges about whether there was any point in writing the history of the war before it had been won. Bridges persuaded him there was. As Hancock later recorded in his autobiography: ' "What did you do in the Second World War?" "I studied its history." That sounded inglorious and rather silly but henceforth it was my task of national service and I took it all the more seriously because it seemed so peculiar.'[35] Hancock's 'national service' as a historian helped to make up for the guilt he felt about escaping real national service – as the youngest son in a family in which the oldest had already gone to war, his Australian parents were able to prevent his conscription. The war history project was peculiar because it involved both the writing of history as it happened and because the history was an 'official' one which involved privileged access to countless government documents as well as the signing of the Official Secrets Act.

There were eventually to be some thirty published volumes. As 'narrator', Hancock acted as 'guide, shock-absorber, conciliator, and educator of both sides' in some of the internecine battles which developed between the historians and the official guardians of the secrets, the permanent civil servants.[36] Three of the volumes were 'synoptic' – that is, wide-ranging in their coverage: Postan's *British War Production*; the volume Hancock co-authored with Margaret Gowing (Richard's biographer), *British War Economy*; and Richard Titmuss's own *Problems of Social Policy*. Looking around amongst his friends and acquaintances for possible names, Hancock was told by Eva Hubback of this interesting young self-taught demographer and social analyst, Richard Titmuss. Eva Hubback, like Richard, was interested in population questions. She was also Principal of Morley College for working men and women (when she was appointed, the only grandmother to be head of a college), chairman of the Family Endowment Society, secretary of the Association for Education in Citizenship and a member of the Council of the Eugenics Society. She couldn't sew or cook, was always half an hour late for meetings, but was a good swimmer. Despite her evident expertise in many fields, with her diffident smile and grey-rimmed glasses she persisted in describing herself as 'just a popularizer'.[37]

Within a few weeks of Eva Hubback suggesting his name to Hancock, Richard and Hancock had met, and Richard had received a formal offer. This amazing stroke of good fortune probably had something to do with the fact that Hancock, being Australian, was outside the British class system, and so was unimpressed by Richard's lack of the usual civil service qualifications. Hancock also had the rare gift of being able to cut through red tape. It seems, though, that he did have to teach Richard some history: 'gave me a lecture on economics and pointed out that life at the time of Domesday was not brutal and nomadic,' wrote Richard to Jerry Morris of Hancock's response to the book he co-authored with Kay, *Parents Revolt*. 'Bad slip there. Neither François [Lafitte] or you pointed it out. And Clarks College did not tell me.'[38] But despite Hancock's general enthusiasm for Richard, the County Fire Office still refused to release him. 'After I had been seen and approved by Hancock and various important people in the Ministry of Health,' wrote Richard to Maurice Newfield,

> the job of compiling the official war history of the Ministry was offered to me at a salary of £700. After the Insurance office had refused to release me the next step was to obtain the approval of the Ministry of Labour to the change prior to my resignation being handed in. Such however is the power of the insurance interests (they have more representatives in the House – over 50 I believe – than any other industry) that I was informed yesterday that the Ministry of Labour would not sanction the change of occupation. I do not intend however to let the matter rest there.[39]

It helped when the insurance world made the connection, via the pages of the *News Chronicle*, between 'Titmuss the writer [and] Titmuss the little insurance clerk'.[40] In January, Richard burnt his boats, along with his pension, and resigned in order to take up Hancock's offer. He did, however, first secure permission for the publication of the two books he was writing. He had no intention of allowing the Official Secrets Act to stem the flow of everything he still wanted to say, which was a lot.

The change of occupation to civil servant (professional grade) proved difficult after seventeen years in the County Fire Office. 'It takes a little while to become acclimatised,'[41] noted Richard. Kay had difficulty adjusting, too, observing to her friend Helen Johnston that the new job 'is not too bad' and she was beginning to get used to Richard 'popping in and out at all times of the day', though he did always seem to come home to lunch when she was out and there was nothing much to eat, whereas if she arranged a lunch he had the habit of not materializing at all.[42] Unsurprisingly, Richard soon regarded himself as 'rather a rebellious' civil servant, and found it 'rather amusing to reflect that after all the rude things I have written about the Ministry in "Poverty and Population" and Infant Mortality I should now be sitting in their offices reading Progress Reports to the Cabinet! I have an hour with McNalty to-day [. . .] He wears boots. I am not surprised.'[43]

Arthur MacNalty was Chief Medical Officer at the Ministry of Health from 1935 to 1940. He then took early retirement to become editor-in-chief of the medical side of the war history, a task that took him a quarter of a century.[44] For Richard, the job grew rapidly, and by May he thought he would probably be editing the history of the social services and education as well. 'My work is extraordinarily interesting,' he told Jerry Morris in June, 'but I am still appalled by the size of the job. I now have editorial responsibility for the Bd. of Ed., part of Home Security and the Scottish Depts. I have proposed tentatively that the volumes should be entitled "The Health and Social Services". I cannot see them being undertaken in less than 600,000 words. A dreadful thought.'[45] By July, he was already annoying the Ministry men: 'I have now completed over 30,000 words on Evacuation. Some of the higher officials who have read it have been kept from their beds!'[46]

One unlikely setting for conversations about the writing of war history was the dome of St Paul's Cathedral. Here Hancock and Richard, among others, had official duties as firewatchers, guarding the cathedral from the effects of aerial attack. The safety of the cathedral had great symbolic importance for Londoners. It was, in fact, hit twice, on 12 September and 29 December 1940. On the first occasion, a bomb big enough to destroy the whole façade landed in front of the steps but failed to explode until it was dug out of the tangle of gas mains, electricity cables and mud and towed away to Hackney Marshes. The second incident was equally serendipitous; an incendiary bomb lodged in the outer shell of the dome, where it started to melt the lead until it fell out and off.[47]

Richard's own spell of duty in St Paul's began in March 1942, when he wrote to Maurice Newfield about it: 'I am a fireman looking after St Paul's Cathedral. It is all very disciplined and efficient and once a week, amongst other strange things like trailer pumps, I patrol the Golden gallery at 3 a.m. and look down on a darkened London and listen to the birds.'[48] He spent about fifty-two hours a month in the dome of St Paul's at night. An official photograph [Plate 14] shows him in a very unmilitary pose and his tin hat, reading out instructions to a group of other tin-hatted, shadowed faces. The job required an intimate knowledge of the cathedral, its 36 separate staircases, the position of the fire hydrants, and how to operate the quite complicated machinery. The position of the hydrants, pumps, etc. was marked clearly on hand-drawn plans provided by the St Paul's Surveyor's Office in June 1940, inside which Richard kept his own detailed notes. There was also a set of instructions: 'St Paul's: its shape and geography. Notes on learning the Building', which invited the firewatchers to think of it as a 'ship with a series of decks'.

Hancock, Richard's co-firewatcher, recalls getting 'plenty of fun' out of those Wednesday nights when it was his turn for duty. He called it 'the best club in London' and remembered that 'We had a cubby hole in a corner of the crypt which we assumed to be no part of holy ground and towards midnight we used always to gather there for talk and tea and sometimes even for rum, of which we had a bottle or two put away for occasions of unusual stress or jubilation.'[49] To pass the monotony of nights when there were no bombs to watch out for, lectures were given by members of the Watch to their colleagues; topics ranged from 'women in romantic poetry' to 'aluminium and its future possibilities' and the solar system.[50] During the service of thanksgiving held when the war was over, it was noted that the St Paul's fire guard watch had on three occasions saved the building from the effects of bombs. The Dean, W. R. Matthews, remarked: 'But I know very well that it was not the thought of gratitude or praise from men that moved you to come here night after night and to endure the hardships and dangers of the watch. You felt that something beautiful was threatened, you felt that something which stood for much that is noble and venerable in the life of England was threatened, and you rallied to its defence.'[51]

But even with the more congenial and stimulating occupation of the war history, and the opportunity to sip rum with his co-firewatchers on unconsecrated ground, Richard was still labouring away at odd moments with his other books and general campaigning activities. During this period, he and Kay published the only book they would jointly author, *Parents Revolt*. Richard also took over much of the management of the wartime work of the Eugenics Society. He was extremely active in Sir Richard Acland's Forward March Movement, which proselytized a new morality and common ownership of all industry as the only answer to the disorders of the world. In 1943, the results of Richard's long-drawn-out investigation into the social patterning of health and illness was published. He began a series of articles with Jerry Morris, which laid the foundations

151

of the new discipline of social medicine. Of course, now he was in the Cabinet Offices not so many of the invitations to speak and write could be accepted, and Kay, as secretary, wrote to explain; to Mr H. E. Roff of the Purley Rotary Club, who wanted him to speak about the falling birth rate: 'My husband [. . .] is very sorry but he is engaged on very special work in Whitehall and will not have any time to spare';[52] to Mr Myant who wanted a thousand words on infant mortality for the University College Hospital magazine, 'He is now attached to the Offices of the War Cabinet for special work [. . .] The infant mortality material is in the publisher's hands and will probably appear under the title of POOR CHILDREN DIE. When we cannot say.'[53]

The two driving forces of Richard's intellectual and political life at this time were the concern with the future of population, and the distaste for the culture which produced the Second World War. These two themes were connected. An article in the *New Statesman* which he published in August 1941 called 'The end of economic parenthood' spelt out his view of the connection, which he knew few people understood:

> Man's desire to serve the community – and one way in which he can best do this is by consciously and deliberately desiring the continuance of his own kind – has been increasingly negatived by a society which tells him to seek his own interest, individually and nationally; to regard wealth as an index of biological success; to attain power through wealth; and to relegate morals to a two-hour session of platitudes on the seventh day. For a century we have preached the value of morals and practised the immorality of acquisitiveness [. . .]
>
> Modern war is a temporary index of a morally unhealthy society; a declining replacement rate is a permanent expression of the same thing. The former results from man's physical control over the internal combustion engine, the latter from control over fertility. In both cases he is destructive of life; he kills the living and destroys the desire to reproduce . . .[54]

Altruism was the cornerstone of a rational civilization. Acquisitiveness was its enemy. Richard's lifelong attack on the dominance of the

profit motive owed much to the influence of the socialist historian
R. H. Tawney, whose slim volume *The Acquisitive Society* was first
published in 1921.[55] For both Tawney and Titmuss, capitalism was
wrong chiefly on moral grounds. Its opposite was not the political
and economic system of communism, but the moral structure of
altruism. From the point of view of the failing birth rate, sufficient
altruism would avoid war and guarantee that enough babies would
be born. Altruism was also the moral key word of the movement
founded in 1940 by Sir Richard Acland, whose book outlining his
ideas, *Unser Kampf*,[56] sold 75,000 copies in its first three weeks.
Acland, a Liberal, had been elected as MP for North Devon in 1935.
He was the son of a long-established landowning family, and had
inherited from his father a baronetcy which had been created in 1643
for services rendered by the Acland family to the Royalist cause in
the Civil War. Acland became persuaded of the value of socialism in
1936, and in 1940 was converted to Christianity.[57] In *Unser Kampf*,
he set out the fundamental causes of the war with Germany as beyond
any conception of party politics. Like Richard Titmuss, he saw the
immorality of the war as deriving from the amorality of the current
social and political order. The key error was the self-seeking of both
the individual and the nation, which produced both the world-wide
problem of economic recession and unrest and the ultimate breakdown of peace. The only solution was a 'new standard of morality'
based on the ethical principles of Christianity; the commandment
Love thy neighbour as thyself' would reinstate a moral altruism
'hich had largely been forgotten by the churches themselves. Only
'1 a creed would adequately oppose the economic structure of
'poly capitalism in which it was every man's duty to advance
..is own private interests.

The sympathy between the views of 'the two Richards' led Acland
to ask for permission to print 3,000 copies of Titmuss's *New Statesman* piece. Richard Titmuss had first contacted Richard Acland when
Unser Kampf was published, as many other people had done.

> When I was in the House on Thursday to attend the meeting
> on Family Allowances I sent a card in but apparently you
> were in Committee.
>
> First, I wanted to thank you for 'Unser Kampf'. Although,
> as a Liberal, I may diverge somewhat on a few side issues

nevertheless I accept your major argument for Common Ownership with all that implies in national and international relations. If a majority of the Liberals *and Labour* accept your case then it seems to me that a Lib-Lab Front on Common Ownership must become a reality.

A lot of my friends who are Socialists and with whom I have discussed the book want to know whether any *organised* body of opinion is to emerge. Even if everybody who reads it attempts to influence other people that in itself is not enough. The whole world-wide case has got to be kept alive – the one really frightening thing about this country to-day is the apathy that prevails over everything political and social. Most people just cannot visualise a better world – the peak of their dreams is just a few more shillings every week and that at the expense of somebody else [. . .]

Have you contemplated any sort of political organisation? What is to be done to convert other Liberals?[58]

Acland orchestrated these personal contacts in order to establish the nucleus of an organization which could advance his ideas. The Forward March movement united a wide range of intellectuals, writers, industrialists and politicians, including Ritchie Calder, Tom Balogh, Victor Gollancz, Lord Horder, Eva Hubback, Kingsley Martin and the Labour politicians-to-be Richard Crossman and Douglas Jay. According to François Lafitte, the main aim of the movement was to try to recall the Labour Party to its proper duty in the political lacunae left by Labour putting socialism 'into the refrigerator' for the duration of the war, and the Communist and Independent Labour Parties both adopting a 'futile attitude of war resistance'.[59] Many of Richard's friends were more sceptical than he was about the advisability of choosing 'Russian solutions'.[60] To Maurice Newfield, Richard waxed enthusiastic about the newly formed 1941 Committee and its propaganda, which he thought 'should be powerful'. Although many of the names were still secret, he could tell Maurice in confidence that Horder was one of them.[61] The membership of the Forward March movement and the 1941 Committee overlapped with other intellectual and social circles in which the Titmusses moved, particularly the Eugenics Society. Even Dr Birch turned up again, with the endorsement of the 1941 Committee's work by a body called the Christ and Unemployment Crusade to which Birch's name was attached as editor.[62]

Acland invited Richard to be a signatory of a document called the 'Manifesto of the Common Man' setting out the aims of the movement. Richard agreed, becoming thereafter progressively involved in the necessary committee work, sending Acland's book and associated propaganda to many of his friends and acquaintances, and substituting for Acland as a speaker when Acland went into the Army. By May 1940, he had arranged for Newfield to introduce Harold Laski and John Strachey, both of whom Newfield knew personally, to Acland with a view to a substantial publicity drive.[63] At this time it seemed to Richard that there was a real possibility of a strong parliamentary opposition on the broad principles of *Unser Kampf.*[64] By April 1940, the title Our Struggle had been chosen in preference to the German form. Later on, Acland's initiative was known as the Forward March Movement (from Churchill's famous 1940 speech: 'long live the forward march of the common people of all lands towards their true inheritance'). By 1942, Richard, along with his friend François Lafitte, was responsible for framing Forward March policy. An ambitious programme of national groups and mass publicity was drawn up, with the aim of getting candidates elected to Parliament. An alliance was formed with J. B. Priestley's progressive 1941 Committee, and a Nine-Point Declaration was issued which they intended to serve as a platform for Left candidates at by-elections; the nine points included common ownership of services and industries, elimination of red tape in the civil service, post-war plans for free full state education and a civilized standard of living for everyone.[65] In mid-1942 the Forward March movement and the 1941 Committee merged to form a new political party called Common Wealth, under Priestley as Chairman, though many people thought of Common Wealth as Acland's 'Christian Communist Party'.[66]

Kay was a bystander in these events. It's hard to tell what she really thought, though her letters make it clear that she enjoyed vicariously some of the personages and happenings they involved:

15 September 1941, KCT to Katie Miller
Dear Mother,
I don't see a ghost of a chance of coming down to see you

again this week as we are still hoping to get away for a weekend at the farm early on Friday so I thought I would tell you all about things.

I'm feeling rather tired to-day as I seem to have had so many broken nights [. . .] Acland came in about 2 o'clock on Sunday morning bursting with news about the Conference and we sat and talked over cocoa and sandwiches before I put him to bed on the camp bed in the lounge. He left Richard behind as he said it was very necessary he should stay over Sunday to prevent the conference slipping back on the resolutions they had got through on the Saturday. Apparently the two Richards, Gollancz, François and Wilfred Brown were a very effective ginger group and did their best to rattle Priestley and Edward Hulton off their fences. Gollancz, Brown and Acland all left on Saturday night leaving Richard and François to continue the battle alone and R. came home very late last night, having to knock me up as he had given Acland his key the previous night, full of excitement with the continuation of the story. Apparently François was too exhausted to get up on Sunday morning and R. had to tackle Priestley and Hulton alone. He seemed quite satisfied with the result. It seems to me that the Acland crowd wiped the floor with the others and Acland told me he was writing Priestley to tell him to go back to his books as his 1941 Committee would be useless if it could not take bold actions and make bold decisions. It's funny to be a looker-on. Picture Post may have photographs of the Conference this week. Their star photographer was there and followed Hulton and Priestley around. I should think they will take care to keep Titmuss out of it, and probably all of his followers of whom there were many, but one never knows. I dare say we shall be chewing the whole thing over again as there is a meeting at Brown's factory at 5.30 when R. and Acland are to speak. I shall probably go and we shall probably return to the Browns for a meal afterwards [. . .]

Mrs Hubback has a new hat – like an Admiral's turned round the other way in R's description and he said she wore a dreadful brown woollen costume that was always rucked up somewhere. Having no time for private discussion during the weekend they are meeting for tea one day this week as she is writing a new book on Family Allowances and they want to make sure that their two new books don't cover the same ground.

R. just in – 3 p.m. – some typing to do for him.

Much love, Kay

Picture Post did indeed feature nine photographs of the conference. The largest showed fifteen men and four women in relaxed postures, many behind clouds of pipe or cigarette smoke, debating the Atlantic Charter; Mrs Hubback appeared in her hat sipping tea with a friend, and supposedly talking about family allowances.[67] One of the men in the photographs was probably Wilfred Brown, who was managing director of the Glacier Metal Company in West London and known for his study of industrial psychology. The Glacier Metal Company was run in a co-operative way, with a regular news bulletin to which the workers contributed and which during the war ran with the slogan 'It All Depends on Me'. Brown got a peerage in 1964, which would not have gone unnoticed by Kay, who must have wondered about Richard's own chances.

The Forward March movement eventually fizzled out. The merger of the different strands was unsuccessful (Richard sat on the Merger Committee with 'the rest of the boys').[68] The imminent disbanding of Common Wealth was announced in *The Times* in April 1944.[69] Although Common Wealth candidates would continue to be put forward at by-elections, socialists and radical liberals would also be supported. The main reason given for the movement's decline was lack of money. The following year Common Wealth was still going, but had decided to pledge its support to Labour candidates.[70] The post-war Labour government made the movement's separate radical-ism redundant. Acland himself left the Liberal Party in 1942 to represent the Common Wealth Party, but went on to become a Labour MP in 1945.[71] (To show that he meant what he said, he left the family's considerable North Devon estate to the National Trust.)

Richard Titmuss's own association with the Forward March movement was weakened by his role as official war historian. From mid-1942 on, he felt he could no longer afford to be identified publicly as a radical.[72] This was noted by Kay in some comments she added to the files after Richard's death:

> My recollection of the period (which was largely during the blitz) was of frantic activity at Gerald Rd [where Acland lived] – so much talk and so much paper. I think Richard knew quite early that the Common Wealth movement would not get very far, but for a time it provided him with the feeling of trying to do something for the country & we must remember his job was Insurance – War Damage Claims which was unsatisfying.
>
> As is evident from a read of these papers Acland was an idealist – Wilfred Brown tried to be practical but was very busy with his Glacier Metal Co [...] After the war when Acland gave away his inheritance in Devon Richard acted as referee for a job in the teaching profession for him. He visited us several times [...] & was full of rather wild Christian ideals talk.

H. G. Wells, who belonged for a while to the 1941 Committee, described it as a 'well-meaning (but otherwise meaningless) miscellany of people [...] earnestly and obstinately going in every direction under their vehement professions of unity'.[73]

Richard's major personal project in 1942 was a slim volume called *Parents Revolt*.[74] This started out as *his* book, and became *theirs*, in the sense that it carried both their names, but, as Kay's December 1941 letter to Kasso in Canada made clear, she'd typed rather than composed it. The history of its publication went like this. In early 1940, Frederick Warburg of Secker and Warburg had raised with Richard the possibility of a book on population problems, and he wrote again in August 1941 following the publication of Richard's article in the *New Statesman*.[75] The contract with Secker and Warburg was in Richard's name, but when the book was about to be printed he wrote to the publishers to request that Kay's name be added. Unhappily, many reviewers forgot Kay's authorship: 'Parents are in Revolt and Mr Titmuss knows why,' ran the headline in the *Catholic Herald*.[76] The publishers' own treatment of the second author didn't help, for they added insult to injury by omitting her name from the dustjacket, and then going on to advertise the book as written by a

Richard and *Mary* Titmuss.[77] The error was echoed by many reviewers.

The subject of *Parents Revolt* was the long-term decline in the birth rate. Why was this happening? What did it mean? What consequences were in store for 'civilization'? Richard's concern with the 'quantity' of the population stemmed originally from his insurance interests. One of his first publications in the *Insurance Record*[78] had somewhat uninterestingly, but predictably, in view of his occupation at the time, attempted to calculate the impact of long-term population changes on fire and accident insurance. But the Titmusses were by no means alone in being concerned about a falling population. During the 1930s the newspapers were full of headlines about population problems, not only at home but in France, Italy, Germany, Sweden and other countries. In April 1942, Richard had written together with Lord Horder a letter to *The Times* in which they were pleased to add Mussolini's Italy to the list of nations incapable of replacing themselves.[79] When Richard gave a talk to the British Social Hygiene Council in June 1942, the proceedings were widely reported in the press under headings such as 'White Races Birth-rate Problem'[80] and 'White Parents Are "On Strike"'.[81] Richard himself attracted considerable attention by mentioning the one and a half million fewer babies in the same breath as one and a half million more pet dogs. '15 Dogs in Place of One Baby' declared the *Daily Mail*[82] with dramatic but unmathematical verve.

The pronatalism of *Parents Revolt* developed at a time of widespread concern throughout Europe about a changing demographic structure. This was taken to mean not only proportionately fewer births but an increasing burden of elderly people, which would bring obvious, deleterious social consequences. The population debate tapped into long-standing histrionics about the ebbing vitality of nation states, and drew both on right-wing concerns about the threat to nationalist power and on left-wing ones about the imminent failure of capitalism. Like eugenics (with which it overlapped both intellectually and socially), the fear of population decline appealed to both conservative and socialist attitudes: the former used it to encourage upper-class breeding, the latter to oppose individualism as the enemy of a healthy birth rate. In between, there was a liberal position which caricatured declining fertility as an obstacle to social reform; an ageing population could not be a reformist one. Like this assumption about age, much of the population debate at the time was constructed of non-sequiturs. A characteristic of the anxiety about population decline for over a hundred years was the ease with which the qualitative was read into the quantitative; fewer numbers were taken automatically as marking a moral decline; metaphors of 'breeding' and 'stock' crept in, suggesting that it was the 'best' people who were failing to reproduce, and the 'worst' who were threatening to overcome them. Paeans to procreation were thus rarely 'simple' pronatalism. They often, also, had a military purpose. The military was linked to the eugenic; only healthy armies could win wars; and only healthy populations were worth fighting for.[83]

Without appreciating this background of metaphor, it's difficult to understand today why so many people got so worked up about the birth rate then, particularly since with the wisdom of hindsight we can see that at the height of their concern the birth rate decline actually reversed itself,[84] so that most of their clever predictions turned out to be wrong anyway. The Titmusses themselves contended that this matter of the birth rate was 'of even more vital importance to the destiny of man than the tragedy of war'.[85] Capitalism was 'a biological failure', promoting the extinction of the entire social order. This somewhat surprising answer seemed to place the Titmusses firmly on the political left. But, on the other hand, their preoccupation with the falling birth rate of *some* countries, rather than (or as well as) the rising birth rate of others, suggested a right-wing nationalism. The arithmetic of their concern with fewer births – most pronounced among the better endowed classes and likely to produce a steadily deteriorating population in the qualitative sense – was also uncomfortably undemocratic.

Just as the Titmusses were not the only ones to be concerned, they were not the only ones to publish on this topic. Indeed, it was hard to find anyone who was anyone who didn't write either about the birth rate or eugenics or both. Alexander Carr-Saunders published *The Population Problem* in 1922. A zoologist and barrister, Carr-Saunders was a convinced eugenist who believed that biology held the answer to social problems. Maynard Keynes, the economist, was at school with him and recalled his being a slow beginner, taking a long time to decide what he wanted to do, and then reaching Malthus by reading Darwin, which repaid a debt, as Darwin had developed his own theories by reading Malthus.[86] Carr-Saunders's panoptic vision of the problem of population was conceived during the First World War when he was forced to spend an idle period at a depot at Suez.[87] In 1923 he took up a chair of social science in Liverpool and in 1937 he became director of the LSE after William Beveridge. He was, by all accounts, a perceptive and kindly man, a walker, like Keith Hancock, in the Welsh hills and other places, and if his teaching at Liverpool on the country's first social science degree was marked by too much enthusiasm for eugenics, at least it was enthusiastic.[88] Carr-Saunders was to assume great significance in Richard's post-war life as facilitator of his appointment as professor at the LSE in 1950.

In 1934, Enid Charles published a book called *The Twilight of Parenthood*. Charles was the wife of Lancelot Hogben, a virulent anti-eugenist with whom Richard would later cross swords. In her book she predicted that the population of England and Wales would decline to half the size of greater London (i.e. 6 million) in the next two hundred years.[89] Her position on the social group differential favoured environmental rather than genetic explanations. She quoted her husband on this, tongue-in-cheek:

> No single group has the monopoly of all the virtues. It is quite possible that the distribution of genes among the Scotch tends to favour a rather higher general level of intelligence than would be found among negroes educated in the same way. One can be open to be convinced that this is so, and retain a personal preference for generosity, cheerfulness, a sense of humour, vocal music without the accompaniment of bagpipes, and the restraint which permits a man to listen to a joke without explaining the point of it to its inventor.[90]

The last chapter of Charles's book picked up the theme of changes in the position of women, particularly the exodus of women from the home to seek paid work. She saw free enterprise as counterproductive to social planning, and argued that the laissez faire economy which encouraged women to go out to work should be replaced by social policies, such as family allowances, which would offer practical help. The Titmusses would later express similar views.

There was much speculation about why middle-class women weren't having as many babies as they used to, but very little empirical investigation. In his speech at the 1942 British Social Hygiene

Council conference, Lord Horder highlighted 'passive resistance' on the part of would-be parents as the main underlying cause. François Lafitte said women didn't have babies because of home-making difficulties – 'the pram racket, enormous prices for equipment – and because of the marriage bars, which are a scandal in a country which calls itself democratic'.[91] Demographer David Glass referred to a 'personal investigation' of his which showed that parents were affected by the fear of war.[92] Biologist Lancelot Hogben considered it was all due to separate sleeping arrangements, bedside lights and too much washing.[93]

On the whole, the problem was treated as one of 'man's' decision to avoid parenthood, in the usual sense of 'man' being intended to embrace women's motives as well. A fascinating survey of the birth rate, social conditions and women's experiences had been conducted in 1914 by Ethel Elderton, who was a Galton Fellow at the University of London, but few people appeared to be aware of it. Elderton's survey in the coal-mining and textile-producing areas of Lancashire and Yorkshire identified as important factors in lower birth rates the increased cost of living, women's employment in the textile trades, and the practices of family limitation by both abortion and contraception, which seemed widespread.[94] When the pioneers of the Peckham Health Centre in London repeated in 1935 a study originally undertaken in 1929 of contraceptive habits in the area, they reported a substantial lifting of the taboo on birth control. One sign of this was that chemists now exposed for sale, and actively advertised, popular brands of contraceptives without fear of offending the public.[95] However, this interpretation might have been a bit over-optimistic. When Richard wrote a pamphlet on population for Eva Hubback and her Association for Education in Citizenship in 1943, they asked him to remember the susceptibilities of the Roman Catholics and substitute the term 'planned family'.[96] Richard was outraged: 'It is for the Churches to face up to the truth – not for us to avoid it.'[97] He himself became actively involved in the contraceptive market in 1942 when the Family Planning Association wanted an investigation into a new chemical contraceptive called Volpar (the name was derived from 'voluntary parenthood'). Volpar became something of a cause célèbre in birth-control circles, with Marie Stopes expressing in the pages of the *Lancet* the view that Volpar (which contained mercury) was almost certainly injurious to women's health.[98] As 'the founder

1 *Left*: Richard and Kay Titmuss, 1970

2 *Below*: Richard Titmuss as a child (on right) with his brother and sister

3 Richard Titmuss with his mother, 1936

4 *Left*: Kay Miller, aged fifteen, with her mother and younger brother

5 *Below*: International Youth Tramps, 1934. (Richard Titmuss on right, Kay Miller at back, right)

6 Visit of HRH the Duke of Kent to Fulham Fellowship for the
Unemployed, 1939. (Kay Titmuss in centre, Richard Titmuss at
back, left)

7 The Rev. R. S. Birch

8 *Right*: Richard
Titmuss on a walking
tour of Germany, 1935

9 *Below*: World Youth
Congress, Geneva,
1936. (Richard Titmuss
and Kay Miller in
centre)

10 Barton Hill farmhouse today

11 Barton Hill Farm today: 'Happy Valley'

12 Barton Hill Farm in the 1930s: Richard Titmuss fetching water

13 Barton Hill Farm during the war: Kay Titmuss (on right), the 'maid' and the 'landgirl'

14 Firewatching at St Paul's Cathedral during the war (Richard Titmuss standing)

15 *Left*: Richard with Ann in London, 1944

16 *Below*: Kay with Ann in Wakefield, 1944

17 Richard and Kay drawn by Ann, *c.* 1958

of the Mothers' Clinics', Stopes deplored the failure of the FPA to 'follow the fundamental policy of safe C.B.C. [constructive birth control] clinical work – namely, that (apart from rubber) nothing is advised for use by the clinic patients in the vagina that the practitioner advising it would not himself be willing to masticate and swallow daily for long extended periods'. This was presumably why Blacker, amongst others,[99] ate the stuff. The publicity Stopes used for her clinics advised mothers that Volpar was 'extremely bad and unreliable' – they should refuse it and use instead 'our safe greasy Solubles with the cap supplied by the Clinic'.[100] The Eugenics Committee voted £250 in support of the FPA's investigation, and Richard was enlisted to help with the planning and statistical analysis of the study. The FPA were particularly keen to examine the efficiency in preventing pregnancy of something called 'Tropical Volpar' which had so far been tried only in India and Tanganyika, but which laboratory tests suggested might be superior to any other form. In September 1941, Richard wrote to Margaret Pyke outlining a study proposal: of 2,000 married women, all new patients, 1,000 should be advised to use Volpar and 1,000 another contraceptive chemical. Patients should be allocated alternately to the two groups by means of a card system.[101]

Claims about the effectiveness of the 'New Chemical Contraceptive' were published in the *Lancet*, where the support of the Eugenics Society and the National Birth Control Association (President Lord Horder) was noted disapprovingly in some quarters. Nothing seems to have come of Richard's Volpar investigation or, if it did, there is no record left in the files. In 1949 Volpar Paste and Gels with their 'essential killing substance' of phenyl mercuric acetate were both on the list of approved contraceptive products. A survey of FPA clinics funded by the Eugenics Society showed both to be at the top of the list of the chemical contraceptives used.[102]

But if the declining birth rate in the 1930s clearly had something to do with women's experiences and behaviour, the links between the vital statistics of demography and women's social and economic position were not made by British writers. This task was left to the Swedish social reformers Alva and Gunnar Myrdal, who made the connections most ably in a book called *Crisis in the Population Question* which was published in Swedish the same year as Enid Charles's *The Twilight of Parenthood*.[103] The Myrdals' book advocated full-scale social reforms for averting the crisis which took account of the needs of both mothers and children.[104] Like the Titmusses, they were a couple, but, unlike the Titmusses, they did not make the legendary mistake in their book of assuming that man and wife are one, or that the interests of the family unit are necessarily the same as those of its individual members.

In Britain, the principal population experts (apart from Enid Charles) were men: Carr-Saunders, David Glass and R. R. Kuczynski. All three worked at the LSE. Robert René Kuczynski came to England from Berlin as a political refugee in 1932, published a series of books on population, and was largely responsible for getting demography accepted as an academic subject. He became its first Reader at the LSE in 1938,[105] when he embarked on a massive study of the demography of the British Empire, which was completed after his death with the assistance of his daughter Brigitte.[106] Kuczynski's major contribution to the debate was a technical one. He introduced the concept of the 'net reproduction rate' (NRR) which offered a more exact calculation of the likely trends in population than existing methods. The net reproduction rate concentrated on the female population aged 15–45 and sought to determine how many girls a woman would give birth to in the course of her reproductive life. The technique was widely used from the late 1930s on to predict population trends, and Kuczynski had brought it with him from Germany, where he had learnt it from the director of the Berlin Statistical Office, with whom he had worked as a young man in the late 1890s.[107] The NRR was quite easy to calculate, once one had information about the fertility of different age groups. But as these were not available for England and Wales until 1939, the standard practice, curiously uncommented on by most, was to use the rates for Sweden instead.[108]

An NRR of one meant that the population was replacing itself; at less than one it was not. However, all these fancy calculations had a fatal flaw in them. Because the statistical projections extrapolated from *current* birth and death rates, on the assumption that these represented a closed system which would not be influenced by external factors, they were almost bound to be wrong. For instance, the birth rate in the 1930s was low mainly in the 20–30 age group, leaving time later on to catch up on births which had been delayed due to the Depression. Richard had noted this tendency in his work on German health statistics. His jubilant discovery that at no time since Hitler came to power had the German birth rate been high enough to replace the existing population drew the attention of 'one of the "high ups" at M.O.I. [The Ministry of Information]' who was excited by its propaganda potential.[109] It was the cohort of young people who delayed childbearing during the 1930s who were mainly responsible for the 1940s boom; in Britain, the upturn started the very year *Parents Revolt* was published. By the time the work of the Royal Commission on Population was under way in 1943-4, the attention of demographers had turned to nuptiality as one 'external' factor that was likely to have a significant impact on birth rates.

Kuczynski and Richard met some time in 1941. By early 1942 they were lunching together regularly: 'He really is charming and I enjoy sitting at his feet,' wrote Richard to Maurice Newfield.[110] Richard seems to have got to know David Glass somewhat earlier. Glass was employed by the Eugenics Society as a research assistant to carry out some research into European population policy. His academic life began with a research assistantship to William Beveridge and he remained connected to the LSE for fifty years, going on to do a pioneering study of social mobility in Britain.[111] He and his wife Ruth feature in the Titmusses' later letters to one another. Like Kuczynski, Ruth was a German refugee; a member of a prominent Jewish family, at Berlin university her studies of youth unemployment had been abruptly interrupted by the rise of the Nazis. Her first husband was Henry Durant, a pioneer of public opinion surveys. She divorced him in 1941 and met David Glass while working at Columbia University in the United States.[112] When news of David Glass's marriage reached Maurice Newfield and Richard, they were apparently not keen to meet his new wife.[113]

Groups and organizations devoted to particular versions of the population problem proliferated during this period. Carr-Saunders's view on population, particularly as expressed in his 1935 Galton lecture for the Eugenics Society, 'Eugenics in the Light of Population Trends', led directly to the formation of the most influential and long-lived of these organizations, the Population Investigation Committee. Theoretically separate from the Eugenics Society, most of the PIC's members were eugenists, and the committee's work was financially supported by the society, as well as by private donation (some from Eugenics Society members; Laurence Cadbury paid

Glass's salary for two years himself). The remit of the PIC was mainly research: 'to examine the trends of population in Great Britain and the Colonies and to investigate the causes of these trends, with special reference to the fall of the birth-rate'.[114] It first met in June 1936 with Carr-Saunders as chairman, Blacker of the Eugenics Society as general secretary and David Glass as the committee's research secretary – a full-time paid appointment. The results of David Glass's researches, *The Struggle for Population*, came out in 1936, carrying an introduction by Carr-Saunders which bemoaned the imminent failure of Britain to supply the Empire with enough of the right breed of citizens.[115] Another body was set up at the same time as the PIC, the Population Policies Committee; this was the joint brainchild of the Eugenics Society and Political and Economic Planning. Richard and Kay's friend François Lafitte was the secretary of the PPC.

This was the framework within which *Parents Revolt* came to be written. Beatrice Webb's preface must have helped to sell it. Inspired by an inquiry about his work she had made via the *New Statesman* in 1941, Richard had written to her in February 1942 enclosing the manuscript and requesting 500 words from her in support of the book. At first she regretted that she was not fit enough to take on the task, being 'well over eighty years of age' and having spent the last two months writing a forty-page introduction to the reissue of her own *Soviet Communism: A new civilisation*.[116] But eventually she did write, not 500, but 700 words. Richard was angry that, in order to save paper, the publisher cut the extra words so that the preface could be set on one page. Beatrice Webb's text highlighted the implication of the falling birth rate for 'the survival of the white race' (yet again), and ended by pointing optimistically in the direction of the Soviet Union, whose economic system, she suggested, might by the end of the century result in three hundred million well-educated and healthy human beings.

Everybody's Weekly summarized the main themes of *Parents Revolt* with two photographs of children playing at the seaside and a well-appointed couple stowing leather suitcases carefully in the boot of a shiny new car.[117] The reviews themselves were mixed. The *New Statesman and Nation* complained that the book wasn't original,[118] and that not enough attention had been given to the emancipation of women as a factor producing reluctant parenthood. *The Times*,[119] the *Spectator*[120] and the *Fortnightly Revue*[121] all observed that the biological failure of capitalism was strictly an unproved thesis. Since the whole nineteenth century had been 'immensely acquisitive and competitive [...] and immensely fertile', the religious newspaper the *Tablet* argued that the thesis was actually disproved.[122] The *Lancet* found the argument stimulating, but complained that there were too many statistics.[123] Under the by-line 'Racial Suicide', the *Western Telegraph* deemed the book 'very instructive and [...] topical [...] far and away the best book as yet written on the subject'.[124] The nursing journals considered the book essential reading for nurses, the social work journals commended it to social workers, and the *Medical Officer* prescribed it for all who worked in the health services.[125]

In the wave of publicity generated by the book, Richard took part in a BBC discussion in November 1942 with the title 'Too few babies?'[126] Many people wrote in after the broadcast. Laurence Cadbury pointed out that the motive of keeping up with the Joneses was unlikely easily to be obliterated,[127] and what about the importance of domestic service and help in the house? Shouldn't this be made more available to parents? Richard thought this had some appeal.[128] As to keeping up with the Joneses, what he really aimed for was a different standard of values relating to happy family life: 'i.e. gardens, creative work, public service and citizenship'.

Other listeners' letters made different points. 'You appear to have the myopic outlook of a church-mouse,' noted B. Hardcastle of Burgess Hill. 'Anyone up in the first elements of ethnic sociology will tell you of the great laws governing racial growth and decline [...] We are now going over the crest of a mighty wave and a movement from east to West of all Aryan civilisations.'[129] Hitler had been sent to help with this move. The British Empire was irremediably in decline (because too many Englishmen were marrying Eurasians), and the new race was now in America, where the best of the 'old puritan stock' had gone. The French, Italians and Spanish were all decadent, and so dying out; the British upper classes were 'over-bred' and 'over-brainy'; insanity, cancer and false teeth – all signs of racial degeneracy – were everywhere. The writer enclosed a news cutting bearing the headline '100,000 FORCED BACK TO THE SLUMS' next to which he wrote 'where they breed like rabbits'. An anonymous mother from Bristol remarked that she was one of the nation's unfits, having been worn down by constant child-bearing, and shouldn't Mr Titmuss consider the physical well-being of women before he advocated a return to the days of non-birth control?[130] An alternative view identified domestic architecture as the problem:

> There will never be more than one baby in the middle class family, until they stop building those silly houses all over the country that the middle class are buying, the ones I mean, and there are hundreds of them, two sitting rooms, two bedrooms and that useless Kitchenette. My idea of a house for the middle class, is a large bright kitchen, where everyone can have their meals, and where a woman can do a good day's washing if she wants to ... plenty of bedrooms, and above all somewhere to keep the Baby carriage which no-one seems to think when building these houses.[131]

An 'impregnating machine' from Cornwall took issue with the Titmusses' argument about the acquisitive society,[132] observing that 'bacteria, small insects, flies, herrings, rats, rabbits, pigs, and monkeys' all have high birth rates and are very acquisitive. What was needed was a reversion to barbarism, 'in which the animal follows the sexual impulse of the moment without thought for the morrow'. A farmer's wife and mother of three from Devon took up the point about domestic help: 'Have you ever thought,' she asked, 'what it is to be so ghastly *tired* all the time that you cannot enjoy your children?' Her house was large and inconvenient (farmers picked the land and their wives just got the houses that went with it), and after a summer helping make hay and harvest oats, looking after livestock and horses and mucking out stables, as well as caring for the children, she didn't wonder 'that we mothers ask: Is it good enough?'[133] Then there was the problem of the men. Women want to have children, but they need, as well as economic security and peace, marriageable men – that is, men who are willing to be dependable fathers rather than just husbands.[134] *Parents Revolt* prompted one young man in Sydenham to want to write a sequel called 'Bachelors in Revolt' which would be about the 'economic and sexual persecution' of single men. He'd never asked anyone to get married or have children, so why should he be taxed to help them? Marriage should be abolished, and so should organized religion, particularly Catholicism, as

Catholics were much given to ignorant and stupid breeding, thereby leading Britain into a state of starvation, at worst, and, at best, an unhealthy dependence on foreign imports and the Papacy.[135]

One deeply felt and unsigned letter written on a scrap of lined paper, torn out of a notebook, went as follows:

> Dear Mr Titmus, I was very interested in your talk you gave on the BBC Friday night, why should we have more children when times are so hard I have 6 children ages 12;10;8;6 and twins 6 months I have 3£ a week to keep us all 8 of us all told my hubby 6 children & myself I have had no new clothes for 13 years I only get what I can pick up at jumble sales for a shilling or two which is not very often so I don't think anyone should have any children until they are sure you are going to get something to help clothe them and give them more food it's not fair on the children they are made to suffer as well as their parents What have I nothing at all only hard work and worry wondering where the next pair of shoes etc is coming from. I have four girls and I hope they will take my advice and not have any children until everything is different for them. Why let the old age pensioners have it all their days are done our childrens just beginning and you are relying on the future generation for all things my advice is to all those getting married don't have children.
>
> You can publish my wording if you like in the 'Daily Mirror'.

These letters received no response, as Richard records that he decided to 'go all academic and not answer them'.[136]

Parents Revolt was well received among Kay and Richard's friends; Ursula Grant-Duff found it 'absolutely convincing'; Eva Hubback commended it as excellent and marked by a felicity of phrase; Maurice Newfield called it 'a brilliant and most penetrating work'. Kuczynski thought it magnificent. Cadbury was full of praise. But Richard and Kay liked best the reaction of 'a married friend of ours who having finished the book told us that she felt as though she ought to rush off and have a baby straight away'.[137] Personal copies went to Galia Morris, the Lafittes, and other old friends and family, including Richard's mother, Kay's own mother and father, and Aunt Lilian at

Barton Hill Farm. With their copy, Kay wrote a letter to her parents. She was full of news about Richard's achievements in getting into print, but wanted also to mention her own first appearance on an important social welfare committee. There was no doubt, however, about *Parents Revolt* being a book Kay felt she wanted to own jointly with Richard:

24 July 1942, KCT to Katie and Thomas Miller
Well, here is your book. I feel that the occasion demands a special letter and there is much that I would like to put into words, but there are many things on my mind this morning [...] The book is a real milestone in our lives and now it is being launched it is only natural that we should feel some trepidation about its reception. For the first time the Titmusses express without restriction their dissatisfaction with the world order, both social and economic. We risk much in doing so [...] It is a comfort to know that two people at Forest Hill will think no differently of us for having written it. Whatever happens the experience will be worth it [...]

It is strange that just at this moment I should make my first appearance on the Administrative Committee of the C.O.S. I can't say that I relished the experience yesterday [...] A Medical Officer of Health a few days ago described Richard as a cat among the pigeons. That rather expresses my feeling about my presence at the Committee yesterday. However, I was quite overwhelmed by the reception I was given. That I should receive such a welcome I had no idea. One matter arose on which I had quite a lot to say and to see the faces of those old charity administrators all round the table turned to me gave me a funny feeling. I carried my point too.

I wish I could show you a copy of the Lancet but we have only one. In the same copy is an excellent and praiseworthy review of Bill's [le Gros Clark's] pamphlet on his research into school meals, and an article on industrial health by Dr Garland who is also a friend of Richard's. Following the leader on the Rheumatism article is another on Bill's work so we can regard this issue of the Lancet as almost a family affair.

Maurice and Sigrid [Newfield] are in town. His first visit

for two years. And we are lunching with them to-day to discuss 'Birth, Poverty and Wealth' [...]

There are many more things I could tell you. I would like to come down for another nice quiet day at Marler Road. Thursday last week really stands out as a delightful time. I haven't touched the piano and 'Donkey Serenade' since! Perhaps we take life too seriously but we can't help the way we are made.

P.S. An amusing touch. Priestley and the Archbishop of Canterbury will receive their copies as you receive this.

Mother and Father's reply was stiffly appreciative. It was the book itself and what it symbolized, rather than its content, which impressed them. Kathleen's PS had made its mark:

26 July, 1942, Katie Miller to KCT and RMT
Dear Kathleen and Richard,
Thank you very much for the book & Kathleen's most interesting letter. I feel my powers of expressing myself are quite inadequate & I cannot claim any part in the literary talent she evidently possesses. I have nearly finished the book & Father has been reading it this morning. We both find it most interesting, well written, & easy to read for that type of book. I have more & more admiration for Richard for the amount of work entailed in getting the material together, & sincerely hope you will reap a rich reward [...]

It is amusing & highly complimentary that we should receive a copy of your book at the same time as such important & public people.

Much love & all good wishes, Mother.

Father has just told me he thinks it a most brilliant book.

In a letter to Maurice Newfield, Richard anticipated the reaction of many eugenists to the book.[138]

They won't like Parents Revolt. They won't take to it however the pill is sugared. But boiled down [...] what does it amount to? We don't like monopoly-capitalism and we say so. Here we are joined by the Archbishop and by the F.B.I., who in their report on reconstruction go all emotional about the 'little man'. We deplore money values and we suggest that man does not live by bread alone [...] One day we really must have a four-cornered talk about all this. I realise that you cannot go all the way with us in some of the things we said. I also realise that we all have a bit of Ernest Benn in our make up. But unless we can re-state Liberty in its modern context the others will get away with it by taking Liberty in its 19th century garb and that will mean the end of it so far as we are concerned.

Copies of the book went to a wide range of academics, politicians and civil servants; even to the Prime Minister. One found its way to Carr-Saunders. 'I am not altogether happy,' wrote Carr-Saunders to Richard, 'about linking up the economic diagnosis with the explanation of the population situation. Surely this is carried too far. Take the teachers – a very infertile group – but blessed (if that is the right word) with security. In one place you suggest that they are specially tempted towards competitive spending. But is this true; and even if they do succumb to a car, is this really to be ascribed to the working of the capitalist system?'[139] There had, after all, he pointed out, been population crises in Greece and Rome, and there was currently one in Polynesia. These could hardly be blamed on capitalism.

In these ways, Richard Titmuss's radicalism upset not only those in Whitehall, but the inner circles of the Eugenics Society whose acceptance of him had been so crucial to his own success. It was around this time that Richard joined the Labour Party.[140] But he did help the Eugenics Society in other ways, as we shall see in the next chapter.

Meanwhile, through all these statistical and domestic preoccupations, the war went on. The period between the springs of 1941 and 1944 was a long haul. The resoluteness of Londoners to stick to their ordinary ways of living as much as possible was symbolized by Big Ben, which had its face scarred when a bomb passed through its tower, but nonetheless struck the hour correctly a few minutes later.[141] Food was a problem; it had replaced the weather as the main topic of conversation. In March 1942, Kay wrote a long letter to Kasso in Canada:

13 March 1942, KCT to Kathleen Hobday in Canada

Faced with the problem of giving you three months' news I am wondering how much you hear of us over here. I have no means of telling so must just pick out items that I think may be new and give you our personal and family news, and it's quite a job to know where to start. On thinking things over I find that we know very little of what is happening in Toronto. We did see that you were having a black-out test some time ago and we have recently heard from Dr Hutton of a very interesting experiment in the feeding of pregnant women!! I read too the other day that you were to have no new taxis on the roads and I believe there is some petrol rationing. Can you still get your peace-time variety and quantities of food? It is really laughable but one's mind – if one is a housewife – returns constantly to the food problem these days. We have to do a good deal of planning to make things go round now so many things are only obtainable on our point rationing scheme, and it means a careful watch on the larder. Rice, lentils, beans, etc. tinned meat and fish, fruit, peas, etc. are all on the point system. We have 20 points a month each and if you buy a tin of meat bang goes 20 points. In a few weeks white bread is to disappear and any buns or scones the pastrycooks make will be of brown flour too. That, I think, is a very good thing and I think now the shops have so little to sell many of them should close and so release people for more vital work. Our potatoes and carrots have lasted out the winter but are now so old they are not very appetising and there are very few green vegetables to be had. I have just taken over an uncultivated garden about 3 minutes walk away and hope before long to have some home-grown lettuces and lots of other things to give us a bit of variety. We have both suffered quite a lot recently from indigestion but our diet may not be altogether to blame. We seem to have been living under strain for so long. This winter has been the longest we have ever lived through and we look forward to the spring with quite a childish anticipation. The weather has been exceptionally severe and there have been so few bright days. To-day it really feels as though things will be green again before many weeks are past and we feel quite encouraged: so much so you see that I am spending the evening writing to you instead of taking an hour's rest before going to bed.

Father is now working very long hours in the Income Tax Office at Camberwell and both he and Mother look very tired, but he feels he is doing his bit as he is replacing a younger man. When we went to see them a couple of weeks ago they were without coal and had the workmen in. Under the War Damage Act the house is being repaired. In addition to ceilings which had to be re-plastered one wall (internal) was found to be unsafe and had to be re-done so the place was in an awful mess. However, they are looking forward to the 'clean-up' and having the place habitable again.

Donald is in Scotland but his wife is staying at home and Andrew starts school after Easter. He is growing fast and the trouser and shoe problem gives his mother some anxiety. There is a shortage at the moment of children's clothes and Muriel has put Andrew into corduroys as she thinks they will be toughest. If we buy anything nowadays we have to keep an eye on durability!

Continued March 28th
Your delightful surprise parcel arrived to-day. You've no idea the excitement it caused us. We devoured the chocolate straight away. I shall make jam of the apricots. I have been trying to save a little sugar each week as our jam ration is only 1 lb a month and it is not very good jam either. It has different colours and different labels BUT [. . .] We have not seen tinned lemon juice before. That has been put in our emergency store. Last week when Richard was in bed with a chill and longing for something fruity I felt very glad I had kept just one small tin of mandarin oranges in the refrigerator. They were like nectar but I am afraid they made us long for more.

Richard is now attached to the Offices of the War Cabinet to write the health section of the history of the war. The task is somewhat formidable but it is very interesting work. He has to meet and interview a lot of people and read piles of documents. He has no fixed hours of work which I sometimes think is rather a pity as it is a job to persuade him to take any time for relaxation. Whether he is in Whitehall or at home here in the flat he is nearly always working [...]

I think all London's railings have now gone to the factories. It makes quite a difference to the appearance of houses, parks and squares. The big gates of Hyde Park are still closed each night but the only reason can be to keep the cars from driving through and pedestrians can walk across any time: there is nothing to stop them [...]

I expect you have heard that our basic petrol ration is to be abolished in June which means the end of private motoring. With the difficulties over rubber I suppose it may be many years before the number of cars on the roads reaches pre-war level and I don't know that that is a bad thing. Anyway the roads should be far pleasanter for us on our bicycles this summer if we have any time to use them [...]

War or not, there was still too much work. In a letter to Jerry Morris that summer Richard, not surprisingly, anticipated 'the end of all this nonsense [the war] [...] Shall we all go to (a) Spain (I want to drink Andalusian wine), (b) Italy or shall it be the Austrian Tyrol with Vienna and Budapest thrown in? I don't really mind so long as we can sit in a cafe, drink, argue, dance and generally misbehave [...] (I'm sure that Kay and I are storing up an immense capacity for misdemeanour).'[142] But he despaired of his/their work ever decreasing to manageable proportions: 'The work continues to accumulate. The Beveridge Cte. have asked me for a Report on "Length of Working Life". The B.B.C. have asked for a script for a half-an-hour broadcast to America on Parenthood in War-Time. The War-time Social Survey have asked me for advice on planning an inquiry into the incidence of sickness and illheath (doctors consulted, period incapacitated, cause, age, sex, occupation, income, etc, etc.). Oh Jerry, I do wish you were here to help . . .'[143]

175

SEVEN

—⟶❈⟵—

Nature or nurture?

In November 1940, ten British children arrived in Ontario, Canada, to spend the rest of the war as guests in the homes of Canadian families. Most of them went to Brantford, a town some two hours' drive from Ontario with a population of about 30,000 and an industry based on farm implements and bicycles. The children ranged in age from six months to sixteen. The Canadian host of one of the children, John Mulligan, aged fifteen, later said:

> We of Canada consider it a great honour and privilege to have these fine English boys and girls come into our homes. I might say in my own case, when John Mulligan got off the train in Brantford over four years ago to be our war guest little did we dream that we would become so attached to him and have such a very pleasant four years together. Of course today John is looked upon by Mrs Clarke, my son Jim and myself as a member of the family. He was a very small boy when he arrived here and today I am glad to report is six feet tall and is now in the Royal Canadian Navy.[1]

What John Mulligan thought we do not know. One of the English mothers, whose children Simon, aged ten, and Briony, six, also went to Brantford (though to separate homes), was relieved to report that by December she'd had the most charming letters from their hosts, Mrs Roberts and Mrs Ward, 'and the happiest possible letters from the children themselves. [. . .] my husband and I can now devote our whole time to war work as we are doing, with completely quiet minds.'[2] However, it wasn't all happiness. A young man called Peter Boyd-Bowman, at sixteen the oldest of the 1940 arrivals, got married in Canada four years later and stopped writing to his mother, much to

176

her displeasure. She blamed the corrupting influence of the Canadian family.[3]

Simon, Briony, Peter and John were part of an initiative set in motion by the Canadian Eugenics Society designed to 'save from the Nazi clutch many of the finest children from the Motherland'.[4] It was also a desperate attempt to save the Canadian Eugenics Society, which was in its death-throes and died soon after. The idea was that British children would be provided with wartime homes in Canada by members of the Canadian Eugenics Society. In 1940, William Hutton, a member of the Canadian Eugenics Society executive and M.O.H. for the town of Brantford, cabled Lord Horder in London instructing him to send 250 children for relocation in Brantford – 'the cream of Canadian homes for the cream of British children'.[5] The English Eugenics Society was to select the children, who had to be 'eugenically desirable, i.e. mentally and physically well endowed'.[6] Although poverty was not to be a contraindication,[7] many wealthy and professional families were anxious to have their children enrolled in the scheme. Psychiatrist Eliot Slater wanted to send his sons, Michael and Nicholas, and wrote an extensive account of the family background: his own father, Gilbert Slater, had been principal of an Oxford college; his wife's father was Leonid Pasternak, the Russian portrait painter, and her siblings included Boris Pasternak, '50; healthy; the best known of modern Russian poets'. All of this surely made his children eugenically desirable.[8] In Canada, the host eugenists assumed that social standing would be used as a proxy for eugenic fitness, but that the selection process would have to be discreet, given the negative flavour of eugenics at the time.[9]

A three-man committee was set up by the British Eugenics Society to select children for the scheme. Richard Titmuss was one of the three men; the others were the social psychiatrist Aubrey Lewis (a colleague of Eliot Slater's) and Clinton Chance, honorary treasurer of the Eugenics Society. Ever since a substantial bequest received in 1930 from an Australian sheep farmer, Henry Twitchin, the society had had to look after its money better. Twitchin gave his money to eugenics because he believed he had been born of unsound parents, and inherited all their weaknesses – he never married and wanted to help others avoid unfit parenthood.[10] Aubrey Lewis, also an Australian, was a prodigious scholar and linguist, who started out by studying the aborigines and ended up running a social psychiatry unit at the

Maudsley Hospital in London. He was much impressed by German research on the heritability of mental disorders,[11] and was regarded as the country's leading psychiatrist. Chance, Lewis and Titmuss designed detailed forms for collecting medical and other information about children who might be sent to Canada, with headings which went from the usual 'height' and 'weight' to 'level of intelligence' and the rather more obscure 'movements of expression' and 'furrows and expression lines'. But in practice, the Canadian Eugenics Society seemed to have its way, as the children who went to Canada were all solidly upper middle class.[12] Richard himself wrote to the managing director of the County Fire Office and to Carr-Saunders as the director of the LSE to ask whether they knew of any suitable families among their staff. In the end, not more than two dozen children actually went to Canada out of the 266 (along with 41 mothers) whose applications were sent to the committee.[13] There were problems with some of the Canadian hosts who would only accept certain kinds of guests. Some potential hosts were refused acceptance by the British because their families had connections with Austria.[14] But the bigger problem was that 190,000 British children were already awaiting evacuation and the British evacuation experts couldn't understand why the Canadian Eugenics Society didn't simply open its homes to the first arrivals.[15] The Canadian government also had its own organization to care for British war guests. Ironically, the scheme failed in part because its spirit of private enterprise went against the developing drift towards greater state control.

Eugenics was an international movement, but it took different forms in different countries. One of the attractions of its philosophy was that it could so easily be bent in opposite directions. Thus eugenics could mean working for social reform in order to maximize everyone's chances of developing equally, or it could mean the most autocratic and devastating measures for ensuring that certain social groups did not reproduce. In the early years of the century eugenics was extremely popular in Britain; 1913 even saw the birth of a baby called Eugenette.[16] Most active members of the Eugenics Society shared the same social milieu: they were white, educated, and middle or upper middle class.[17] Perhaps more than anything, a belief in eugenics offered the opportunity to move beyond the divisiveness of party politics. Grand visions could be imagined; improvements, whether in social conditions or of the human 'race', all seemed possible.

The German branch of the eugenics movement, the Racial Hygiene Society, was founded in Berlin in 1905. An international organization also originated in Germany; German eugenists were keen to develop their British contacts. No less a person than Winston Churchill was one of the vice-presidents of the International Congress on Race held in London in 1912. In the years leading up to the Second World War, there were many friendly contacts between British and German eugenists. Both movements had in common a heavy medical membership; doctors at the time were keen to colonize new areas of health such as sexuality, mental illness and deviant social behaviour, all of which sheltered under the eugenic umbrella.[18] Blacker of the British Eugenics Society was in close touch with doctors in Germany who were researching the biology of mental defects. When asked by the chairman of the Departmental Committee on Sterilization to prepare a Eugenics Society brief in 1932, Blacker wrote instantly to Germany for the latest evidence. His correspondent was the man who is said to have drafted the compulsory sterilization law later passed in Germany, who probably at the time had it in his desk drawer.[19] There were many such Anglo-German contacts during the 1930s.

Whatever we might think today, the link between British eugenics and Nazi racism was not straightforward. German eugenists could be as suspicious of the possible link with socialism as some British eugenists were of the association with Nazi racism.[20] On the other hand, the two did not develop entirely without knowledge of each other. People in Britain knew about Hitler's plans for racial extermination of the Jews long before the Second World War started. Reports of individual anti-Semitic events during the 1930s were widely carried by the British press, which acknowledged the general anti-Semitism prevailing in Germany.[21] Events in the concentration camps, and the move from theory to practice regarding the extermination of the Jews, were also covered: 'Nazi threat to kill off all Jews,' said the *Daily Telegraph* in November 1938;[22] 'Hitler's torture system in concentration camps,' reported the *News Chronicle* in October 1939.[23] This latter article referred to the findings of a government White Paper which gathered together information available to the government from various sources, and stated that some of the file was 'unprintable'.[24] There's also some evidence that information about exactly what was happening in Germany was actively suppressed in Britain. The BBC, for example, decided not to broadcast its information about the Holocaust until the war had ended, partly on the grounds that such news might unsettle the progress of the war, and partly because the reports might have been biased by the Jewish tendency to 'exaggerate German atrocities'.[25]

However eugenics was defined, a main plank in the agenda of eugenic social improvement was improvement in population quality. This was why eugenists were interested in the meaning of the overall fall in the birth rate, which concealed a tendency for there to be many births in the lower social classes and not enough in the higher. The increased adoption by working-class parents of birth control was one solution. The other was sterilization of the 'unfit'. The elimination of the unfit from society was something in which many eugenists were interested. In Germany, the gas chambers used to kill Jews were originally built to gas unfit Germans, and by the summer of 1941 some 50,000 had met their deaths this way.[26] Legislation designed to prevent the unfit from breeding was, however, a slightly more socially acceptable technique. Germany's 1933 Law to Prevent Hereditarily Sick Offspring was directly modelled on legislation which already existed in many American states permitting the sterilization of 'defectives'. The last-minute switch from voluntary to compulsory sterilization in the German law was as a result of Nazi medical officials seeing the opportunities of the new law for pursuing a racial population policy. Between 1934 and 1945, 1 per cent of the total German population was compulsorily sterilized.[27] Measures were also introduced for the forcible castration of homosexuals and for preventing marriage and sexual intercourse between Jews and non-Jews. The reason given for most of the German sterilizations was 'hereditary feeble-mindedness' though permission was granted on grounds of eight other conditions, including alcoholism.

At Maurice Newfield's suggestion, the *Eugenics Review* in England published a translation of the German law,[28] undertaken by Mrs Grant-Duff,[29] who was a fluent German speaker, and who made active links between British and German eugenics throughout the 1930s.[30] For example, she arranged for David Glass to visit Germany in 1935 (though he was warned, as a Jew, to be discreet).[31] Mrs Grant-Duff travelled widely in Germany making contacts, collecting information and generally putting people in touch with one another.

The British Eugenics Society had for many years tried to get legislation allowing for voluntary sterilization. The case was summed up by Havelock Ellis in his *The Task of Social Hygiene*, published in 1912: 'The superficially sympathetic man flings a coin to the beggar, the more deeply sympathetic man builds an alm house for him so that he need no longer beg; but perhaps the most radically sympathetic of all is the man who arranges that the beggar shall not be born.'[32] The beggar might not think so. And if this was what sympathetic men did, what would sympathetic women do? In 1934, the eugenist biologist Julian Huxley said that the case was 'overwhelming' now for action on sterilization to be taken. He denied that it had anything to do with politics, except in the sense that a sterilization law would make available to the poor opportunities the rich already had.[33] Some eugenists favoured compulsory sterilization. Among these was George Pitt-Rivers, a relation of Ursula Grant-Duff, who was interned as a political prisoner by order of the Home Secretary during the war because of his Nazi sympathies. Pitt-Rivers's and others' support for compulsory sterilization was rejected by C. P. Blacker, on behalf of the Eugenics Society, as he thought it might alienate the Labour support necessary to get any sterilization law passed.[34]

Throughout the 1930s there were bitter disputes about what should and should not be written in the *Eugenics Review*, and what should and should not be discussed at meetings. For example, in 1935 Blacker wrote to Huxley for advice:

> I understand that you have just come back from Germany, and I want to write to you about a proposal, on which Mrs Grant-Duff is very keen, that we should call a special members' meeting to discuss what is being done in the case of eugenics in Germany [. . .] Mrs Grant-Duff [. . .] has friends in Berlin and is very keen on German eugenics. She wishes to raise the matter at our next Council meeting, and is desirous that the lecture should be given by a Eurasian called Mr Cedric Dover.[35]

Blacker wasn't too happy about the idea, as he understood that what the Germans meant by 'eugenics' was not the same as what the society ought to mean. A refugee from Germany, Dr Felix Tietze, explained the main difference between eugenics in the two countries at a Eugenics Society meeting in 1939: 'Race is the Nordic Race

[. . .] or at least the "German Race", although such a thing does not exist; and Eugenics, or as it is exclusively called in the Third Reich, "Racial Hygiene", is only the science concerned with the promotion of the German nation [. . .] By this restriction the German "Rassenhygiene" excludes itself totally from what is called, internationally, eugenics.'[36] Blacker warned Mrs Grant-Duff that they should try to avoid any show of anti-German propaganda at this meeting. There were two reasons: eugenics needed to be kept separate from politics, and any strong anti-German views might affect Tietze's friends and family in Germany.[37]

Fortunately Huxley advised against Mrs Grant-Duff's proposal.[38] His friend Lancelot Hogben had warned him of the need to distinguish British eugenics from the German kind, and it was Huxley who in his famous Galton lecture the following year made the imaginative leap between the terms 'eugenist' and 'sociologist'.[39] This was where Richard Titmuss came in. For if there was one simple message in all that work Richard had been doing with Kay's wifely help, it was this: that the effects of the social environment were so great and so unequal that something had to be done about them before any input of nature itself could be quantified. The Eugenics Society could lean on Richard's work to get itself out of a tight corner. Reciprocally, Richard himself could further his career by adding to his list of important social contacts and drawing on the help of people with power in the circles he wanted to enter.

But it's quite difficult to work out from the surviving records what the key players, including Richard Titmuss and his wife, actually *believed* about eugenics. While there is evidence that Richard favoured voluntary sterilization, did he, like Clinton Chance,[40] regret his involvement in the Homes in Canada scheme? Only a couple of letters about it survive in the 'pruned' papers bequeathed to me – the rest of the story has had to be unearthed by delving into the records of the Eugenics Society itself. Some personal difficulty for Richard must have derived from his close association with Jerry Morris, who came from a Jewish background; according to Jerry, 'By an unspoken pact, Richard and I never discussed this part of his life – I wanted nothing to do with the E.S.'[41] The definition of eugenics offered by Richard and his friend François Lafitte in their review of Rowntree's second poverty survey of York referred to the twin goals of increasing people's inborn *capacity* for 'wholeness', and helping it to be *realized* by creating the right social conditions.[42] There is a surviving correspondence between Richard and Laurence Cadbury in which the subject of differences between 'negroes' and white people is tossed between them: Cadbury admits that, although he has a high opinion of the negro, there are innate differences.[43] Richard's reply takes the view that 'there are some differences in the innate capacities between negroes and other humans [. . .] but "racial" or "blood" differences as postulated by the Nazis are not important'.[44] In another letter written at about the same time, Richard agrees with the message of Huxley's Galton lecture 'that our primary aim should be to concentrate on producing a single equalized environment in which the inherited qualities of the race could develop under the most favourable conditions'.[45] This makes the problem of nurture by far the most important one for eugenists.

The nub of the question was how many of the differences that exist between people and social groups are determined by nature and how many by nurture. Events in Germany in the 1930s gave a new edge to this debate, especially for eugenists who wanted to go on being eugenists without being accused of Nazism. By the time of the Homes in Canada initiative, Richard had already made friends with many in the Eugenics Society. His 1938 book *Poverty and Population* had drawn positive comments from many eugenists, including Laurence Cadbury, Seebohm Rowntree and Eleanor Rathbone, and the preface solicited from Lord Horder had amounted to Eugenics Society sponsorship. From the early 1940s Richard was a regular contributor to eugenics debates. Together with Eva Hubback and Aubrey Lewis, he had agreed to serve on a sub-committee of the society which would help to make information on eugenic matters available to the armed forces.[46] In 1942, Maurice Newfield, who edited the society's journal the *Eugenics Review*, became ill, and Richard offered to take over as acting editor.[47] Ironically Newfield's illness, tuberculosis, was one of those that used to be considered a hereditary defect, but was later discovered to be due to a bacillus with a propensity to triumph in poor nutritional and other environmental circumstances. As acting editor of the *Eugenics Review*, Richard was in regular correspondence with Newfield as he moved in and out of hospital. Their letters during this period were carefully clipped together by Kay – Maurice's on thin blue paper from hospital, or on notepaper headed with his home address in Essex, and including

183

some from his ever-patient wife Sigrid; some of Maurice's on official Hamish Hamilton notepaper; and the many carbons of the ones Kay typed for Richard. The tone of the letters grows warmer as the months pass, with love and best wishes for better health being exchanged, and Maurice becoming 'such a dear friend' and the wives making comments about what it was like looking after these great and much-too-busy men. Richard wished Maurice lived nearer, as there were so many things he wanted to discuss with him. Kay and Richard were often invited to visit the Newfields in Essex, and Maurice encouraged them with remarks about how the district was held in great favour by cyclists from London. So the Titmusses were still cycling. But then it was still wartime (though there were not too many references to that in the letters), and bicycles were a reliable means of transport.

Newfield enlisted Richard in the main challenge facing the Eugenics Society during the war, as he saw it, which was to 'restate eugenic principles in contemporary terms (which would mean emphasizing far more than we did in the past the eugenic significance of nutritional and other environmental factors), to stress the difference between eugenics and nazi eugenics (butter *not* guns; genes *not* blood; the health of the individual *not* the might of the State)'.[48] In 1943 Richard gave a paper to the Eugenics Society on 'The social environment and eugenics'.[49] He began with the nineteenth-century eugenists and their gloom-and-doom prophecies about social problems, and pointed out that these had not got worse despite the continuation of a high birth rate among the working classes. Moreover, his own researches showed the powerful effects of a poor environment in killing working-class infants. Two strategies would be necessary in future: weeding out the unfit – for which a policy of voluntary sterilization would be appropriate – and improving the social environment. Above all, it was important not to pretend to know what one had no way of knowing, and this included 'the biological endowment and potentialities of the great masses of our fellow men' in the 'vastly unequal opportunities offered by a highly stratified society'.[50]

Richard's paper drew on the work he'd been doing for several years with a grant from the Leverhulme Foundation. He'd started to explain the challenge of this work to Newfield early in 1941: 'The major part of my material is concerned with proving that practically everything published by the Registrar-General and the Ministry of Health on both regional and social class mortality *trends* (i.e. trends in differential mortality) is incorrect.'[51] This may have seemed either idiocy or immense cheek, but the underlying logic was persuasive. The official mortality figures mixed up all causes of deaths. Thus deaths from infection were included with deaths from accidents. It was important to separate these. If all this seemed drearily statistical, Richard found much to enthuse about in the material with which he was dealing. 'Did you know,' he wrote to Jerry Morris, 'that 100 years ago the footmen at Royal Windsor suffered from perpetual sore throats? And that the sore throats remained until 50 unemptied cesspits were discovered under the Castle? And that before the Industrial Revolution the rate of mortality among Peers was higher than that enjoyed by labourers of the East India Company? The Peers suffered a high violence rate – an occupational hazard I suppose.'[52]

The first draft of *Birth, Poverty and Wealth* had been written 'in the strutted basement of a London house during the bomb-littered winter of 1940–1'.[53] Richard's intention in writing it was to address the very questions of nature and nurture that were preoccupying the Eugenics Society. What were the relative inputs to child health of biology and environment? The book was a study of inequality using the statistics of infant mortality; the subtitle 'a study of infant mortality' was added at the suggestion of Kuczynski.[54] It had originally been called *The Impact of Environment on Infant Life*,[55] with the alternative titles of *New Light on Poverty*, *Whom the Gods Love*, *The Conditions of England's Children*, or, simply, and most aptly, and as Kay had evidently preferred, *Poor Children Die*.[56] In his author's acknowledgements, Richard said that he had been substantially helped in writing the book by Jerry Morris, Maurice Newfield and Aubrey Lewis 'and, as in all such work, by my wife's unfailing patience and assistance'.[57] Newfield protested about the inclusion of his name: 'The truth is, I respect your work so much that I get deep pleasure from my small share in it – from giving it the light of day and a form presentable to others as statistically innocent as myself.'[58] Newfield had clearly grown very fond of Richard, and had discovered that (with the exception of Richard's statistics) they had much in common.

Richard argued that the extent to which newborn children die is 'a broad reflection of the degree of civilization attained by any given community'.[59] Factors such as industrialization and housing density are important, but so is the extent to which income, wealth and other material resources are unevenly distributed in the population. The most crucial findings reported in *Birth, Poverty and Wealth* were that the deaths of children were related to the occupations of their fathers, and that the gap between the life chances of working-class and middle-class infants had increased since 1914. Secondly, the social class gap was most pronounced in the latter part of the first year of life, in cities, and for infectious and nutritional diseases. These factors were highly significant, for what they pointed to was the overriding importance of the environment in shaping health. Hereditary differences simply couldn't explain the social class differences, nor the differences between town and country which showed that rural children were generally better off.

This time it was Maurice Newfield, from his sick-bed, who wrote the book's preface. The Eugenics Society helped with a grant of £100 towards publication, for once again Richard had great difficulty in getting anyone to publish his work. The story of how he eventually got the society to sponsor his peroration on behalf of nurture illustrates in microcosm some of the larger debates about nature and nurture that were raging at the time.

As Harold Macmillan had told Richard that his firm would always be interested in anything he wrote, Richard asked them if they would publish the book, but no, during the war they were only prepared to take on bestsellers.[60] In the summer of 1941 Richard sent the typescript to Newfield. In his twin roles as publisher and eugenist, Newfield replied:

> I have *enjoyed* reading this typescript and I have derived great profit from it. If anyone had asked me before [. . .] what had been the trend in class-differences of infant mortality, I should have said with an assurance that exactly matched my ignorance, that thanks to the works of the M. of H. and the local authorities the gap between the rich & poor had narrowed *enormously* since the last war. I feel sure that I would have insisted on the 'enormously'!
>
> What I should like to know now is would anyone have contradicted me? Is the discovery of the widening gap your own or has it been published or hinted at elsewhere? [. . .]

I hope to hear – for the sake of my own self respect – that the discovery is in fact new.[61]

Newfield was very concerned to sort out what Richard was *really* saying about the nature versus nurture argument. As there was now more medical knowledge than there had been, this ought to have benefited poorer people more. However, presumably knowledge only helped in a favourable social environment? Newfield knew that many committed eugenists would argue that the root explanation of the class differences in infant mortality lay in the weaker genetic consti-tution of working-class babies. Here Richard's figures seemed to dispose well of whatever 'miserable justification' such an argument might ever have had.

Richard was overjoyed at Newfield's appreciation of what he was trying to do. He wrote back to assure him that no previous attempt had been made to carry out the analysis he reported in the book:

The impression I have gained from reading quantities of medical papers, Min. of Health reports and so on corresponds with yours. It amounts to something like this – although class inequalities are considerable and consequently there is much to be done, still, there has been a very great improve-ment. This I believe is the sort of thing you felt (and also a number of my friends) until my figures were seen. It would be true to say therefore that my research has been into hitherto unexplored fields. 'Discovery' may therefore be the right word.[62]

The next step was for Newfield to write to Lord Horder in order to secure a subsidy for publication from the Eugenics Society. Horder, as Newfield's own doctor, had just prescribed a stay in a TB sanatorium. Before Newfield went, he wrote to Horder:

In all the flurry of packing I have been neglecting a mission which I undertook on behalf of Richard Titmuss. Some weeks ago he sent me the enclosed typescript of a small work on infant mortality for an opinion. I read it with great care (as you will see from my marginal comments) and formed the opinion that within its restricted field it was a work comparable in sociological importance with the up-to-date edition of Progress and Poverty [Rowntree's *Poverty and Progress*]. It seemed to me that its main thesis – that, contrary to what I imagine must be the universal belief, the class differences in infant mortality are greater today than they were thirty years ago – called for the widest publicity and discussion [. . .] You will find attached to the typescript the copy of a letter in which I suggested, very tentatively, an interpretation of his data. The letter was handwritten and Titmuss's wife, very sensibly, made a copy for him to read![63]

Titmuss's wife always tried to be sensible. As Horder could find no snag in the manuscript, the council agreed to provide a subsidy. On this basis, Newfield went ahead and gave Richard a contract for the book with Hamish Hamilton. However, even that wasn't the end of the story. When the conservatives within the Eugenics Society actually *read* the manuscript, they began to realize what they had done in committing the society to supporting its publication. The minutes of the meeting at which the subsidy was agreed were, according to Richard, 'tampered with'.[64] Chance and Bramwell were particularly opposed. In June 1942, Newfield wrote to Chance at length in the book's defence: 'One thing is surely worth recalling. Whatever the shortcomings of this work on points of detail, it is a more temperate statement, less purple patched, than *Poverty and Population*, on the strength of which Titmuss was invited to join the Society. I don't doubt that it could be made more sober still and cleared of some minor errors; but these changes would only make it even worthier than it is now of eugenic support.' But what *was* 'eugenic support'? Newfield's explanation struggled somewhat tensely with the notion that what was 'eugenic' was not 'political', and vice versa:

I feel very strongly that what unites us as eugenists is not a common view of how society should manage its affairs; nor should our differences on such matters divide us. The things on which we are agreed, namely the principles set out and progressively modified in our statements of aims and objects, are fundamental, but beyond these we may all have our separate views about the kind of society in which these principles would have the best chance of fulfilment. I am not myself among those who believe that this or that social organisation is indispensable to eugenic progress. There may be forms of society hostile to such progress – possibly fascism is – but there are also a wide diversity of social and economic organisations with which eugenists can work to good effect.[65]

The only criteria in judging the manuscript should be whether it was well founded in fact and whether it led to conclusions likely to further eugenic principles. Titmuss's political views were his own business.

Copies of the book with a personal letter went to the usual list of well-connected names: E. H. Carr at *The Times*, Kingsley Martin at the *New Statesman*, Sir Walter Layton at the *News Chronicle*, Clayton Jones at the *Lancet*, Victor Gollancz at *Left News*, Lord Horder, Carr-Saunders at the LSE. Review copies were sent to seventy-one journals, newspapers and magazines – from *The Times* of India to the *Auckland Star*, and from the *Catholic Herald* to the *Journal of Obstetrics and Gynaecology*. As with the two previous books, Richard promoted this one relentlessly. 'Did you see Beveridge's letter on Friday?'[66] He wrote to Maurice Newfield on 26 September. 'Obviously he has read the book but why in the name of everything did he not mention it?'

Carr-Saunders got a copy, not only because of the Eugenics Society link, but because he chaired the Leverhulme Committee to which Richard had to report. He wrote to say he liked the book, but was worried about it. He had a tendency to worry about Richard's books. Of Chapter 7 he wrote, 'the ordinary reader would possibly, or even probably, deduce from this chapter that heredity was of much less importance generally speaking than I believe it to be'.[67] This was just the kind of reaction Richard expected from committed eugenists. Chapter 7, said Richard, had given him a lot of trouble and had been rewritten 'more times than I care to remember'. Moreover,

Drs Lewis, Blacker and Newfield all read it at various stages and helped me with advice on this fascinating problem of heredity and environment [. . .]

I suppose most people approaching this problem for the

first time start off with certain predilections and I am no exception. I did try, however, to give a balanced picture. It may be that my preoccupation with the environmental aspects of infant mortality has so weighted this chapter as to give the impression you received. I should like to correct this impression.[68]

In a letter to Maurice Newfield, he admitted that Aubrey Lewis had actually rewritten some of the offending passages for him.[69] The message was clear: 'the doctors (who know more than I do) helped me, but I don't mind placating you by admitting I may have gone slightly overboard on the environmental point.'

The book had a considerable media impact. The review headings included 'Poor Folks' Babies Stand Less Chance';[70] 'Babies – Beware of Poor Parents!;[71] 'The Babies Who Need Not Die';[72] 'Environment and infant mortality';[73] 'Infant Victims of Capitalism';[74] and 'Poverty as a leading cause of infant death – a disturbing book that must not be shelved'.[75] Mr Titmuss's findings were regarded as 'horrifying',[76] and 'sensational'.[77] The Economist's reviewer noted cattily that 'it hardly needed all these tables to show that the children born to the upper and middle classes have a better chance of survival than those born to the poor'.[78] On the other hand, there were also those who thought the book stood as an 'all-too-rare example of vital statistical material presented in a form accessible to laymen'.[79] The left-wing newspapers especially welcomed Richard's direct demonstration of the gulf between the ruling and the working class. The Daily Worker went so far as to claim that the book showed that 'Ninety thousand babies were murdered in this country in the three years 1930–2 by social conditions which could be remedied.'[80] But many found the conclusion about nurture versus nature too unpalatable. According to the reviewer for the Evening Citizen, the book's stress on the importance of economic conditions completely ignored 'the criminal ignorance and neglect of many mothers', who were resolutely and stupidly fond of giving their young babies 'fish and chips, pickles, strong tea, lollipops, chocolate biscuits and toffee apples'.[81] As to Richard's condemnation of the view that a high rate of infant mortality is good for the race because it eliminates the unfit, the British Medical Journal noted that he was 'forcing an open door here, and may, perhaps, have gone a little too far in his depreciation of hereditary factors. It is surely true that *under equally favourable environ-ments*, selective breeding effects a good deal in producing valuable physical qualities in farm stock or race-horses.'[82] 'One cannot help feeling,' said *The Economist*, who obviously couldn't, 'that the main purpose of the book was not so much to draw conclusions from comparative statistics of infant mortality as to give statistical support to conclusions that Mr Titmuss formed many years ago – that England is divided into the privileged and the under-privileged by the unequal distribution of wealth, and that a new social order is needed . . .'[83]

One of the most flattering reviews of *Birth, Poverty and Wealth* recommended the book for its impressive marshalling of the environmentalist position. Lancelot Hogben, Professor of Social Biology at the London School of Economics, was an ardent anti-eugenist, dubbing eugenics 'an apology for snobbery, selfishness and class arrogance'.[84] He also correctly pointed out that terms such as 'the good of the race' and 'desirable' as in 'desirable social qualities' were matters of taste, not science.[85] A champion of 'ethically neutral' science himself, Hogben had been one of the first boys from a working-class background to go to Oxbridge on a county scholarship. Here he felt himself to be a member of an intellectual elite, but excluded from a social one which wasted its time in rowing and beagling.[86] Hogben was a socialist and a conscientious objector. Many of his scientific and political views were shared with another mathematician and geneticist, J. B. S. Haldane, who held a chair in genetics at University College. Together, Haldane and Hogben formed a fearsome front against the eugenist position.

In *Nature*, Hogben welcomed Richard's book as a 'refreshing indication that there is a rising generation of statisticians and social biologists who have thought their way through the luxuriant overgrowth of misconceptions which Galton's generation planted'. He called the book 'temperate' and 'stimulating', 'lucid' and 'well-documented', and decided that it lifted a class of problems calling for immediate legislative action above the 'fog of political indignation to the level of a factual analysis of human needs': the book deserved a wide circulation among those who espoused what Bacon called the 'true and rightful goal of science'.[87]

The first part of Hogben's review constituted an attack on the 'fascism' of the Eugenics Society. This provoked a counter-attack –

a letter signed by Horder pointing out that the author of *Birth, Poverty and Wealth* was himself on the council of the society, and 'that people like Carr-Saunders, Ryle, Huxley, etc., could not be described as fascists'. When *Nature* refused to publish the letter, Maurice Newfield referred to the episode in the *Eugenics Review* a few weeks later with a certain amount of sarcasm about Hogben. The result of this was that Richard received a 'most fantastic and libellous letter' from Hogben claiming that Richard had deliberately engineered the attack against him.[88]

This story illustrates the weight of passion that attended the nature–nurture controversy at a time when National Socialism in Germany was carrying the nature argument to extreme conclusions. Richard made other enemies because of his views. In 1942 he found himself caricatured as a fascist in a book of essays called *Talks in a Free Country* by a conservative Churchman, Dean Inge – the 'Gloomy Dean' as he was known, a man fond of the Duke of Wellington's alleged remark that the battle of Waterloo was won on the playing fields of Eton.[89] Inge was a keen eugenist of the old school, an early and outspoken member of the Eugenics Society. He contributed the details of his family history to an unpublished investigation (confined to people in 'the educated classes' who had been married for at least six years) of family health inheritance carried out by the Eugenics Society. Inge boasted about his father: 'Fine cricketer. Oxford Eleven. Two first classes in Classics, Oxford [. . .] Exceptionally high character; conspicuous soundness of judgement [. .]' and slightly less about his mother: 'Great mental ability; well-read but not learned. Great strength of will and determination; vehement convictions.'[90] Inge's essays about various social, political and religious issues of the day were written in the style of imaginary conversations between different protagonists, and one was a British fascist called Titmuss, who expressed the view that German youth was physically very fit. Richard's attention was brought to Inge's book by a member of the St Paul's Cathedral firewatching team during a spell of duty one evening. He sought legal advice, and after being told that libel would be difficult to prove, decided not to try to clear his name.

Amongst those who were sent copies of *Birth, Poverty and Wealth* were Professor A. J. Ryle at the Institute of Social Medicine in Oxford, and Jerry Morris, then serving as a major at the 38th British

General Hospital in Bangalore, India. The second significant project Richard accomplished during the war years was in the field of social medicine. Social medicine was a direct progeny of the nature–nurture controversy: a careful, systematic response to the invitation implicit in conservative eugenicism – to prove that nurture counted for more than nature. The term 'social medicine' itself was not much used before 1942.[91] In 1941, Richard joined a group called the Committee for the Study of Social Medicine which met at St Mary's Hospital under the chairmanship of Professor A. St G. Huggett, a physiologist interested in social problems. The group's first home, in 1939, was University College Hospital, according to Jerry Morris, who was a founder member.[92] Richard became Vice-Chair. His view of it was that it represented a collection of about twenty 'progressives' – 'senior men from London Hospitals, M.O.H.s, T.B. Officers, Physiologists, and so on'. They were also fortunate to have got hold of the assistant editor of the *Lancet*, who appeared to be 'a kindred soul'.[93] 'It is called a Social Medicine Group,' wrote Kay to her friend Kasso in Canada of this latest of Richard's ventures,

> and is composed of a number of medical specialists and a representative of the B.M.A. It arose partly I think because a number of people had read R's first book and partly because, to thinking people, social medicine is I believe a natural step forward. Briefly, the group's object is to foster the treatment of an individual taking into consideration his whole environment, economic position, etc. Lectures are being given and a bulletin will be issued shortly. R has been asked to go to S. Wales to lecture one weekend soon. When there is anything published I will see if I can send you a copy. The work is in its infancy but they are a most interesting group of people'.[94]

Richard's work may have alerted some people to the importance of social medicine, but this new view of health had other origins too.[95] It was MacNalty of the Ministry, he whose boot-wearing so impressed Richard, who was responsible for suggesting in 1939 the first chair of social medicine in Britain, at Oxford. This was taken by John Ryle, the son of a doctor friend of Julian Huxley's. Ryle himself was a eugenist and continued to believe firmly in the importance of genetic determinants of health and illness while being seen as the rising star in the firmament of the new social medicine.

The purpose of the CSSM was to discuss ongoing work of the sort Richard and others were doing, to share ideas, get work published, and generally to advance the understanding of social factors affecting health. In the autumn of 1942, when Huggett and Richard sent a letter to members soliciting money to keep the committee going, they listed the achievements so far: a paper in the *Lancet* by Jerry Morris and Titmuss; a survey of the financial effects on the sufferers of TB; work on the social aspects of clothing and war-time feeding in pregnancy; and a survey of diphtheria immunization for children which looked at the best ways of convincing parents to have this done.[96] The main source of income for all this activity had been a gift of £50 from Archie Cochrane, a public health doctor, who was later to become extremely well known in Britain as a pioneer of evidence-based medicine. Cochrane's gift to the CSSM came via his sister, as he was at the time a prisoner of war in Germany.[97]

The paper by Morris and Titmuss looked at juvenile rheumatism, which was the most common serious disease of children at the time, and a disease of which Morris himself had considerable clinical experience.[98] It was estimated to afflict about 2 per cent of children and was linked to rheumatic heart disease, an important cause of deaths from heart disease in adults. Morris and Titmuss judged that altogether juvenile rheumatism was responsible for 2 per cent of all deaths in England and Wales. The cause of juvenile rheumatism was obscure, its diagnosis difficult and its treatment unsatisfactory, but there was no doubt about one thing: deaths due to the condition were about four times more common in the lower social classes. Plotting the social geography of deaths from the disease, which is what Morris and Titmuss did in their paper, showed that the most dangerous places were the rural districts of the depressed areas, particularly in Wales. In other words, poverty was an important cause.[99]

This was the first of three papers on social medicine Richard and Jerry Morris published together. It was accepted by the *Lancet* before Jerry sailed for India in 1942 to serve in the Army, and was the outcome of a two-year mutual instruction process in which the two men taught each other everything they knew about the medicine and sociology of infant mortality, childhood illness, social class and social change.[100] The second Morris and Titmuss paper continued with the rheumatic heart disease theme, and demonstrated more clearly the disease's intimate connections with poverty by looking at the relationship with unemployment over the period from 1927 to 1938: high unemployment was followed by higher rheumatic heart disease mortality.[101] The subject of the third paper in the series[102] – peptic ulcer – deserved to be part of the study of social medicine because peptic ulcer deaths among men had been rising since the outbreak of war; but, as about 1 in 10 of the population had ulcers at some point in their lives, the main interest of the condition lay in the suffering and inefficiency it caused during life. However, the really fascinating thing about ulcer deaths was that, if the ulcers were in the stomach, deaths were much higher among working-class men, whereas if they were in the duodenum the opposite was true, and middle-class men were more likely to die. How could this be explained? As with many such puzzles, the state of Britain's vital statistics was inadequate. There was little information on factors of relevance ('e.g., heritable tendencies, tobacco, the bolting of meals, and changes in diet').[103] Morris and Titmuss were inclined to the view that chronic irritants associated with poverty were important in gastric ulcers, while 'psychosomatic' influences were more important in duodenal ulcers. Deaths were higher in the cities, with the noise and the stress and the general speed of everything. On the other hand, it would be the 'restless', 'energetic' and 'ambitious' types most prone to ulcers who would be most attracted to the cities.

Was Richard thinking of himself here? His own restless and ambitious energy spawned yet more projects in these war years when he was supposed to be single-mindedly concentrating on the war history. The 1940s were the decade of social medicine groups, as the 1930s had been that of population organizations. In March 1942, Richard joined the Nutrition Society, a group formed the previous year 'to advance the scientific study of nutrition and its application to the maintenance of human and animal health'.[104] Richard probably wasn't very interested in the animal aspects, but membership of the Nutrition Society continued the theme of the work he had done with Bill le Gros Clark in *Our Food Problem*. Predictably, he was soon invited to give a talk to the society on the statistics of infant mortality: 'The papers we are going to have are one by Bourne[105] on the development of the embryo treated as a whole, one by Barcroft on the function of the placenta. He says he knows nothing about it, but still. There will be one by Hammond on the birth weight in the animal, and one by myself on the influence of diet, and one by yourself,' wrote St G. Huggett, who seems to have been a founding member of more than one social medicine group.[106] Through a Dr Leitch whom he met at this conference, Richard was put in touch with pioneer obstetrician Dugald Baird, who was then chairing an investigation into the causes of high infant mortality in Scotland.[107] Baird was sent the proofs of *Birth, Poverty and Wealth* and warmed to Richard's argument, which he planned to incorporate in a paper he was currently writing for the Secretary of State for Scotland. But there was also a critical note. Why did Richard say that early infant deaths were due to genetic causes? Could they not equally be explained by environmental deficits affecting mothers in pregnancy?[108]

Birth, Poverty and Wealth and the papers with Jerry Morris were part of an extremely ambitious project which was planned to involve massive health surveys and the framing of laws which would spell out the relationship between health and society. There would be a book, a 'masterpiece on social medicine',[109] and at least 'two readerships, two cottages and two season tickets'.[110] All the signs were good. 'Went with Galia to hear Ryle,' wrote Richard to Jerry Morris:

> Magnificent meeting – crowds standing. Ryle: sane, logical, quietly humorous, states the case (and states it well) for State Salaried Service. Then goes on to S.M. [...] Gives one example – and one only – of how such studies should be carried out – *Morris* and Titmuss have shown us the way [...] G. and I were thrilled. How much would I have given to have seen you there [...] Went to Berterelli's afterwards for a meal as G. was going on night-shift and I was going fire-brigading at St Pauls. Took Huggett with us as he wanted to see me. He was a bit of a nuisance as I would have preferred to talk to G. about you. She is so courageous, Jerry, you have got a treasure. I can guess so much because I know what it is like to leave Kay for a few nights.[111]

The same day, Kay wrote to her mother. Her letter updated Mother on their joint project of Richard's work, and referred with a little displeasure to her secretarial role in it. The Reverend Birch reappears; his love-life was evidently something Kay and her mother discussed. Kay bought a shirt for Richard (always difficult because of his long arms) on a shopping expedition with Eileen Lafitte, who was expecting a baby. An item about the anointing liquid used in the Coronation must have impressed Mother, who was a staunch royalist throughout her life:

8 October 1942, KCT to Katie Miller
Dear Mother,
Just a few news items for you. The Titmice have been written up in a blurb in the NEW YORK TIMES. We have not seen it but the B.B.C. who have a copy told us. They also told us that they were broadcasting to America about our book.

The German birth rate stuff had the leading article in the Times on Monday and an editorial on it. Luckily they were able to publish evidence of the correctness of Richard's interpretation as Goering's paper had regretted the fall in births a few days previously and had stressed the need to catch up after the war! In the Times it was published from 'A Special Correspondent.' Nevertheless a number of people traced it to Richard.

Next week the Lancet are to publish the German tuberculosis and other disease figures. Again the time is opportune as you will have seen from the N.C. this morning that the Medical Research Council's Tuberculosis report is just out [...] We hope that the Minister in his speech in the House will refer to certain aspects of the Report which R has stressed and also to the comparable German figures. Look out for it some time soon and see if you can recognise bits [...]

When next you see Richard ask him for some inside details on the Coronation. He came home this morning full of stories gleaned from the Librarian at St Paul's. Did you know that the anointing liquid was made from a recipe handed down from the days of King Edward III? There is in existence somewhere in London some of the oil from the Coronation of Boadaceia (not spelt right somehow) and the Librarian said the biggest thrill of his life was when he was allowed to smell a piece of paper dipped in this liquid. I guess you and I would love to hear this man talk [. . .]

Birch is married again as we suspected to the Vera woman. A fortnight ago I believe in the Church at Hither Green where he is now Minister. Comment fails me!

The Research Dept. of the Amalgamated Engineering Union rang up to-day seeking information from R. What next? I put them through to his room number. To have all these calls in the evenings is a bit too much [. . .]

We didn't do much shopping on Tuesday. Eileen [Lafitte] and I lunched with Susan [?] at Peter Jones [. . .] and then after purchasing Viyella for the baby at the Army and Navy stores and a shirt for Richard at Austin Reeds (they only had two that would fit him) we met Galia and came home to tea after a visit to D. H. Evans. We had all had quite enough of the crowds by that time. Eileen used up her coupons on nappies as she really couldn't be bothered to see about anything else.

And that I think is all the news [. . .]

Lots of love, Kathleen

It was three years since the war had started. 'Three years of war and no issues clear, no battles won,' wrote Nella Last, a Lancashire mother, in the diary she kept for Mass Observation, 'how long when we *do* start? [. . .] Talk about "new worlds" makes me shudder at the thought of the destruction and the maimed, the spoilt, the shattered, the lives and hopes that will have to be cleared up, patched up, replaced. "Peace in our time" – will our children's children see a clear path out of the morass, a path firm and plain enough to see ahead and plan, with security?'[112] It was almost as though war had become a habit. In London, Harold Nicolson, like Richard Titmuss, took his turn at fire-watching: 'I hear Big Ben chime 9 and 10 and 11. The guns spit and fire all round us, the river lies milkily in the misty moon, the searchlights sweep and cluster [. . .] The guns boom and crackle, the rockets soar [. . .] There is a lull, and then it all begins again [. . .] The deep drone of our own bombers going out to Germany throbs through the night.'[113] Huxley's friend and fellow anti-eugenist J. B. S. Haldane confirmed many Londoners' mistrust in public shelters by sharing the office basement of the Zoo with the Huxley family during air raids. There was a direct hit, which burst a water-main. Huxley led the firemen to the sealion pond – the only source of water left – and they drained it. The camel and zebra houses were also hit, but the camels just sat there as though nothing had happened. The zebras were less quiescent, and the night-watchman reported seeing one cantering through the tunnel leading to the road which circled the park. Huxley and the air-raid squad set off in pursuit and managed to shepherd the animal back before it got as far as Camden Town.[114]

It was the work that got recorded, and the domestic and inter-national incidents of the war, but people's innermost feelings are less accessible to the historian. Kay and Richard Titmuss were having a difficult time. The war was exhausting them, and their minds continu-ally turned to this business of the birth rate. They had discharged their professional responsibility by writing a book about it, but what about their personal one? If the middle classes weren't having enough babies, didn't this include them?

EIGHT
——— ✵ ———

Having Adrian

In June 1943, Richard Titmuss wrote to Maurice Newfield: 'We have some exciting news for you – and for you alone. We are going to have a son – yes, it's got to be a boy [. . .]'[1] In the same month, he also wrote to Jerry Morris in India:

> There is so much news and so much to discuss [. . .] that I do not know where to begin. But I suppose we must have some sort of order of importance – an order which will probably astonish you even if you agree with it. *The Birth Rate*: I can't break this sort of thing gently. I suppose I could insinuate things but that would only infuriate you into sending pre-emptory Cables. Bluntly then, there is going to be a Titmouse. Yes [. . .] Note the correlation with the war news. And with Beveridge. I can almost see the astonished expression on your face. Another candidate for Clarks College [the commercial college where Richard had done a book-keeping course] [. . .] There has got to be at least one boy. Adrian, I think, is first choice.[2]

Richard and Kay had been married for seven years. Childlessness, they had said publicly in print, was a social evil – a sign of the acquisitive and war-struck times. They/he had made this point over and over again: 'There is no place, no time, no room, no rest for culture of the soul in a world swept and tarnished by the virus of acquisitiveness. In this atmosphere parents revolt [. . .] Are we really content to continue to live and move in a society into which children do not fit and man is not man but a misfit?'[3]

Richard and Kay were in no doubt that the major factor behind
the declining birth rate was the spread of birth control, which released
reproduction from 'the dictatorship of Nature'. Yet this didn't really
explain *why* people weren't having enough children – it only told
one *how*. Perhaps sterility was rising? In America, Raymond Pearl
had studied 199 fecund American couples and determined that 301
copulations were required for every live birth.[4] Data from Scotland
were less pessimistic, though not about the relation with age: 71 per
cent of infants born to mothers under 20 made their appearance
within 7 months of marriage, 40 per cent did so at the maternal ages
of 20–24, 17 per cent at 24–29, 10 per cent at 30–34 and 9 per
cent at 35–39.[5] Older mothers were much less fertile. Then the
Titmusses considered the factor of diet. The change to machine-
grinding with metal rollers had eliminated stone-ground flour, which
was rich in the fertility vitamin E. This had happened around 1880,
at the same time as the birth rate in Britain had begun its long
downward trend. But since then the national consumption of vegetables, fruit and milk had gone up, suggesting better, not worse,
health. Thirdly there was 'sex vigour'. In 1662, John Graunt had
observed that 'Anxieties of the mind hinder Breedings'.[6] The twentieth century was a neurasthenic age, and neurasthenia reduces sexual
activity. This could be seen from the fact that both births and suicides
tend to ebb and flow according to the cycle of prosperity. Interest-
ingly, both children and war act to reduce the suicide rate – but
marriage does so only for men. For women, marriage makes suicide
more likely.[7]

Why did Kay and Richard have only one child? Why did they wait
for seven years? (And why were they so sure they were going to have
a son?) My mother used to say, 'We were waiting for the end of the
war.' In the rare embarrassed moments during my adolescence in
which she alluded to the awkward business of sex and reproduction,
she made it clear that, in order to defeat the conception of Adrian,
they had deployed double measures of the rubber equipment whose
source material had so diligently to be protected during the war.
Although birth control was not yet a drawing-room subject, middle-
class women knew where to go to get themselves kitted out, and
using mechanical contraception was not the trial it is these days,
when anything other than swallowing a pill seems too taxing.[8]

Kay and Richard's concerted attempt to conceive Adrian started in early 1942. In October of the previous year, Richard confided in their doctor friend Maurice Newfield: 'We are both very busy but it helps to ease the tension of the crisis in the East. If it was not for the terrifying climax with which we are faced we should both dearly love to have a child. Kay has seen her doctor and we have decided to wait for a few months.'[9] Perhaps he felt a need to explain why two such pro-children people weren't taking their own views seriously. Kay was thirty-nine, and he was thirty-five; time would be running out. By the following April,[10] Richard is writing to thank Newfield for his 'nutritional advice'. The few months had elapsed and nothing had happened: Children could not merely be wished into existence; and the anxieties of the war, as John Graunt said, did not promote easy breeding. Then there was all that endless work the Titmusses were doing. In April, Richard himself was feeling the strain and went to see his doctor, who told him to take a month's holiday 'and added that he would not answer for the consequences if I refused'.[11] In August, Richard wrote Newfield an unusually personal letter: 'The Titmice are in trouble again. Kay has been ordered a month's complete rest by her doctor. He is worried about the functioning of her nervous system. A slight tap on her arm sends her knee into action; digestion is all upset and she is jumpy. She went to see him because we were wondering if we were going to have a small titmice. But no. Is it serious, Maurice? She is being doped with bromide and belladonna.'[12]

Newfield replied a few days later:

We were both grieved, but naturally not surprised, to learn of Kay's breakdown. I am no tele-diagnostician but the symptoms and treatment both suggest the kind of functional nervous syndrome that so commonly develops after prolonged intellectual and emotional stress. It gets better if treated seriously, but not if it is dismissed as unimportant because not organic. If I were your doctor I should prescribe the month's rest for both of you, on the same principle as I used to prescribe sleeping draughts for parents who complained that their children had insomnia . . .[13]

One wonders why they were 'naturally not surprised'. There had been hints of trouble the year before; perhaps this was why. Did the bromide and belladonna work? They sound like fairly drastic remedies.

Richard himself identified two causes of Kay's condition in his letter to Newfield: too many visitors, and the anxiety of the war. Ministry of Information surveys provided evidence that women *were* more depressed by the war than men[14] – but, on the other hand, this might have been because they tend to be more depressed anyway.[15] Kay left little record of how she felt, or why she felt it. She destroyed all her diaries from these years, except for one, a little blue-silk number for 1941, which lingers on, probably forgotten by her. This records 'depression' and other miseries explicitly a number of times. There is also another mystery: a code of two letters – 'S' and 'D' – attached to different days. Each occurs fourteen times over the course of the year, with 'D' following 'S' after an interval of between two and five days. Judging from the notebook diary of 1943, 'S' stands for sex, as the 'S' recorded on Saturday April 24 predated my (slightly early) birth by thirty-eight weeks and two days. Does 'D' signal 'depression'? If so, why does depression follow sex in this apparently systematic way? And if 'D' means something different, what does it mean?

Writing to Kasso in Canada in early 1943,[16] Kay called this period in her life 'a summer of illhealth' which forced her to lead a 'very secluded life', giving her 'an excellent opportunity to do some serious reading'. She referred to her nervous system having been 'seriously out of order', with the result that many months later she still had to keep the brake on. The failure to get pregnant would itself have been a cause of strain, given Kay's age; she had to look no further than the computations of fecundity that surrounded her in Beaumont Court to see that this was one area of life in which the eugenists' arguments about biological determinism carried some weight.

Something that many people commented on at the time was the failure of the eugenists themselves to live up to their proclaimed standards of fertility. The Newfields, for example, had only one child. According to writer Robert Graves, who stayed with them in 1942, this was something of a 'family joke'. Graves himself already had several children, although he belonged to a social group – professional writers – eugenists deemed 'notoriously unfertile'.[17] Eugenist Havelock Ellis was impotent as well as childless. Galton, the founder of eugenics, had no children because he caught VD in the Middle East – but his wife restricted most of her public complaints to his work, with which she got absolutely fed up.[18] Lancelot Hogben, a professional anti-eugenist, and his friend Haldane were not above a few nasty quips. Haldane's answer to the problem of the low birth rate among the more prosperous classes at least had the merit of logic: 'If the rich are infertile because they are rich,' he observed, 'they might become less so if they were made less rich.' This made the inheritance of property eugenically undesirable. One might even go so far as to say, 'that a large part of the eugenic movement is a passionate protest against the hard fact that the meek do inherit the earth'.[19] But, as Haldane went on to note, the contradiction between social and biological success isn't peculiar to our own civilization. The qualities people most admired in the Middle Ages were holiness in the clerics and valour in the nobility. But the clerics were celibate, and the English nobility wiped itself out in various battles. Hogben's wife, Enid Charles, might have been speaking for herself as the mother of four children when she noted that 'High fertility is undoubtedly a handicap to vocational advancement in adult life.'[20] She pointed out that the low fertility rate among the professional classes was 'chiefly proclaimed by persons who themselves belong to the professional class, often by those who are themselves conspicuously infertile'.[21]

Marriage to Richard had brought many benefits for Kay: intellectual stimulation; a passport to new social circles; the opportunity to mix and mingle with and count as friends some of the most influential people of the day. It brought extended horizons to the daughter of the travelling salesman from Forest Hill. Her own desire 'to do good', though acted out in many practical ways with the charismatic Reverend Birch in Fulham, lacked any anchor in a systematic, forward-looking political vision; it was specific rather than general, treating the cause instead of framing the remedy. Richard's politicism, his earnest, probing concern not only to establish the facts of things which people said they knew but usually didn't, but to go further than this and inquire into the underlying causes of behaviour, made him not only a 'natural' sociologist, but someone for whom the study of values was indistinguishable from the examination of facts. In studying values, you had to understand the ways in which the beliefs and opinions informing individual behaviour were derived from the wider cultural mind-set. Ultimately, of course, the personal *was* the political – though that particular discovery would have to wait for another social revolution – one that the longed-for Adrian would, with all the unplanned ironies of history, herself espouse.

So being Mrs Titmuss meant social mobility, of a kind. Mr Titmuss had been socially mobile in marrying her, but then he had taken her along with him, a willing partner, into echelons of thought and power and social connection of which she never would have dreamed. Would she have dreamed of having her name attached to that of Mrs Sidney Webb? Of writing to the Archbishop of Canterbury? Of supping with the King's doctor, of being on forename terms with the sons and daughters of lords? Could she for one moment have imagined idling down the Thames with the daughter-in-law of Havelock Ellis, or seeing Eva Hubback's astonishing hats, or exchanging letters with the crazy Sylvia Pankhurst or the serious Eleanor Rathbone, or feeding cocoa to a baronet bedded down on the camp bed in her lounge? Could Kay in her wildest dreams have understood that the man she married would end up in an office in Whitehall, be privy to the secrets of government, write the social history of their lives even as they were lived, being remembered for this thereafter and rewarded with his very own title of professor? And if all of this was attractive enough on its own, she must have had the heady sense of being at the forefront of the tide that was bearing Britain into the visionary state of welfare it would become – with education and health and a more-or-less decent standard of living the right of every citizen.

Alva Myrdal, whose book on the population crisis written with her husband Gunnar had predated the Titmusses' own, published with a British colleague, Viola Klein, a book called *Women's Two Roles* in 1956. The copy I have of this is my father's. Next to it on the family bookshelf was the contentious *Modern Woman: The lost sex* by Ferdinand Lundberg and Marynia Farnham; and Eliot Slater[22] and Myra Woodside's *Patterns of Marriage*, a text about the eugenic side of marriage dedicated to the memory of Maurice Newfield. Later on, and quite mysteriously, Betty Friedan's *The Feminine Mystique* appeared on the shelf alongside, fated to jostle for space with Dorothy Davis's *A History of Shopping*. The basic thesis of *Women's Two Roles* was that the social position of women had been transformed in two distinct phases since the mid-nineteenth century: phase one saw the admission of women to the world of masculine jobs, provided, on the whole, that the women were unencumbered with family ties. In phase two, which was still going on, came the attempt of a growing number of women to combine family ties with employment. Myrdal and Klein's account was, as many critics observed, a fairly middle-class view. But they did say that what all this added up to was really only a recapturing of the position women were in before the industrial revolution divided life into the two spheres which could so conveniently be allocated on a gender basis: women and the home; men and the world.[23] The gendering that happened before that didn't so neatly separate men and women into public and private spheres.

The two-roles situation created all sorts of dilemmas for women. At the time Myrdal and Klein published their book, they considered the main ones to be psychological, and thought the old hostility to professional women was a thing of the past. In this they were unduly optimistic. It wasn't a thing of the past then, nor is it now. 'My family had expected me to become Madame Curie and Hedy Lamarr wrapped up in one,' said an American college student interviewed by the American sociologist Mirra Komarovsky in 1946.[24] She was lucky – most families would have expected a housewife and mother as well. But the point was made: the cultural expectations women encountered, and their own more-or-less conscious aspirations which settled around these, would enforce and reflect a series of dualisms no man would face – between being a woman and being a person; between being a carer and being the cared for. It is significant that Komarovsky repeated her study forty years later and found essentially the same state of affairs.[25]

The two things which are bound to cause an epidemic of hostility to women are the aftermath of war and the spectre of organized feminism. The 1920s had both. Women's magazines, a barometer of women's situation, were happy to report that 'The tide of progress which leaves woman with the vote in her hand [. . .] is ebbing'; instead she was being projected back into a 'deep, very deep sea of femininity'. It was 'Mrs Fluffy Femininity' who carried off the prizes.[26] *Housewife*, launched just before the outbreak of the Second World War, venerated, as its name suggested, housewifeliness in women above all else – for it was this, and only this, that produced pleasant homes and happy men. *The Lady* abandoned its articles on women's employment and substituted features on dressmaking, complete with packages of paper patterns. The choice was between a career and marriage, and there were no prizes (except to Mrs Fluffy Femininity) for guessing what real women would choose to do. During the war years, the promulgation of practical ingenuity for the homemaker was actively encouraged by the Ministries of Food and Fuel and Power, who used women's magazines unashamedly as propaganda outlets: 'Women were told how to make "fruit" flans with carrots and brassieres out of lace curtains (good for upholding morale if nothing else).'[27] The importance of food, of scrimping and saving, and eating lots of carrots, certainly emerges in Kay Titmuss's letters to her friend Kasso in Canada.

The 'first wave' feminism that had gained women the right to be guardians of their children, to attend university without fear of being de-sexed in the process, to train and be recognized as professionals, to own property by themselves, and to be given the vote, wasn't dead; it had just gone underground. Some underlying objection to the way women are defined in what *Parents Revolt* and many other texts of the times called monopoly capitalism is a feature of the system itself. You can't have one – capitalism – without the other – a feeling that some people have a worse deal than others.[28] But class, race and sex oppression were invisible in the moral rhetoric of the time. This was despite the fact that there were still feminists around, even if some of them were prone to funny hats. Eva Hubback herself was parliamentary secretary of the National Union of Societies of Equal Citizenship, formerly the non-militant wing of the suffrage movement. In 1927, NUSEC followed the path of American feminist organizations in splitting over the issue of equal rights versus social reform feminism. The straw that broke the feminist camel's back was protective legislation for women workers. The equal rights contingent saw this as impeding women's earning capacity, but reformist feminists thought it necessary to protect the interests of women in the family. Eleanor Rathbone was a leading figure in 'welfare feminism', and she believed that the way ahead lay, not in allowing women to become like men, but in recognizing the value of the role they performed at home, and in giving it proper economic support. The conflict was over spheres of independence: Rathbone and her followers saw ensuring women's domestic independence from men as a necessary first step, which, by dissolving the argument for a family wage to be paid to men, would eventually lead to equal pay and equal status for women outside the home. But others put it the other way around: the first task was to ensure equality outside the home and then women would become equal inside it.[29]

The other thing that happened to feminism in the inter-war years was its voluntary co-option by the birth control movement. Whatever the likes of Richard Titmuss and his wife said about the falling birth rate, working-class women wanted what middle-class women had: access to birth control. But birth control was not politically, religiously or medically acceptable, and so it did very much have to be campaigned for. Maurice Newfield wrote books in defence of birth control under the assumed name of Dr Michael Fielding. The fact that Newfield and Fielding could not acknowledge their relationship reflected the ardent anti-birth-control spirit of many elements at that time, including in the Eugenics Society, which was divided on the subject of deliberate family limitation, and appointed a special committee to make sure Newfield didn't import too much of his pro-birth-control mission into his editorial work for the society. One problem for everyone was that birth control could be linked with negative eugenics, as much as it could with the positive promotion of women's health. This made it difficult for feminism, or any truly radical political position, to be compatible with the view of social reform offered by eugenics.

Women themselves have always tended to be defined in terms of their capacity to have children. It is for this reason that being able *not* to have children – 'negative' feminism – has been prominent as an objective whenever the frustrations of women have surfaced in a political form. While the 'barren' Hitler's encouragement of breeding in (the right kind of) women was widely viewed as repugnant, other cultural and social developments during the 1930s and '40s served to stress with a new urgency the primacy of women's maternal functions. The returning heroes were one reason – jobs were needed for the men, and happy havens of homes staffed by smiling women. But there was also Freud; the new 'science' of psychoanalysis did, whatever Freud's original intentions, definitely uphold the equal-but-different view of the sexes, if not the unequal-*and*-different one. Emma Goldman, who was Freud's almost exact contemporary, could find nothing very new about psychoanalysis at all when she went to talk to him.[30] But 'It is probably fair to say that no other single scientific theory has so much affected the outlook of the present generation,' wrote Viola Klein, Alva Myrdal's collaborator, in 1946.[31] Perhaps the second most striking aspect of the Freudian mythology (the assumed pre-eminence of the phallus being the first) is that the work of civilization is men's business, requiring as it does a sublimation of instinct of which women aren't capable, given that the family is their prime purpose in life. Which comes first – the identification with the home, or the reluctance to sublimate – is another matter.

By the time we come to the much-quoted *Modern Woman: The lost sex*, written by two American psychiatrists and published in 1947, the implications of wholesale unreconstructed Freudianism are there in the title: women are lost if they pursue anything other than a purely domestic function. Appendix III, 'Facts and Statistics Reflecting Unhappiness', puts the falling birth rate second only to divorce as a cause of malaise. While a lot of children doesn't mean a happy marriage, childlessness indicates an unhappy one. Since there's no evidence that either men or women have become inherently less fertile, the failure of women to give birth must be due either to disease or emotional disorder. As disease is on the decrease, disordered emotions have to be the explanation. The logic is perfect:

> As all practising psychiatrists know, women physically able to bear children give all sorts of reasons for not having them. And the reasons given almost invariably betoken emotional disorder. Some of them are: husband does not want any or wants only one, which brings up the question of why the wife accedes to this ruling; married late and involuntarily is not having children (why was marriage delayed?); husband is much older and is probably infertile (why was a man so much older chosen for marriage?); wife has a job or profession and cannot take time off to have children (why does the woman emphasize job or profession?); husband, though healthy, cannot hold a job and be depended upon for income, necessitating work by the wife (why was such a husband chosen?); there is no husband because men available do not appear suitable as husbands or cannot be induced to propose (which brings into question special standards of suitability and inability to bring a desired male to the point of proposal).[32]

That it is all women's fault shouldn't surprise anyone. Nor should it amaze that it is also women who are the victims, violating their own nature by refusing to become mothers: 'a mature woman without children is the psychological equivalent of a man without the male organ. A child is the woman's power in the world. Often this is a great power, as witness some men born of women: Aristotle, Jesus, Shakespeare, Beethoven . . .'[33] Actually, all men are born of women. Including Adrian, for whom an impressive future was expected, as 'a mighty fine social reformer'.[34]

Kay Titmuss was not a feminist, and her husband was not a feminist sympathizer. But as a student of society, he couldn't fail to note that the peaks and falls in the position of women, although not nearly as fascinating as those in the birth rate, did bear some connection with these, and also had some claim to be a subject in their own right. In 1952, Richard was invited to give a lecture in honour of the memory of the suffragette Millicent Fawcett. This prompted him to systematize his academic thoughts about women, making him one of the first people in the post-war years to do so. Like Virginia Woolf, he noted the frequency with which 'women' turned up in the card indexes of libraries – 10,600 times in that of the New York Public Library – and how infrequently 'men' did – 446 times.[35] As a historian, which the position in Whitehall had made him, he found the progress in women's situation over the previous eighty years a 'supreme' example of 'consciously directed social change'.[36]

Most of Richard's lecture on the position of women hinged, as might be expected, on the birth rate; some of it was about women's tendency to be less wealthy but also live longer (there were those, especially in America, who, with a logic almost as perfect as Lundberg and Farnham's, viewed propertylessness as necessarily extending life); and the rest of it dealt with the increased popularity and changed expectations of marriage. Men were expected to push prams, and some of them now did so. Richard noted that compressed childbearing and improved health would give women something like half their lives free for non-domestic work, but he failed to discuss the implications of women's two roles. Indeed, he could hardly be expected (then) to understand how women's caring functions extended far more widely than the simple physical care of dependent children, to include a lifetime commitment to the care of dependent men, relatives and others, who for one reason or another were unable fully to take care of themselves. His basic error lay in seeing social progress as something unitary and guaranteed by the political and moral arithmetic of the welfare state. Within such a framework, it was easy to suggest that equality had broken out in the family. It also made it difficult to see that beneath the superstructure of social policy lay an extremely inegalitarian system, wherein production fed inexorably off reproduction along gender lines. Men were the producers and women the reproducers. As a later social analyst would put it, the position of women as domestic labourers imposed 'specific forms of alienation, intensified by an ideology of hetero-sexual and monogamous life', taking not only a physical but a 'psy-chic' toll.[37]

Was Kay Titmuss's functional nervous syndrome related to this psychic toll? Richard's friend, psychiatrist Aubrey Lewis, had not been able to find any increase in neurotic conditions during the early years of the war. Those at the front line of the civil defence battle seemed particularly free of any neurotic reaction. And as before the war, most of those complaining of neurosis were women; women who'd been neurotic before the war were likely to visit their doctors with neurotic complaints during it.[38] The diagnosis and labelling of women's problems has a long history of its own. Until the mid-nineteenth century, men were more likely than women to be diag-nosed as mentally ill or insane. Then four things happened: mental illness became the province of the medical profession, women were denied access to medical education, some started to organize on behalf of their rights to be educated, employed and have political rights just like men, and hysteria and neurasthenia were invented as novel illnesses. As with Lundberg and Farnham, mental breakdown in women came to be seen as caused by women's denial of their own nature. It could even be passed on from mothers to children – indeed, this process was said to be one of the main causes of the preponder-ance of women in mental institutions[39] – an explanation that would probably have struck the right note with some of the difficult eugen-ists with whom Richard tangled. Of the two new diagnoses, hysteria was particularly applied to working-class, and neurasthenia to middle-class, women: 'neurasthenics were thought to be cooperative, ladylike and well-bred, "just the kind of women one likes to meet with," one doctor declared, "sensible, not over sensitive or emotional, exhibiting a proper amount of illness [...] and a willingness to

perform their share of work quietly and to the best of their ability."'
Indeed, 'Physicians often contrasted the hysteric's *belle indifférence*
and moral turpitude with the neurasthenic's "refined and unselfish
nature".'[40] Most neurasthenics in America (from whence the term
originated) were female, educated, urban and middle class. Interest-
ingly, both New Women such as Beatrice Webb and Virginia Woolf,
and Old Women such as mothers, suffered from it. Charlotte Perkins
Gilman's classic story, 'The yellow wallpaper', recounts the unhappiness of a new mother, who was treated by further compulsory con-
finement to the home, and by the dictum that any form of creative
work would be bound to tip her absolutely over the edge.[41] But if
nervous disorder became, in some way, the mark of women, this had
to be because they were more or less universally frustrated: either
they had too much to do at home and were denied a sufficient role
outside it, or they didn't have a role at home at all. Either they didn't
have children or they did. Kay Titmuss's mentor, the Rev. Birch,
used the term 'neurasthenia' freely in his book *Psychology and the
Individual*, and in various vignettes from his own counselling practice
trumpeted a decidedly restrained role for women. There was, for
example, 'a married woman who said she could not attend to, or
remember, her ordinary household duties; the strain and the worry
were really getting on her nerves, and in the end she broke down.
Tonics helped for a time but did not remove the symptoms. The
real cause lay not in her stars but in herself. She wanted to carry on
her business.' As she clearly couldn't do this and be a good housewife
and mother, the home had to win: 'the energy directed to that single
aim brought back harmony'.[42] However you saw it, being a woman
was a fairly sizeable problem.

And so it must have been a problem for Kay. Although many
women experienced an increase in their freedom, independence and
economic status during the war through the extended employment
opportunities it offered them, for Kay it was the opposite. Gone were
the days of happy busyness in Fulham with Dr Birch, when she had
been occupied with many useful tasks and had a sense of her own
self-worth. Already by September 1940, after months of evacuation
to Bedfordshire and a barely satisfactory role helping Aunt Lilian,
the feeling of being a 'discontented dishwasher' was intensifying.
The psychological process is charted in the letters. 'My job seems to
be developing as the one who sits and waits,' she wrote in her diary.

To Kasso in Canada, she said that she'd come back to London because Richard needed her. She found it strange to occupy the role of 'looker on'. It seemed that wherever she turned, it was primarily the kitchen that called. There were few glimpses of her active pre-war role. In the summer of 1943 she was able to help a colleague of Richard's in the insurance world who was sacked for ' "playing about" with a messenger boy & rejected by everyone'. 'He sought refuge with R,' noted Kay in her diary.[43] She managed to talk to his parents and get them to understand and accept their son back. 'There is an exhilarating feeling about tackling a job for which I am fitted,' she declared. Something of the same feeling probably attended her cycling round London for the Westminster Citizens' Advice Bureau on behalf of the homeless.

Any other work tended to be Richard's, not hers. Kay worked on all Richard's manuscripts, not only typing, but checking, rewriting and correcting – all that painstakingly detailed work which often takes authors much longer than their original creations. She also typed all Richard's work for the Eugenics Society and the *Review*. Her role in the gigantic correspondence between Richard and Jerry Morris was of the same order – typing, communicating, commenting, arranging. She typed most of Richard's letters, which he often dictated directly to her. Sometimes she even transcribed handwritten letters sent to Richard, so that he would be able to read them more easily. She dealt with much of his correspondence – invitations to speak, to write papers, inquiries about his work, letters in response to it. But in this labour Kay was not alone among wives; most in their circle did the same. It seems to have been totally accepted that the principal work was whatever the men were doing, and that the women, when not occupied domestically, would help the men. In no case was it the other way around. Although there were women who had careers of their own, either they had husbands who also had careers, or they were single. The model of marriage that propped up this system of wifely labour avoided any notion of unfair treatment by stressing the companionate nature of the relationship between husband and wife: the sharing of ideas, the constant conversation, the mutually held values. The submersion of her work in his was hidden by a veil with 'equality' writ large all over it. For, after all, it *was* the women who were the practical ones, so this was a division of labour that could be expected. Jerry Morris, induced to speculate on the nature of women and men by his observations of life in India, wrote to Kay from Calcutta in June 1943:

> As you've heard I'm on a course in Calcutta so I'm seeing the world. I wonder what you'd make of this place. What, e.g., would you do about the spitting? It's an old Indian habit and is spread among all social classes [...] I'm not worrying about aesthetics (the Indians know as much about that as we do) but officially there are 100,000 TBs in this town and everybody is spitting all over the place [...] The cholera hospital reminded me of those pictures, you know, of the history of medicine books. It's the second outbreak in 6 weeks. They lie in rows, dehydrated to the bone, the flies buzz gaily round while with pre-Listerian technique the staff administer life saving Calcutta tap water into their veins. You're a *practical* person, like Galya (unlike me, and I think, R). What would be your reaction to all this?[44]

As Richard had noted, Jerry's Galia was a 'treasure'. Both the women and the men agreed implicitly that there would, and should, be an unequal division of labour in marriage. The men's letters refer to the women's labours in a casual taken-for-granted way. Richard, for example, in his letter confiding in Newfield about Kay's break-down, notes, with no sense of self-contradictory irony, that Kay has now finished dealing with all the revisions to the manuscript of his *Birth, Poverty and Wealth*; he is sending on to Newfield the revised text. However, in view of Kay's health, he will prevent her working on it further. The previous month all this had been arranged in another letter: 'I find that I have collected a little more material [for *Birth, Poverty and Wealth*] – only a little – which Kay will be sending you very shortly. She will also be sending you her alterations and marking any passages that need your attention.'[45] Newfield had written to Kay in almost instructional tones: 'All I ask is that you should send me the material piecemeal, first running through it yourself to make any revisions that come easily off the pen and to mark passages that you would express differently if you had the time and energy to spare. I would then do the rest.' Newfield seems to have felt some need to defend his asking this of Kay. He himself was 'struggling, for several hours every day, with a large (about 150,000) work on

War Surgery, written by a Catalan surgeon in a language he imagines to be English, bless his innocent heart'.[46] But Richard's resolve to stop Kay working on *Birth, Poverty and Wealth* didn't last very long. In November, he explains to Newfield that 'Kay or I will have to go to the R.S.M. on the bibliography [. . .] The index we will do when the thing is in page proof.'[47]

The division of labour may have been accepted, but so was the tendency of the wives, like parents, to revolt from time to time. 'I'm always thinking of the jolly (if bad mannered) times we've had together,' wrote Jerry Morris to Richard on his journey out to India in April 1942, 'particularly one Saturday night we did statistics instead of taking the girls to the theatre. Rather chilly atmosphere, don't you remember?'[48] Much of the work the women had to do was, after all, pretty boring stuff. Of 'his' book, *Parents Revolt*, 'Kay finds it much more interesting to type,' Richard had noted the previous year, 'there are very few statistics and some of the chapters, "The Naughty Nineties", "Some Red Herrings", etc., appear [interesting] to her. Well, it is a change after typing statistics for five years of married life.'[49]

About the delay in the publication of *Birth, Poverty and Wealth* caused by the Eugenics Society fracas, Richard tells Newfield: 'Kay is getting very cross about the book, [. . .] she has, she tells me, already typed it three times.'[50] 'You will notice that I have typed this,' he observes of a letter in the same month. 'Kay strikes by retreating to (a) the garden – vegetable or (b) the allotment – vegetable. She is digging for something or other. I think it's more to do with keeping the Titmice well than Victory.'[51]

Newfield hand-wrote many of his own letters in order to save 'my overworked Sigrid'.[52] In the files of the Eugenics Society, there is a miserable correspondence about getting Sigrid paid for her secretarial work.[53] In one of these letters, written during the last years of Maurice's illness, Sigrid confessed, 'I don't mind the nursing and the cooking – but I can't tell you how I hate having to mix it with office work.'[54]

Like Kay Titmuss and Sigrid Newfield, Galia Morris typed Jerry's papers for him, and acted as research assistant for the social medicine work he and Richard were engaged in over this period. When Jerry went out to India, he missed Galia's secretarial help, telling Richard, 'This is my first experiment in typing these damn things so please be lenient. Alternatively send Kay out here where I can assure you she will have a very warm welcome.'[55] When Richard complains that Jerry didn't spot the error about Domesday in *Parents Revolt*, Jerry pleads 'very sorry and silly', and asks Kay to 'be an angel, I mean even more of an angel, and type out a copy of the reviews for me'.[56] When Jerry and Richard do eventually hire a research assistant to help with their work, Marie Meinhardt, she unfortunately has a complicated pregnancy and then a stillbirth, and so the quality of the work isn't as good as it might have been. When Richard alludes in May 1943 to Kay's unhappiness about typing yet another book, Jerry inventively suggests that Richard should 'get Meinhardt to do this as part of her work'.[57] Marie is paid; Kay isn't. The work is the same.

All this duplicates the role of wives outside the Titmusses' circle of friends, though sometimes there was a bit of secretarial wife-swapping going on. Julian Huxley recalls taking a chalet at Diablerets in Switzerland one winter with his brother, Aldous, and Aldous's wife, Maria; D. H. Lawrence and Frieda had a chalet nearby: 'we all began a cheerful three weeks together. Aldous and I wrote hard till lunch, while Juliette was busy typing my script and Maria that of *Lady Chatterley's Lover* for Lawrence.'[58]

Both outside and within the Titmusses' circle, the wives' work didn't stop at typing: 'It was *very* disappointing that you couldn't manage Saturday but lucky for you to be under Kay's watchful eye,' wrote Newfield from his sanatorium in Sussex to Richard, who himself was not well, in March 1942. 'If I had listened to Sigrid, take this for a warning, I shouldn't be in this place today. When she begged me to go slow I would counter with "it's only a chill" or some remark equally cretinous [...] I would beg of you not to come until you are better, but Kay's letter made it quite clear that you wouldn't get the chance!'[59] The women kept their eyes on the men, in more ways than one: 'I am so sorry Maurice that you are having all this trouble [with the book again],' wrote Richard a few months later. 'I expect Sigrid is as cross about it as I am [...] My love to you both and especially to Sigrid whose task in keeping one or both eyes on you is about equalled by Kay's job.'[60]

These divisions of love and labour were the context in which Kay and Richard struggled with the problems of Kay's health and Adrian's conception. Kay saw a number of doctors, and received much medical advice. By the autumn of 1942, she was considerably improved: 'We are both feeling better for a week on holiday. Cycling and on the river and plenty of sleep. We stayed in Windsor and went to have a look at the playing fields of Eton. I wonder what we should have been like had we been educated in that cloistered atmosphere?'[61] Her illness had become his; he was feeling the strain as well. By November he was telling Maurice, 'Kay is very much better but still has to be careful to rest in the afternoon, and to "pack up" any job she is doing as soon as she begins to feel tired. She has not returned to her social work but there is, of course, plenty of other work for her to do here. I'm very busy in Whitehall and have very little time for the things I want to do and I find I am very tired in the evenings and need a lot of rest at weekends.'[62] Kay never returned to social work again, though she did attend committees for a while. In March of the following year, Richard wrote to Maurice: 'I must say how grateful I am for all your help in advising Kay [. . .] We think it would be as well now to wait and see what nature can do if we try to take things a little more quietly [. . .] May we report to you later.'[63] According to Richard's letters to Jerry Morris in India, Jerry had also been consulted about Kay's health, and he had written to one of his medical friends about her, who reported by aerograph to Jerry in India; and Jerry had also been passing on vitamin advice.[64]

One of the doctors Kay went to see was Dr Aleck Bourne, who rose to fame in 1938 when he invited prosecution by carrying out an abortion on a 14-year-old girl who had been assaulted and raped by several soldiers from a London barracks. Ahead of his time in his understanding of the role of psychological factors in reproduction, Bourne defended the case on the grounds of the risk to the girl's mental health, but only escaped conviction because of the physical dangers of childbirth at such a young age.[65] Remembered for the courage with which he challenged the law, Bourne was not in favour of abortion on social grounds. He had many interests. In 1942, he wrote a Penguin Special entitled *Health of the Future*, which considered the issues of both poverty and eugenics, and contained an account of the 'functional nervous syndrome' from which Kay had suffered, and which Bourne blamed on 'the modern way of life which involves so much anxiety, unhappiness, fear, hurry and tension'.[66] Inside the book, my mother pinned a note: 'A delightful & remarkable man. After examining me in his private consulting room (Wimpole St I believe) I well remember his advice to the effect that he

saw no reason why I should not have a child but if I really wanted
to become pregnant I must take life more easily. He was right of
course.' Of course he was.

The news of the pregnancy was greeted warmly by Kay and
Richard's friends. 'Dear Kay and Richard, We were so happy to hear
about the dear little Titmouse,' wrote Newfield, going on to engage
freely in further medical advice:

> I simply can't tell you how happy and how excited. All we
> could do was sit up in bed, sip our morning tea, and repeat
> [...] 'how marvellous, how absolutely marvellous'. Dear
> dear Titmice, look after each other very carefully, take no
> chances (but on the other hand plenty of vitamin E and other
> vitamins too, for good measure) and don't be so sure it's
> going to be a boy, for how can you be sure so early, that it
> won't be a pair, boy and girl? And thank you both for giving
> us your special confidence. We feel the rich satisfaction of
> the newspaper editor who has an exclusive story – limited
> just a little by the knowledge that we can't use it.
>
> By the way: Glaxo laboratories do the best lines there are
> in vitamins – i.e. Adexolin capsules for vitamins A & D,
> Nicorbin capsules for B_1, B_2 and C, and Wheat Germ Oil
> Extract G.L. for vitamin E. All three preparations for mummy
> and the first two for daddy.[67]

'The news of Kay is really rather overwhelming,' wrote Jerry from
India, 'and I can't say how pleased I am [...] So Adrian it will be
[...] You're absolutely right to insist on nothing but the best and
are really lucky to have Bourne personally interested . . .'[68] Bourne
did look after Kay personally; there were no tedious ante-natal visits
or long-drawn-out, assembly line hospital visits. Richard worried
about the chances of twinning, which were higher with age. Bourne
arranged for a bed in the Lindo Wing of St Mary's, which wasn't
cheap at 50 guineas. Richard wrote to Jerry:

> You know Beveridge ought to have had a kid before he wrote
> his Report. Something less nonsensical than £4 might have
> resulted. Apart from that we are going to be overcrowded

here. It looks as though the brat will turn me out of my 'sweat-hole'. Where the typewriter and desks and papers and other nonsense will go I don't know. I think I shall have to move my research equipment into the bath as we don't keep coals. You know what this means, my boy, more housework, taking over the allotment, changing nappies and all the rest. But we will try and not bore our friends with it all and allow the kid to dominate our lives . . .'[69]

The suggestion of bored male bonhomie is at odds with the loving tone of the letters to Kay. Space was a problem; the flat in Chiswick had only three rooms, and it was in the small second bedroom, tucked in by the lift shaft, that Richard kept all his work. Jerry consoled Richard about the financial side of things: 'With all the money you're making from these trifles Adrian will be able to go to Winchester. Don't tell G. but that's where he'll bully Willie.'[70]

While the men exchanged plans, Kay kept a diary of her pregnancy:

April 24: At farm for Easter. S. [sex?] on Sat. Cycled & danced at Offley. 16 days later (Mon May 10) R went to Cambs & I went to stay with Mother. On Tues May 11 (2 days after I on 9th) first felt odd. Tummy v. upset. Saw Dr Meyer about indigestion on May 19th. By May 24th suspicious & thinking in a disturbed way – reluctant to undertake the task.

May 31st: Feeling nausea & more certain in my mind. Visited Mother June 1st v. faint. Kept it from her. V. faint & full of nausea until June 5th. Sense of smell v. acute. Saw Meyer June 7 for confirmation & arranged to see Bourne June 11th. By this time swelling visible & skirts tight. Amused to hear Esther Killick Huggett's wife & Dean of Royal Free Med School, also aged 40 under Bourne at St Mary's for August.

Bought maternity dress at Peter Jones.

Have forgotten to mention the morning gasping for breath in the first weeks & how I had to go out & stay out for some time as soon as I got up.

June 23: Have been away to farm for a week of bad weather. Large appetite. Quite well except for a bit of indigestion.

Told At Lillian & today Eileen. Chosen names Adrian or Ann.[71] Told Newfield & had a charming letter from him [. . .]

July 1st: Appetite & size continue. Reluctant to be more than a cow. C.O.S. takes a back seat in my mind. Miss Forrester [?] to supper last night & told her the news.

July 16th: Nothing to wear now but one maternity dress & have had to buy belt. Just had lunch with Susan Stamforth [?] & made 1st purchase of 4 ozs blue wool. Baby's ration book issued today.

Oct 15: Much increased in size since last entry & Adrian is kicking vigorously. Clothes problem relieved by gift of skirt & smock thro' Galia & from her also 2 large pairs of pants which are closed & not yet worn – weather still mild & pruritis makes restriction inadvisable.

From G.[Galia] at Banstead 2nd hand pram cover. Coats, & pillow cases – from Mother blankets & sheets & shawls & my old cot eiderdown with promise of nursery chair. Utility Dayella nighties & day gowns. Today bought towels for the infant and find only 14 coupons left 12 of which must go on nappies. 12 Harringtons thro' Miss Scott [one of 'the girls' – the health visitors – who lived upstairs] & 12 more must be obtained somehow. V. lazy but v. well except for left leg & swelling in l. External genitals. Rather impatient – 25th week & according to the books & accepted theory, 15 to go. A little alarmed at the impending responsibility. A separate nursery much desired but not possible. Still attending C.O.S. Cttees but rather irregularly.

That autumn Richard became ill with what was diagnosed as infective hepatitis. Newfield, who was consulted, arranged for him to have a proper clinical examination at a cheap rate. When Richard mentioned in a letter to Newfield in December that Kay and Adrian were blooming, Newfield responded with: 'My dear Richard, How can you throw us into such a flutter? Do you mean that Kay and Adrian are blooming together or separately? I usually look down the first column of the Times but don't tell me I've missed something. Anyway, together or separately may they thrive and go from strength to strength – but if it is separately may I send them a copy of The Nursing Couple?'[72]

Richard had another problem. He had seriously begun to worry about whether he was adequately equipped for the academic work he was doing. There had been traces of this concern earlier. Was his lack of education not a formidable handicap? A few weeks before Adrian was due to be born, he wrote to Jerry:

> Now for a little confession. I have had the 'glooms' lately and badly [. . .] My particular worry is, broadly, education. It gets a bit tiresome you know, to be constantly meeting people who will talk about things on which you know literally nothing. I am always being reminded about this 'educational inferiority'. It applies to literature, history, 'the arts', and, nearer home, to statistics. It sometimes makes me despair of getting, and holding, a worthwhile job after the war. I feel I want at least a year at a university and six months intensive study of mathematics and statistics.[73]

What had sparked this off was a meeting Richard had recently had with a group of people working on infant mortality in Birmingham. They were using a new statistical technique called 'multiple regression equations', about which he knew nothing. Either this was a great invention or a piece of nonsense; if the former, then some of the calculations Richard was doing in his work with Jerry would have to be redone. Matters were probably not helped by the fact that Jerry himself had recently been promoted: 'Salaams I bow to the Great Ones, O Major,' wrote Richard when he heard. 'I was brought up you know to bob and curtsey to my betters [. . .] Think what it means to me my boy; I shall now be able to talk (loudly) of "my friend, *Major* Morris". You are definitely Class I – the social differential widens.'[74] Jerry replied to Richard's letter about his need for university training in no uncertain terms: 'It's time to call a halt to this nonsense [. . .] Life is quite sufficiently unpleasant and unhappy without one's dearest friend developing an inferiority complex under one's very eyes. This sort of thing has happened so often before in History that I oughtn't to have been surprised! The self educated man made to feel inferior by the products of certain universities and especially when this poor self educated bloke has the cheek to know so much more about *their* subject than they.'[75] A 'smattering of culture' – for this was all that Richard was coveting – could easily be acquired. But six months at a university wouldn't make him happier, Jerry wrote, because he'd realize how unsatisfactory it all was – no substitute for 'the genuine and massive substance of the scholarship and originality which is *your* contribution, your *great* contribution'.

Richard's physical illness, and his psychological concerns, coincided with Kay's imminent motherhood. The many letters between Richard and Newfield during this period are actually a patchwork of two births, hers and his: *Birth, Poverty and Wealth* was being processed by Newfield at Hamish Hamilton. Maurice wrote: 'A few points arising from your [. . .] free copies list for B.P.W. (1) Why Clayton Jones and not the *Lancet* direct? (2) Anything you'd particularly like me to say in the covering letters? (3) Why *Daily Herald* and *Daily Worker* but not *News Chronicle*? [. . .] Much love to all the Titmice – mature and embryonic.'[76] And later: 'Congratulations on B.P.W.'s birthday. Don't stop at one child, will you?'[77] Richard replied: 'How nice of you to write on B.P.&W.'s birthday. I hope there will be many flourishing ones for H.H. and the author.' But he had to remind himself not to take on too much extra work: 'I have to remember running the allotment on my own, spilling History, and learning to do things with nappies.'[78]

Aleck Bourne wasn't himself present on that foggy morning in mid-January when Adrian was born. After the birth, Richard, Bourne and the doctor who had deputized for him gossiped around Kay's bed. Arthur St G. Huggett, who worked at St Mary's and whose own wife was about to give birth there, visited Kay regularly. If the sex of 'Adrian' was a surprise, no one left any record of this. A female friend, Anne Carr, the wife of E. H. Carr, assistant editor of *The Times*, wrote consolingly to observe that 'There's everything to be said for a girl first. They are easier at parturition, they are easier to rear and they are more perfect companions at an early age [. . .] Kay will enjoy dressing Ann.'[79] On Ann's birthday, Richard was written to by the Women's Advisory Committee of the London Labour Party and asked to introduce a conference discussion on problems of infantile mortality. It was but one item in a stream of such invitations which these days he was increasingly turning down. His job on the war history was all-consuming; he dreamt, ate and wrote history, and in any time spare from that he dreamt abut his social medicine work with Jerry. Now he had fatherhood as well. Two weeks after Ann's birth, he told Jerry what this 'new statistic' was like: 'it has been all rather hectic becoming a father. Kay came out on the 13th day and I have now had two pretty broken nights. She is an angel during the day but a bit "windy" at night. I've taken charge of the sterilising and bottle preparation Dept – National Dried Milk which she has taken to beautifully. She is really quite adorable not a bit like a withered apple as some people say of all new statistics. Kay is still a bit shaky but I am glad to say that there do not appear to be any complications.'[80]

Maurice Newfield made 'Ann and her intelligent parents' a present of a book called *The Intelligent Parents' Manual* by two Americans, Florence Powdermaker and Louise Grimes. The book was full of common sense about babies' need for love, and perhaps rather less on the topic of how to avoid spoiling 'him'. The birth of a baby brought a new feeling of responsibility, warned Powdermaker and Grimes: 'the mother to protect and care for the new baby well, the father to earn a sufficient livelihood to meet the additional bills'.[81]

Four days after Ann's birth, a new series of heavy raids on London began – the 'little blitz'. Explosions near the hospital didn't help with breastfeeding. Kay and Richard also blamed staff mismanagement. This made Richard want to carry out (with Jerry) 'a field survey of the quality of maternity services'. Meanwhile, the birth had generated a new 'angle on the man-power situation' – another candidate for Richard and Jerry's research:

It took me two hours to register Ann. When I got to the Office I found a queue of women (straight from Hospital on their 10th day) standing on their feet (with their babies – husbands being in the Forces) waiting patiently for the Registrar. Some of them were breastfeeding in the corridor. They had to have their ration books, etc at once. After I had talked to them I kicked up a row and was thoroughly rude and threw the W.C. Offices about quite a bit. But the poor old Registrar (who had to handle births, marriages and deaths) was professionally about the standard of the L.A.'s rat-catcher. He put me down as a 'temporary princi*ple*'. That is how our vital statistics are collected [. . .] Another job for us: survey the quality of Registration.'[82]

Ann gained four ounces a week on National Dried Milk. ('At ½d a week. Why do we allow so many parents to be bamboozled into buying expensive baby foods at 10/- a week? It can't surely be vested interests can it?'[83]) In February and March the Germans continued their new offensive on London with bigger and more destructive bombs. The noise was horrendous. In February, a thousand Londoners died.[84] The worst night was 14–15 March with no fewer than a hundred bombers over London. This newly concentrated attack, after four years, affected people's morale. Food was scarce again after the cold winter which followed a summer drought; the water supply in London was affected, and bomb damage to the mains aggravated the problem. Kay was so upset and distressed that Richard had to evacuate her and Ann to Bedfordshire:

> It really was getting her down – she was in a bad state when we moved a fortnight ago, complete with masses of things for the kid, to the farm. She is happier there with little Ann but it is a cock-eyed place in which to look after a small child. No weights, no hot water (in fact very little water at all), no milk (only one old cow), no clinics, no doctors who will call, no teats in Bedfordshire whatever, etc. etc. And I might add no coal or oil. So you can imagine how busy I am at the week-end relieving Kay a bit and busy during the week searching for teats and nappies and things. It's a fitful sort of existence; I now sleep 3 nights at Chiswick, 3 in Bedfordshire and 1 at St Pauls. [...] my state of mind is hardly conducive to quiet, reflective, research.[85]

A week later the water on the farm failed completely:

> Kay and I set off in the evening pushing the pram containing 27 empty pint beer bottles. We pushed and rattled the lot for 3 miles and then washed them all and filled them from a spring well. Then we pushed the lot back again. Everyone else on the farm was quite content to drink out of a dirty old cattle well (which had given up dead cats) [...] The result was of course that I got no work done. But we should not grumble; there are others much worse off than we are. Ann is favouring me with the most adorable grins and

chuckles partly because I am now quite good at (a) feeding and (b) nappy changing.[86]

A bomber had blown up over the farm, drenching it in petrol, and then dropping a blazing tank into the kitchen garden. Richard and his cousin Bob had the uncomfortable task of searching for unexploded bombs. In mid-April, Kay and Ann went back to London, where they stayed until the summer. Then in July they moved up north, to Wakefield in Yorkshire, to stay with Kay's relatives.

NINE

───⟫✦⟪───

Is she still squeaking?

Richard took Kay and Ann to Wakefield in early July 1944. 'My darling,' he wrote on his return to the London flat, 'It is still here – just as we left it – and so it will be. But it seems strangely quiet and empty. I've been half expecting to hear my little watering-can's burbling irruptions [. . .] And I almost tiptoed into the study [where Ann slept]. But from the bottom of my heart I'm glad that you are both safe in Yorkshire. You can tell Auntie Nora and Uncle Bert so. It will make this existence just bearable.'[1]

Between mid-June and the end of July, a million and a half people, mostly mothers and children, left the city in a series of 'unofficial evacuations'. There was also a resumption of official evacuation, particularly of schoolchildren, as the government's by now well-tried evacuation machinery came into effect to meet a new German threat. After they were variously called V1s, doodlebugs and buzz bombs, the Cabinet ruled that the new pilotless planes capable of delivering long-range bombs should be officially known as flying bombs.[2] The point about flying bombs was that they came in daylight as well as at night. Furthermore, their path from the coast turned previously safe areas of the countryside south of London into 'bomb alley', so the government nomenclature of reception, evacuation and neutral areas had to be revised. In Sissinghurst in Kent, Harold Nicolson recorded in his diary the arrival of a flying bomb on 24 July:

> At 4.45 this morning I am suddenly awakened by the sound
> of a flying bomb zooming over my head. I do not wake up
> with any start, but quite calmly and completely. As I hear it
> (a few seconds only), it cuts out and I know that it is about
> to descend. I bury my head in my pillow and then comes

226

quite a small crash and no sense of blast through the room. But a second later I hear things falling and splintering in my sitting-room and I get up to look. The shutters have been thrown open and the iron bars smashed out. Only one pane is broken. My lovely apothecary pot with lilies in it is also destroyed.[3]

The first bomb reached London on 12 June. Like Harold Nicolson, who went back to sleep after the bomb had shattered his apothecary pot, people seemed remarkably philosophical about it. As war historian Keith Hancock remarked in his autobiography, the British had early on in the war developed a habit of *not* running when the sirens went that seemed strange to some of their European allies.[4] But by the summer of 1944, one of the things that helped people to put up with the new menace of flying bombs was a general feeling that the war would be over soon. At the same time, the nearness of the end made it difficult to put up with the renewed attack. People expected peace.

Kay and Richard found this new separation – her in Yorkshire, him in London – difficult, though justified by the need to protect baby Ann from the bombs. They wrote to each other almost every day: a total of 108 letters and postcards survive for the period from July to October, 1944.[5] Kay and Ann went to live with Kay's Aunt Nora and her husband Bert, who'd made their home in Wakefield, a small market town in the West Riding of Yorkshire, lying on the river Calder eight miles south of Leeds. In the 1940s, Wakefield's main industries were coal, iron, glass, chemicals, engineering, boiler manufacturing and woollens. It had a compact but unremarkable cathedral which sat on the hill in the old part of the town, and now, in the 1990s, queens it over modern shopping centres. On the other side of the river, Thornes Road snakes out of the city with an air of assertive lower-middle-class prosperity. Opposite Bert and Nora's house was a large city park with a mock-Tudor bandstand, tennis courts and a putting green. Bert, an electrical surveyor, had built the solid redbrick house and the squat bungalow next door, where Bert and Nora's son Brian later lived with his family. Nora, a small-boned woman with dark eyes and a pert face and figure, was very like her elder sister Katie, Kay's mother. Little is known about Uncle Bert.

Bert worked in the coal industry, overseeing the electrical instal-
lations in nearby Bolsover colliery and later acting as a travelling
surveyor for an insurance company covering machinery and boilers
in the mines. The coal industry was under strain during the war.
With structural weaknesses inherited from the struggles of the Great
Depression combined with an ageing and demoralized labour force,
and primitive mechanization due to undercapitalization, coal production fell. There was a litany of industrial disputes, and high absen-
teeism. It was neither a profitable nor a safe industry. Bert's obvious
concerns about it are marked by a single carbon copy of a letter
Richard wrote to him in June 1942, following a conversation they
had had 'about this question of coal production'. The issue of concern to Bert was that some collieries were deliberately working poor
seams. Richard felt they ought to do something about this, and
offered 'to get my friend, Sir Richard Acland, M.P. to ask a question
in the House'. He asked Bert to give him in confidence the names
of the culpable colliery owners, and promised to burn any such
information.

Wakefield was a long way from London, but the North was not
immune from air attack. Indeed, in September 1940 Nora had written to her sister Katie in London about a German plane that dropped
a few bombs in the park opposite.[6] But it probably seemed a safe
enough retreat to Kay. Having Ann to look after, she must have
been forced into a focus on the present which denied, or at least
ignored, the reality of war. Babies do not know about these things.
Like Louie, in Elizabeth Bowen's *The Heat of the Day*, who gives
birth to little Thomas Victor in July 1944, and takes him from the
London hospital where he was born directly 'into abeyance in a
Midland county', Kay must surely have been heartened and impressed
by 'the baby's intention to survive'.[7]

On 3 July, Richard left Kay and Ann in Wakefield, and returned
to his overcommitted life as war historian, part-time writer on population and social issues, night-watcher at St Pauls, tender of the
Turnham Green allotment, and dutiful family man. In the same week,
he might sleep in four or five different places, and this had been
going on for many months now. In March, Maurice Newfield of
the Eugenics Society, writing to Richard for advice about a paper
submitted to the journal, asked, 'Where do you live – and when do
you live there?'[8] In July, Richard wrote to Jerry Morris in India

despairing of his 'nomad life', trying to live normally in abnormal circumstances.[9]

Some of the same characters who peopled the 1939 letters appear in this next series. There is still 'The Parent' (Richard's mother, in Mill Hill, North London), and 'Father' and 'Mother' or 'the parents' (Kay's parents, staying in Wakefield at the beginning of the summer but threatening to move back to their temporary home in Hayes, West London). Kay's brother Donald and his wife Muriel are the target of some not-too-kind remarks. Richard regularly visits his brother Harold, and Harold's wife Blue and daughter Margaret, in Watford. The Titmusses are in regular contact with François and Eileen Lafitte; Galya/Galia and Jerry Morris are now more dominant figures. There's no longer any trace of Dr Birch in the narrative. Eugenics and the population problem are still very much at issue. David Glass and Jurgen Kuczynski perform on both these stages, with their respective families. There are also some new characters: 'Lakey' – Miss Lake – Richard's overworked cabinet office secretary, called upon to perform a multitude of non-secretarial duties; the mercurial Keith Hancock, overseer of the war histories and Richard's new boss, and Keith's wife Theaden, a BBC producer, judged by the Titmusses to be unsuitably lacking in maternal instinct; the 'Great White Chief', Sir Edward Bridges, secretary of the War Cabinet and the person ultimately responsible for the civil histories of the war; and Denys Hay, an Edinburgh historian also involved in the writing of the civil histories, his wife Gwyneth, and their three children. Then there is the community of people who lived in 'The Flats', most significantly, the two health visitors upstairs – 'Bunny/Bunnie' and 'Scotty/Scottie' (both spellings were used). Elizabeth Coales and Muriel Scott used to run a welfare clinic in Chelsea and although elderly, were often referred to as 'the girls'. They advised on Ann's welfare and shared the windowless corridor of number 5 with Richard on the worst nights of the bombing. Last but not least 'Mrs W.[Walton]' cleaned the flat, and her family were invited to bath and stay there when their own house was bombed.

Richard wrote to Kay as soon as he got home to London from Wakefield after a tiring train journey. One imagines him struggling off the crowded train at St Pancras and through the blackout back to Chiswick and the empty flat. At the station he saw Huggett, who was awaiting the return of his doctor wife on the same train. Unlike

Kay, Esther had left her children up north and returned to bomb-struck London to get on with her work. Just as this probably seemed unremarkable to the Huggetts, so the Titmusses' own division of labour seemed unremarkable to them. Richard's 3 July letter went on:

Lots of phone calls to-day. Kuczynski rang up – his wife had been ringing the flat to inquire after you and Ann. He was delighted to know that you had gone away. Lunch with him on Wed. Hay rang to say that another Flying Bug had demolished the glass, etc., at their Highgate flat just as it had been put in. He was annoyed. Sarah's school damaged and the family still at Gerrard's X. Lunch with him tomorrow. Glass rang to say he was very worried – they have been staying at Tonbridge (travelling up and down every day) but now have to move. Has not got anywhere to send Helen so will have to bring them back to Hampstead. Lunch with him on Thursday [. . .] Lakey overjoyed to see me [. . .] I thought I should have to handle one of those embarrassingly tearful scenes – wiping tears away with the blotting paper – but I kept my distance. What a useful barrier a desk can be. Looks tired out poor girl [. . .] restaurant she was in on Friday lost its glass. Refuses to go away for holiday from parents. Dad won't move. She thinks it's lovely that Mrs T. and little T. are in Yorkshire. Now she wants to do my shopping for me. I shall have to re-register at the Army and Navy [. . .]

Hancock, I hear, is puckishly cheerful through all the gloom and enjoying living dangerously. Bunny has been away for 3 days in Essex and came back to-day. They depart on Friday [. . .] Parcel from Jerry – Bitter Marm. and chocolate – what a blessing. Lots of bills, books and papers to read, insurance and what-not in the post, but nothing else of inter-est. Joan [Harman, Richard's relation who was running her husband's butcher's shop] has not had her clothes off for 3 weeks she says. Mill Hill and Watford O.K. but rather tired keeping the dogs pacified. Both want me to sleep but shall probably go to Harold on Thursday. He is on holiday and says that the piles are better. (Just discovered the tap in the study running vigorously and won't turn off. What have the girls been doing? Must ask them [. . .] O dear, another job).

Mother has been ringing Cockernhoe. Two bugs in Luton. What excitement. B. H. [Barton Hill] in the Front Line – or nearly. One bug between Stopsley and Luton of all places and the other in the Dunstable Road. Of course Hit[Hitler] is aiming at Parsonage Farm. Not a word from Lilian. I hope the chickens are shelter-proofed [. . .]

Good-night my darling and God bless you both. Don't fret and give sweetie-pie a kiss from daddy.

R.

Richard wrote again the next day. Although the news of bombs in London was bad, at least it justified Kay and Ann's retreat to the North:

4 July, RMT to KCT in Wakefield
Only one day [. . .] But I must not start counting. Two important items of news: I have had the dripping tap stopped by Taylor and I have at last traced that noisome taste in the pantry. It's that pestilential moth stuff of yours; yes, it is. I check it up by sticking my nose first in the pantry and then rushing round to my wardrobe. Surely it wasn't necessary to put moth balls among the butter? Anyway, I want an antidote please. It is bad enough wearing them but when it comes to eating them as well [. . .] In confidence, all London mothers and children now being registered for evacuation; the populace is getting the jitters – I am not blaming them. Nasty business on Saturday in Peabody Avenue – about a 1000 homeless – even the P.M. went down to inspect. One outside the Air Min. at 8.30 yesterday morning killed about 40 going to work. One in the middle of Hertford. One between Turnham Green Stn. and the Chiswick Perambulator Co. Have not inspected the damage yet [. . .] But the war news is magnificent especially from the East. At the present rate of progress the Russians could be in East Prussia in about 10 days. There is no doubt this time that the Germans round Minsk are thoroughly demoralised. Another extraordinary important event is the Danish strike in Copenhagen. The Germans have actually given way to all the Danish demands! I am really very hopeful.

Hancock wants me to go to supper one night (he thinks I have nothing to do) [...] Now I must go and get myself an egg; afraid I shan't get round to the allotment to-night. St Paul's to-morrow, Watford Thursday.

And Kay replied:

6 July, *KCT to RMT in London*
Such a comfort to hear from you. Sorry about the moth stuff. There's none in the larder but there is some in clothes in the top of the cupboard [...] Is there a gap thro' which the smell is passing across the china? Stuff it up with paper. I don't really want my fur coat disturbing but if it is too bad move the things into the hall cupboard where the tools are.

Is Peabody Avenue in Scottie's area or is it Leicester Square way? [...] I hope the enclosed [photographs] will please you. Aren't they delightful? Will send 2 or 3 to Galia to see before passing them on to Jerry. Other folks will have to wait till we have paper. Lakey might try a few shops if she is not too distraught [...]

Cut the girl's hair yesterday to stop it falling so near her eyes when it is untidy & she looks much better for the trim [...]

I seem to be going about with a dull ache inside me wondering all the time if you are safe [...] If this goes on for long it will be terribly hard to bear [...]

Only a bit of C.'s[Chamberlain's] speech on the 1 p.m. news. Gather the F. bomb is far more serious than we at first supposed. That the war news is good is small comfort to me with you in London. I'm quite primitive about it all.

Nothing I think will prevent M. & F. returning to Hayes next week.

[...] Should be glad of the bickipegs in the big tin in the sideboard sometime. It's time she had something more than a tin to bite. Could Lake pack them up & send them?

Apart from the bombs, the war news was good. More than eight hundred and fifty thousand of the Allied army had disembarked in

France at the end of June. The Russians were into Poland. Richard was counting, as usual:

5 July^e, RMT to KCT in Wakefield

A line before I go to St P. A quietish night but busy again to-day. Nothing very close since 2 rude noises last evening. One simply cannot check up where they all come from unless one spends the whole day – as some people are – telling F. Bug stories. Kuczynski & I discussed to-day casualty figures. After pooling our knowledge we estimate 2000 killed per week in Southern England [...] What queer limits this war has for the plodding historian.

I learnt to-day the extent of the housing damage. It is incredible so don't let it be talked about for heaven's sake. In just under 3 weeks ½ a million homes damaged! That may mean ⅕ of all houses in Greater London [...] You must use your own discretion about how much of all this you indicate to the parents. If they are determined to go back there is no sense in alarming them. On the other hand I wish they would consider for a moment staying in a hotel in North London (say Edgware) & father could then travel Underground nearly all the way to Camberwell.

[...] Kuczynski thinks the Germans have introduced their weapons now in order to soften public opinion *against* prolonging the war, i.e., may make the peace terms *earlier* & not perhaps so severe. I wonder. He argues that they have suffered a major military disaster in the East.

How are you feeling my dear? *Please* not depressed. We will all be together again very soon. How is sweetie pie & is she missing her Daddy?

Joke: 'There will always be a Southern England'.

But in Southern England – in Britain as a whole – morale was low. People couldn't understand why effective steps hadn't been taken against the new weapon. Wild rumours circulated: a quarter of a million casualties, two of Churchill's daughters killed. Londoners had had enough. In Chiswick, Richard grappled with the personal aspects of nutrition and plotted weekends in Wakefield. The strategies he adopted to protect himself – hiding behind a wall in the office, taking the Underground rather than the bus – were a measure of Kay's anxiety for him:

6 July, RMT to KCT in Wakefield
Although it is getting late what do you think I am doing? Cooking a chop, fried onions & pots! My first *full* meal in the evening this week [...]

By now you will have heard the P.M. He does not under-estimate the seriousness of it. It was a clever speech though – he did not really give much away especially on housing. Can we really be parted for 2 months? I wonder. The only thing to do if we have to hang on for Ann's sake is for me to take 2 or 3 weekends. But let me know what you think before I say any more [...] We are going to have a move at St P. Everyone on a damn silly rota of 1 hour's patrol round the dome. I was on 3–4. Meant about 2½ hours sleep before 3 & I did not go to bed afterwards. At 10 had a grandstand view of a Bug from the roof. It came out after the clouds & swept over the dome – about 300 ft. above. We chased round the Dome – quite safe darling – & saw it fall steeply & hit Hatton Garden neighbourhood. Fearsome looking bomb. Anyway, am feeling a bit tired tonight – hence the onions. It was very good – the chop & onions I mean [...]

I've moved the furniture round in the Office. I'm now safely tucked right away in one corner behind a 10 inch wall & Miss L. is in another corner. I'm also greatly limiting my bus-rides, going by underground if possible, having lunch in restaurants with basements & so on. You see, I am doing as I am told darling.

[...] Hancock pugnaciously cheerful & careless. Takes all his clothes off & gets into pyjamas in this glass flat of theirs. It's surprising how many people do take their clothes off. But I don't.

Picture Post offered me 15 guineas for a *framework* of an article on 'A Children's Charter'. 1300 words & they polish. I shall do it this week-end – it will pay a number of tickets won't it?

What other news now? Mrs W. home to-day. I wrote her

a note & left a £1 but she says Mrs T. will pay her when Mrs T. comes back. Is that the arrangement? [. . .]

I am now going to ring up the parent & then go to bed. The girls are coming down.

Oh for a sight of sweetie-pie's little face & to hug you darling.

. Becoming a father had sensitized Richard to a whole new range of practical issues. His *Picture Post* article looked at what Britain's children could expect in the brave new post-war world, and is distinctly visionary even from the vantage point of the 1990s. They could anticipate a greatly improved medical service, with 'a free Family Doctor' for everyone. The second thing children needed was more difficult: a society designed for them and their needs. People with children should not find themselves worse off than those without. Better housing and family allowances were obvious necessities. The places where children lived and spent time must be safe, with measures taken to reduce the risk of road accidents. Cinemas, shops and clubs should have creches so that children wouldn't have to be dragged by mothers round shops or left by fathers outside public houses. Day nurseries, already part of 'our national system', should be supplemented with short-stay full-time nurseries to help families with crises such as illness. And why could suitcases and trunks be taken free on the London Underground when prams had to be paid for?[10] Kay later corrected him on this point: there was a charge for large trunks.

She was preoccupied with thinking up what reasons Richard should give Hancock and the Ministry for taking one of the overcrowded trains up to Wakefield. A new wave of evacuees was expected there:

8 July, KCT to RMT *in London*
2 months! Impossible! Waves of anxiety keep coming over me & make me feel quite sick. Ann's sweetness makes it worse. You are such a perfect father. She's asleep with the sun on her legs. Grand day after a soaker yesterday.

Shall expect you weekend after next if you have not arranged Scottish business or to bring your work up here. M. of H. officials too busy to help a historian or atmosphere not conducive to writing are possible approaches to

H.[Hancock]. Think up something. You know what we said at the beginning of the war. No-one shd stay if they can work elsewhere. It's just foolish pseudo duty stuff.

F.[Father] insists on returning. M.[Mother] doesn't want to go. We're quite helpless. Poor little soul [. . .]

What of this new evacuation. 800 expected here at the Rest Centre tomorrow [. . .]

Sweetie-pie promoted to a 2-course dinner with only a little bottle to finish. Yesterday potatoes and spinach followed by semolina pudding & fresh strawberries. No indigestion & she just lapped it up [. . .] I could do with my new shoes. The old ones got soaked yesterday. Will do if you come when I suggest. Hope you got the snaps today.

Will weigh A today & add a note before posting this.

Am writing Mrs W. to tell her to take the money from you and to come Thurs. only.

A gained 5 ozs.

This letter crossed with one of Richard's in which he hesitantly voiced an alternative to Wakefield: that Kay and Ann should move in with his brother Harold and Harold's wife Blue, in Watford. Richard also needed some serious advice from Kay on gardening:

8 July, RMT to KCT in Wakefield

Sorry, I missed writing yesterday. I had meant to do so about 4 o'clock but then I had to see Hancock and it was a rush to get off to Watford [. . .]

A bad day yesterday and last night apparently but no bombs at all at Watford and only a few in the fields around. Blue and H. both offer you and Ann Watford as long as you like and will turn over a room to you. So if it should become impossible to go on living without you and Ann well then [. . .] But not yet dear. It's been extraordinary to-day; nothing since the all clear at 6 this morning and it is now 8.30. I got home from the Office at 2.30 (calling on my way at the allotment) and had lunch off cold chop (cooked at 7.30 on Thursday morning), lettuce, cabbage, radishes off the allotment and tomatoes that Lake had bought for me. I was

longing for some green stuff – hardly nothing all this week
and that very tired. I have just spent a couple of hours on
the allotment so had better report. It looked a wilderness of
weeds when I got here. But having cleared some of the muck
away and found 1 good row of peas and 3 disappointing; 4
good rows of beans and the diseased row had recovered
somewhat and has flowers over it; hardly any sign at all of
carrots, onions (O dear), spinach, beet and leeks. Planted
out 30 good, strong cabbages, weeded, and tied up all tomatoes. Now I want your advice. The tomatoes look quite
good but have sprouted into 3 and 4 stalks and seem to be
growing outwards instead of up. A lot of flower on them
and quite a number of small and fair sized green tomatoes.
Now what do I do? Will it kill them to break off the subsidiary
stalks? Some marvellously fresh radishes, several good lettuces
(had a good cos) but best of all are the cabbages. They look
grand. Masses of rhubarb some of which I have brought
home for the girls and for Hancock. Hancock has invited me
over [. . .] to-morrow evening at 7; I don't particularly want
to go as have so much to do but suppose I must. Well,
darling, there will be something from the allotment for you
when you come home; you will be back before the beans
and tomatoes are over. [. . .] I hope we don't lose any stuff
but the door is now wide open for shelterers. They were all
sitting outside with their baggage waiting for the siren to
go; the kids playing on the green and mothers as near to
the shelters as possible. The sun was shining and everything
looked quite normal except few people about and I felt rather
sad and lonely. There was a cricket match on the green and
a dance at the Town Hall this evening while evacuees are
being registered to-day and all day to-morrow. What an
incredibly stupid world it is – even our tomatoes have to go
wrong because of it.

The war news is still good and even the pessimistic
N.S.&N. [*New Statesman*] thinks that it is quite possible that
it will be over before the leaves of autumn fall. I hear good
reports of falling German morale in Normandy.

[. . .] I've started the Picture Post article and hope to
finish it to-night and to-morrow morning. If I do and if no

buggers about I shall get the bicycle up and go for a short ride.

Is it really only six days since I left? It seems like an eternity. How much has Ann grown and is she still squeaking? O dear I mustn't say anymore except to sigh to see you both and send my love.

Instead of seeing them, two days later he got the photographs of Ann which Kay had posted:

10 July, RMT to KCT in Wakefield
They're marvellous. O but she is sweet. Even Lake went into raptures so I sent her out to photographers to cool off [. . .] I think I like best the one with you standing Ann on the ground. She has the inquiring 'what is it all about' look that I remember so well [see Plate 16]. And the one with me has come out very well even to that engaging grin. I wish we could photograph the squeak. Please do thank Uncle Bert [. . .] Last evening was an awful bore. First Hancock did not come for nearly an hour so I talked to Mrs H. (he is having his head modelled) [. . .] H. seemed determined to play the cheerful, inconsequential, small boy & Mrs H. was bored. So was I. I cycled there & took some rhubarb & radishes from the allotment.

Lake has brought me to-day some cake & pastry. On Friday she came with 1 lb. of tomatoes. I made her take the money. N.B. I must bring her rhubarb. What a world!

[. . .]Have you made any financial arrangements with Auntie, dear, & do you want any money before the next 10 days or so?

She didn't, but she was determined to argue with him about when he was coming to Wakefield:

11 July, KCT to RMT in London
You say Thurs 27th. I still say Thurs 20th & then again for August Bank holiday if we have to stay so long.

[. . .] Re – tomatoes. If that is all we have spoilt we'll do v. well. Take a middle line. Leave the side shoots which have fruit formed if they look like developing & take the others off. Just do what seems best. It won't kill the plants but they have of course wasted some of their energy in producing them.

I like being with Ate. U.B. was away for last night visiting his parents in Nottingham & she said after 28 yrs she hated parting for a night. They understand how we feel – how lonely you are & I don't have to bottle myself up so much.

Ate & I had a fish & chip supper which I fetched & we ate by the fire on our knees. We'll have some when you come.

Brian is bringing a Canadian home for the weekend so we'll be busy – such a baking there'll be.

A had raspberries (juice) from the garden & we've black-currants too.

Horribly cold. I could do with my winter vests. I'll have to give you a list.

Richard and Kay's circumstances – his in the public world of government, and hers in the private world of the semi opposite the park in Wakefield with Uncle Bert and Auntie Nora and Ann sitting in her pram in the kitchen – produce a matching dialectic: between his accounts of national and international events, and hers of purely domestic ones. Richard was making lists of a different kind. Apart from the Whitehall job and the allotment, there were many other things people wanted him to do, and then friends would keep asking him out, out of kindness, no doubt, taking pity on him for being all on his own:

12 July', RMT to KCT in Wakefield

It's hard. Very hard to-day. My *worst* day I think. The world seems so empty, fallow & purposeless without you. It isn't only Ann – it's both of you together. I am finding it awfully difficult to settle to work. Just counting days. But I suppose I shouldn't grumble.

A quiet night – the second I think without any incidents in London. It certainly has been less intense since last Friday

[. . .] Hayes rang this morning & we exchanged news. Had to say I would go & spend a night there perhaps next week but with all these invites & you away I shall never get any work done. I can't make up my mind. The W.[War] O[ffice] want me to do an ABCA [Army Bureau of Current Affairs] about 5000 words. 20 guineas. Shall I or shan't I? I've already got to do:

> Royal commission
> Fertility Inquiry
> Disease mortality
> NcNalty
> 1 Health Education lecture

You tell me.

Had lunch with Hay & Christopher Hill (History teacher at Balliol). Hill talked about All Souls Fellowship. Advises me to push Hancock. (Serious). Five years. Extras for living out of college. Recognised as only part time. No supervisions.

Just got your Monday letter [. . .] What about Ann's bibs with sleeves dear? Let me have a list & I will post if you want them before I come.

Although Richard was only two years into his Whitehall job, it was by its very nature a temporary one. If the war was nearly over, then so would his job be. Since he'd given up the security of his insurance post, which included relinquishing all his pension contributions, the question as to what would happen next to Richard Titmuss was becoming an urgent one. Kay shared this concern, but for her the overriding issues continued to be of the everyday domestic variety:

12 July, KCT to RMT in London
Beloved,
[. . .] Your picture of the cricket on the green made me homesick [. . .] Ate is round at the Rest Centre getting ready for 500 evacuees expected today.

Do bring some work up here. Never mind the puckish. H. I'm sure you'd do just as much as in town.

Don't forget there's a new pair of socks in the case by the

tool box. You may need them and you can bring me the
holy ones to darn. Cold here – v. cold. Fire every day. We're
both well and longing to see Daddy. You should see me sit
up alone now. AOL

Kay

Give Lake your cooking fat ration.

Because of the flying bombs and the possibility of rocket attack,
many people were leaving London – a million, it was calculated, left
before August.[11] The only good thing about this was that the
food queues shortened. London wore an air of tiredness and
desolation. There was even talk of evacuating the civil servants.
Kay's parents' home in South London was bombed again. From
Jerry Morris in India came a welcome food parcel, and some clothes
for Ann:

13 July, *RMT to KCT in Wakefield*
Darling One,
Your Tuesday letter arrived this morning and Wednesday this
afternoon. The post is queer. About 20th or 27th: travelling
is hell now – I don't even know whether I shall get to Luton
to-morrow. More evacuees are going out now (mainly
North) every day than during the 40–1 blitz & far fewer
trains. But I shall see & come up if I can [. . .] A lot on with
Hancock at the moment: cabinet ctees discussing Historians,
publications, 'advance' short histories, etc, etc. This won't
last long but it might hold me up. We will see from day to
day. Thanks for tomato note but don't know when I shall
get round. There is so much to do & everything takes longer.
And now I generally have to have two talks every evening –
Hayes and Mill Hill.

[. . .] Quieter at night – noisy during day [. . .] Tower
Bridge hit, Stamford Brook, several round Chiswick & about
20,000 houses *per day*. London getting appreciably emptier.
Restaurants easier.

Picture Post delighted with my stuff but that's all I've
done since I left Wakefield. The Glasses to-morrow night
but refused to stay. Could not get out of it. Prefer my bed
in the corridor. St Pauls in revolt last night. Me on from

241

5–6. Very sleepy to-day. Very busy unfortunately. About 1 cwt. of Cabinet Papers to read. Sorry about telegramese.

All my love to both of you,

R.

13 July, KCT to RMT in London

Beloved,

What a joy your letters are even when they present me with problems. Will sleep on ABCA.

Enough money thank you. No arrangement yet. I buy what I can. She will take something for gas etc. I am sure. Have to be tactful.

Got a pottie today at last [. . .] Don't be forlorn darling. It won't be long & A is safe. You haven't the anxiety I have.

I shouldn't go to Hayes. You've enough running around. 26 Marler [Kay's parents' home in South East London] has had further damage. Front bay blown out & back door I believe.

[. . .] Are you coming next Thurs?

AOL

Kay

14 July[e]*, RMT to KCT in Wakefield*

Beloved,

A marvellous present from Jerry. *, 2lbs of lump sugar & – best of all – a lovely babies suit for Ann. Pink – with blue kisses on the front, some sort of wool – fluffy material & lined, 4 pieces, trousers, double-breasted [?] coat, gloves, & hat. I think she'll like it for the winter. I'll bring it with me [. . .] Here is my P. Post thing. You will see I've learnt something from Ann already.

Mrs W came yesterday & got my rations (I had left it at the girls for her on Wed.). 3 chops & *. Shall never eat it all & it won't keep. Taking some * to Glasses to-night but had a little for breakfast. After writing me a little note she casually mentioned that they had been blasted the day before – windows, ceilings, doors, etc. And yet she came to 5 B.! What devotion [. . .] Things are very trying with the History at the moment.

[...] Should know by Monday morning whether next Thursday will be possible. Anyway, it won't be long.

Quiet last night but busy to-day.

My love, kisses & everything else to you both.

R.

Richard was torn between the desire to spend time with Kay and Ann and the overwhelming business of the war history. The nights at St Paul's didn't help his exhaustion, even if it was 'the best club in London'. His boss in Whitehall, Keith Hancock, later recalled what it was like emerging from a night of duty in the cathedral to a normal day at the office. 'After our stand-to I used to drink tea, talk a little and then make my way to the War Cabinet Offices for a hot bath, a canteen breakfast and the day's work. As likely as not I would see my official chief, Sir Edward Bridges, waiting his turn for the bath and looking just as fresh as I felt tarnished.'[12]

Although Richard wrote about his feelings missing Kay and Ann, the rest of his letters tended to be factual. What did he feel about this business of writing a history of everything that was going on around him? It was, after all, a massive enterprise to have taken on, and one for which he was largely untrained. And how did it feel, after all that talk about the need for more middle-class babies, to have one but rarely see her? Richard's next letter to Kay recounted a brief interlude he had in Luton with his friend Fred Grundy, who was M.O.H. there, and with whom he was working (in whatever spare time he might have) on a social survey of the area:

16 July, RMT to KCT in Wakefield

I am writing this in my bedroom at the Grundy's. They have been most awfully kind. One is surrounded here with every comfort. The garden is magnificent, food and drink excellent [...]

I had a terrible journey. I got to St P.[Pancras] at 8 o'clock Sat. morning. Had to queue for 3½ hours. Train was even more packed than the one we were on. First stop Luton. Many local trains have been taken off. Parts of the long distance trains are being reserved for official exercises. If it is still like this during the week I doubt whether I shall get on the train to Wakefield. I am going to make enquiries at the

Ministry to-morrow & also send Lake to find out about trains on Thursday. I thank Heaven we got you & Ann to Wakefield when we did.

I am now faced with (1) this Cabinet – History – Hancock business this week (2) trains (3) Horder has asked to see me this week – when & what about I don't know – it's mysterious (4) getting rations: Monday not home until 7. Thursday promised to go to Wakefield. Wed. St P. Thursday – if I come – I should have to leave about 6.30 for the 10.30. But if it comes to that we must scrap meat ration this week or let Mrs W. have it.

O dear, I am getting awfully tired of all this complicated organising that has to go on all the time [. . .] At 11.30 Hancock on the phone [. . .] Hancock said he had lots to talk about & because it was so hot he wanted to be 'naughty'. Proposed we both went off at 2 to go to swimming pool at Roehampton & borrow costumes & towels. Met him at 2 & counter-suggested Chiswick. So home we came. Went in the bath at 3 & bathed, had tea & talked history & post-war until 6. Took him to allotment [. . .] An immense amount of 'coming-&-going' on at present about the History. He wants me to meet Sir Edward Bridges (you know – Secretary to the War C.) on Friday. Told him my problem re Wakefield & how hard it is. Asked me to postpone till next week & then home several days. So that is that darling. I shall come a week on Thursday even if the heavens fall. If I can't get on early one I shall catch 11.15 Thursday night arriving 5 o'clock Wakefield in time for Ann's feed. Longing to see you both [. . .] Will tell you all about Hancock & Grundy then. Nothing definite but both encouraging & promising. (I want a greenhouse for you sweetheart).

[. . .] Must tell you what an ugly child Peter Grundy is. Ugly, unfair flesh, sore, red bottom. We or you know better.

[. . .] Mother has had letter at last from Muriel who is fixed up till mid-Sept. She wants to ask her to make a birthday cake for Andrew this week!!! I told Mother it was dreadful & not to make one. I expect she will. Tell Auntie Nora this horrific story. Shall post this at 8 o'clock in the morning.

17 July, KCT to RMT in London
Dear Daddy,
How do you like the new designation?

[. . .] I think you'd better cancel my request for winter vests & bring my summer wrapper (yellow flowered – bottom drawer) & old sandals (grey, hole in toe).

A is feeling the heat – only wanted milk for lunch. She sat up for 1 solid hour & wouldn't lean back against the pillow; she is a picture. Bring your shorts. You can wear them in the garden without embarrassing anyone I am sure.

Are you coming? By the time you get this you will have decided about this week. I try to think each morning that we're one day nearer the end of the war. Is a major battle developing in Normandy that may be decisive?

We must take A to the seaside & build sandcastles next summer [. . .]
AOL
Kay

18 July, *RMT to KCT in Wakefield*
Dear Mummy (?),
Well what does this sound like? Just got your Monday letter. I will change the list over to summer things. I have wondered how Ann was taking the heat [. . .]

This is a heartache darling. To think of 4/5 blessed days with you and Ann! Of course I will bring my shorts. We will go to the park, drink tea and beer & perhaps to pictures again all on our own.
Your devoted R.

Motherhood was Kay's full-time occupation. Just as Richard had no training for his job writing the war history, few women know how to look after babies until they have them. Ann was an easy baby to care for; at least none of those problems Richard told Kay about in their friends' households seemed to be arising in Wakefield. The childrearing manuals of the 1940s that Kay would have read were still strongly in the 'behaviourist' tradition of J. B. Watson. Babies were expected to fit the world they were born into, and to this end consistent and predictable patterns of stimulus and response were expected. A 'good' child rarely cried, became self-sufficient early in dealing with small problems, didn't demand 'spoiling' by adults, ate what she was given, slept when expected to, and generally moved smoothly from one developmental milestone to another. This vision of untroubled independence was reinforced in the dictates of New Zealand doctor Truby King, whose amazingly simplified idea of childhood took root as an ideal in many parents' minds.[13]

Kay felt pride in motherhood:

19 July, KCT to RMT in London
Your Sun-Mon letter a great joy but how I long to know more of the H-G discussions [. . .]
So Peter G. has a red sore behind has he. I'm surprised at his parents. Can't be good for his health or his temper.
Don't let them rush you into anything over the History. I expected sudden activity near the end of the war. You must tell me something of the interview with Bridges and with Horder.
Muriel's name is muddier than ever in this house.
Have heard from Galia – better for a week in Devon & from Madge [Sandor] who has been with N [her husband] in Grasmere for a fortnight. A wail of a letter from Eileen. Really F. is the limit to let her be in such a state & not to find somewhere else for her to go. Nicky a constant trouble at nights. She is worn out & F. sleeps in the kitchen at weekends so *he* won't be disturbed [. . .]
Had a charming letter from Mrs W. who says she is mending your socks.
Weather cold again. It will have to be winter vests. I'd rather like my blue (wedding) coat. Do you think Miss L. would make a parcel of it & let's risk it in the post. It's rather bulky & I don't want you to be burdened with much luggage especially as you must bring papers to work on till over another weekend. One just won't do.

There was a danger that Richard would be burdened with more than luggage, but he turned the prospect down:

20 July[c], RMT to KCT in Wakefield

Feeling a bit limp this afternoon. Not a lot of sleep at St P. last night & rather noisy. We staged our revolt & are to discuss with Allen ['surveyor' of St Paul's Cathedral] next week. Hay has been working to 1 every night marking exam. papers, & Gwyneth has cystitis. There are also 4 children in the place. So they have decided they must get away so Gwyneth can go into hospital. They hope (?) to get up to Newcastle by the Flying Scotsman on Monday. Hay is dreading the journey & I have offered to help them across London.

I have been asked to act as escort to 40 kids next Thursday (when I casually mentioned I was off to Wakefield). Free ticket & seat but one has to go to the school. I don't think I shall – too much of a strain despite the sociological interest. But I am coming next Thursday whatever happens. I am, quite honestly, very optimistic about the war. I think it *may* collapse suddenly any time now. It is probable that some German approaches have already been made. Anyway, I think so although I may be wrong. Their outlook is utterly hopeless. I am not seeing anyone to-night as I want a rest at No.5 although it will mean 2 telephone talks. To-morrow I have to prepare for the great white chief – Sir Edward.

Only 6 more days & then we can all love one another again.

22 July, KCT to RMT in London

Well – how soon now? Days, weeks, months? Is it a good thing they didn't kill him or doesn't it matter much one way or another. Will the Luftwaffe really obey our orders to bomb Germany if it comes to it? V. interesting that all this is happening as you forecast. Do you remember my asking you if you would be able to know when the end was near as you did the beginning.

[. . .] If you think we can come home within 2 or 3 weeks don't bother about anything but my shoes.

Rather impatient at no one to talk to about events. Daily Mail does cramp its readers' views. Auntie wants us to supply Germans with ammunition to finish themselves off. I pointed out she'd have to allot it to both sides, to which suggestion she had no objection – but there we are.

Joy [Bert and Nora's daughter] is in London for weekend with Cyril & returns Mon. Will let you know what is her experience of getting back. If it's v. bad perhaps you'd like to consider fathering 40 C.

A. has just had her first taste of cheese – mixed with potato. She took it without pulling a face but her mouth opened wide for semolina & fresh strawberries.

[. . .] Five more nights & then –

Plans for Richard's next trip to Wakefield were overshadowed by the German news. Working in Whitehall, Richard was often privy to information about the progress of the war he couldn't put in his letters. But he told Kay as much as he could:

22 July[e], RMT to KCT in Wakefield
There has been a lot of activity this week, and the nights have been exceptionally noisy [. . .] I expect that anything I say here will be out-of-date by the time you get this letter. I should expect the revolt to be 'played down' a bit over here as, during the next few weeks, a blanket of silence descends on Germany. Nevertheless, it means (1) that some of the ablest German generals have decided that Germany has completely lost (as Ludendorff had decided in July, 1918), this event is the best comment we have yet had on the use of V1 V2 V3 as military weapons, that no one in the German Army will trust anyone else (and you cannot fight total war on three fronts by telephone and the confirmation of orders to the High Command), that is probable we shall soon be in touch with a German 'Badoglio'. Incidentally, you don't announce small revolts at 1 o'clock in the night. In my view (and of course it is only a guess) organised fighting by the German Army will have ceased within two months. You will be interested to know that on Wednesday I said to some of the boys at St P. and also to Lakey that it was probable that some revolt against Hitler was already stirring in Germany. Consequently, my stock has gone up. (It is a

repeat of the Hess Business you know – pure luck). So cheer up darling, we will celebrate on Thursday.

[. . .] The Waltons have been blasted again. I have asked her if she wants any money temporarily. The girls are coming home on Wednesday [. . .] Must continue this at Office as now 8.45.

The Monday: 9.45. No fresh news. As I expected 'a blanket of silence'. I think the Germans on the Eastern Front are the big hope. The German Communists will just allow the Germans to take power and sign the Armistice. Then will begin the fight for political power. If – & it is a major if – anything? should happen in the next day or so I will arrive before Thursday. But in any event I shall be with you on Thursday (have decided against looking after 40 kids). *Don't worry* in the meantime. I do not intend to become a casualty after lasting so long.

Richard's reference to small revolts announced in the early hours of the morning was to Hitler's broadcast on 21 July revealing an attempt on his life by Colonel Graf von Stauffenberg. Von Stauffenberg had put a bomb in a despatch case in Hitler's map-room. Three officers were killed; Hitler's legs were burned, his right arm temporarily paralysed and his ear-drums pierced. The culprit fled to Berlin where he was captured and executed the same night.[14] The possibility of a German revolt against Hitler was now widely contemplated in Britain.

Kay was still full of domestic plans:

24 July, KCT to RMT in London
You will stay 1 week + 2 weekends won't you? I'll be *cross* if you want to go back before a fortnight today. Take leave if you can't do work. Remember H–K [Hancock] said a month. It's important to save us anxiety & I'm sure you need a good break & some good sleep.

The list is as follows:
2 Pink Woollen Vests (1st drawer left side)
New shoes
Wool for Ann (one of the drawers in her chest)
Custard Powder (some packets near flour in cabinet)

*Blue coat if possible

And of course Ann's new things from Jerry.

Wear your thicker raincoat if it's back from cleaners (buttonless if need be only bring the buttons with you). It's cold out here.

We'll buy you some new slippers. Have seen some nice ones & some posh ones I want.

Almost counting hours now.

*If too bulky perhaps you could manage red jersey & check skirt from case near tool box. Would like them v. much & furry coat too. It's so cold.

Don't bother about any food. Bring book we can get rations here.

But despite Kay's pleading, Richard spent only four days in Wakefield. He told Jerry Morris about his visit in one of his many letters to India, boasting about Ann's spectacular progress in trying to talk at 6½ months, and threatening to walk before she crawled. He also wrote to Jerry about their peptic ulcer paper (due out 'any Friday now') and their paper on rheumatic heart disease which had been held up because the printers had been bombed. The eminent statistician A. Bradford Hill had asked him to give a paper to the Royal Statistical Society on social mobility and deaths from violence. The Luton investigation was proceeding, and he and Grundy were busy working on the lay-out for a punch card system capable of recording multiple items of social and medical data relating to births and infant deaths. His ABCA pamphlet was published in December: *Fewer Children: The population problem.* Was he thinking of Ann when he wrote, 'The first thing we have to realise is that the population aged over 25 in 1970 is already born.'[15] But whatever he himself realized, the problem was still one of the underpopulation of the 'white' compared to the 'coloured' races which threatened Britain's post-war task of leading 'to adulthood a vast Colonial Empire'.[16] Richard welcomed the appointment of a Royal Commission on Population, but observed that both Sweden and Russia had ambitious population programmes aimed at addressing the central question: why have children gone out of fashion?

Along with the anticipation of the war's imminent end, went the projection into a post-war future. All the talk now was of reconstruction; there was an atmosphere of hope about correcting some of the social problems revealed by the war. But for Richard, still embroiled in sorting out the problems of the war history, all this seemed a very long way away. He went back to London on 2 August, and wrote reflectively to Kay the next day. His wife and child pulled him one way, and the grand project of the war history – getting grander by the minute – pulled him the other. But their friends' experiences continued to convince him that he'd done the right thing in insisting on the separation; Kay's worries about his safety would just have to be coped with. Her letter voicing these, to which his 4 August letter responds, did not survive:

3 August⁵, RMT to KCT in Wakefield
It's a bit early in the afternoon but I wanted the pleasure of writing to you as the next best thing to hearing your voice. I could not sleep at all last night – from 2 o'clock (I was on from 12.30–2) I just lay & pictured you and Ann together. I had, and still have, a clear photographic picture of Ann: Ann screwing up her face, blowing semolina violently & all the rest. It was a nasty, dirty night. It was dark, very dark & misty with low clouds & many more got through. Between 11.30 & 5.30 59 passed over or near the Cathedral. The previous 'high' was 42.

[. . .] Hancock has an Administrative Secretary – Sir Quinton Hill. I met the gent this morning. A most forbiddingly traditional Civil Servant – all stripes, grey hair, spruce, correct & inhibited. Hancock told me (confidentially at midnight that he was a failure at M. of Food & with Sir William*). Wormald refuses to have him as 'Father Confessor' – wants me instead. I will only have Hancock. More talk on 'Synoptic History'. Hancock has a plan for me to write a Grand Vol. I – a broad, sweeping reconnaissance [?] on the Home Front at War – the Family under Fire, Civil Defence, Social Services, Health & Nutrition, Education, Welfare & what-not. You know, looking analytically at England of the Common Man, what the Government did or did not do [. . .] If it comes to this he says he will have to make me Director of the Education & C.D. Histories or some such title. Target date to come. Also, he wants to come &

swim at 5 B this week-end. No peace at all except with you
& Ann.

4 August^e, RMT to KCT in Wakefield
Just had your letter. It makes me ache to think of you worrying. But, darling, do remember that I work in a very safe
building & sleep in one of the safest places [. . .] I used the
corridor last night & [. . .] I slept like a log from 12–6.
Didn't hear a thing. There were some F.B.'s but it was light.
Weather made a lot of difference I'm sure. And to-day it is
really *hot August* & I feel all hot & sticky. Not a siren since
6.30 this morning. Maybe the better weather will mean fewer
F.B.'s – it is certainly going to help a hell of a lot in Normandy. Even Kuczynski – that cautious one – says the end
is rapidly approaching. I had a most interesting lunch with
him to-day. (Remind me to tell you.) He also asked me to
a meal next Friday evening.

    Glass in a frightful mess over Helen & Ruth, so is Lafitte,
so are the Townsends [Beaumont Court residents, note in
KCT's writing] etc etc. *It is a blessing* darling that you are
not. Glass wanted me to agree to joint occupation of a cottage
near Gt Barfield. I said *NO*. It would have meant turning
you into slavery.

    More talky-talky over History. Will tell you over week-end.

In the hot August weather, taking her baby out in the park for
her first summer, Kay allowed herself to fantasize about happier times
ahead. But the rain in London drove Richard off the allotment into
the pub:

5 August^e, KCT to RMT in London
Not surprised at H's last suggestion. Could see it coming
[. . .]
    A & I had from 1 pm together yesterday when A & U
went to Leeds. Oh she was sweet. She ate her first Ovaltine
rusk very nicely with obvious enjoyment but not exactly like
a lady. Crumbs everywhere. So sorry you missed it.
    It's very hot & when she wakes we're going to feed the
ducks on the shady path by the lake. Great excitement the

252

other end of the Park with donkey rides & roundabouts & swings. Where will we 3 be next Aug Bk holiday I wonder?

5 August, RMT to KCT in Wakefield
A quiet night and nothing since 7.30. Hancock coming this afternoon so may not have time to catch Saturday post. More good news from Germany showing how widespread discontent is. War Office think ABCA excellent but still has to go through censors. Spent ½ hour on allotment last night in rain. So fed up had to go and have one pint of B. Lots & lots of peas, beans, rhubarb, etc. Distributing & eating them. Something like 100 tomatoes looking better than next door neighbour who can't leave his alone. Write and tell me about planting out leeks and sowing fresh seeds – I've forgotten.

All my love. Only 12 days now.

Richard's next letter returns to the unresolved business of his future. The comments on the Hancocks' relationship are interesting. Richard understands his need for Kay:

6 August[e], RMT to KCT in Wakefield
My darling,
It is Saturday evening & nearing 10 o'clock. I'm tired & waiting for the girls to come down so I can go to bed. It has been dreadful this evening without you. I've felt lost & aimless. Tried to work on the McNalty MS but hopeless. I did so want to talk to you. The Hancocks came at 3 & stayed to 7. Although it has been a lovely day I found it a strain. Mrs H. is so jumpy & upsetting. She cannot help W.K.H. like you help me. We sat & sun-bathed (went in once), had tea (Auntie's cake came in *very* useful as the bread was stale), & talked.

H. said very suddenly: 'I've written a report on Titmuss for Sir Edward today.' Me: 'An interesting one?' H.(slowly) 'Yes – you would find it interesting.' Then he went on to say that it was all about what was to happen to me when the wicked Nazis have been beaten. I gathered he says that he (H) cannot advise me *not* to go back to insurance unless the Cabinet are prepared to do something about the future security of Titmuss. They must realize that if they want T. to write Synoptic History on *The People & Five Years of War Strain* it will put back his work & mean a longer term of employment. I gather that at least Sir Edward wants such a History. Well – we shall see. I expect, as always, things will turn out differently from what we expect.

Sunday morning 8 o'clock Waiting for the girls to get up! [. . .] After breakfast I shall write to Jerry & then I may go to Mill Hill & get that done. What a bore! 7 dogs to see I suppose. But once done I shall not go again for months.

[. . .] I saw sweetie-pie in bed last night.

God bless you both.

All my love.

R.

In her domestic setting, Kay calls forth sustaining images of the family being together with its own patch of land – little England and everything right with the world:

6 August^e, KCT to RMT in London
Beloved,

The cool of the evening sitting in the garden where we have been since lunch & Ann has been nearby all day. I'm lonesome & homesick. I love you so much a fine sunny summer day is more unbearable than a dull one. Will we ever have a secluded patch of our own grass with our own fruit trees? When & if I'm sorry A. will be beyond the pram stage. She has been a little jewel. At tea time seemed to be so happy to be with us eating her rusk, & went off to sleep without a murmur.

Uncle Bert has a table & is working at his reports & Auntie is mending – a very domestic scene. I haven't been able to pay for anything but our own rations this week. She wouldn't let me but I have given her my new silk dress that I had only worn once. She looks very nice in it & is very pleased with it. I don't know what else I can do.

Will write tomorrow but want to be sure of a letter awaiting you on Tues so here we are – just a bit of inconsequential

chatter. Sad that I can write nothing else to one I love so
much – my heart is so full [. . .]
    AOL
    Kay

Mon.
Your Fri & Sat. stuff has come this morn. Bless you. Dull &
misty but looks like being hot again. Glad you turned down
cottage with Glass's. It wouldn't work but I certainly should
have to.

It wasn't clear why sharing a cottage with David and Ruth Glass
would be quite such a burden.

The dark skies and driving rain of June and July which had led
Kay to call for her woollen vests had now given way to an archetypal
English summer. While Kay reflected on her dreams for their own
patch of grass with fruit trees on it, Richard meditated in a significant
letter on the deeper meaning of life as a middle-class family man. It
wasn't fantasies of family life this time, but real practices and values
that seemed at odds with those of his own background, now he'd
built a new life for himself with Kay – if only he had a chance to live
it properly:

7 August, *RMT to KCT in Wakefield*
Beloved,
It is a wicked shame that we should have to be separated
during such a marvellous week-end [. . .] it seems an eternity
without you. Ann is important – I've thought about it a lot
– but you are infinitely more important – another 30 years
& – who knows – all eternity *together*. But to miss a few days
– a few hours – is all wrong [. . .]
    Saturday you've heard about. Sunday – my God, what a
day! – was spent at Mill Hill. Pity alternating with impatience,
disgust & frustration. I stayed the night but left at 8.45 on
the excuse (a lie) that I was to see Hancock. I could not bear
it any longer. They do not feel or think as we do – they have
not the remotest conception of what life *can* mean. The
tragedy is that they do represent a group – and a considerable

one – in the community. What a gimcrack civilisation we have built – what values! For example, 8 out of 10 in the road – & presumably in the neighbourhood – not only *tip* the milkman 1/- a week but never query the bill so as to get extra milk.

So I got back to 5 B. early in the morning. It was glorious: I could not bring myself to work, the allotment seemed futile so I took refuge in action. I cycled to Runnymede. A puncture half-way there which I mended successfully & then my back brake snapped. It would of course. Needless to say it was nostalgia all the way. I spoke to no one. Settled down by the river & read all the afternoon. It was so hot that I had to go in to get cool twice. The place of course was crammed. I thought of you and Ann in the Park & wondered how she was taking the heat.

[. . .] At 6 this evening – and a glorious evening – I could not count more than 5 people in the garden. The pool deserted. That gives you some idea of what evacuation has meant here. There were few F.B.'s yesterday; only a small number in the night (very distant ones at Mill Hill) & only 1 short warning to-day. With this clear blue sky they don't send them over.

H. rang up to-night as he was fire-watching. Back from his holiday & had left Blue at Oxford for another week. They had one F.B. in Garratts Lane – ½ a mile away – which killed 51 people last week – slum property. So Watford isn't a safe area.

[. . .] Any list this time darling? Lard, custard powder, fruit (from Jerry), Mazola Oil?

I must now do a bit of McNalty. Will write about the war later darling but I'm very hopeful. Soon events will crowd in upon each other thick and fast. Think of a river in flood & then, after minor trickles, the dam bursts. God bless you both my darlings. 10 days.

R.

She must have lived for his letters. She was inconsolable without them. It was difficult not to blame Ann for making her Richard-less:

8 August, KCT to RMT in London

This morning is probably the first time I have wakened rejoicing that a holiday is over. We had a pleasant day: U.B. & I went to the fair & the dancing + joined the throng of hot holiday makers in the Park. The triumph was being able to buy as many plums as we wanted in the morning. By 4 pm there were hundreds queuing for them. At. & Ann spent that afternoon bottling them. I couldn't forget you alone at B.Ct & felt v. sad. I know I'm naughty to moan so much: it's worse for you alone. I have the wench & the pleasant companionship of A & U. but – well. I shall always be unconsolable without you. Soon it will be a week only & then we can begin to count hours.

[. . .] Leeks. 1" apart and 9" between rows. Make holes and rest plants in with drop of water. They root themselves then.

9 August, KCT to RMT in London

I know I've thought about it a lot & today was inclined to be impatient with A for keeping me from you. We never thought somehow that this situation might arise.

Striking development in her personality. At. says she's never seen such an expressive face on one so young & is never tired of watching her. We took her in the Bank yesterday & the remarks (quite audible) were interesting. 'Just look at that baby – isn't she canny? She's only a young baby you know' & several more in the same strain mixed up with the usual 'Isn't that a bonny baby?' sort of thing.

The longest week I've ever spent. Darling don't you think you'll have to bring some work up here for a bit. After all it won't be long now before the damn bursts will it?

A impatient. Taking her to post.

Throughout their separation. Richard assumed the role of 'kinkeeper' more usually taken by women. His next letter, with its description of Katie Miller fully clothed sleeping among lace pillows, would have delighted her sister Nora in Wakefield:

9 August, RMT to KCT in Wakefield

Just a brief line to let you know early that everything is O.K. after staying night at Hayes. They were delighted to have me. Mother and father both looked tired but they had adapted themselves wonderfully. We talked of many things. And we all slept together downstairs. What a world it is! Thinks of 7 years ago. And now, Father Me and Mother (in the corner) sleeping in clothes in beautifully laundered sheets and lace pillows. Enormous dinner and enormous breakfast (with new scones). Oh dear 7 days.

It's a wonderful image: Richard sharing a room with Kay's upright Victorian mother and father fully dressed in their pristine makeshift beds.

But Kay had 'the wench' to console herself with, and all the wench's impeccable babyhood achievements:

10 August, KCT to RMT in London

Now for the important news. Your daughter has cut a tooth & there is another nearly through. She looked v. pale yesterday but was quite merry & bright: just refused her rusk at tea time. In the evening she wakened at 8 + for 2 hrs cried on & off. I picked her up once + comforted her & she gave me such a sweet smile when I put her back in her cot. She tried to go to sleep but her mouth wakened her each time she dozed off. I brought her downstairs to feed her at 10.30 & had a look & there was the tooth sticking thro'. She went down like a lamb at 11.15 & I didn't hear a sound till 7.15 this morning. It's 12 now & she's been asleep since 10.30 so the other one isn't troubling her much. How's that!! No fractiousness, no sore bottom, no diarrhoea, not off her food. I do rather regret that E.[Eileen Lafitte] is missing the lesson on how it can be done. Of course we may have trouble with some. Can hardly hope to get thro' without but it's a good start. U.B. was so excited about it. He tells me he finds himself looking in all the prams he sees as he did when Joy & Brian were babies. They'll be sad here when we go.

A week today. That's what I'm living for. Are we going to sweep on to Paris now? When do you think the damn will burst? Can you be sufficiently optimistic for me to not give you a list of things to bring? Have you had some more dried fruit from Jerry? Eat some & you might bring a bit. Ate. is v. well stocked but custard powder is not available. Perhaps Mrs W could get some at Oakesholts for you to bring.

11 August*, RMT to KCT in Wakefield
It was marvellous to get your letter with the news about our daughter. What a darling she is to be so good [...]

I think you must expect to be away another month darling so let me know what you want me to bring. Not that I expect to leave you for a month after next week-end!

I wish now I had never introduced the H's to the pool. They are coming Sunday morning & afternoon. It's a curse not being left alone. From 4.30 on Sunday I'm committed to the Dubners [Sam Dubner was a colleague on the St Paul's watch] at Hampstead after putting them off time and time again. To-night – meal with the Kuczynskis. Work, the flat & allotment suppers of course but it can't be helped. By the way, I've let myself in for something else! Not much though so don't be cross. A 6 minute dialogue on the Forces Brains Trust 'Answering you' on this family business. With a Major Richard Bennett. Tell you more next week [...]

Present arrangements are to catch the 11.15 next Thursday but shall write tomorrow.

12 August*, RMT to KCT in Wakefield
Interesting evening at the Kuczynskis! They live in poverty with large German furniture & an enormous and dusty library. Mrs K. is a first-class painter & has done an excellent drawing of her husband. But she is a bad cook. I came home with indigestion and had to get up at 2 for magnesia. They sent their love to you both.

According to present arrangements the girls go to Chalfont on the same day as I travel North. They don't want to – in a way – but I think Bunny should go as she looks tired.

We will talk about the war next week. But I am waiting for the Russian offensive to start again – I think they have been re-grouping & bringing up their supplies. In France anything may happen but the situation is extraordinarily interesting. Although the Germans are still fighting well their defences are getting awfully thin.

It's overcast and dull to-day. I hope therefore that the H's change their minds tomorrow. I'm getting a bit tired of Synoptic History – & any sort of History from the north.

I took beans & rhubarb to the K's. And at home had the first ripe tomato! Shall I bring any with me?

[. . .] Only 5 more lonely breakfasts now.

12 August*, KCT to RMT in London
A is v. pale & won't eat her vegetables the last 2 or 3 days. Can you find the iron tablets in the kitchen & bring them? It's the other tooth no doubt. She still weighed 16 lbs at Boots today.

I would like the No.12 needles from the front of the top drawer of Ann's chest. There is a gauge there to tell the size but At. Elizabeth will help you. I think in the ex-glory hole of mine near the wireless (the wooden rack) there is an envelope with some felt slippers for Ann waiting to be stitched. If so, please bring them.

Lovely summer day but a bit windy. V. tired [. . .] Are the F.B.'s slackening?

14 August*, RMT to KCT in Wakefield
A *most* trying day yesterday. The H's from 12–4 & I left them there and then the Dubners. Will tell you more on Friday.

A somewhat noisy night & early morning. The crockery and the chairs jumped about but nothing broken. Don't know where they fell.

News good – & it will be better I think. My guess is you will have news of another invasion landing before I arrive. Anyway, I'll bet half-a-pint.

Kay's imagination of how the future could be made her strict with Richard: he must tell Hancock they *had* to spend some time together:

14 August^e, KCT to RMT in London

It's a heavenly day & I just ache with the beauty which emphasises the loneliness. I have a longing to be with you & Ann on a secluded little garden of our own with the bees humming among the flowers around us & apples & pears & plums on the trees. Or in Geneva or anywhere among snow capped mountains. Reading a novel about the life of a Swiss guide & it brings back to the memory the days like this you & I have spent abroad.

So you think we may have to endure another month. I want my whole home & as you can't bring that I don't think there's anything else. 8 weeks on Sat. It's a long time to be away from one's precious home. But I shouldn't complain [. . .]

Don't let H keep you for anything. Tell him the truth. Tell him we must have a few days together to refresh our souls & that history will suffer if we don't. Does he realise how much we complement each other & how we discuss everything? You must now be in contact with him enough to talk of these things. Don't worry about the pool. Fine weather won't last long & I imagine it is the pool & garden that attract him. Or am I wrong?

Could I read in bed with a bicycle lamp? I'm so long going to sleep & I can't see with the light here. Is there one on your hat shelf or on the cupboard above it? I don't like to ask Nora to move the light if it's another month. Well!!

They had five days together. Kay was finding it harder and harder to be away from Richard. When he went back to London this time, he promised to return just over a week later. A trip to North Wales with the Hancocks was on the horizon, and he wasn't looking forward to it. Kay speculated on the nature of Hancock's interest in Richard – was it something of the same that she herself felt? Richard, suffering from the pangs of paternal deprivation, didn't answer. The truth of the matter was that he was entirely in Hancock's hands, not only as regards whether he went to Wales or not, but what he might be doing for the rest of his life:

26 August*, RMT to KCT in Wakefield

I looked forward to a note from you to-day & there it was on my desk. I'm glad that 'morbidness' is a little less acute. Ann must be such a comfort. I had a queer experience yesterday. I was walking down V. St. behind a woman carrying a rather lovely baby about Ann's age. I suddenly felt like saying 'Do you mind if I hold your baby a minute?' The Ann substitute.

Now I must tell you about the Hancock business. Early Wed. evening he asked if I had decided about N. Wales. I told him – about you & Ann & said I was sorry. He replied that he fully understood, etc. At 11 he suggested that he & I should walk round the Crypt & talk. Then he told me what he had been doing about me:

1. Talked to the Warden of All Souls who was greatly interested. Long discussion about possibilities of research at All Souls and at Nuffield College under Clay (the Bank of England adviser who is looking for a few people like me after the war). Hancock has now put all this in writing (with lots about me) to All Souls. Thus: 2 possibilities.

2. Long minute to Bridges about me. Said it would be disastrous if I went before History completed. Therefore the Cabinet Secretariat must scratch their heads if they want to keep me.

3. Has spoken to Compton (head of the Central Stat. office which is definitely to be maintained and expanded after the war). Compton said he would be 'lucky' to get me.

As best I could I said how grateful I was. H. said he was doing all this for 2 reasons: his own interests & as a friend. Then we went back & heard the 12 news about Marseilles, Rumania, etc. Suddenly H. began to talk again about 'working too hard & learning to play again'. Then said he had a new idea. Briefly, it was that I should do a week's work in North Wales. This of course he admitted was an excuse but said I could do some 'background reading & talking'. It was all very difficult & embarrassing – coming as it did on the heels of everything else. I felt it impossible to refuse again. Why he should be so insistent I don't know & why he should want me there with Mrs H. I don't know. I don't want to fish & I want to get away from History. But there it is. I shan't look forward to it. Another snag is that he is vague about the date. Talks about 8th to middle of Sept but much depends on his getting papers from the General Staff to read as he is taking 2/3 weeks & Miss Eyre will be sent for.

Please let me know whether you think I have done the right thing. This may alter the date of visit to Wakefield but I shan't leave it longer than we arranged.

What else now? Collected 66 ripe tomatoes last night. What a diet I shall have! The cabbages seem to be rotting with lots of earwigs in them. Any suggestions?

No Mrs W next week as Mr W & Lester on holiday. She has left lots of soap-flakes for you. Does Auntie or do you want them?

Would you please let me know number of Ann's Savings Certificates. If not with you it should be on list.

Had lunch yesterday with Richard Bennett. Frightening news about Army Education. Each ABCA now read by Minister *. My ABCA going through the mill. More revision this week as Bennett is very keen on it. I wonder whether it will ever see the light of day [. . .]

Hours & hours yesterday with Sir Quinton (who thinks that someone will *hang* if my evacuation history is published – he says it was exciting & excellently written – so he says). Also with Major Kohan (M. of Works historian), * & Wormald. On Monday night 'Worms' & I are touring London's new deep shelters.

Apart from this 'toing-&-froing' I am feeling very lonely. With the girls away, Lake on holiday & H. taken up with Blue's relatives, I do not always know 'what sort of a night it was'.

[. . .] Fabian meeting last night. Mrs Hubback sends her love, Hay does & Frank [?]. They all want to see Ann again. So does her father – rather badly.

O darling – to-morrow I shall hear your voice.

In the last two letters in this series the anguish mounts:

26 Augustᵉ, RMT to KCT in Wakefield
My own Darling,
Back again on the typewriter you see. Been on it a large part
of the day. It has been a lonely day I'm afraid. I was at the
Office this morning – when I wrote my first letter to you.
Had steak, beans, tomatoes and potatoes and actually gravy
for lunch. But the latter was the texture of porridge that Ann
prefers. Then stewed rhubarb. I brought some back last night
– thought I must eat it. I was careful not to put too much
water in (and plenty of sugar) and it is very good. But how
glad I shall be to have a partner again – not just to hand it
over to you again – but to have a partner. I've revised ABCA,
re-written the broadcast, written to Newfield and read 200
pages on housing. And now I want someone to play with.
Glass rang me up. They are in trouble again. He says he just
can't afford to go on paying £4 a week extra for Helen and
Nannie in Lincs. and went off the deep end because he can't
get a billeting allowance for them and not pay any contribution. So Helen is to come back from Lincs. and be sent
down to Kent again. What a life, and what practice as opposed
to all their theories.

You will have heard from the wireless that we have had a
lull since yesterday morning. Of course I expect that the main
reason is the exceptionally good weather and clear sky, but
there is just a little hope dodging about that it may mean
something else (i.e. moving the sites). Let us see. Bulgaria
and Rumania are going to help a lot. It means of course
another Front – and a big one – on the S.E. For morale it
is also very important. The 1918 sequence had to happen
first [. . .]

O darling I mustn't be sentimental any more but what
cruelty it is to separate us.

All my love, Richard

29 August, KCT to RMT in London
Beloved,
It is cruel. That is just the word for it [. . .] Can't give all
the time I would like to this letter. 'Tis mid-morn. A. asleep
but likely to wake up any minute. She sleeps far less during

the day now. She's lovely – looks very fit & I don't care what she weighs. How's that for the Lafittes? Poor little Helen. They should never have brought her into the world.

Re future near & far. You can't do anything else but accept the N. Wales I am afraid. *BUT* it may not materialise. If you do go make up your mind to revel in the change of air & scene. I'm puzzled a bit about it. I can only think that with the closer relationship he finds something of what I find in you & wants more of your company. From the history view-point he feels he can rely on you to carry on & if he can arrange satisfactorily with Bridges you will be his right hand through months maybe years of difficulties. He knows as well as we do that criticism will be acid & he thinks in you he has someone strong who is prepared to face it & carry on. I hope the All Souls comes off. With that as a mainstay we might have a little peace & quiet. Otherwise no. If you remain a C.S.[Civil Servant] you will have so many enemies. In any case I expect we will have lots of troubles. ABCA points the way. Disgusting. My temper will be as sorely tried post-war as war. Together with Ann to play with we shall manage to cope with them all. Not to be able to talk to you today is making me feel quite ill.

Have just hung out nappies under a doubtful sky. I'm furious at the waste of time watching the weather & turning nappies in the evening round a small kitchen fire. When I've a hot cupboard at home & constant hot too!!! Such a waste!!

Back to Wales & your visit here. Could you not join him from here if need be. You're due here 9th aren't you?

I do hope I can be back by end of Sept. Will send you a list of clothes you *must* take for fishing. You will have to have two pairs of shoes. I should worry if not. Must get new brown ones. Would like to be in at the buy if possible.

No soap flakes required. Ann's Certificate no is not on the Bank slip re-purchase & I have not the numbers on my list. You'll have to get particulars from the Bank & you'd better let me have them. Curse this business. I'm in an awful temper.

Shall probably try & ring you on Thurs even on the chance of finding you in [. . .

Before I slept last night I thought of our home & our bed

all unoccupied & I ached to be there with my own things around me – even a sight of the tomato stain on the wall would be welcome. I hope A behaves herself on the return journey. I'll be quite unmanageable.

I know the news is good but it's not quick enough for me & I'm fearful of the frightful climax. Paris is just a forerunner of Berlin in a year's time I suppose. They'll no doubt clear the French F.B. sites & then we'll be in doubt about others & there'll be a few sent over & a lull & then a few & it will all be so maddeningly indecisive.

What will you do with me? I need you so badly. Think of it this letter is my only outlet today.

Yours in suppression & loving you so much.

Kay

Running through both Kay and Richard's letters was a shared concern for the safety of their friends, sheltering either in London or out of it, the men anxious to tuck away their wives and children out of the path of bombs, but not always able to ensure this, and everyone carrying the burden of the fear that the war might at any moment shift the temporary separation of families into a more permanent one. As any mother would have done, Kay wrote of Ann's developing personality, of the food she ate, the sleep she took, the clothes she wore, the way she responded to the world around her. She could console herself with the fact that Ann was a good and undemanding baby; her efforts to be a good mother and to put her duty to Ann before her desire to be with Richard seemed to be paying off. But when she wrote to Richard about Ann and other domestic matters, Kay was conscious both of the enormous interest such topics hold for new parents and of the 'inconsequential' nature of her 'chatter' ('Sad that I can write nothing else to one I love so much'). Her world had reduced itself to the walls of 85 Thornes Road and the daily tending of a small baby. While Richard shared her interest in Ann's development and felt keenly the pain of being separated, he'd now become the representative of the public world to his little family. It was he who bore them news both local and global: recitations of bombs falling, houses ruined, conversations in Whitehall, forecasts of peace on the Western Front, projections of the kind of future the Titmusses could expect to have once the war was over. And he himself was forever the historian, observing and recording even as he lived and wrote – some of his letters to Kay were written, to save paper, on the backs of pages of analyses of billeting figures composed for his war history. He needed the war to write his history, but war was at the same time the enemy, imposing divisions between Richard and Kay that didn't exist before. In the same way, they needed a child to make themselves into a family, but the child herself was responsible for an irremediable separation between their roles.

Paris had been liberated on 25 August, and there were hopes of the Allies ending the war at a single blow by crossing the Rhine from Holland into Germany. Anti-aircraft guns at the coast had got very efficient at destroying flying bombs, and then Montgomery's offensive in the Pas de Calais disabled the launching sites. On 7 September Duncan Sandys on behalf of the government announced that the 'Battle of London' was over. Richard and Kay began to plan their own private evacuation of Wakefield for the end of September.

TEN

❄

Doing half my job

The news of the war was good the day Richard went back to London in preparation for the dreaded trip to North Wales with the Hancocks. At one o'clock it was announced that the British Army had occupied Brussels, and hostilities between Finland and Russia were over. The news in the evening was that British troops had crossed into Holland. Some 300,000 German prisoners had been taken in France alone. The German Army was in disarray. There was now hope that the era of flying bombs was over. From his privileged position in Whitehall, Richard could report to Kay rumours of surrender on 5 September and the hopeful sign of the formal disbanding of the Cabinet Flying Bomb and Rocket Committee, an ad hoc grouping set up in the summer to plan for the consequences of a major German rocket attack.[1] A waxwork exhibition of German atrocities was on display in London: 'Horror of the Nazi concentration camps,' said the advertising boards. 'Come inside and see real Nazi tortures, flogging, crucifixion, gas chambers, etc.'[2]

Writing to Richard to thank him for the spinach which had arrived safely in Wakefield, Kay, from her nexus of domestic concerns, hoped that Hancock would cancel Wales and that she and Ann would soon be back in London to celebrate the end of the war. But 'Too optimistic, I suppose,' she noted, even as she wrote this. Richard was feeling very depressed about it all. He was having a bad time in the Ministry with threats of censorship about the narrative of government policy and mistakes he would be allowed to tell, and he had a problem with his health as well. Kay had put him in touch with a Dr Meyer, who had been recommended by Birch.[3] On 6 September[4] Richard wrote to Kay before his night-time sojourn in St Paul's:

I don't think that I shall ever allow again anyone – whoever he is – to stand between you & I. That is how I am feeling to-day. Very low. Partly because of work – the unending vista of concentrated thought about the origins of muddle – & partly because of this ulcerated business of mine. It's not that I'm feeling ill [...] but that it is a little disturbing. It still bleeds when I go – or want to go. Meyer was not at all disturbed about it. Said it was common & recommended a little Agarol each night & this ointment twice a day. I've used it but I suppose it hasn't had a chance yet. I did not ask him how much blood one can continue to lose like this without carrying any ill effects. I suppose just because I'm tired it distresses me. Anyway, in my opinion the best answer would be 2 days in bed on fruit juice & no solids to give the apparatus a rest. And that is what we'll do if it is no better when you come back. And please be sure dear that if I do not feel well in Wales then I shall make it an excuse to come home before the end of the week & then fetch you & Ann home to comfort me. Silly, isn't it?

[...] Hancock (would you believe it) has gone to Wales to-day & I am to follow with Mrs H. on Friday morning [...] No other news of any significance. The Lafittes are at 33 Broadhurst Gardens, Eastcote – I saw them leaving the flat on a visit on Monday evening. Eileen very excited about telling me all about Nicky. F. thinks he is going to be such a marvellous cricketer as he is good with a ball. I wonder.

All my love to you & darling Ann, R.

Richard went on the train to Wales with the 'chattering' Mrs Hancock. There he was exposed to an example of a marriage he would not wish to emulate, and to further scheming about the place of his own volume in the overall plan of the civil histories of the war:

10 September, RMT to KCT in Wakefield
I don't quite know where to start [...] We did not get to P.[Penmachno] until 8 o'clock. I was awfully tired, with a headache, bored with Mrs H., longing to be rude instead of polite & cursing everything & everybody. And it was so

cold! I couldn't get to sleep. Yesterday was somewhat better although still cold but with some sun (& rain). H & I walked to Bulls-y-coed & back in the morning – about 9 miles. Climbing & steep most of the way [. . .] one (!) half pint, I could have drunk 3. In the afternoon H went fishing & I retired to the bed – but found it difficult to sleep without you. In the evening – a little walk & one half pint again [. . .]

It isn't really a farm you know, not by our standards. 13 acres, 5 cows, a few sheep & chickens. A small cottage with 3 bedrooms, half way up a steep hill. The food though is wonderful – if only you were here I should enjoy it. Plenty of lovely home made butter, oceans of thick cream with everything & good cooking. The shortages are of course sugar & meat.

As to H & Mrs H the atmosphere is at times 'tense'. It is quite a revelation. They can have absolutely *no conception of our relationship.* I have not yet had a single question about you & Ann. In the train, twice there were delightful babies. Mrs H. took not the slightest notice – ignored their smiles & noises. I found it strange.

Here there is a dreadful amount of talk about *sleep & beds.* If one wants to go to bed early the other doesn't. Last night H. went off (& so did I) at 10.30. Mrs H. (dreadfully tired) was 'just coming'. For the next hour I heard H. thumping on the floor of his bedroom to get up his wife to bed. This morning: both slept badly. Mrs H. wanting to move into a hotel. H refusing to move. And so on.

Can you interpret this? First thing yesterday H. told me his dream. He was playing cricket & bowling. He had difficulty in bowling because there was not much room to run (? the bed space). The first 2 balls the batsman stopped. At the third one the batsman put out his chin & the ball went straight in his mouth: Hancock said 'How's that' & the umpire said 'Out'. The ball was found behind the fellow's teeth. Tell me what you think.

We have had one talk about history. Bridges has accepted one plan & it is practically certain to go through the Cabinet Cte. The 'Advance' Volumes – Hancock, Postan, Titmuss.

Each of us is asked to give a paper to the next Conference of the Economic History Assn. at which all the peers of the historical world will be present. I am to start looking for a Research Assistant (£1000 – £500 on War Cab. scale). H. wants me to get him or her within a month.

But I can't see yet this Volume – I can't see *how* it will be written. *What* it will contain. I haven't any sort of Plan in my mind. And so I am not happy about it.

It's about time for lunch so I must stop [...] I'm sorry Ann has been a bit fidgety. We must get the play pen (Hay has the high chair for us). And, of course, darling I will help you with *everything* in the flat. Only to have you near once more.

This was in response to Kay's happy anticipation that she would soon be able to make new net curtains and take 'that awful black paper' off the windows in the flat – Richard would help, wouldn't he? She'd been to Wakefield station to find out about trains, and had wept to see the platform crowded with mothers and children waiting for the London train to come in. Although the government was not officially recommending a return of evacuees yet, as Richard was later to narrate in his war history,[5] this was another example of a good plan made to look like a bad one, because people simply did not behave as they were supposed to. During the winter of 1944–5 hundreds of thousands returned prematurely to a dilapidated London and to their families. Once again Richard and Kay joined the crowd. Just as Kay had come back to London during the phoney war in 1939–40 and in time for the bombing, now there was no stopping her enthusiasm for an end to the separation she found so painful:

10 September', KCT to RMT in Wales
Darling I'm so excited I don't know how I'll get through next week. Grand Sept. day here. V. cold with a frost this morning. We have a continuous fire. Nice & warm in one room!! Our house must have central heating.

Better bring your big ruc-sac to pack things in & the smaller one too in case we need it.

A is sitting up in the sun in her pram watching the kids

271

next door [...] Nearly at the end of this correspondence business thank goodness. Oh Richard!!

While Kay was occupied with high chairs and the date of the return to London, Richard and Hancock went fishing, and enjoyed the countryside:

11 September, *RMT to KCT in Wakefield*
How I wish you and Ann were with me. It has been a glorious 2 days. Very cold in the mornings & evenings but lovely in the day. Yesterday afternoon we went for an 8 mile walk & took our tea with us. H. & I went 'worming' for trout but no luck. In the evening we had 2 hours on my History. Helpful, but as I told H, I can't see the plan yet. Have you had any ideas yet about my Research Assistant? He (preferably a he) must be good & do research work – not just taking over a block [...]

Intellectually I find this a bit of a strain. The weather has of course eased things a bit & the atmosphere is a little less tense. But I shan't be sorry when Saturday is here. I definitely return on Sat. & must then get busy booking Yates [car driver to pick them up from St Pancras]. *Please write & tell me the train we are catching* [...]

We took lunch out to-day & picked blackberries. A lovely walk. From 5.30–8.0 H. & I went harvesting, i.e. helped the farmer to get his oats in. The frost each night is so severe that the crops are not dry until after tea. We had a bathe this afternoon. V. cold but refreshing.

[...] I've found a farm here where you & Ann & I can stay. A lovely place with a little river for Ann.

Oceans of love & kisses for sweetie-pie.

In response to the mass exodus back to London, the government's propaganda machine had come into action to persuade people against returning. Kay wanted Richard to reassure her: she depended on him to know the truth about the public world of history and war and politics.

11 September^e, KCT to RMT in Wales
Darling. It is O.K. for us to go home isn't it? Feeling a bit windy on account of statements in Press asking evacuees to stay put. Is the warning really because of housing difficulties or is there likely to be another snarl of an angry heart? Don't want to risk another exit [. . .]

Find I no longer care about bombing of German civilians. Feeling v. much 'let them have it'. Vindictiveness due to what Londoners have had to suffer. We have had to stand a lot on account of bad choice of leaders + why should they escape for the same mistake. Has the war made me vicious? I'm actually rejoicing at the thought of it being carried into Germany.

[. . .] Do write & reassure me of the wisdom of returning.

12 September^e, KCT to RMT in Wales
Papers full of bad travelling conditions back from Leeds. Are they exaggerating? Will definitely ring Mon. & again later in week if you have not had time to probe matters fully. It is silly to come back if another week or two will give time for danger to pass don't you agree? Also, I want to be sure the crowds have gone. We don't want another 'sardine journey'.

[. . .] We'll have some pints soon. Glad the food is good that's something. Dream quite obvious. Poor souls – what a mess.

Don't worry about the Volume. It will be very different working on it when we three are together again & you & I can talk things over in our easy chairs when S.P. is tucked up in bed.

The images of a cosy domestic life are powerful: once the family is together again everything will be all right. Kay tried to respond to Richard's request for help in untangling Hancock's plans for his war history. Where was the research assistant to come from? 'He or she is to be no makeshift. You must have the right person.' She was ill with a stomach bug – the problem with motherhood was that you couldn't even take a day off. Her mother had written to her with news of mysterious explosions in London and saying 'the time is not ripe for our return'.

The mysterious noises took the form of 'a thunderclap, followed by a noise like a faraway express train'. The press were instructed to treat them as town gas explosions, but in November Churchill admitted in the House that their origin was a new rocket attack. This was to continue past the end of the year; in all, 1,054 rockets fell on Britain, about half on London.[6] The main damage was not to the British morale but to houses; by the end of September 1944 a total of 1.1 million houses in the London region had been totally destroyed or seriously damaged by the German air attack.[7] Thousands of builders, condemned to spend their nights in Wembley Stadium or some other improvised camp, were drafted in from the provinces to embark on a programme of major repairs. The main civilian casualties from the rockets were 168 people doing their Christmas shopping in Woolworths in Deptford; another 120 ended up in hospital.[8]

Richard knew about the rockets before everyone else did and told Kay about them on the phone. In their letters the explosions were referred to as 'IT'. The first rockets landed on London on 8 September, the day the government announced the formal end of its evacuation scheme. The areas affected were Chiswick and Epping. 'Curse these bloody people,' said Richard. Kay and Ann's return would have to be deferred; he would visit Wakefield for a weekend instead.

18 September, RMT to KCT in Wakefield

I've been so worried about you. Nothing since Thursday morning when you told me about being sick. I've been imagining all sorts of things & wondering how I could find out and whether I should come up to W. straight away. I sat and watched the phone last night praying that you would ring. And now I am hoping that you ring to-night. If you don't I shall send a telegram. I am definitely coming on Friday & will let you know later what train.

Now I suppose you will say that you are worrying about me. I'll give you the 'low-down' on Friday (don't want to commit to paper). But for your ears it is 2. Only a very small number so far but enough to keep you & Ann away. Far less need to worry than during the small F.B. days – these are so few. Perhaps 5 a night on S.E. England. So don't worry darling [...] Now let us assume that from this week-end you may have another 2/3 weeks. Let us look it in the face, darling, & be cheerful. Well, that & the weather being so is there anything you want me to bring? Clothes I mean. Spinach? Tomatoes? Runners?

I shall try & catch the 10.30 Friday or if not the 1.40. I prefer to meet you (& probably Ann) at the Station you see. But will send P.C.

Don't forget: we must have time to talk this week-end.

Review of BPW [*Birth, Poverty and Wealth*] for you to read. Macintosh just appointed to the Chair of Pub. Hlth. at London & regarded by Lewis, Jerry and others as the Chief hope of British Medicine in the future.

18 September, KCT to RMT in London
It is hard. Just back from a vain endeavour to phone you (2 hour delay on line) [...]

Oh, the ups & downs of this life [...] Is it any wonder I've lots more grey hairs?

[...] Today I met a sad couple. Baby 14 months old & he has to go to the Far East. They have till Thurs. We are better off than that provided you are safe at the end of the madness beloved.

I must change my tune & talk of precious Ann. She's grown up with a bow on her hair to keep it out of her eyes. Her playtime is an exhausting business. You'll be wanting more tea to help you to recover when she's gone to bed. She got herself in an 'orrible mess today in the garden pulling mint to pieces & trying to eat it while we gardened [...]

If we have to plan several weeks more here & you come next weekend please bring A's 3 white frocks made of stuff like her nighties AND my 2 pink winter vests if you can find them in the kitchen. Then we'll manage.

Urgent. Money please. £1 left.

Darling it will be soon won't it? And then don't let us part any more – ever. So tired of perpetual wireless programmes I don't want to hear. Time I had some beer & went to Chis. Emp. & sat on a cttee, & cooked my family a meal. Oh Richard!!

This was to be Richard's last weekend visit to Wakefield. During it, he and Kay discussed how he should respond to Hancock's plans for the war history. He was still endlessly busy. While the war history was his official full-time job, he had two other major irons still in the fire: the social medicine project with Jerry Morris, and his work for the Eugenics Society. In September the *Medical Officer* at last published his and Jerry's paper on social factors and rheumatic heart disease. The paper followed their earlier one on juvenile rheumatism and both had been a struggle to put together, with many passages travelling to and from India on the famous aerogrammes. When Richard told Hancock this in Wales, Hancock thought it a tremendous achievement in such difficult conditions.

As Richard noted in his 18 September letter to Kay, his book *Birth, Poverty and Wealth* was still getting attention, not least for its disputation of the eugenic view that working-class infants died because they came from inferior stock. Ursula Grant-Duff of the Eugenics Society proposed a meeting on infantile mortality. Blacker was unsure whether the lowering of infant deaths was desirable on eugenic grounds, given who would be likely to survive in these circumstances.[9] Ursula proposed a Dr de Swiet, M.O.H. for Paddington, as a speaker, and Richard was called on to arbitrate. Unsurprisingly, he had no time for any other extra-curricular work, and turned down invitations such as one to speak at Leeds University on any aspect of population[10] and another from the journal *Mother and Child* to write on any topic related to maternal and child welfare,[11] a subject with which he was considerably occupied, both personally and professionally.

Returning to the flat, via the allotment where he filled his empty rucksack with 629 green and yellow tomatoes, Richard decided they all needed a definite target for Kay and Ann's return home. He wrote to Kay proposing 9 October, or, failing that, 16 October – his birthday. Things might be moving on the what-do-we-do-with-Titmuss-after-the-war front; Hancock was talking to Clay about a fellowship for him at Nuffield. A proposed part-time appointment as statistical adviser in Luton working with Fred Grundy displeased Hancock, who felt it should be put off until Richard had made more progress with the history. Richard wondered whether Ann looked round in bed for him after he left Wakefield. Wednesday 27 September began for Richard with the grading of the tomatoes:

RMT to KCT in Wakefield

So many are split and will go bad. Decided to pick out all good ones and separate to ripen. I shall thus be living on a diet of half tomatoes. The Townsends [flat neighbours] back with a front page story in D.T. of '4 days behind the German lines'. Haven't read it. The baby is a noisy one – I heard it at 11.30 last night.

Great rush to-day about everything affecting me. 9.30 with Grundy to Lyons and 2 sessions with H on my plan. You were quite *right*, beloved: he likes it much and has made few changes and then only English (not that we were wrong anywhere). I am glad he is pleased with it. Sir Edward is to read it to-morrow. The vital Cabinet meeting is next Tuesday.

The upshot of my talks with Grundy and H. comes to this. Appointment as Adviser to Luton Corporation on statistics and social surveys. Six months and then see. Time: about 4 days a month – some Sats. and evenings. This will keep the thing alive until say June 1945. Payment: retaining fee or honorarium. Now how much for say 6 months. 650? 675? or what? Must include travelling. Let me know as I am going to the Public Health Ctee. at Luton next Tuesday at 6. Staying with Grundy the night.

[...] Mrs H has come back from Anglesey with dreadful cold. Poor W.K.!

About 4 people are wanting me for week-end. M. Hayes. Connie. Meinhardt. Hay etc. Shall probably refuse the lot; do McNalty and go home and drink with Harold Sat. night.

[...] Oceans of love to you and Annpenny.

There was one bright spot on their social landscape: Bob Farr of Barton Hill Farm, where Kay had stayed at the beginning of the war and when Ann was a few weeks old, was getting married. She went out to buy him and his prospective bride a present. She also splashed out on a coloured dress for Ann – 'hellishly' expensive at 30/- plus 5 coupons, but a fee Richard had recently received from the BBC for a broadcast would cover it, wouldn't it? Uncle Bert and Aunt Nora, despite their kindness, were beginning to irritate Kay with their *Daily Mail* politics:

28 September[e], KCT to RMT in London

D.M. [*Daily Mail*] shouting about how S. Security *could* provide us with more children. Absolute blarney. A.N. & U.B. not much better. I'm naughty & have developed counter measures. When A.N. reads me a bit from the D.M. completely ignoring the fact that I'd absorbed the contents in a scan through earlier in the day I insist on reading a bit from N.S. [. . .] On several occasions I haven't voiced an opinion but have asked a few careful questions which have been a bit disturbing to the other side. Don't worry I won't overdo it. It's just a new game I play all by myself.

[. . .] Tomatoes. What a total. Hope I can make us some of our favourite soup.

[. . .] Afraid the infant didn't look for you in bed on Mon. You hadn't become a habit in 3 nights I suppose.

29 September[e], KCT to RMT in London

A. has a 4th tooth. She was quiet all night yesterday but (did I tell you) cried about 20 mins during the evening. That was all & it was through this morning.

What developments!! You have managed Luton business v. nicely I think provided you don't land yourself in for weekends there. Presumably some of your part of the job can be done at home. Have arrived at a figure of £100 in this way.

If full time say £840 per year.

I.e. per month of say 24 working days £70

Present arrangement say, 6 working days per month £17.10.0

Multiply by 6 £105.0.0.

Suggest you throw in travelling & charge £100. Just had an idea. Could it be arranged they paid expenses? Would it save paying so much Income Tax as would it come to the same thing if you can step up return expenses for job. What a curse not to be able to talk it over.

Did not mention you in letter to Bob – whether or not you would be at wedding I mean. Didn't want to involve you in any difficulties.

I believe Brian [Nora and Bert's son] is coming on leave

Oct 10th. It would be nice to leave him his home & mother to himself. Do you think we might make it Oct 9th?

[. . .] We won't bother with Rose Hip Jelly thank you. U.B. has picked some & for the entire evening they've been topping & tailing them. AND I've done some, & they aren't finished yet & its 10 p.m. I've a reaction against domesticity. I'm still prepared to cook us all meals & keep us clean & tidy but it must be in the simplest way possible. We'll buy A some Rose Hip syrup this winter & some blackcurrant puree.

And I don't want such a big garden after all. Let's have a big bit of lawn when we have one. Plenty of room for A. to run about.

What are Lafittes doing about returning to Chiswick?

The end of the correspondence is in sight. In the last few exchanges, there is a long letter from Richard which spells out some of the parameters of 'our war history'. He's proud of the job Kay is doing up in Wakefield, still bothering about the outside world as well as successfully mothering Ann – at least successfully compared to his brother's wife. He's beginning to realize that the book he's writing may turn out to be a classic in social history and the job he does on it may affect his and Kay and Ann's lives in a fundamental way:

30 September^e, RMT to KCT in Wakefield
At last I have some time to write to you properly. I have got the wireless on because it is so lonely, and although I am surrounded with a medley of books and papers I do not feel like work. It is hell isn't it particularly in these quieter moments?

First of all let me try and put the situation to you. For about a week after the first 10 days or so there were no 4's. I have now learnt (what I did not know before and therefore alters what I have told you) that 4's have continued to arrive – but not in the London area. A few a night are hitting England – where, I really don't know, but suspect E. Anglia. Whether these are coming from inside Ger. I don't know and I don't know whether anyone else does. What the next few months will hold is just anybody's guess and there is no point in my arguing the debit and credit sides. What is apparent are the warnings from prominent people that the war may last into 1945. At the moment we are right in the middle of one of these well-known stagnation periods. I should guess that before the bad weather really arrives – say within the next three weeks – we shall see a big offensive launched from the West and by the Russians from the East. Meanwhile, we are having the usual dose of about 5–10 FBS a night. Note that these like the others are all at night or in the evening, i.e. darkness. In the Chiswick Emp. last night with H. we had two alerts and another one early this morning. Nothing to be heard and each one lasted not longer than about 15 mins. Frankly, this sort of situation – sporadic odds and ends – may well last for another 2/3 months. What then do we do? I have told you the worst. On the credit side we have the unknown factors. It seems to me that we have two alternatives: 1. To continue to hang on like this, perhaps for the winter, reviewing the situation from week to week, with a fortnightly or three-weekly visit from me. 2. To return home in a fortnight leaving behind as an insurance the stated possibility that you and Ann may return at any time possibly without more than a few hours notice. Of course there are a great many factors to be considered; your safety, Ann's health and safety, both your health in Wakefield, feeding in the next two months, and the effects on both of us of separation. I need not say anymore because you can weigh them all up just as I have tried to do. It is awful though. Now write and let me know what you think. But – I know what you are going to say [. . .]

The Allotment: What do I do with full-grown carrots, beetroots and youngish onions? Can they be stored?

H. and I had a quiet evening; a few drinks, Chis. Emp. and then I made omelettes for both of us – he enjoyed his. He is very worried abut Margaret and Blue. Blue is in a highly nervous, irritable condition. Margaret I am afraid has gone wrong. Physically she is, according to H. perfectly sound. But she won't take solids, she insists on being played with (or having toys) when she is fed, she won't sleep during

the day, she always wakes up at 4 in the night, she screams
if she does not get her own way or what she wants, potting
takes an hour quite often and is then a failure and generally
(so thinks H.) she is miserable and fractious most of the day.
In other words, she is wearing Blue out who, to get a little
peace and quiet, gives in after perhaps a refusal for half-an-
hour. It seems to me that this inconsistency is fatal. Surely,
it is better to give in at once and so lessen the importance
of things rather than this half-hearted struggle?

Would you advise a fortnight's regime of strictness, of
suffering screams until Margaret is quite exhausted? Or
should we not say anything until we have seen them? In any
case you had better not write to Blue. But let me know what
you think. H. is awfully afraid of having a spoilt, wilful child.

No, darling, my pride (or whatever you call it) is not hurt
because Ann did not look round for me. But it is natural
that I should feel sorry about it; that I should want to share
her with you. This is all part of *our* war history.

I wanted to hug you when I read about your 'little game'
with B. and N. I feel so proud of you when I think how easy
it would be just to sink into a coma of the daily round;
thinking and bothering nothing about the outside world. O
darling how lucky I was [. . .]

I am now going to have a shot at the last bit of McNalty.
Then to phone Hayes and get some supper. To-morrow I
suppose the parent will come. At any rate I shall have discharged my duty (if she does) for some time. To-morrow I
will get some spinach and post it off to you on Monday.
Tuesday night I shall stay at Luton and I suppose I had better
put in a short appearance at the wedding. That means that
on Monday I must pack for Wednesday at St P.

[. . .] Both Hay and Chester (Hancock showed it to him)
like my Plan very much. All round approval in fact. It *could*
of course be a book that might become a classic in Social
History. I realise its immense potentialities and importance.
In other words, the quality and quantity of my work in the
next 18 months may well settle the rest of our lives together
– and Ann's. But I am full, very full, of doubts about my
capacity. I know you will help dear; help to shut me up in

the bedroom and a lot more. But essentially I have got to worry all this out myself; all the concentrated thinking, most of the ideas and so on. And, at this moment, I don't feel like it. But that is enough for to-night. I will add a line or two to-morrow.

Sunday morning. It is a glorious morning; it would be of course. I would much rather it have been wet and miserable – that might have helped me to settle down. And if it had been wet the parent would not have come. As it is I shall have to go and meet her I suppose. But she cannot stay after about 5 fortunately.

I rang Hayes last night just as they had come in from the pictures. 'The Song of Bernadette.' Father said it was a miserable film and that when he goes to the pictures he goes to be amused. Anyway, he seemed to think that Mother enjoyed it. I expect you will have heard from her about all the activities that are going on for the rehabilitation of Marler Road and the search for a flat. The flat business seems to be pretty hopeless.

I've finished grading the tomatoes and have washed up the things since Friday. Chops for lunch, beans and pots. If the parent wants a sweet and does not like stewed rhubarb she will have to make something. I shall leave that to her. It will keep her busy [. . .] said he rather ruthlessly. Well, it is a shame, having to live like this.

A couple of days later he wrote to thank Kay for her computations re the Luton job. He agreed with her: they must make domestic life after the war as simple as possible. If it occurred to him that his growing reputation might make this difficult, he didn't say so:

2 October, *RMT to KCT in Wakefield*
I can see that the minimum must be £100 and your idea about expenses is a good one. I would rather they paid expenses as the I. Tax people are bound to be difficult about such unusual claims.

I am not surprised, darling, that you are suffering from a reaction against domesticity. You have had such a time of it for 4 months. I completely agree; let us make it as simple as possible, enjoy Ann, have some colour and friends while we can and do something useful. Yes, after my experiences with the allotment I too don't want an acre of a garden. Just enough to experiment with.

I forgot to leave with you the Times on HSC [review of the rheumatic heart disease paper]. Here it is and you might also like to read Postan's article on War Production. Now I must get some soup and write to Jerry. Just had an Am from him and this is what he says about my news of the History. 'Here is the most thrilling thing that could have happened, the most amazing (considering the public school you were at), and you don't seem at all excited. This volume will be in every single public library in the country, in every town hall, in the syllabuses of umpteen university courses, part of the training of umpteen public health workers, social workers, and L.G. officials [. . .] Tell Kay from me that you are the most unspoilable person that ever was.' It isn't that as I've told you. But it is nice of him all the same.

[. . .] Lilian rang at 10.30. Would I deliver the toast of the bride's father & mother!! Both wanted me to. Of all the infernal cheek! I refused. There is to be a reception – 60 people – Joan & Gordon going to B.H. to-day – & Meg – & Peter is to be a page!! What utter nonsense! If I go – and I suppose I should put in an appearance – I shall have some funny stories for you.

Kay's last letter spoke of the tensions in Wakefield, with Uncle Bert and Auntie Nora understandably wanting their house to them-selves again. This, after all, was what Kay herself wanted: to be with Richard in their own home doing all her job rather than just half of it:

3 October', KCT to RMT in London
My dear Husband,
Your letter came yesterday afternoon and I have now read it five – or is it six times. Bless you for every word of it. Darling it is so sad. Our situation I mean. I am afraid I broke down and had a bit of a cry when it came and I told Auntie all about it. She admitted what I have been feeling for some

days now that (more or less though in not quite so many words) they will be glad to have their home to themselves again and I know they would both prefer to have Brian here without us. It is only natural after all this time. Just put us in their place. At the same time she said how sorry she was for us and how she understood and that we really must not add to our burden of decision by considering them. She really was very sweet about it and it would be quite all right if we had to come again. But oh darling I couldn't. Not in the winter up here.

I am afraid I have spent a good deal of the night thinking things over and I think I have faced up to the kind of home coming it will mean. I have weighed little Ann on one side and you on the other (I do come sort of in between I know and felt almost torn in two at times). After all the position is really immeasurably better than when we returned home before. Whatever they try to do to us now they can't keep it up for long. I think the all important thing at the moment is the effect of separation on us. We have reached the limit and must be together again. If I had known what Ann's first year would bring forth, I should certainly not have had the courage to produce her.

Now to get on with the business. I can't see that the additional few days under your plan make so much difference to the situation [. . .] I am in favour of 9th *if* you have no appointments for Sat and could come up here then [. . .] It will make a difference here when Brian comes. If I stay I shall feel horribly in the way. A. will have to go into the end room – with the risk of the what not chain waking her as it is so near. Also I do feel she should be in a big cot as soon as possible now. But still we'll stick it out if we have to. I talked to Auntie about Brian and how we would like to help and that if you could talk with him you would know better what he was fitted for and so on in order to cover your being here 13th – 16th and she said she would like you to know him etc. I have done my best darling.

[. . .] We can talk about Margaret and Blue. It makes me rather frightened about my capability of handling Ann. I do so want to bring her up well. I feel that the war situation must have affected Blue. I am sure you are right. Inconsistency is fatal [. . .]

If you are not coming this weekend if you have time bury beetroots. Cover them with soil and mark the spot. That is to keep the frost out of them. Dig up carrots and onions.

Darling, I want more than anything else in the world to be with you, to have you working in the flat and cook you meals and take you cups of coffee and give you lots of hugs. And I want to read what you are writing and discuss it with you. I'm only doing half my job and have been living on that basis for too long. And I want to see mother and father and lots of our friends.

A. is awake and I must get the orange juice and take this to the post. She is in her pink outfit. Very cold wind. It fits her nicely but the leggings are a bit queer.

Shall now try & look forward at least a year. All this will be past history & have sunk into insignificance.

So full of love for you sweetheart.

Yours, Kay

It did. The letters were consigned to the brown suitcase, where they stayed for over forty years, though who knows how many times Kay (or Richard) took them out and read them as a record of those early months of parenthood, when Richard's writing of 'the' war history seemed no recompense for the quality of the one they were forced to live. On 9 October Richard brought Kay and Ann back to London. Brian Buckland was left to enjoy a quiet time with his parents unencumbered with the cries of a baby who might be woken at the pull of a lavatory chain, and the troubles of a couple who had been apart too long. Back in the flats, Richard did all the 'concentrated thinking' he needed to finish his 'amazing' narrative of the life and times of the wartime government and of families just like, and unlike, his own; and Kay, presumably, cooked his meals and looked after the baby, and talked to Richard about his work in the evenings. That winter of 1944–5 was the coldest for fifty years. There was little fuel, and food shortages, particularly of fresh vegetables, must have put a premium on the yield of the allotment on Turnham Green. For Christmas there was hardly a turkey to be had, and the toy shops were virtually empty.

Towards the end of his war history, in a chapter called 'The Last Phase', Richard would later observe that 'Nothing has so far been said about the difficulties which children and parents may have encountered in resuming relationships at the end of evacuation [. . .] A few questions and a few tentative generalisations must, therefore, suffice. Whether or not an emotionally abnormal situation developed in a home depended on many factors; predominantly on what separation had meant to parents and children. But that is merely the opening question.'[12]

ELEVEN

—⟫⟪—

The road to Acton

Richard's 'opening question' about the meaning of the war to parents and children is only one of many posed by the narrative of this book. In writing it, I had a number of different aims. The first was to do my mother's frustrated attempts to tell the story of her/their lives some justice by collating from the carefully pruned contents of the brown suitcase an account of how it all was – meeting the gangling, argumentative young Dick Titmuss with his purple prose and his aspirations to be more than an insurance man; working for peace and for the successful publication of his peregrinations through the emerging world of demography and social policy; having a baby while the bombs dropped and there seemed no greater idiocy than believing that their civilization would have a future; and particularly – because it belonged to that independent identity of hers which predated her meeting with Richard – all the labouring with the Rev. Birch and the shoe-mending and knitting of the unemployed men and women of Fulham, which brought to Kay as their self-appointed welfarist many small victories of money raised and men sent to the country for the open air who got jobs as well, and women who, despite being over thirty, got themselves retrained as chiropodists, much to the chagrin of the local labour exchange, which wasn't nearly as efficient as Kay Miller in re-organizing people's lives.

All my mother's throwaway remarks – 'Resolve to set about planning the book which is to be written one day'; 'I will write and write in future'; 'What of the writer?' – have now borne fruit, of a kind. Whether she would have approved of the result is another question. But if I'm convinced of one thing, it is that my mother left me the suitcase because she wanted her story to be told. She could have left the contents of the suitcase to someone else. More obviously, in view of her pruning tendencies, she could have thrown it all away. She knew the kind of line I was likely to take. She was well aware that I would notice that shift of position from Richard Titmuss trying to get a look into the important world of Kay Miller which is depicted so wonderfully in the photograph of the Duke of Kent in Fulham, to the world of Richard Titmuss and his important work helped by the ever-patient Kay, which becomes the narrative and meaning of their marriage thereafter. The fact that *he* became her work was something *she* was proud of; but it didn't give her the same satisfaction as the work she once had which was her own. Most of all, perhaps, my mother wanted me to know the person she was before I was born. Her wish to write was, I believe, about reclaiming some creative sense of herself as the agent of her own life. The Kay Titmuss who wrote to her husband from the solid little house opposite the park in Wakefield was not the same as the Kay Miller who wrote in 1934 of the deplorable way in which men put women on a pedestal and lose sight of their own capacity to know themselves. She who railed against Richard's inability to tie himself to her in marriage and his eternal messing around with unpublishable pamphlets on unchristian themes was distinguished later for the wholly uncritical regard in which she held all his ventures.

There are many more chapters in the lives of Richard and Kay Titmuss beyond the narrative of this book. I've dealt only with the years from 1934 to 1944; he died in 1973 and she in 1987, so there's quite a story still to tell. But the story in this book is not only about the beginning of it all; it's also the *essence* of what happened afterwards. Without it, what came next can't be understood.

My father was fond of signing the prefaces to his later books, 'R.M.T., Acton'. The house with the yellow door, in front of which the Titmusses are poised the day he got his CBE, was on the borders of middle-class Ealing and working-class Acton. When he'd become a professor and his expertise was properly acknowledged, 'Acton' sounded more impressively egalitarian; whereas when he was still climbing the ladder, it was better to describe the flat in Chiswick as near the comely Kew Gardens (rather than, as in fact it was, near Acton). The second task of this book has been to describe that very project of developing the career of Richard Titmuss that became Kay's own. It's the story of the road to Acton. Who was Richard Titmuss? Where did he come from? How did he get there? These questions, only partially answered in the official fable of Richard Titmuss's rise to fame, receive a somewhat fuller answer here. It's a complex answer, dependent as it is on the annexing of Richard Titmuss's wife's energies to the bettering of his career and the unashamed, though at times nicely subtle, plundering of the social and material resources of the semi-rich and powerful. But at the same time, we can see the intellectual shape unfolding: out of the keen young insurance man who computes life expectancies for fun in his spare time, from the tight-collared Mr Titmuss of the Young Liberals and the Fleet Street Parliament, who speaks with passion about why we should not all be cannon fodder, comes the respected author of *Poverty and Population*, and of *Birth, Poverty and Wealth*; the writer of many well-honed articles and many well-targeted letters to newspapers; the recognized population expert and pronouncer on matters of social class and policy; the historian with an office in Whitehall, and with friends among the clever and famous; the man with a great academic career stretching ahead of him, including guaranteed channels to the ears and minds of holders of political and social power. The story of Richard Titmuss is about his ideas and about his beliefs; the expertise he was able to build up, the imaginative vision of society he projected. But it's also the story of how this expertise and vision crossed the line that divides the unknown from the known. He could have remained unknown, but he didn't. Why didn't he?

Unlike many of the people whose names appear in this book, Richard Titmuss didn't have a public school education and he didn't go to university. He couldn't rely on Eton or Winchester or Oxford or Cambridge to provide the easy camaraderie that helps to make a successful public life in the class-bound society of Britain. In discovering the huge disparities in life chances between those at the bottom and those at the top of the social scale, he was at the same time commenting on his own lack of fortune in not being born at the top. Awareness of class was central to his intellectual perception of society. But it was also constantly felt as an aspect of his own life.

The third aim that underlies the writing of this book was to look at what the story tells us about certain aspects of the history of the twentieth century. Here I have in mind not class as Richard Titmuss understood it, but a different meaning of class: the divisions between men and women. The thesis is simple, but disturbing: none of the major traditions of British party politics has been centrally concerned with inequalities between men and women. As a consequence, there has been no concerted attempt to tackle them. Therefore, we still live in a gender-unequal society. I think the story of how both Richard Titmuss's work and his relationship with Kay developed shows how limp the liberal/socialist vision really is when confronted with the enormous socially structured inequalities which divide the genders. The concern with pronatalism, with the competitive nature of capitalism, and with the unequal effects of the social environment which marked Richard's work during the period covered in this book appeared radical to some and not to others. It was radical to those in the eugenics movement who believed in the concentration of 'good' genes among the socially well-endowed. It wasn't radical enough to those who thought they could see clearly that eugenics wasn't the same as social science. And one way in which it wasn't radical at all was in its perfect sublimation of the interests of women as a class in the survival of the bourgeois family. From this point of view, the story of Kay and Richard Titmuss's relationship is a case study in a particular practice of social relations – one which aligns domesticity with women, and men with the public political world – one which says in marriage there are two people, a man and his wife.

Women are more interested in families than men, because more of their lives and labours and loves are bound up in them. But the family as an institution is not woman-friendly. There is a tension in there between the rights of women to be free and to be themselves, and the need for somebody to be devoted to the welfare of the family.[1] Perhaps the most striking aspect of all that debate in the 1930s and 1940s about the falling birth rate and what was to be done about it is the way it bypasses women as the key actors.[2] It's women, after all, who still bear children, not families. The Titmusses and their friends (and enemies) spoke of families as little entities with minds of their own. When Richard wrote their book, *Parents Revolt*, he turned reproduction into a political matter – something governments ought to be concerned about. But from this politicization he omitted gender. There were only parents, not mothers and fathers. There was no sense of division within families, of *her* interests not being the same as *his*. The mark of a good marriage was that they were. But whose interests dominated whose? The answer, so far as the Titmusses' own marriage is concerned, I think is clear. In this respect, they weren't unusual; far from it. And that's the point: in following tradition, they weren't breaking away from it, and this espousal of traditional values weakened the quality of the political imagination (*his* or *hers*) brought to bear on public issues.

There were other models of marriage around them. There was sociologist David Glass and his sociologist wife, Ruth; there was social biologist Lancelot Hogben and his demographer wife, Enid Charles; there was historian Keith Hancock and his wife Theaden, the BBC producer; there were the two doctors, Arthur St George Huggett and his wife, Esther Killick. Two of the women in this quartet didn't even change their names. But the Titmusses' closest friends – Maurice and Sigrid Newfield, François and Eileen Lafitte, and Jerry and Galia Morris – were all couples in which the wives didn't at the time pursue separate professional lives. The variety of patterns outside the inner circle did offer actual choices to be made; one has only to read Dora Russell's relentlessly political autobiography[3] to see that. But there's no equivalent in the Titmuss letters of the moment in Dora and Bertie's relationship when they have their first argument about tying up parcels. When he asked her to tie up a parcel for him, 'I suggested that he might tie it up himself. "I have never," he said with great dignity, "tied up a parcel in my life and I am not going to begin now." With equal dignity I replied that I had not married him to tie up his parcels.'[4] There's scarcely a hint of the possibility of female independence, and no suggestion of feminism, in the Titmusses' letters. There aren't any choices to be made. Or, rather, the choices were made when they chose each other. The wife's work served the husband's, providing for him that eponymous thing, a *refuge*. There are many famous examples: H. G. Wells, patient of the Titmusses' friend, the eugenist Maurice Newfield, had a wife who 'accepted his tumultuous infidelities, and in her own exquisite manner had created for him and their two boys a home of great beauty, a place of *refuge* from the noisy public world';[5] Julian Huxley, whom the Titmusses knew, praised his own wife who 'always supported me against carping critics [. . .] accompanied me on many of my travels [. . .] bore patiently with my humours and faithfully tended me through my periodic bouts of depression [. . .] Most important of all, her love has helped me to acquire inner peace and understanding, and has given me a *refuge*.'[6] Ruth Guiness, eugenist statistician R. A. Fisher's wife, bore him eight children, cared for them and him and his home, looked after the mice and the crops that were the subject of his experiments, tended the poultry and the garden, read him *The Times* every morning, listened to all his ideas, and entertained his friends at weekends. When, exhausted, she excused herself briefly one afternoon, having been ordered by her doctor to rest, he accused her of not loving him.[7]

My mother kept a file of obituaries, torn out of newspapers, in which she lodged the records of the deaths of the people she and Richard had known. Two of the obituaries she preserved are those of Alva and Gunnar Myrdal, the Swedish population experts and social reformers. They were an example of a couple who spanned both public and private worlds; they were parents and Nobel laureates – he in economics in 1964 and she in peace in 1968. Unlike Richard and Kay Titmuss, the Myrdals made intimate connections between the population crisis and the archaic position of women. In *Nation and Family*, published in 1945, and incorporating the argument of her earlier book with Gunnar on the population problem, Alva said:

> If society wants to encourage and not punish family building, it will have to give men and women freedom in their efforts to have families and to support them. The forced celibacy or sterility among wage-earning women is a sign of society's incapacity to adjust itself to modern conditions. A population policy of democratic vision thus creates a new stronghold for married women's fight for their right to work. At the same time the frontier among feminist groups should be shifted in order to denote this new interlocking of individual and social interests. What is to be guarded is not so much the 'married woman's right to work' as the 'working woman's right to marry and have children'.[8]

This, of course, would mean changing men as well: 'parental discomfort, work and constraint' would all have to be equalized, with fathers taking a greater part in childcare, and taking it in turns with mothers to wake early in the morning and stay home in the evenings. The list of necessary reforms was comprehensive: free health care for all mothers and children; subsidized housing for families with children; free school meals and children's clothes; free state education from nursery through to professional training; subsidized or free holidays; increased security of employment for parents; shared social responsibility for children with handicaps.[9] Many of these reforms were translated into practice in post-war Sweden and remain part of the welfare state there today. The differences between what the Titmusses represented and what the Myrdals did were two; first, after her part in *Parents Revolt*, Kay Titmuss retired from the intellectual scene; second, the Myrdals turned a concern with population into a practical social policy whose major platform was attempting to do something about the position of *women* in the family.

In 1944, when this book ends, the war wasn't even over. But most people believed it soon would be; they looked forward not only to peace but to the possibility of making Britain a better place to live in. In November, Winston Churchill, newly back from Moscow, spoke in the House of Commons of tradition being 'the flywheel of the state'. He beamed at his co-politicians and told them all, 'We are a decent lot. All of us. The whole nation.'[10] There began to be talk of an early election. Richard and Kay Titmuss and baby Ann went back to London to get on with their lives. Kay and Richard stopped writing letters to each other, and Kay put her diary away, though she did get it out for a few moments four years later to note despondently: 'What a waste of a book. Found it in a drawer. Life has changed since the last entry. Ann is now 4½. We have had a spate of holidays: Norfolk, Cornwall & the farm. Weather appalling. The coldest since 1922 in July. We are all well & R is struggling to complete Vol I of the history.'[11] It shouldn't have surprised Richard to find there were problems with publishing the history. He had a trail of unpublishable books behind him, and his war history was too intimate, too revealing a book for the Ministry – full of gossip, rife with unflattering facts. Only after Keith Hancock threatened to resign did publication go ahead.[12] By then Richard was about to move on, and all Hancock's efforts on his behalf had paid off. After a short spell running a social medicine research unit with Jerry Morris, in 1950 Richard joined Carr-Saunders's LSE, the academic home of so many of those who flit in and out of the Titmuss letters. But what happened next is another story.

Some of the peace and reconstruction Richard and Kay had hoped for had come to pass. In 1942, William Beveridge had published his Report on Social Insurance and Allied Services, the writing and researching of which he'd been very reluctant to take on, expecting far more from the War Cabinet, and recalling, with his friend Keynes, their successful part in the running of the previous war. Beveridge may have cried from disappointment when they gave him the job,[13] but it was a job well done in the sense that the Beveridge Report was subsequently seen to lay the framework for the post-war welfare state. Although it didn't establish the National Health Service, or provide safeguards against mass unemployment, it did institutionalize the important idea that every citizen had the right to a decent standard of life. Beveridge explicitly considered women's needs, but the language in which he did so was that of companionate marriage; it was in this setting, their proper one, that women had the right to expect fair shares. The Beveridge reforms were intended to help the tired housewife who'd spent too many hours touting her ration books around during the war.

Then, in 1945, there was the landslide victory of Labour, totally unexpected by the Conservatives, but presumably reflecting the mood of the country for a break with the past. Clement Attlee's government rapidly introduced the 'from the cradle to the grave' security that had been the goal of many British social reformers. The last plank of this, the National Health Service, came into force the day Kay wrote her last despondent diary entry. So this should really have been a day of celebration.

It must have seemed, then, that a good deal of what Richard Titmuss and his wife had hoped for had come to be. It was a time of consensus, of optimism. But a welfare state based on the two-roles model of women was to be a disappointing chameleon, a deeply flawed emblem of man's belief that in providing for his fellow men he would also treat women with the human respect they deserved. Post-war Britain was an era of deceptive ideology for women – a time when they were told they'd won their battles, they were equal now. The six years of Attlee's government were ironically a time of great cultural conservatism. Out of this stagnation came the 'permissiveness' of the sixties. But this was ideology, too – a sinister boil breaking on the carcass of British imperialism.[14] The Festival of Britain in 1951 summed up the Labour Government's achievements – universal state education and health care, the nationalization of key industries. It was a celebration of an inward-looking nationalism, the illusion of equality. It was that very illusion of equality that bedevilled women, but it came to them with all the authority of tradition as their parents had lived it. The cosy dream of the happy family in the little house was the landscape of all good women. Not even the crowning of a woman as head of state – the coronation of Queen Elizabeth II in 1953 – disturbed the idyll, for the queen had a family, too – indeed, the queen *was* the family, the family was the commonwealth, a commonwealth of nations, all friends together under the same flag.

In all this women were strangely classless. Family life retained its status as haven: consensus and harmony were thought to reign in the kitchen as well as the nation. Hoovers arrived, which was good for women's two roles. Men went on having one. The welfare state supported 'the family' but only if it was a conventional one. What developed was a sequential arrangement for women, whereby a period 'at work' would be followed by one at home rearing children and another combining motherhood with part-time work. This gave women the idea they had the best of both worlds, but (or therefore) it co-existed with massive formal and informal discrimination against them in almost every field. At the same time, the cultural symbol of The Family became more important, as emotional attachment (later 'bonding') between mothers and children was discovered, and as psychiatrists spoke out on behalf of children, which meant saying something about their mothers, too. And as life got more compli-cated, the private world of the family assumed even greater signifi-cance as the source and support for personal identity. Any claims women might have made for greater autonomy irrespective of their family roles were countered by the need to 'rebuild' family life.[15]

Beneath all this history lurks a constantly disturbing question: are women citizens? The Victorians had been sure that they weren't. In the Second World War, they undoubtedly were, though the achieve-ments of women in taking over men's roles and responsibilities are mostly limited in this book to Kay Titmuss's sporadic existence as a single parent. But there's the nub of the problem. Equal for women means being like men. Equal for men doesn't mean being like women. So long as men and women inhabit different spheres and there is no *collective* lifting of the boundaries between the home and 'work', the public world will be the important one and the private world of the home will only shadow it as a poor relation. As feminism has taught us, western political thought 'rests on a conception of the "political" that is constructed through the exclusion of women and all that is represented by femininity and women's bodies [. . .] Manhood and politics go hand in hand [. . .] women have been designated as the upholders of the private foundation of the political world of men.'[16] It goes back to Greek society – to the age of Plato. Man's public speech happened outside the household in the *polis*. Only free men could speak. Women and slaves were confined to private realms of discourse: 'Their tongues were silent on the public issues of the day. Their speech was severed from the name of action: it filled the air, echoed for a time, and faded from official memory with none to record it or to embody it in public forms.'[17] '*Faded from official memory*' is a highly loaded phrase in the light of some of the material drawn on for this book.

It would take a lifetime to 'tell the full story of the public and the private', [18] and I'm definitely not trying to do that here. But there are many different ways of understanding the dialectic between the two spheres. The one Richard Titmuss later developed would gloss over the gender division, and would focus instead on the contribution of formal and informal fiscal systems to keeping alive and unhealthy those same social inequalities he'd first spotted as a hard-working insurance clerk in the 1930s.[19] In such a paradigm, women simply disappear within the word 'social'. All the caring they put in both at home and elsewhere becomes something too private really to speak about; at least not of the same order as the welfare provided by the state. And so it remains the case that, 'despite the scale of collective reproduction in welfare, the huge budgets of education, housing, health, income maintenance and the personal social services, most of welfare/personal production and reproduction still takes place within the home. It is here that the redistribution between wage labourers and their economic dependants takes place, so that in return for subsistence the wage labourer exchanges housework, child care and sexual servicing with the wife-mother.'[20] There are obviously good reasons why Richard Titmuss didn't notice this, intellectually speaking. His own wife protested against housework, calling herself a 'discontented dishwasher', but this was an appellation that belonged to their private relations. Yet at the same time there's a curious split, for in Richard's later work on blood donation the 'altruism' of the 'good' society is the core of a desirable morality.[21] Who cares, then? In the pages of this book who was looking after whom? Altruism –

giving – lies beyond the fiscal framework, it isn't part of economics. And so women aren't either. The British Labour Party socialism, with its touchingly naive faith in democracy and its limpid semi-Christian values which Richard Titmuss found his way into, let him down when it came to an intellectual understanding of why some people are more equal than others.

D. A. Riesman's account of Richard's views on welfare and society ends with a statement that takes me back to the beginning of this book. 'Perhaps in the last analysis,' says Riesman, 'Titmuss can only fully be understood if one interprets his life's work as an attempt to find a collective response to Cain's perceptive question on the nature of social welfare: "Am I my brother's keeper?"' [22] As Richard's daughter I find myself excluded from much of the language he used to describe social relations. There's a nice irony in the naming of the computer software used by my cousin Andrew to record his part of the family history, 'Brother's Keeper'.

It's hard to write about one's parents. It's easier to tell their story as they told it than to comment on it. Yet to tell it as they did isn't necessarily interesting to other people; biographers must produce art as well as chronicles. Retiring one's own judgement from the scene is the traditional biographer's art. But like so much of what appears as objectivity, this stance may be only the veiling of hidden bias; one may not pronounce, yet one selects, and it is, like Kay Titmuss's pruning, in the gaps through which other versions of history may be glimpsed, that perhaps the really interesting truths lie. But if biographers are charged with a duty not to suppress the truths they glimpse, where does this leave the filial biographer? [23]

In her memoir of her parents, Margaret Mead and Gregory Bateson, Mary Catherine Bateson observes that it's *only* the daughter who can know as much as can be known about her parents. There's a continuing responsibility which flows from this – there are tasks connected with one's parents' legacies that simply can't be done by anyone else. But there's also, and very importantly, 'no perfection to enshrine and no orthodoxy to defend'. [24] The narrative of my parents' relationship unfolded in these pages is primarily the one my mother wished to leave. I can't defend it as orthodoxy: because it's her story, there's also the real possibility that it is in some senses a false one. The trail of her prunings – letters thrown away, the tell-tale hints of the little blue silk diary that evaded destruction – may lead into quite another forest; but so faintly now that I can scarcely even see the trees. The letters in this book tell a love story; Kay and Richard undoubtedly loved each other. But the downside of love – the fear of dependency (on both sides), the flashes of hate – isn't there. It's unreal. Of course, two people in love who are separated and who communicate through letters don't waste time being negative. Yet, still, I wonder. This is where another layer of complexity comes in. I've written this book as Kay and Richard's child, but I'm also me: and the fifty-two years I've lived since I blew semolina bubbles in the Wakefield kitchen bring another kind of experience to bear on the meaning of the past.

Separating the 'autobiographical' from the 'biographical' element during the writing of this book hasn't been easy. There *is* a difference, though stories about one's parents may say more about oneself than stories told consciously about oneself.[25] My mother wasn't alone in leaving me a bundle of papers with vague instructions about possible meanings. Writer Christopher Isherwood's mother left her son letters and a diary, kept regularly for seventy years, with the words, 'Perhaps someone will be glad of it, some day.'[26] Like the brown suitcase: that's for you. Nigel Nicolson's sensitive *Portrait of a Marriage* was based on an unpublished autobiography he discovered in a locked Gladstone bag after the death of his mother, Vita Sackville-West.[27] The fact that these women left hoarded writings, that they were reticent even about their own wish for some sort of memorial, must be seen as an integral part of the narrative of their lives.

Christopher Isherwood, the son, doesn't appear as 'I' at all in the book he wrote based on the papers his mother left him: Christopher calls himself Christopher. In this book I have mostly called myself 'I'. The 'he' of Isherwood's book and the 'I' of this one mark a gender difference. But some steps of this dance are to the same tune. There is, for example, the essence of the filial dialectic itself: Christopher Isherwood, the son, repelled by the militaristic uppercrust masculinity of his father, adopted an anarchic homosexuality; Ann Oakley, the daughter, reacting against the constrained life for women inscribed in her mother's life and letters, tried to do something different in hers, including puzzling in private, and in public, about the nature of these differences between men and women. In his account of his parents, Isherwood is inclined to believe that his mother got the better bargain, whereas Oakley's perception is that her mother got the worst in that distributive (un)justice system known as marriage.

So my interpretation is my interpretation. Just as my mother pruned the papers she left me, so I in turn have pruned them. It would have been quite impossible to include everything. My interpolation of an authorial voice has framed the contents of the papers, my parents' history, in a vision which overlaps with, but is not the same as, theirs. I haven't been as 'dutifully selective'[28] as William Beveridge – or, rather, perhaps I've operated with a slightly different sense of duty from his. Parts of the book are my mother's story told through my eyes. Parts are my father's, but again my perceptions are tangled up with his. When I put the two together, I come up with a story like an iceberg, in which what we see only points to more which we can't see, because it's hidden, though from time to time we may catch glimpses of bits of it through the ever-changing prism of the waves.

'Childhood spirals around me like smoke. I cannot see myself clearly in the glass.'[29] Nor them. As a child, I was aware that the most vital of my father's relationships were not with adult women. The greatest emotional affect lay in his relationships with men. It was there that the sparks flew, that excitement existed. By comparison, the relationship with my mother was flat, like a spent chord. She'd really ceased to share his political and intellectual interests,[30] though the division of labour they lived by still held marriage up as a joint enterprise: man and wife at one in everything. She was cross a lot of the time, as I remember it. She was cross, some of the time, with me. For me, there was always a gap between the public face of the family – well-ordered, conventional, successful – and the private enclosure in which resentments and differences were fought out – verbally most of the time, but sometimes physically as well. I felt it didn't work, and that I was caught in the trap of their attempts to force it to. Later on, when I had left their home, their marriage remained a mystery to me. As Enid Bagnold, a writer whom Kay much admired, once said, 'One has no idea what goes on between married settled people. Once a pair has reached 20 years they have closed the front door.'[31] Marriage, and particularly marital sexuality, is a very under-studied subject in the welter of personal issues people research and write about these days.

As their child I come back, again and always, to the joint project of their marriage. To me as a child this meant a mother who was always there in a physical sense and a father whose comings and goings were the high points of both our days. What I carried out of those early years was the perception of my mother as a dependent and frustrated woman and my father as a clever, charismatic man whose undoubted love of power was combined with a deep sensitivity to others, but whose treatment of me and my mother was riddled with all the ambivalence he felt, like many men, towards women. Whatever my parents believed had been equal about their relationship in the beginning I did not feel as their child. For me, the eager rhetoric of equality was always divorced from the sad practice of inequality. In resolving not to be like my mother, I also resolved not to be like my father. The two drawings of my parents reproduced as Plate 17 were done when I was about fourteen. My parents are both working, but he's bent over a book or his normal pile of papers, and she, wearing an apron, has her hands in a washbasin scrubbing clothes. I never saw her poring over papers – nor, for that matter, do I recall ever seeing her reading a book. My father never washed clothes, except when he was on his trips abroad, when the new drip-dry polyester shirts that came in in the 1950s were greeted by Kay as a godsend.

The rhetoric of the 'joint project' of marriage is there in the Titmuss letters: the stress on *complementarity*, the protest against the babble of the maritally quarrelling Hancocks who can have no conception of the Titmusses' own relationship as one in which everything, theoretically, is shared. As a matter of fact, had the Titmusses attended more to what was going on in the Hancocks' relationship, they might have seen a different picture. When Hancock moved to London from Birmingham and took up his employment in the War Office, he took a lower salary than he might have done because he didn't want to make any profit from the war. So his wife Theaden had to turn voluntary work into paid work. Her job as a talks producer for the BBC Overseas Service meant long hours 'under rackety conditions', getting home late in the evening and still having housework to do. Like Kay, she suffered from nervous exhaustion and had to be rescued by two kind Hampshire ladies who took her into their home for rest and convalescence.[32]

While in those years few would have criticized the notion of jointness that informed this conception of marriage, plenty have done so since. What is joint is not equal. Where roles and labours are divided, there are, almost inevitably, inequalities of power. Lives lived in parallel by married men and women are unequal because women work out their destiny within marriage, whereas men decipher theirs despite (or because of) it. Transactions apparently of love are as likely to be those of power. Love is invoked particularly at those moments where shifts of power occur, and where there is some reason to disguise them. He loves her, and she responds, especially when she merges her identity with his.

What children experience is the *relationship* between their parents. For them, this is a thing indistinguishable from the parents themselves. Even when one or both parents are absent, there is still the conjectural relationship. But if it's hard for children to understand when their parents don't seem to love them, perhaps the hardest thing of all to understand is that our parents began by loving each other and not us. All children are intruders. They're like common thieves who steal what isn't theirs, who claim attention and love and make a fuss when they don't get what they want, or take it anyway. Then they set up house with their victims and never leave. Parents are never free of children. But children are never free from parents, either. The relationship between one's parents can be expressed as the daily non-equivalent realities of being mothered and fathered, and in the form of webs and myths and lies: what one's parents believed about themselves and each other, what they each said about this. The tales they told, the dreams they believed. The people they were, and those that they hoped to be, particularly perhaps that persona – sexual, social, emotional, material – that they sought to become in living with each other and having a child together. Most of my childhood was lived after this book finishes, and I can't consciously remember that part of it chronicled here. I remember only the austere art deco meanness of the flat in Chiswick. I do remember fragments of some of the people who feature in my parents' letters. There was Carr-Saunders, for example, in his guise as LSE director, to whose Christmas parties for staff and children I went, and at which, every year, I wanted to be given the fairy off the top of the tree. But Carr-Saunders never gave it to me. There was Bill le Gros Clark, of *Our Food Problem*, blinded and maimed by a firework as a boy, on whose lap I was made to sit as a little girl; I can remember the rough, worrying smell of his clothes even now. (At least, I thought until I did the research for this book that he'd been blinded

301

by a firework as a boy; it was only when I read his official biography that I learnt he'd been hurt as a soldier on the last day of the First World War. Did I remember what my mother said correctly? Did she get it wrong? It certainly put me off fireworks for life.) I *think* I remember Keith Hancock, but I can't be sure; I certainly remember historian Denys Hay, on whose work about that period I've drawn in this book. Separated from his own children during the war, Denys would come home with my father to bath me in the evenings. I don't remember the eugenists, but there is a squinting photograph of me with Margaret Gowing, who wrote the British Academy biography of Richard, on a Cornish beach backed by the house where Eleanor Rathbone wrote *The Disinherited Family*.

But the smoke of childhood still spirals – really as well as symbolically; what can I see beyond the smoke rings? Reading the letters and the papers around which this book has been written has helped me to understand better how the development of my parents' relationship is also the story of the evolution of Richard Titmuss, expert on the welfare state. More fundamentally, there may be something about such an activity of coming to terms with the past.[33] In writing a book about his parents, based on the letters they wrote to each other when his father worked in India, William Beveridge found this was simply a way of getting to know them. *India Called Them* he named it,[34] though India called his father rather more than his mother. The title was suggested by Beveridge's sister, Jeanette, who married R. H. Tawney – a man whom Richard Titmuss much admired, but who considered all women fools.[35]

We take the material our parents give us, and the opportunities and constraints we feel around us, and make what we can of it all. Most of us find out who we are and what we want to be only by living it. This living includes the perpetration of mistakes and a constant reflecting on the past. The past, our perception of it, enters when we least expect it. Its elisions and insertions slip through barely open doorways, usually unbidden, and more like fortune-tellers than like ghosts. The presence of the past is not about the past but about us now.

I am the product of my parents' marriage in more ways than one. It perhaps goes without saying that I don't recognize myself in the Adrian whose birth my parents so eagerly anticipated in 1943; nor have I been the great social reformer their friend, Jerry Morris, promised them I would be. I am a social reformer of a different kind. I never had a chance to find out what my father thought of this, as he died before either he or I knew what I would become – though the signs were there. My mother, like Simone de Beauvoir's,[36] was often shocked by what I said and published, but proud of, and flattered by, my success. If I can't see myself in Adrian, I clearly recognize myself in the baby they describe: so impatient to grow up that she threatens to walk without crawling; with a face so prone to expression she has to cover it in meetings even now, half a century later, to avoid others reading her opinions there like an open book. I enjoy cycling, and didn't understand how much they did until now. I have an inordinate fondness for spinach, too, and it wasn't till I read these letters that it occurred to me this could be due to the emotional aura surrounding my mother's serving it to me in Wakefield, in the little kitchen with Uncle Bert watching, the spinach freshly extracted from the package my father had lovingly dispatched from the Turnham Green allotment in between his war-history writing and fire-watching duties.

But I might have liked spinach anyway. Who can tell? There's something awfully cloying about baby Ann's goodness, though. Going down like a lamb, sitting like a little jewel, wearing a bow in her hair, Sweetie-pie just lapping up her dinner. And there's something unpleasantly self-congratulatory about the way the Titmusses so easily condemned the errors of other parents: poor little Peter Grundy with his sore red bottom; the Lafittes' Nicky, who couldn't have been half as clever as they pretended, and whose mother should have taken a lesson or two from Kay in how teething could be managed; Richard's niece, Margaret, who went horribly wrong because of her mother's inconsistency in dealing with her; and last but not least, poor Helen Glass, daughter of a professional couple, who should never have brought her into the world at all. Even more reprehensible were those who weren't openly interested in children: Theaden Hancock who went on the train with Richard to North Wales and couldn't exclaim, as he did, over the babies who shared the carriage with them. The Titmusses moved in curiously childless circles, as Robert Graves observed of his friend Maurice Newfield, who had only one child to his many, despite being such a good eugenist.

I wonder now why such nastiness to other people was necessary. Why not more charity? One answer comes from Simone de Beauvoir's comment on her mother: 'It is impossible for anyone to say "I am sacrificing myself" without feeling bitterness.'[37] You can believe in the nobility of devotion but have other desires, too. As for children, well, children differ; some are easier to bring up than others. Certainly, the pressure to be good was a dead weight on my shoulders for many years and I haven't quite got rid of it yet. Perhaps there's something *especially* good about female only children subjected to a lot of comings and goings in childhood. Perhaps they know it's pointless to complain about it; the point is to try to be the pleasure one's parents hoped for, for as long as one possibly can.[38] Or maybe some of this is the child's reaction to the parent's (mother's) depression. I'm struck by the way in the letters all this praising of Ann for her goodness and all the unkindness to other people are threads woven in with the fabric of how the middle-class family *itself* is imagined: small, self-sufficient, inward-looking; a selfish cosiness represented in a train of epitomic little England images – a little house with a 'secluded' patch of lawn and a few fruit trees where the bees hum quietly among the flowers; sandcastles by the sea in the summer. 'England, Home and Beauty', as Lord Horder put it, quoting from someone else, in a slim paperback published in 1945 called *Rebuilding Family Life in the Post-War World*. We go from love of our family to love of mankind and nation, and this is no sentimental nonsense but a healthy and constructive thing.[39] Sir Arthur MacNalty of the Ministry put the same thing differently when he wrote, quite unequivocally, 'The family is the unit of race.'[40]

The Sweetie-pie of the letters is definitely not me now. Sometimes I doubt that I ever was a real person to them, though they would – and did – hotly contest this. But I was their/her validation – living proof that parents shouldn't revolt, that there was a new England to be built out of the ruins of the war. Like Alva and Gunnar Myrdal's second child, who was called 'Krisan' or 'Little Crisis' because of her appearance the month after her parents' book *Crisis in the Population Question*,[41] I felt I was produced to prove a point. I was also my mother's reason for being separated from her husband. She was torn between us. It must have been hard not to hold it against me. I wonder perpetually about the meaning, not only of the pruning that went into the leaving of the brown suitcase, but of some of the annotation that went on. I especially wonder about a passage my mother underlined in one of my father's letters to her: the one written on 7 August 1944 to Wakefield: 'Ann is important,' he wrote, 'I've thought about it a lot – but you are infinitely more important – another 30 years & – who knows – all eternity *together*.' His premature death from lung cancer unfairly gave them only twenty-nine, though I can't say whether his plans for eternity came off. But why did my mother underline this when she was in her eighties and I was in my forties? What was it she thought I needed to know and in relation to what other truth might I have needed to be told it?

Lovers look inward; their gaze is at themselves. But that's another aspect of the narrative of these pages I find it hard to understand. While the Titmusses struggled with their separation, and went on working and publishing both tracts of the times and messages with more longevity, millions of people – killed, maimed, rendered childless, parentless and homeless – were far worse off than they were. They lived through a period when fourteen of Europe's democracies became dictatorships.[42] Events in Germany defied description. Where in the Titmusses' work and consciousness was that moral sentience they so championed in *Parents Revolt*, and why did they so endlessly go on about the selfishness of people in not having babies instead of that lack of fellow feeling that is far more immorally expressed in killing people? It's uncomfortable to realize that their vision of the 'good' society was fundamentally a vision of their own country[43] – her quotes from Kipling, her lack of sympathy for the German victims of war, his willingness to die for England (not that there was much chance of that in the County Fire Office). My parents' emotional nationalism cut them off from other parents and children. It also separated them from their own relations as they grew to feel fewer and fewer bonds with their own families of origin; and Kay's victory over 'the Evil One', Richard's own mother, became – almost – complete. Moving into the intelligentsia must have been a real barrier to intra-family communication.

The Titmusses didn't have a particularly difficult war. They lost no loved ones; he didn't fight; they were never separated for more than a few weeks at a time. And yet it was all Sturm und Drang. We're used to thinking of the war as a time when women leapt into action – into uniform, into the factories, on to the farm tractors, taking over all the men's jobs and doing them just as ably and with great results for their self-esteem. But none of this happened to Kay. She did help with the children evacuated to the family farm in

Bedfordshire, and she did help with the homeless in London, but there must have been a great deal more she could have done, particularly after the retreat to Wakefield, when she had but one baby to look after and Auntie Nora to help her. What Kay didn't do in the war is only one of the unanswered questions framed in the course of writing this book. Indeed, I recognize that the book probably raises more questions than it answers.

The son of Fritz Haber, the man who invented chemical warfare during the First World War, and who was involved in secret German chemical rearmament in the 1920s, wrote a biography of him.[44] On the centenary of his father's birth he attended a celebration at the lecture theatre of the University of Karlsruhe where his father had taught at the turn of the century. Two young men appeared on the rostrum with a banner claiming that Haber was a murderer. His son thought this was a lie, but discovered it wasn't. Parents have secrets from children, which may be hard to assimilate. My parents' preoccupation with eugenics is a puzzle to me. I try to stand back and see it as a movement of its era in which Right and Left contested the battleground and Richard Titmuss bravely stepped in there with his social statistics and brought fresh air, with speakers such as Margery Spring Rice, and his panegyric about the environment, and was welcomed with open arms by Maurice Newfield and some others, but found his eugenist credentials severely criticized by those with a more obstinate belief in genes. Titmuss's ascent to fame would have pleased the more old-fashioned C. P. Blacker who approved of those who rose in the social scale as having more socially valuable qualities.[45] That he considered these largely innate would have puzzled the Titmuss and Farr families, given as they were either to farming or to drunken idleness; and Kay Titmuss herself might not have agreed, in view of the role she carved out for herself as the environment which permitted a flowering of potential in Richard that might otherwise have lain dormant in the chilling soil of a different marriage. William Beveridge thought the 'middle' class of independent workers, including farmers, a 'natural' breeding-ground of individualism[46] – and perhaps he was right, though not about the 'natural' bit.

So Richard Titmuss was a child of his times; and his wife as well. We/I need to see them as much as they were then as through the non-rosy spectacles of half a century on. If the welfare state was founded on the three Ps of philanthropy, patriotism and patriarchy, does it matter? What matters, of course, is that its failures stem in part from its weaknesses. The re-privatization of welfare that's going on now shows us what little distance we have travelled in facing up to the tensions hidden in such words as 'community'. Similarly, the trend among 'respectable' scientists towards the idea that human behaviour is better explained by genes than by environment sounds like a debate, dressed up in smarter technical language, right out of the pages of the *Eugenics Review*.[47]

As I said, my parents might have seemed different to other daughters and sons. Writer Antonia White, alias Eirene Botting, had two daughters who remember her differently. Susan Chitty's biography, *Now to My Mother*,[48] declares on its first page, 'Antonia White was not a good mother to me'; Lyndall Hopkinson's was called *Nothing to Forgive*. Actually Lyndall shared with Susan the feeling that it had been hard to love their mother. Antonia wrote both her daughters a letter asking to be forgiven which they read after she died. Lyndall went home to Italy and re-read all her mother's works: 'The only "revelation" [. . .] came from recognising how similar some of her feelings for her mother were to mine about her in my teens, though she wasn't afraid of her as I was, instead she despised her mother and treated her in a dismissive way. Of course I knew that Antonia, like me, had preferred her father: it was the recurring theme in her novels, and her morbid feelings for him had been the cause of many of her neuroses in later life.'[49] Sue and Lyndall had different fathers, but Antonia's mothering of them was distant, intermittent and mostly handed over to other people. Her life was dominated by madness, the writing of a small amount of transparently autobiographical fiction, love affairs, abortions, and a self-centred religiosity. She thought unselfish mothers made execrable company. Daughter Sue took an overdose when she was twenty-one and came round to see her mother and father at the foot of the bed 'looking like a normal mother and father. Not that I had ever consciously wanted such a thing.'[50] She and her mother didn't meet for five years: 'My success was her failure.'[51] Daughter Lyndall was also prone to depression and read in her mother's diaries after her death that her mother wished she had never been born. But her portrait is a compassionate one, whereas her sister's is not. What was unforgivable to one child was understandable to another.

The father of French psychoanalysis, Jacques Lacan, was also the father of two daughters, one by his wife and one by his mistress, the first of whom he largely disowned. Both wrote biographies. The one by the mistress's daughter, Judith,[52] is hagiographical and makes no mention of her half-sister at all. The book by Sybille, Lacan's 'legitimate' daughter, is, as might be expected, full of conflict and despair.[53]

Just as striking are the different recollections of Alva Myrdal by two of her three children, Jan[54] and Sissela.[55] Like Susan Chitty, Jan cut off all contact with his mother for some years, beginning when she was Minister of Disarmament, and he was a political campaigner involved in denouncing the Vietnam war, promoting the rights of Palestinians and publicly opposing the foreign policy of the government to which his mother belonged. He thought she preferred the government to him. While his sister saw the whole episode as a misunderstanding, for Jan it fuelled his deep-seated feeling that 'Not many children have survived a mother who saw her son as a kind of laboratory animal for behavioural studies and a father who did not conceal his contempt for the being he and his wife had brought into life.'[56] The compassionate version, Sissela's, begins, like that of Antonia White by Lyndall, with the sadness of the maternal death, proceeding backwards into an understanding of the project of life. Jan's, like Susan Chitty's, begins and ends with the brutality of childhood. Alva had told no one he was going to be born. He was never really convinced she was his mother. She couldn't take care of children. The fact that she taught courses in child psychiatry and parenting was 'an example of black and surrealist humour'.[57] She had cold fingers. 'I was a mistake.'[58] When the school psychologist said he was emotionally disturbed, Alva instituted the family hour: 'It was the hour before dinner. The governess turned my sisters over to her. Alva had allocated twenty minutes to each child. She played with Kaj for twenty minutes. Then she read Sissela a fairy tale for twenty minutes, and finally there were the twenty minutes spent with me. But she had a hard time discussing steam engines and such, and I couldn't talk to her about the things I thought about, because she didn't understand.'[59]

In Sissela's book many of the experiences recorded by Jan appear in a different light. For example, in 1967, when Alva and Jan fell out, Alva didn't know Jan had just been arrested in a Vietnam demonstration. Sissela sees that Alva's children called forth a conflict in her: between being confined and being free. It's as a woman she understands this. Jan, on the other hand, cannot free himself from the image of the rejecting mother and the too critical father who hectored his son throughout his childhood for everything from eating too many meatballs to using too much of his mother's time to having been born with a half-closed rectum which the doctor had had to force open. 'A certain inferior slag falls from every social class.'[60] Perhaps the Myrdals weren't above eugenics, either. But Jan points out that Sissela's first book, 'When she was an American and over 40, was about lies.' She dedicated it to her husband – but if Jan had written a book about lies and dedicated it to his wife she would have filed for divorce. Sissela is like Alva and Gunnar, 'phony as a three-crown coin'.[61] Of course, to those outside the culture from which Jan writes a three-crown coin could be real. Sissela's second book, published after Jan Myrdal's *Childhood*, was called *Secrets: On the ethics of concealment and revelation* and was dedicated to her parents.

What Sissela's biography of Alva seeks, most of all, to understand and demonstrate is her mother's unique fight to have and hold two roles – to be both Peer and the Solveig waiting at home of the Peer Gynt story:

> Throughout her life, Alva pressed for explanations about what it means to be a woman. With no models and little support, she broke out of the stereotypes for femininity that surrounded her when she was young. She wanted to make room in her life for both love and work, as Freud put it, but aimed for a quality and an intensity with respect to each that few dare to seek even now. She came up against nearly every obstacle that can confront one who set herself such goals. Each time she overcame one of these obstacles her world expanded; yet each time the difficulty of making everything fit took on new dimensions. Husband, family, work, larger causes – how does one reconcile obligations and challenges that seem to pull in so many different directions?[62]

With difficulty. Though she is best known in this country as co-author of the pre-feminist classic *Women's Two Roles*, Alva Myrdal's *Times* obituary was headed 'Tireless advocate of disarmament'.[63] She was leader of the Swedish delegation to the Geneva Disarmament

Conference and deputy leader of the Swedish delegation to the United Nations General Assembly. It wasn't easy to achieve what she did. There were moments in her and Gunnar's relationship when she had self-consciously to lift herself out of the mould of subjecting herself to his life and become the subject of her own.[64] She might not have liked that paragraph in Gunnar's *Times* obituary, also preserved by Kay in the year of Kay's own death, 1987, which noted that 'His wife Alva [. . .] was of one mind with him and took an active part in much of what he did.'[65] Hers didn't note that he was of one mind with her and shared in her work. In all its weighty cultural symbolism the joint project of marriage remains sequestered on the rock of male identity and achievement.

Who knows how different this book would have been if I'd been my brother or sister?

I found my justification for writing this book in Sissela Bok's comment: 'If we knew about people only what they wished to reveal, we would be subjected to ceaseless manipulation; and we would be deprived of the pleasure and suspense that comes from trying to understand them.'[66] Richard Titmuss's ideas generated controversy in his lifetime, so it will be no surprise if the development of his career and his relationship with my mother as described in this book seem controversial to some people, too. There's no sense in which I wanted to write a 'critical' biography of my father (or my mother) – using 'critical' in the accepted negative sense – though doubtless that is what some of the book's readers will pick up. I don't believe we should never speak ill of the dead, and although Richard Titmuss was a saint to others,[67] he wasn't one to me. He was that much more interesting persona, my father. In his writings he is to me now sometimes sharply original, always a wonderfully scrupulous collector of social facts, usually interesting and often witty: in his work there are some very fine examples of what not having a formal education can do for you. But equally I've no doubt that sometimes what he wrote wasn't original, and some of it was wrong. He was wrong, for example, in much of what he claimed about the rise and fall of birth rates.[68] Sometimes he recycled other people's ideas, as we all do. His appeal to moral values hid an intellectual discipline that was weaker than it might have been. It was perhaps in the linking of facts with values and of both with hard-nosed policies in the real world of human behaviour that he most excelled.

310

I owe an enormous amount to both my parents, and perhaps the true texture of that debt has only now emerged from my reading of their letters and papers. But I've also had to come to terms with the fact that, in some fundamental way, in my own life I always seemed to disappoint them. The personal testimony of the material I've used to write this book has enabled me, rightly or wrongly, to read the private problem in the public story. Committed to a different-therefore-unequal model of male–female relations and to a political agenda which loses some of the most deeply experienced inequalities of our time in a rhetoric of paper-thin democracy, my parents seemed unable to allow me the same freedom to reject this as they themselves exercised in believing it.

This, perhaps, is an essential part of the parent–child dialectic. Writing this book has made me wonder what my own children might do about me one day. But we have to tell the truth as we see it; I believe that, and I expect they will, too. The real challenge is to tell the truth but be charitable with it; to see that life as it is improvised within the framework of certain rules is generally a matter of people doing the best they can in the circumstances.

My children may want to go back into the past one day, and, if so, this book should help them to do it. For me it's been mostly an intellectual journey – one I did in my head while sitting in mounting panic surrounded by gigantic quantities of papers; a journey accomplished much too fast, because of the other obligations of my life, and which became in its worst and best moments a living obsession. To break the fatigue this brought I did make a few real journeys. I went to look at some of the places that feature in this book; to Bedfordshire on a glorious summer day when the countryside was just as I remembered it from the summers of my childhood spent there, and where it was easy to see Kay and Richard on the dipping hills behind the farm picking the burrs of blackberries from each other's hair; to Wakefield on a pouring wet day to search a map in a modern shopping centre, surrounded by Yorkshire men eating faggots and gravy, for a road that didn't seem to exist because my mother's handwriting was capable of at least two interpretations – and then finding the house on a long wet road leading out of town bedecked in a garish new frontage and wearing not quite that aspect of cramped poverty I had imagined.

I also went back to the Flats in Chiswick to re-meet my childhood,

311

and Kay and Richard's time there. I cycled through London on a warm spring bank holiday, when the parks were full of cramped flat dwellers, and the first armies of tourists, guide books in hand and fat white sneakers on their feet, and couples who thought they might be in love, and couples who thought they might not be, and stooped fathers practising the art of pushchair-steering, and mums with schemes for an episode or two of temporary freedom. My parents would have approved of my cycling. But I chose that means of transport in order to get a sense of moving from one part of the city, where I live now, to another part, where I first lived: to go through time, backwards.

My route took me through Camden and down the edge of Regent's Park, and then I crossed the Marylebone Road, competing with hot motorists in their inefficient combustion machines, and went towards Paddington, from thence to the edge of Hyde Park, down the Bayswater Road, past the pavement artists and the picture sellers with their gaudy displays, through Notting Hill and the peppermint palaces of Holland Park, to the roundabout which leads to the seedier Shepherd's Bush. There's a tricky bit of cycling here, for the road divides four ways, and mine was the second right towards Chiswick. A minute later the doctor's surgery which had administered so many medical rites to me and my first two children more than a quarter of a century ago appeared on my left. Almost opposite was the mean little street they decided to name after Richard Titmuss. It's squeezed between a pizza parlour and a cut-price food store, with the sign 'Titmuss Street' hung underneath a much grander one for Weetabix: 'Stay trim – lift a spoon in the morning.' There were lilac trees in bloom on the Goldhawk Road, and the air freshened up on the edges of one of London's first garden suburbs, leafy Bedford Park. I turned right and then sharp left and skirted the common ground between the road and the railway. Here I had once pushed babies in prams and thought about milk and night needs, and all the troubled business, which had occupied Kay, of childhood immunization and married women's work. Up the hill by Chiswick Park underground station – strange how steep I remembered it, but it isn't, it's only a little climb really; where you used to look down on the Chiswick Empire, home of a child's thousand Arabian nights, and where Richard strayed to get away from the exhaustion of the war. At the border of the next patch of grass, a sign says 'Welcome

to Turnham Green. Hounslow Arts and Recreation Department'.
This is where my father grew the spinach and the tomatoes to contest
the vitamin C shortages of wartime; this is the path he walked to
and from the flat to post his letters to my mother up north, to and
from the writing of the war history in that room in Whitehall with
the distempered ceiling, to and from his sojourns in the dome of
St Paul's Cathedral. The Green is all smooth gleaming grass now,
well kept, with dark green seats and litter bins, with no sign of any
allotments anywhere, and the paths cross it cleanly from corner to
corner.

The Flats loom out of the sky above the Turnham Green walkers,
a monolithic slab of dirty-red brick and square enamelled window
frames, three blocks joined together in a euphonious art deco cacoph-
ony: Beaumont, Belgrave and Beverley Courts. They look quite smart
now, art deco buildings having returned to fashion, and repainted
as well. I remember them as dark and depressing. Something about
them always frightened me. I cycle round the monolith, going down
the 'Private Road garages only' side entrance, and passing faded
blue-grey doors which haven't been repainted since my childhood,
and crossing the concrete where I fell and scarred my face for life in
1949, and the garage where my mother skinned rabbits and hung
up their fur to dry thereby putting me off meat also for life. But it's
all different now. Instead of the easy cries of children and the open
traffic in and out of the big garden with the swimming pool, there's
an awkwardly railed-in silence. There are tall fences topped by barbed
wire. The front door of the Flats, which swung open easily and in
my childhood memory is always swinging open, squeaking a bit as
it does so, is now a security system with a gigantic row of intercoms.
You can't get in without being the right person. I'm not; I can hardly
press button 5 and announce that I've come to look at my childhood,
can I? So I peer through a pane of glass to the side of the door and
I can see the hallway where time stands still on the polished lino and
the dark wood doors; the front door of Mr and Mrs Needham's flat,
where my friend Patricia lived, and between their and our own front
door, which is hidden from view on my right, the lifts with their
terrifying enclosures and endless even louder squeaking – the music
I listened to in my cot in the small bedroom beyond the bathroom
with the window facing the backside of Beverley Court, the one my
father had to move his papers out of when I was born. I wish I could

see into the gardens now, but there's no way I can. Instead I have to make do with my memory of a safe place where children played and where my mother at the kitchen sink could call to me through the window. My father's presence in the flat is scarcely felt, but I can sense hers. I'm aware of the polishing and the food preparation, the silence of the sitting room with the square table laid for dinner and the radio with the knitted front and the comfortable round knobs – so easy to get hold of, unlike all these little black plastic devices now. I can smell apple pie and rabbit stew. In the air of the corridor, windowless, lurks the memory (not mine, for I wasn't there) of the nights when that was where people slept to get away from the bombs and the falling glass from blown-in windows: 'the girls' from upstairs, and Richard Titmuss, writing to his wife of domestic and non-domestic things – what to do with the tomatoes and was it safe for mothers and children to come home?

It's all laid out exactly as it was, the war-time and post-war austerity combined with my mother's parsimoniousness to create a landscape of figuratively smooth places, where no child or man might catch or hurt themselves, where no sparkling bits of dust would risk being inhaled to interfere with the clean interior pinkness of family life.

This is where it happened, but this is the past. I cycle round again and take a photograph. I'm struck, for what feels like the first time, by the contrast between the huge slabs of the Flats and the cosy Victorian cottages in the surrounding streets – architecture on two quite different scales. Did I think about the other kinds of lives lived in the little houses then, or was my own the only one I knew?

I went to school here, too. Beyond the period of the letters, my parents found a little private school for me which they didn't approve of, but all my friends went there, and so I was sent there, too. My old school, Oxford College, has become the local Labour Party headquarters. In between times it was a women's refuge. The building, grey and rather depressed-looking, like the Old Guard of the Labour Party now, and not unlike the Gestetner duplicating machine of the Rev. Birch story, would have a lot to say if it could speak.

I put a jersey on against the rising wind, and cycle to the middle of the green to refuel (with a carton of out-of-date orange juice) for the return journey to the land of the north. I see again with my real eyes and those in my mind the representation of my childhood before me like a museum piece: Mummy and Daddy together or apart in

314

Number 5 Beaumont Court, living their lives and bringing up their little daughter, and writing letters to each other, and telling tales of love and duty and puzzlement and ambition and understanding. It is with me – all of it – as though it were yesterday, which it was: all time, that we sense, is past time. The other sort we only dream about.

Up Chiswick High Street, but where is the department store where my mother and I used to order Cash's name tapes to sew into my school clothes (ANN TITMUSS in red block letters, repeated over and over again, to make a point of some kind), and where they passed money backwards and forwards in little boxes on overhead wires like the ones that used to pull London's trolleys? There's a Marks and Spencer now, and even a smart blue Dillons bookstore. Mylo's, which sold me a million pale yellow ice creams, has gone the way of many small businesses. The upper reaches of the High Street have become quite posh, with pavement wine bars and people sitting at little round enamel tables, and sunshine lighting up the green of wine bottles, and turning even plain wine glasses into gems of colour. I take a different route back: Hammersmith and Olympia and Kensington this time. Poor Albert has quite disappeared inside columns of scaffolding. Barkers, which was a real treat to shop in, is still there, but it's much too flash now to resemble its past self. I cross the little bridges by the Serpentine. The crowds seem to thicken – there are people wandering everywhere, and they don't hear the cyclist's gentle approach, for we are nearly silent invaders. I want to stop and enjoy the sights, have a Mylo's ice cream, but on I go – I promised to be home. I am, you see, a good woman, too – though in my own way.

Everything fades into a prosaic battle with the traffic. Everyday life is back again. But it always was – that's what this book is about: the mediation of our understanding by the way our lives are lived, both how we choose to live them and what is chosen for us. The responsibility of parents in this business is only matched by that of children – to remember whatever they can, and to reach their own kind of understanding, to compose this along with the rest of their lives, from whatever bits of the past they are able to find scattered about them.

NOTES

CHAPTER ONE: Opening
the Suitcase

1 J. Harris, *Unemployment and Politics: A study in English social policy 1886-1914*, Oxford, Clarendon Press, 1972.

2 P.Shore, *Tribune*, 13.4.73.

3 *The Times*, 7.4.73.

4 *Guardian*, 7.4.73.

5 D.Piachaud, *New Statesman*, 12.4.73.

6 Shore, op. cit.

7 P. Cosgrave, *Spectator*, 14.4.73.

8 Piachaud, op. cit.

9 Lord Collison, *The Times*, 12.4.73.

10 J. Vaizey, *Financial Times*, 10.4.73.

11 Shore, op. cit.

12 In his early years, Richard was known as 'Dick' and Kathleen as 'Kathleen' or 'K'. Later on, he became 'Richard' and she became 'Kay'.

13 J. B. Elshtain, *Public Man, Private Woman: Women in social and political thought*, Princeton, New Jersey, Princeton University Press, 1981.

14 V. Walkerdine, H. Lucey, *Democracy in the Kitchen*, London, Virago, 1989.

15 M. Stacey, 'The division of labour revisited or overcoming the two Adams', in J. Finch, P. Rock (eds), *Practice and Progress: British Sociology 1950-1980*, London, Allen and Unwin, 1981.

16 H. Graham, *Women, Health and the Family*, Brighton, Sussex, Wheatsheaf Books, 1984.

17 There are moves to correct this now.

18 S. Walby, *Theorizing Patriarchy*, Oxford, Blackwells, 1990.

19 C. Delphy, D. Leonard, *Familiar Exploitation*, Cambridge, Polity Press, 1992.

20 Kay also kept carbons of the letters she typed for Richard, which is why the correspondence in his papers is unusually complete as well.

21 Unless otherwise indicated, all correspondence and other material cited is from this collection or from other Titmuss papers held by the author.

22 D. E. Smith, *The Everyday World as Problematic*, Milton Keynes, Open University Press, 1987.

23 D. Sheridan (ed.), *Among You Taking Notes ... The wartime diary of Naomi Mitchison*, Oxford, Oxford University Press, 1986.

24 R. Broad, S. Fleming (eds), *Nella Last's War*, London, Falling Wall Press, 1981.

25 A. Oakley, *Taking It Like a Woman*, London, Jonathan Cape, 1984.

26 V. Woolf, 'The new biography', *New York Herald Tribune*, 30.10.27.

27 J. Fisher Box, *R. A. Fisher: The life of a scientist*, New York, John Wiley, 1978.

28 H. Bosanquet, *Bernard Bosanquet: A short account of his life*, London, Macmillan, 1924.

29 M. Cole, *The Life of G. D. H. Cole*, London, Macmillan, 1971.

30 P. Rose, *Parallel Lives*, London, Chatto and Windus, 1984.

31 M. Gowing, *Richard Morris Titmuss 1907-1973*, Proceedings of the Royal Academy, London, Volume LXI, 1971; D. A. Riesman, *Richard Titmuss: Welfare*

and Society, London, Heinemann, 1977; J. Vaizey, *In Breach of Promise*, London, Weidenfeld and Nicolson, 1983; J. Kincaid, 'Richard Titmuss', in P. Barker (ed.) *Founders of the Welfare State*, London, Heinemann, 1984.

32 Gowing, op.cit.

33 Brian Abel-Smith was a co-student with John Vaizey at Cambridge and later a colleague of Richard Titmuss's at the London School of Economics and a close family friend.

34 Vaizey, op. cit., p. 75.

35 Gowing, op. cit., p. 29.

36 J. Brannen, K. Dodd, A. Oakley, P. Storey, *Young People, Health and Family Life*, Buckingham, Open University Press, 1994.

37 W. de la Mare, *Poems for Children*, London, Constable, 1930, pp. 118–19.

38 R. Fraser, *In Search of a Past*, London, Verso, 1984, p. 6.

39 M. Proust, *Remembrance of Things Past:1*, London, Penguin, 1983, p. 48.

40 Ibid., p. 49.

41 A. Christie, *An Autobiography*, London, Fontana, 1978.

42 M. Mannes, *Out of My Time*, London, Victor Gollancz, 1972.

43 G. Greer, *Daddy, We Hardly Knew You*, London, Penguin, 1990, p. 12.

44 C. Crawford, *Mommie Dearest*, New York, Berkley Books, 1978.

45 K. Chernin, *In My Mother's House*, London, Virago, 1985.

46 See, e.g., M. B. Belenky, B. M. Clinchy, N. R. Goldberger, J. M. Tarule, *Women's Ways of Knowing*, New York, Basic Books, 1986; C. Gilligan, *In a Different Voice: Psychological theory and women's development*, Cambridge, Mass., Harvard University Press, 1982.

47 L. M. Brown, C. Gilligan, *Meeting at the Crossroads*, New York, Ballantine, 1992, p. 2.

48 N. C. M. Hartsock, 'The feminist standpoint: Developing the ground

for a specifically feminist historical materialism', In S. Harding, M. B. Hintikka (eds), *Discovering Reality*, Dordrecht, Netherlands, D. Reidel, 1983, p. 299.

49 E. Martin, *The Woman in the Body*, Boston, Beacon Press, 1987.

50 Brannen et al, op. cit.

51 B. Adam, 'Social versus natural time', in M. Young, T. Schuller (eds), *The Rhythms of Society*, London, Routledge, 1988, p. 213.

52 W. de la Mare, op. cit., p. 120.

CHAPTER TWO: 'K' and 'Dick'

1 For details of the Farrs' family history, I am indebted to information supplied by Susan Harris.

2 C. Lamb, *The Essays of Elia*, London, Grant Richards, p. 109.

3 See Chapter 8.

4 M. Gowing, *Richard Morris Titmuss 1907–1973*, London, Proceedings of the Royal Academy, Volume LXI, 1975, p. 3.

5 Maude Titmuss to RMT, 6.2.37.

6 Lucy Masterman's husband, Charles, was a well-known Liberal politician who died in 1927.

7 R. Llewellyn, *How Green Was My Valley*, London, Landsborough Publications, 1958.

8 Mrs Pethick Lawrence, *My Part in a Changing World*, London, Victor Gollancz, 1938.

9 See Chapter 3.

10 KCM to Helen Johnston, 2.10.34.

11 RMT to KCM, 27.8.34.

12 KCM to Helen Johnston, 3.11.35.

13 KCM to Helen Johnston, 10.3.36.

CHAPTER THREE: Her work and his

1 R. G. Walton, *Women in Social Work*, London, Routledge and Kegan Paul, 1975.

2 B. Wootton, *In a World I Never Made*, London, Allen and Unwin, 1967, p. 56.

3 L. Krey, *And Tell of Time*, London, Collins, 1938.
4 Marion Milner published initially using the pseudonym Joanna Field.
5 J. Field, *An Experiment in Leisure*, London, Virago, 1986. The page number of this quote is missing and I have not been able to find it.
6 Women were included, though they were not the main focus.
7 H. Pelling, *Modern Britain 1885–1955*, Edinburgh, Thomas Nelson, 1960, p. 30.
8 R. S. Birch, *Psychology and the Individual*, London, Sampson Low, Marston & Co, 1930, p. 15.
9 W. D. McNaughton, *The Scottish Congregational Ministry 1794–1993*, Glasgow, Congregational Union of Scotland, 1993.
10 A. J. P. Taylor, *English History, 1914–1945*, Oxford, Clarendon Press, 1965, p. 284.
11 'Unemployment Scheme', *Fulham Chronicle*, 30.11.34.
12 *Fulham Chronicle*, 30.3.34.
13 *Fulham Chronicle*, 8.6.34.
14 Rev. R. S. Birch, MA, PhD, 'Unemployed in Fulham', n.d.
15 *The Times*, 9.2.39.
16 W. C. Johnston, *The Society of Writers to His Majesty's Signet, With a List of Members and Abstracts of the Minutes of the Society, the Commissioners and the Council, and the Early History of the Scottish Signet*, Edinburgh, Edinburgh University Press, 1936; *The W. S. Society & The Signet Library*, brochure, 1995; *Who Was Who Volume III*, London, Adam and Charles Black, 1941.
17 Undated. Helen's letters often were.
18 KCM to Helen Johnston, 22.4.34.
19 The Gas Light and Coke Company.
20 KCM to Helen Johnston, 2.10.39.
21 'Unemployment Scheme', *Fulham Chronicle*, 30.11.34.
22 KCM to Helen Johnston, 22.12.34.
23 Ibid.
24 KCM to Miss Neville, Secretary of the Winter Distress League, 11.4.34.
The 'collecting boxes' were distributed by the Mayor to local organizations.
25 KCM to Helen Johnston, 22.12.34.
26 KCM to Helen Johnston, 16.3.35.
27 KCM to Helen Johnston, 18.6.35.
28 'The Mayor of Fulham's Unemployment Scheme', undated paper, probably April 1935.
29 KCM to Helen Johnston, 18.6.35.
30 International Youth Tramps brochure, 1936, Youth House, 250 Camden Road, London NW1.
31 Mayor of Fulham to Dr Birch, 1.10.35.
32 KCM to Helen Johnston, 3.11.35.
33 KCM to the Mayor of Fulham, 10.1.36.
34 KCM to Helen Johnston, 10.3.36.
35 Ibid.
36 See Chapter 4.
37 KCM to Helen Johnston, 8.4.36.
38 The manuscript, *Crime and Tragedy*, was never published: see Chapter 4.
39 KCM to Helen Johnston, 15.6.36.
40 KCM to Helen Johnston, 21.7.36.
41 International Federation of League of Nations Societies, Geneva, leaflet, 1937.
42 Germany and Italy were on the organizing committee, but withdrew in July.
43 Taylor, op. cit., p. 353.
44 KCM to Helen Johnston, 21.7.36.
45 KCM to Helen Johnston, 4.11.36.
46 KCM to Helen Johnston, 6.12.36.
47 *Fulham Chronicle*, 7.1.38.
48 'Fulham Fellowship for the Unemployed', paper, 5.3.38.
49 KCT to the editor of the *Fulham Chronicle*, 17.3.38.
50 *Fulham Chronicle*, 27.1.39. Both the *Chronicle* and the *Fulham Gazette* carried reports of the Duke's visit on 27.1.39, and this description draws on both.
51 *Fulham Gazette*, 27.1.39.
52 KCT to Helen Johnston, 9.7.39.
53 KCT to Helen Johnston, 25.3.39.
54 KCT to Helen Johnston, 9.7.39.
55 Dr Birch to KCT, 11.3.40.

56 See Chapter 6.
57 KCT to Sydney Hurford, 10.6.43.
58 Ibid.
59 This was not true, I was named but we never worked together.
60 There's no evidence that this was so.

CHAPTER FOUR: His work and hers

1 *News Review*, 25.6.42.
2 *New Scientist*, 18.12.58.
3 RMT to J. N. Morris, 17.1.42.
4 *New Scientist*, op. cit.
5 RMT to Mr Thubrun of the *Post Magazine*, 21.10.43.
6 *Post Magazine and Insurance Monitor*, 6.11.43.
7 RMT to 'Burton', *Insurance Record*, 4.10.43.
8 See Chapter 3.
9 J. M. Henderson to RMT, 13.5.32.
10 There's no evidence of a family connection to either William or Samuel Farr.
11 RMT to the editor of the *Hendon and Finchley Times*, 27.7.35.
12 P. Clarke, *Liberals and Social Democrats*, Cambridge, Cambridge University Press, 1978, p. 4.
13 RMT to M. Newfield, 6.3.41.
14 KCT diary, 3.9.41.
15 Sir Henry Tizard, *Current Biography, 1949*, New York, H. W. Wilson Company, 1950.
16 R. M. Titmuss, 'The birth rate and insurance', in *Post Magazine and Insurance Monitor*, 19.12.36; R. M. Titmuss, 'Vital statistics', *Insurance Record*, December 1937.
17 *Brideian*, September 1935, p. 5.
18 Ibid.
19 See R. Scott, *Elizabeth Cadbury 1858–1951*, London, George G. Harrap, 1955.
20 See Chapters 3 and 8.
21 M. Ceadel, *Pacificism in Britain 1914–1945*, Oxford University Press, 1980.
22 A. J. P. Taylor, *English History 1914–1945*, Oxford, the Clarendon Press, 1965, p. 361.

23 A. Calder, *The People's War*, London, Granada, 1971, p. 27.
24 H. Pelling, *Modern Britain 1885–1950*, Edinburgh, Thomas Nelson, 1960, p. 90.
25 Taylor, op. cit.
26 *The World Youth Congress*, undated, p. 1.
27 British Youth Peace Assembly, *Aims and Objects and Standing Orders*, brochure, undated.
28 British Youth Peace Assembly, *Twelve Point Charter*, brochure, undated.
29 RMT to Joan Peel, secretary to the Youth Charter Group of the BYPA, 31.3.40.
30 RMT to B. Carrett, 28.5.37.
31 Helmut Blume to RMT, 18.3.40.
32 Jessica Dixon to RMT, 23.3.40.
33 *Crime and Tragedy*, p. 6.
34 Ibid., p. 9.
35 World Youth Congress, *The Signpost No. 11. A guide for preparation of the World Youth Congress. August 31st–September 7th 1936*, p. 1.
36 *Crime and Tragedy*, p. 9.
37 Ibid., p. 72.
38 Ibid., p. 77.
39 St Pancras Peace Council, undated.
40 *Crime and Tragedy*, p. 93.
41 Ibid., p. 87.
42 Cambridge scientists, *The Protection of the Public from Aerial Attack*, London, Victor Gollancz, 1937.
43 *Crime and Tragedy*, p. 88.
44 Ibid., pp. 105–6.
45 Ibid., p. 108.
46 Ibid., p. 105.
47 RMT to the Secretary of the Peace Pledge Union, 30.12.36.
48 A. Cummings to RMT, 2.10.36.
49 D. Woodman to RMT, 10.12.36.
50 RMT to Sylvia Pankhurst, 6.11.37.
51 Sylvia Pankhurst to RMT, 17.11.37.
52 Erik Warman for Stephen Aske to RMT, 5.11.37.
53 RMT, letter to Union of Democratic Control, 30.11.36.
54 F. le Gros Clark, R. M. Titmuss,

Our Food Problem, London, Penguin, 1939.

55 RMT to the County Fire Office, 6.4.39.

56 RMT to the Clerk of the Grocers' Company, 1.2.39.

57 RMT to the editor of *Picture Post*, 16.2.39.

58 R. M. Titmuss, *Poverty and Population*, London, Macmillan, 1938.

59 Macmillan, leaflet advertising *Poverty and Population*.

60 See Chapter 5.

61 See Chapter 6.

62 *Chester Chronicle*, 12.11.39.

63 *Yorkshire Observer*, 21.11.39.

64 *Daily Herald*, 28.10.39.

65 *Sheffield Telegraph*, 3.11.38.

66 *Newcastle Journal*, 8.4.39.

67 *Medical Press*, 29.5.40.

68 C. J. Ward to RMT, 5.10.36.

69 Youth House lecture series, London, Youth House, 1936.

70 B. H. Gore to RMT, 17.9.36.

71 RMT to B. H. Grove, 19.9.36.

72 Liberal Summer Schools, preliminary announcement, Cambridge, 3–9 August 1939.

73 See Chapter 2.

74 See Chapter 5.

75 See Chapter 6.

76 RMT to Laurence Cadbury, 18.6.39.

77 Richard Titmuss, 'Grey Rampart', undated manuscript.

78 He resigned from the Society shortly before his death in 1973.

79 RMT to Bill le Gros Clark, 19.9.38.

80 Frederick le Gros Clark, *Dictionary of National Biography*, 1971–1980.

81 Le Gros Clark and Titmuss, op. cit., p. 178.

82 'Deputation Committee', 19.3.37.

83 R. M. Titmuss, '193 years out of date', unpublished paper, n.d..

84 R. M. Titmuss, 'Medical statistics in wartime', *British Medical Journal*, 18.10.41 (letter).

85 RMT to the editors of the Population Index, 22.3.39.

86 RMT to the Secretary of the League of Nations, Geneva, 16.5.39.

87 E. Huws Jones, *Margery Fry: The essential amateur*, London, Oxford University Press, 1966.

88 RMT to M. Fry, 23.1.39.

89 M. Fry to RMT, 25.1.39. Mannheim, to whom Richard subsequently wrote, replied that it was all too complicated to sum up in a few sentences, and proposed a meeting.

90 RMT to the Rt Hon. Sir Montague Barlow, 18.2.39.

91 RMT to G. Marsh, 7.12.38.

92 RMT to G. Marsh, 28.1.39.

93 G. Marsh to RMT, 27.3.39.

94 RMT to G. Marsh, 14.5.39.

95 RMT to H. E. Magee, Ministry of Health, 24.1.39.

96 RMT to N. W. Posthumus, 5.2.39. There is no record of an answer.

97 Marie Meinhardt's lasting appreciation was marked during the writing of this book by a very substantial bequest made on her death to a fund established in Richard's memory at the LSE.

98 R. M. Titmuss, 'Health under the Nazis', *Truth*, 23.8.40.

99 R. M. Titmuss, 'Recent German vital statistics', *Lancet*, 10.10.42, p. 434.

100 R. M. Titmuss, 'Hitler's man-power problem', *Spectator*, 20.10.39.

101 See, for a discussion, D. Dwork, *War is Good for Babies and Other Young Children*, London, Tavistock, 1987.

102 R. Floud, K. Wachter, A. Gregory, *Height, Health and History*, Cambridge, Cambridge University Press, 1990.

103 RMT to the Director-General of the Medical Division, the War Office, 28.3.39.

104 Director-General of the Medical Division, the War Office, to RMT, 31.3.39.

105 See Chapter 6.

106 RMT to R. Acland, 14.8.38.

107 On 23.12.38, Acland sent Richard

a copy of a letter from H. H.
Hobbs, private secretary to Sir
Victor Warrende at the War Office,
to this effect.
108 RMT to R. Acland, 11.2.39.
109 R. Acland to RMT, 16.2.39.
110 Richard met the editor, Sydney
Elliott, at the National Liberal
Club, which shows the importance
of his political contacts.
111 *Reynolds News*, 7.5.39. A paper on
'Man-Power and Health' was also
published in the *Spectator*, 26.5.39.
112 RMT to Horder, 30.4.39. While
Horder was sympathetic, he was,
'[. . .] alas! [. . .]"over my ears"
and, as you know, I am in the "other
House"' (Horder to RMT,
6.5.39.). The *News Chronicle*,
Manchester Guardian, and *New
Statesman* joined the ranks of those
who didn't want to publish
Richard's articles on the health of the
army. In May, the *Spectator* took
'Health is Man-power' for five
guineas.
113 Undated letter.
114 Major-General Alexander to RMT,
26.5.39.
115 RMT to Major-General Alexander,
3.6.39.
116 Attributed to Alexander Carr-
Saunders, obituary of Professor D.
Glass, *The Times*, 27.9.78.
117 Ronald George to RMT, 15.12.40.

CHAPTER FIVE: What love can do

1 V. Brittain, *Testament of Experience*,
London, Virago, 1979, p. 213.
2 Richard was wrong about this.
3 L. Davidoff, J. L'Esperance, H.
Newby, 'Landscape with figures:
Home and community in English
society', in J. Mitchell, A. Oakley
(eds), *The Rights and Wrongs of
Women*, Harmondsworth, Penguin,
1976.
4 'Barton Hill Farm, Hexton',
undated leaflet; thanks to Susan
Harris for providing a copy of this.

5 J. G. Dony, *A History of the Straw
Hat Industry*, Luton, Leagrave Press,
1942.
6 R. M. Titmuss, *Problems of Social
Policy*, London, HMSO, p. 32.
7 Ibid. Information on the evacuation
is taken from *Problems of Social Policy*
unless noted otherwise.
8 F. Grundy, R. M. Titmuss, *Report
on Luton*, Luton, Leagrave Press,
1945, p. 23.
9 Ibid.
10 Titmuss, op. cit., p. 111.
11 Ibid.
12 Ibid., p. 137.
13 A. Noakes, *The County Fire Office
1807–1957: A commemorative
history*, London, H. F. & G.
Witherby Ltd, 1957.
14 Ibid., p. 172.
15 Grundy and Titmuss, op. cit.
16 F. Grundy, *A Handbook of Social
Medicine*, Luton, Gibbs, Bamforth,
1945.
17 *British Medical Journal*, 10.9.60,
p. 812.
18 RMT to Goodman, 30.10.39.
19 H. Ellis, *My Life*, London,
Heinemann, 1940, p. xiii.
20 Richard never learnt to drive.
21 See Chapter 6.
22 *News Chronicle*, 16.10.39.
23 A. Calder, *The People's War*,
London, Granada, 1971,
p. 72.
24 Titmuss, op. cit., p. 171.
25 RMT, manuscript letter,
'Evacuation: Opportunities and
problems', 27.9.39.
26 RMT, manuscript letter, 'Dispersal
and return', 28.10.39.
27 RMT to le Gros Clark, 7.12.39.
28 See A. S. Williams, *Women and
Childbirth: A history of the
National Birthday Trust Fund*,
forthcoming.
29 RMT to J. Rhys Williams, 11.10.39.
30 J. Rhys Williams to RMT, 17.10.39.
31 See Williams, op. cit.
32 Calder, op. cit., p. 81.
33 RMT to S. Rowntree, 19.10.39.
34 R. M. Titmuss, 'Hitler's man-power

problem', *Spectator*, 20.10.39, pp. 539–40.

35 R. M. Titmuss, 'The penalisation of parenthood', *Truth*, 24.11.39, pp. 571–2.

36 U. Grant-Duff to KCT, 18.4.40.

37 Obituary by C. Dover, *The Times*, 21.2.59.

38 R. S. Birch to KCT, 19.9.39.

39 G. Myrdal, *Population – A problem for democracy*, London, Humphrey Milford, 1940.

40 See Chapter 6.

41 M. Spring-Rice, *Working Class Wives*, Harmondsworth, Penguin, 1939.

42 F. Galton, *Inquiries into Human Faculty*, London, J. M. Dent, 1883, p. 17.

43 D. J. Kevles, *In the Name of Eugenics: Genetics and the uses of human heredity*, New York, Alfred A. Knopf, 1985, p. 8.

44 P. M. H. Mazumdar, *Eugenics, Human Genetics and Human Failings*, London, Routledge, 1992, pp. 7–8, 274.

45 M. Heseltine, *Eugenics Review*, 41, 1949, p. 109.

46 R. Graves, *Eugenics Review*, 41, 1949, p. 107.

47 RMT to M. Newfield, 7.12.39.

48 M. S. Teitelbaum, J. W. Winter, *The Fear of Population Decline*, London, Academic Press, 1985, p. 61.

49 F. Lafitte, interview with A. Oakley, 7.3.89.

50 Kevles, op. cit., p. 71.

51 Obituary, *Daily Telegraph*, 24.4.75.

52 See Chapter 6.

53 C. Bertram, *Eugenics Society Bulletin*, September 1975.

54 See Chapter 6.

55 Obituaries, Byrom Stanley Bramwell, *Eugenics Review*, January 1949, pp. 184–91.

56 Thomas Jeeves Horder, *Current Biography 1944*, New York, H. W. Wilson Company, 1945. The story of eugenics is taken up again in Chapter 7.

57 Barnett House Study Group, *London Children in War-Time Oxford*, London, Oxford University Press, 1947, p. 31.

58 See, e.g. G. F. McCleary, *The Maternity and Child Welfare Movement*, London, P. S. King, 1935.

59 RMT to McCleary, 13.3.40.

60 Calder, op. cit., p. 128.

61 N. Nicolson (ed.) Harold Nicolson, *Diaries & Letters 1939–45*, London, Fontana, 1970, p. 66.

62 Calder, op. cit., p. 149.

63 R. M. Titmuss, 'Can the poor save?' *Spectator*, 23.2.40.

64 A. M. Jones (letter), *Spectator*, 1.3.40.

65 R. M. Titmuss (letter), *Spectator*, 8.3.40.

66 R. M. Titmuss, 'The Health and Physique of British Youth: A memorandum based on recent official statistical evidence,' unpublished paper, n.d.

67 M. D. Stocks, *Eleanor Rathbone: A biography*, London, V. Gollancz, 1949.

68 E. Rathbone, *The Ethics and Economics of Family Endowment*, London, Epworth Press, 1927.

69 Eleanor Rathbone to RMT, 30.4.40.

70 Calder, op. cit., p. 99.

71 Ibid., p. 128.

72 RMT to L. Cadbury, 15.5.40.

73 L. Cadbury to RMT, 20.5.40.

74 G. Harman to G. C. Touche, 22.3.42.

75 Ellis, op. cit., p. 43.

76 Ibid., pp. 68–9.

77 Stocks, op. cit., p. 279.

CHAPTER SIX: *Parents Revolt*

1 The Rev. Birch had returned to Scotland for two years.

2 R. M. Titmuss, *Problems of Social Policy*, London, HMSO, p. 286.

3 D. Russell, *The Tamarisk Tree: My*

School and the Years of the War,
London, Virago, 1980, p. 18.

4 A. Calder, *The People's War*,
London, Granada, 1971, p. 215.

5 P. Ziegler, *London at War 1939–
1945*, London, Sinclair-Stevenson,
1995, p. 130.

6 V. Brittain, *Testament of Experience*,
London, Virago, 1979, p. 284.

7 M. D. Stocks, *Eleanor Rathbone: A
biography*, London, V. Gollancz,
1949, p. 280.

8 Ziegler, op. cit., p. 70.

9 Calder, op. cit., p. 331.

10 Titmuss, op. cit., p. 263.

11 Unidentified news cutting: 'The
Angel reveals her blitz secret'.

12 Calder, op. cit., p. 261.

13 V. Glendinning, *Elizabeth Bowen:
Portrait of a Writer*, London,
Weidenfeld & Nicolson, 1977,
p. 149.

14 Calder, op. cit., p. 258.

15 E. Bowen, *The Heat of the Day*,
Harmondsworth, Penguin, 1962,
p. 87.

16 Calder, op. cit., p. 201.

17 RMT to M. Newfield, 26.4.41.

18 Titmuss, op. cit., p. 350.

19 RMT to M. Newfield, 10.6.41.

20 RMT to J. N. Morris, 7.12.42.

21 Mrs Dobson to RMT, November
1941.

22 KCT to Mrs Dobson, 12.11.41.

23 'Report on Returns of Material
Relief given in January by the
North St Pancras Committee of the
Charity Organization Society
1943', and 'Report on Returns from
Chesterfield Borough Welfare
Committee January–March 1943',
unpublished manuscripts.

24 RMT to J. N. Morris, 14.12.41.

25 RMT to H. E. Magee, 5.6.40.

26 RMT to the External Registrar,
University of London, 26.11.40.

27 RMT to M. Newfield, 6.3.41.

28 D. Hay, 'British historians and the
beginnings of the civil history of the
Second World War', in M. R. D.
Foot (ed.), *War and Society*,
London, Elek, 1973.

29 J. Huxley, *Memories*, London, Allen
and Unwin, 1970, p. 140.

30 W. K. Hancock, *Discovering
Monaro: A study of man's impact on
his environment*, Cambridge,
Cambridge University Press,
1962.

31 Obituary of W. K. Hancock, T.
Millar, *Guardian*, 19.8.88.

32 Hay, op. cit., p. 45.

33 W. K. Hancock, *Argument of
Empire*, Harmondsworth, Penguin,
1943, p. 152.

34 W. K. Hancock, *Country and
Calling*, London, Faber and Faber,
1954, p. 105.

35 Ibid., p. 197.

36 R. J. Hammond, 'British wartime
food control: Some addenda to an
official history', *Food Research
Institute Studies*, Vol. III, no. 3,
November 1962, pp. 183–94.

37 Obituary, Mrs Eva M. Hubback,
Eugenics Review, 41, pp. 141–2;
Evening News, 26.2.45. The
reference to Eva Hubback's lateness
comes from a letter from C. P.
Blacker to M. Newfield, 15.7.49
(Eugenics Society Archives, ES
C.247).

38 RMT to J. N. Morris, 6.9.42.

39 RMT to M. Newfield, 28.12.41.

40 RMT to J. N. and G. Morris,
29.1.42.

41 RMT to Bridgman (County Fire
Office), 13.3.42.

42 KCT to Helen Johnston, 10.2.42.

43 RMT to M. Newfield, 6.2.42.

44 Arthur MacNalty, *Dictionary of
National Biography 1961–70*.

45 RMT to J. N. Morris, 20.6.42.

46 RMT to M. Newfield, 3.7.42.

47 Ziegler, op. cit., pp. 122, 144.

48 RMT to M. Newfield, 6.2.42.

49 Hancock, *Country and Calling*,
pp. 193–4.

50 'Appendix I Lectures'. London,
St Paul's Cathedral, undated.

51 Address at the Service of
Thanksgiving for the St Paul's Fire
Guard Watch 1939–1945 on
Tuesday, May 8th, 1945, The Day

of Victory by W. R. Matthews, KCVO, D.Litt., DD, Dean of St Paul's.

52 KCT to Mr H. E. Roff, 10.11.42.

53 KCT to Mr M. Myant, 26.2.42.

54 R. M. Titmuss, 'The end of economic parenthood', *New Statesman and Nation*, 9.8.41, pp. 130–1.

55 R. H. Tawney, *The Acquisitive Society*, Cheltenham, Cheltenham Press, 1921.

56 R. Acland, *Unser Kampf*, Harmondsworth, Penguin, 1940.

57 P. Addison, *The Road to 1945*, London, Pimlico Books, 1994, p. 158.

58 RMT to R. Acland, 17.2.40.

59 F. Lafitte, *Left News*, April 1942.

60 Bill le Gros Clark to RMT, 17.11.39.

61 RMT to M. Newfield, 7.2.41.

62 F. W. Tilley (corresponding secretary of Christ and Unemployment Crusade) to R. Acland, 10.4.41.

63 RMT to M. Newfield, 2.5.40.

64 RMT to M. Newfield, 19.5.40.

65 Addison, op. cit., p. 159.

66 R. Acland, *The Times*, 15.10.43.

67 *Picture Post*, 27.9.41.

68 RMT to J. N. Morris, 19.7.42.

69 'Common Wealth Party Funds: Sir R. Acland's warning', *The Times*, 10.4.44.

70 *The Times*, 8.1.45.

71 He resigned ten years later in protest against the Labour Party's position on nuclear defence.

72 RMT to R. Acland, 5.6.42.

73 Quoted in Addison, op. cit., p. 189.

74 The title had no apostrophe, though one printer (*Wiltshire and Gloucestershire Standard*, 10.10.42) gave it one, and the reviewer, a Rev. J. A. Thomas, apologized for this to Richard (J. A. Thomas to RMT, 27.10.42).

75 F. Warburg to RMT, 13.8.41.

76 *Catholic Herald*, 25.9.42.

77 *Sunday Times*, 9.8.42.

78 R. M. Titmuss, 'Insurance and depopulation', *Insurance Record*, May 1937, pp. 152–3.

79 Horder and R. M. Titmuss (letter), 'The birth rate', *The Times*, 20.4.42.

80 *Glasgow Herald*, 8.6.42.

81 *Daily Record and Mail*, 8.6.42.

82 *Daily Mail*, 8.6.42.

83 M. S. Teitelbaum, J. M. Winter, *The Fear of Population Decline*, London, Academic Press, 1985.

84 Ibid., p. 9.

85 R. Titmuss, K. Titmuss, *Parents Revolt*, London, Secker and Warburg, 1942, p. 14.

86 *Eugenics Review*, 59, 1967, p. 5.

87 A. Carr-Saunders, *Dictionary of National Biography 1961–70*.

88 *Eugenics Review*, 59, 1967, p. 7.

89 E. Charles, *The Twilight of Parenthood*, London, C. A. Watts, 1934, p. 75.

90 L. Hogben, *Nature and Nurture*, quoted in Charles, op. cit. p. 135.

91 *Glasgow Herald*, 8.6.42.

92 D. Glass, *The Struggle for Population*, Oxford, Clarendon Press, 1936, p. 88.

93 D. J. Kevles, *In the Name of Eugenics: Genetics and the uses of human heredity*, New York, Alfred A. Knopf, 1985, pp. 178–9.

94 E. Elderton, *Report on the English Birthrate*, London, Dulau, 1914.

95 I. H. Pearse, 'Observations on the population question', a memorandum presented to the Royal Commission on Population, November 1944.

96 A. B. White to RMT, 28.2.42. The pamphlet was published in the 'Unless we plan now' Handbooks for Discussion Groups series (R. M. Titmuss, *Problems of Population*, London, English Universities Press Ltd, n.d.).

97 RMT to A. B. White, 11.3.42.

98 M. Stopes (letter), *Lancet*, 10.1.42, pp. 58–9.

99 SA/EUG/P.52.

100 SA/EUG/D.37.

101 RMT to M. Pyke, 15.9.41. This was

an unusual early example of a randomised controlled trial.

102 SA/EUG/D.18,24–5.

103 A. Myrdal, G. Myrdal, *Crisis in the Population Question*, 1934. The book was not published in English. Its substance was contained in a book by A. Myrdal, *Nation and Family*, London, Kegan Paul, Trench, Trubner, 1945.

104 See Chapter 11.

105 *Eugenics Review*, 40, 1947, pp. 88–9.

106 Robert René Kuczynski, *Dictionary of National Biography 1941–50.*

107 The director, Boeckh himself may have got it from Britain's William Farr (F. M. M. Lewes, 'A note on the origin of the Reproduction Ratio', *Population Studies*, Vol. 38, 1984, pp. 321–4).

108 David Glass (op. cit., p. 6) simply maintained that '[. . .] conditions in Sweden in the last sixty years have probably been very similar'.

109 RMT to M. Newfield, 9.8.41.

110 RMT to M. Newfield, May 1942 (undated).

111 Obituary of Professor David Glass, *The Times*, 27.9.78.

112 Ruth Glass, *The Annual Obituary*, 1990, pp. 169–71.

113 M. Newfield to RMT, 4.12.42.

114 C. M. Langford, *The Population Investigation Committee: A concise history to mark its fiftieth anniversary*, London, PIC, 1988, p. 5.

115 Richard Titmuss joined the committee later as a representative of LSE but was on the advisory board of the committee's journal, *Population Studies*, from the outset in 1947.

116 Beatrice Webb to RMT, 7.3.42.

117 *Everybody's Weekly*, 7.11.43.

118 *New Statesman and Nation*, 5.9.42.

119 *The Times*, 8.10.42.

120 *Spectator*, 30.10.42.

121 *Fortnightly Review*, September 1942.

122 *Tablet*, 26.8.42.

123 *Lancet*, 14.11.42.

124 *Western Telegraph*, 5.9.42.

125 *Medical Officer*, 3.10.42.

126 'Too few babies?' *Listener*, 19.11.42.

127 L. Cadbury to RMT, 14.11.42.

128 RMT to L. Cadbury, 17.11.42.

129 B. Hardcastle to RMT, 20.11.42.

130 Anon. to RMT, 14.11.42.

131 A. Bennett to RMT, 15.11.42.

132 Anon. to RMT, 8.3.43.

133 Mrs Yandle to RMT, 13.11.42.

134 'Mrs CLR' to RMT, 14.11.42.

135 'P. M.' to RMT, 25.8.42.

136 RMT to J. N. Morris, 16.11.42. It isn't a necessary characteristic of academics that they don't answer letters.

137 RMT to M. Newfield, 8.8.42.

138 RMT to M. Newfield, 7.9.42.

139 Carr-Saunders to RMT, 9.8.42.

140 KCT to A. H. Halsey, 20.1.81.

141 Ziegler, op. cit., p. 160.

142 RMT to J. N. Morris, 19.7.42.

143 RMT to J. N. Morris, 10.8.42.

CHAPTER SEVEN: Nature or nurture?

1 Mr Clarke to C. P. Blacker, 22.8.44, Eugenics Society Archives, SA/EUG/D.97.

2 Mrs Vigers to Mrs Collyer, 22.12.40, SA/EUG/D.95.

3 Mrs Boyd-Bowman to C. P. Blacker, 1.9.44, SA/EUG/D.95.

4 RMT to M. Newfield, 88.8.42.

5 A. McLaren, *Our Own Master Race: Eugenics in Canada, 1885–1945*, Toronto. McClelland and Stewart, 1990, p. 148.

6 RMT to M. Newfield, 7.9.42.

7 Editorial, 'Homes in Canada', *Eugenics Review*, 32, 2, 1940, p. 47.

8 SA/EUG/D.95.

9 McLaren, op. cit., p. 148.

10 D. J. Kevles, *In the Name of Eugenics: Genetics and the uses of human heredity*, New York, Alfred A. Knopf, 1985, p. 172.

11 P. M. H. Mazumdar, *Eugenics,*

Human Genetics and Human Failings, London, Routledge, 1992, p. 213.

12 McLaren, op. cit., p. 149.

13 F. Schenk, A. S. Parkes, 'The activities of the Eugenics Society', *Eugenics Review*, 60, 1968, pp. 142–59.

14 Eugenics Society meeting, 1.8.40, SA/EUG/D.91.

15 McLaren, op. cit., p. 149.

16 Kevles, op. cit., p. 58.

17 See, e.g., G. Jones, *Social Hygiene in Twentieth Century Britain*, London, Croom Helm, 1986; D. Mackenzie, 'Eugenics in Britain', *Social Studies of Science*, 6, 1976, pp. 499–532.

18 P. Weindling, *Health, Race and German Politics between National Unification and Nazism 1870–1945*, Cambridge, Cambridge University Press, 1989.

19 Mazumdar, op. cit., pp. 206–7.

20 Weindling, op. cit., p. 7.

21 A. Sharf, *The British Press and Jews under Nazi Rule*, London, Oxford University Press, 1964. See also F. Honigsbaum, *The Division in British Medicine*, London, Kogan Page, 1979, chapter 27.

22 *Daily Telegraph*, 11.11.38.

23 *News Chronicle*, 31.10.39.

24 Sharf, op. cit.

25 *Independent*, 9.5.95.

26 Sharf, op. cit., p. 88.

27 Weindling, op. cit., p. 533.

28 *Eugenics Review*, 25, 1933/4, p. 179.

29 C. P. Blacker to M. Newfield, 18.8.33, SA/EUG/C.243.

30 See the letters in SA/EUG/C.132.II.

31 C. P. Blacker to U. Grant-Duff, 21.8.35, SA/EUG/C.132.II.

32 H. Ellis, *The Task of Social Hygiene*, London, Constable, 1912, p. 401.

33 *News Chronicle*, 24.11.34.

34 C. P. Blacker to G. Pitt-Rivers, March 1932, SA/EUG/C.273.

35 C. P. Blacker to J. Huxley, 7.5.35, SA/EUG/C.105.

36 F. Tietze, 'Eugenic measures in the Third Reich', paper given to Eugenics Society meeting, 17.1.39.

37 C. P. Blacker to U. Grant-Duff, 23.12.38, SA/EUG/C.132.II.

38 Huxley to C. P. Blacker, note in Eugenics Society files of telephone conversation, 7.5.35.

39 J. Huxley, 'Eugenics and society', Galton lecture, *Eugenics Review*, 27, pp. 11–31. Richard met Hogben at the suggestion of Hogben's medical brother, Hamilton, some time in late 1943 (RMT to H. Hogben, 25.9.43).

40 C. Chance to C. P. Blacker, 9.7.43, SA/EUG/C.64.

41 J. N. Morris to A. Oakley, 14.5.95.

42 R. M. Titmuss, F. Lafitte, 'Eugenics and poverty', *Eugenics Review*, 33, 4, pp. 106–12.

43 L. Cadbury to RMT, 23.2.42.

44 RMT to L. Cadbury, 2.3.42.

45 RMT to C. O. Carter, 3.3.42.

46 Eugenics Society meeting, 14.7.42.

47 RMT to L. Cadbury, 22.10.41.

48 M. Newfield to RMT, 6.10.39.

49 R. M. Titmuss, 'The social environment and eugenics', *Eugenics Review*, 36, 2, 1944, pp. 53–8.

50 Ibid., p. 57.

51 RMT to M. Newfield, 3.2.41.

52 RMT to J. N. Morris, 10.8.42.

53 R. M. Titmuss, *Birth, Poverty and Wealth*, London, Hamish Hamilton, p. 9.

54 RMT to M. Newfield, 25.1.43.

55 RMT to M. Newfield, 21.6.41.

56 RMT to M. Newfield, 3.7.41.

57 Titmuss, op. cit., p. 9.

58 M. Newfield to RMT, 11.2.43.

59 Titmuss, *Birth, Poverty and Wealth*, p. 11.

60 RMT to M. Newfield, 21.6.41.

61 M. Newfield to RMT, 12.6.41.

62 RMT to M. Newfield, 21.6.41.

63 M. Newfield to Lord Horder, 11.8.41.

64 RMT to M. Newfield, 22.5.41.

65 M. Newfield to C. Chance, 12.6.42.

66 Beveridge's letter in *The Times*

(24.9.43) argued for a 'concentrated attack' on infant mortality and all its causes 'on a broad front', which would cover better health services, better nutrition, better housing and better education.

67 A. Carr-Saunders to RMT, 26.8.43.

68 RMT to A. Carr-Saunders, 30.8.42.

69 RMT to M. Newfield, 3.7.42.

70 *London News*, December 1943–January 1944.

71 *Daily Herald*, 20.9.43.

72 *News Chronicle*, 30.9.43.

73 *British Medical Journal*, 18.12.43.

74 *New Leader*, 15.1.44.

75 *Nursing Mirror*, 4.12.43.

76 *John Bull*, 16.10.43.

77 *New Statesman and Nation*, 9.10.43.

78 *The Economist*, 30.10.43.

79 *Friend*, 28.1.44.

80 *Daily Worker*, 1.3.44.

81 *The Evening Citizen*, 5.1.44 op. cit.

82 *British Medical Journal*.

83 *The Economist*, 30.10.43.

84 L. Hogben, *Nature and Nurture*, London, G. Allen and Unwin, 1939, p. 33.

85 Mazumdar, op. cit., p. 155.

86 Ibid., p. 150.

87 *Nature*, 23.10.43.

88 RMT to J. N. Morris, 28.3.49.

89 Kevles, op. cit., p. 63.

90 W. I. Inge, SA/EUG/F.3.

91 J. Lewis, *What Price Community Medicine?*, London, Wheatsheaf, 1986.

92 J. N. Morris to A. Oakley, 14.5.95.

93 RMT to R. Acland, 2.6.44.

94 KCT to Kathleen Hobday, 12.6.41.

95 See D. Porter, 'Changing disciplines: John Ryle and the making of social medicine in Britain in the 1940s', *History of Science*, xxx, 1992, pp. 137–64.

96 A. St G. Huggett and RMT to members of the CSSM, 18.11.42.

97 Letter to members of the CSSM, 18.11.42.

98 J. N. Morris to A. Oakley, 14.5.95.

99 J. N. Morris, R. M. Titmuss,

'Epidemiology of juvenile rheumatism', *Lancet*, 18.7.42, pp. 59–65.

100 J. N. Morris to A. Oakley, 14.5.95.

101 J. N. Morris, R. M. Titmuss, 'Health and social change: 1: The recent history of rheumatic heart disease', *Medical Officer*, 26.8.44, pp. 85–6.

102 J. N. Morris, R. M. Titmuss, 'Epidemiology of peptic ulcer: Vital statistics', *Lancet*, 30.12.44, pp. 841–56.

103 Ibid., p. 849.

104 From honorary secretary Dr L. J. Harris to RMT, 6.3.42.

105 See Chapter 8.

106 A. St G. Huggett to RMT, 18.11.42. Richard's paper was called 'Stillbirth and neo-natal mortality' and was given on 6.2.43.

107 RMT to M. Newfield, 9.2.43.

108 D. Baird to RMT, 16.3.43.

109 KCT to J. N. Morris, 16.11.42.

110 KCT to J. N. Morris, 5.12.42.

111 RMT to J. N. Morris, 8.10.42.

112 R. Broad, S. Fleming (eds), *Nella Last's War*, London, Falling Wall Press, p. 221.

113 N. Nicolson (ed.), *Harold Nicolson Diaries and Letters 1939–45*, London, Fontana, 1970.

114 J. Huxley, *Memories*, London, Allen and Unwin, 1970, p. 254.

CHAPTER EIGHT: Having Adrian

1 RMT to M. Newfield, 11.6.43.

2 RMT to J. N. Morris, 27.6.43.

3 R. Titmuss, K. Titmuss, *Parents Revolt*, London, Secker and Warburg, 1942, pp. 122–3.

4 Ibid., p. 88.

5 Ibid., p. 89.

6 J. Graunt, *National and Political Observations upon the Bills of Mortality*, London, 1662.

7 Titmuss and Titmuss, op. cit., p. 93.

8 See N. Mitchison, *You May Well Ask*, London, Flamingo, 1986, p. 34.

9 RMT to M. Newfield, 11.10.41.

10 RMT to M. Newfield, 1.4.42.
11 RMT to W. Brown, 6.4.42.
12 RMT to M. Newfield, 8.8.42.
13 M. Newfield to RMT, 13.8.42.
14 P. Ziegler, *London at War 1939–1945*, London, Sinclair-Stevenson, 1995, p. 82.
15 L. M. Verbrugge, 'Gender and health: An update on hypotheses and evidence', *Journal of Health and Social Behavior*, 26, 1985, pp. 156–82.
16 KCT to K. Hobday, 23.2.43.
17 Robert Graves, obituary of M. Newfield, *Eugenics Review*, 41, 3, 1949, p. 107.
18 D. J. Kevles, *In the Name of Eugenics: Genetics and the uses of human heredity*, New York, Alfred A. Knopf, 1985, p. 9.
19 J. B. Haldane, *Heredity and Politics*, London, Allen and Unwin, 1938, p. 124.
20 E. Charles, *The Twilight of Parenthood*, London, C. A. Watts, 1934, p. 130.
21 Ibid., p. 134.
22 See Chapter 7.
23 A. Myrdal, V. Klein, *Women's Two Roles*, London, Routledge and Kegan Paul, 1956.
24 M. Komarovsky, 'Cultural contradictions and sex roles', *American Journal of Sociology*, 52, pp. 182–9.
25 See M. Komarovsky, *Women in College*, New York, Basic Books, 1985.
26 C. White, *Women's Magazines*, London, Michael Joseph, 1970, p. 99.
27 Ibid., p. 123.
28 See J. Mitchell, 'Women: The longest revolution', *New Left Review*, 40, 1966.
29 See O. Banks, *Faces of Feminism*, Oxford, Martin Robertson, 1981. These conflicting contentions earmark the central debate of feminism which has never been resolved.
30 G. Steinem, *Moving Beyond Words*, London, Bloomsbury, 1994, p. 33.
31 V. Klein, *The Feminine Character*, London, Kegan Paul, Trench, Trubner, 1946, p. 71.
32 F. Lundberg, L. F. Farnham, *Modern Woman: The lost sex*, New York, Harper and Bros., 1947, pp. 395–6.
33 Ibid., p. 396.
34 J. N. Morris to RMT, 17.7.43.
35 R. M. Titmuss, 'The position of women', in R. M. Titmuss, *Essays on the Welfare State*, London, Allen and Unwin, 1958, p. 89.
36 Ibid., p. 88.
37 H. Rose, 'Re-reading Titmuss: the sexual division of welfare', *Journal of Social Policy*, 10, 4, 1981, pp. 477–502.
38 A. Lewis, 'Incidence of neurosis in England under war conditions', *Lancet*, 15.8.42., pp. 178–83.
39 E. Showalter, *The Female Malady: Women, madness and English culture, 1830–1980*, London, Virago, p. 123.
40 Ibid., pp. 134–5.
41 C. P. Gilman, 'The yellow wallpaper', *New England Magazine*, January 1892.
42 R. S. Birch, *Psychology and the Individual*, London, Sampson Low, Marston, 1931, pp. 65–6.
43 KCT diary, 13.6.43.
44 J. N. Morris to KCT, 23.6.43.
45 RMT to M. Newfield, 18.7.42.
46 M. Newfield to KCT, 18.7.42.
47 RMT to M. Newfield, 16.11.42.
48 J. N. Morris to RMT, April 1942.
49 RMT to M. Newfield, 28.12.41.
50 RMT to M. Newfield, 26.5.42.
51 RMT to M. Newfield, undated, May 1942.
52 M. Newfield to RMT, 1.4.43.
53 M. Newfield to C. P. Blacker, 26.8.35, Eugenics Society Archives, ES C.244; S. Newfield to Miss Collyer, 9.11.37, ES C.245.
54 S. Newfield to Miss Schenk, 30.10.47, ES C.246.
55 J. N. Morris to RMT, 13.7.42.
56 J. N. Morris to RMT, 23.10.42.
57 J. N. Morris to RMT, 29.5.43.

58 J. Huxley, *Memories*, London, Allen and Unwin, 1970, p. 160.

59 M. Newfield to RMT, 25.3.42.

60 RMT to M. Newfield, 22.5.42.

61 RMT to M. Newfield, 7.9.42.

62 RMT to M. Newfield, 22.11.42.

63 RMT to M. Newfield, 30.3.43.

64 J. N. Morris to RMT, 13.4.43.

65 Obituary of Aleck Bourne, *British Medical Journal*, 11.1.75, p. 99.

66 A. Bourne, *Health of the Future*, Harmondsworth, Penguin, 1942, p. 42.

67 M. Newfield to RMT, 14.6.43.

68 J. N. Morris to RMT, 17.7.43.

69 RMT to J. N. Morris, 27.6.43.

70 J. N. Morris to RMT, 13.8.43.

71 Ann was a family name.

72 M. Newfield to RMT, 8.12.43.

73 RMT to J. N. Morris, 4.1.44.

74 RMT to J. N. Morris, 10.8.42.

75 J. N. Morris to RMT, 30.1.44.

76 M. Newfield to RMT, 19.7.43.

77 M. Newfield to RMT, 1.9.43.

78 RMT to M. Newfield, 2.9.43.

79 Anne Carr to RMT, 20.2.44.

80 RMT to J. N. Morris, 31.1.44.

81 F. Powdermaker, L. I. Grimes, *The Intelligent Parents' Manual*, London, Heinemann, 1944, p. 11.

82 RMT to J. N. Morris, 31.1.44.

83 RMT to J. N. Morris, 19.2.44.

84 A. Calder, *The People's War*, London, Granada, 1971, p. 641.

85 RMT to J. N. Morris, 14.3.44.

86 RMT to J. N. Morris, 28.3.44.

CHAPTER NINE: Is she still squeaking?

1 RMT to KCT, 3.7.44.

2 A. Calder, *The People's War*, London, Granada, 1971, p. 645.

3 N. Nicolson (ed.), *Harold Nicolson: Diaries and Letters 1939–45*, London, Fontana, 1970, p. 395.

4 W. K. Hancock, *Country and Calling*, London, Faber and Faber, 1954, pp. 184–5.

5 Not all of these are quoted in this and the next chapter.

6 K. L. Miller to KCT, 21.9.40.

7 E. Bowen, *The Heat of the Day*, Harmondsworth, Penguin, 1962, p. 329.

8 M. Newfield to RMT, 27.3.44.

9 RMT to J. N. Morris, 8.7.44.

10 *Picture Post*, July 1944.

11 P. Ziegler, *London at War 1939–1945*, London, Sinclair-Stevenson, 1995, p. 301.

12 W. K. Hancock, *Country and Calling*, London, Faber and Faber, 1954, pp. 195–6.

13 C. Hardyment, *Dream Babies*, London, Cape, 1983.

14 Nicolson (ed.), op. cit., p. 394.

15 R. M. Titmuss, *Fewer Children: The population problem*, Army Broadsheet on Current Affairs, 1944, p. 8.

16 Ibid., p. 11.

CHAPTER TEN: Doing half my job

1 R. M. Titmuss, *Problems of Social Policy*, London, HMSO, p. 428.

2 P. Ziegler, *London at War 1939–1945*, London, Sinclair-Stevenson, 1995, p. 309.

3 This suggests she was still in touch with Birch, although there is no surviving correspondence. Letters were obviously thrown away; one of Kay's to Richard in October 1944 was written on the back of one from Helen Johnston, but these letters were not kept.

4 Estimated date.

5 Titmuss, op. cit., p. 434.

6 Ziegler, op. cit., p. 298.

7 A. Calder, *The People's War*, London, Granada, 1971, pp. 649–50.

8 Ziegler, op. cit., p. 298.

9 C. P. Blacker to U. Grant-Duff, 4.10.44.

10 Honorary secretary, the Union Sub-committee for Social Reconstruction to RMT, 17.8.44.

11 Secretary, *Mother and Child*, to RMT, 13.9.44.

12 Titmuss, op. cit., p. 434.

CHAPTER ELEVEN: The road to
Acton

1 C. Degler, *At Odds: Women and the
family in America from the
Revolution to the present*, New York,
Oxford University Press, 1980.

2 J. M. Winter, 'Socialism, social
democracy, and population questions
in Western Europe 1870–1950', in
M. S. Teitelbaum, J. M. Winter
(eds), *Population and Resources in
Western Intellectual Tradition.
Population and Development Review*,
Supplement, Vol. 14, 1988, New
York, Population Council.

3 D. Russell, *The Tamarisk Tree, 2: My
School and the Years of War*,
London, Virago, 1988.

4 D. Russell, *The Tamarisk Tree, 1: My
Quest for Liberty and Love*, London,
Virago, 1977, p. 160.

5 J. Huxley, *Memories*, London, Allen
and Unwin, 1970, p. 160.

6 Ibid., preface.

7 J. Fisher Box, *R. A. Fisher: The life
of a scientist*, New York, John Wiley,
1978, pp. 390–1.

8 A. Myrdal, *Nation and Family*,
London, Kegan Paul, Trench,
Trubner, 1945, p. 121.

9 Ibid., pp. 131–2.

10 N. Nicolson (ed.) *Harold Nicolson:
Diaries and Letters 1939–45*,
London, Fontana, 1970, p. 417.

11 KCT diary, July 1948..

12 M. Gowing, interview with A.
Oakley, 28.7.94; CAB.103/408,
Public Records Office.

13 J. Harris, 'Social planning in war-
time: Some aspects of the Beveridge
Report', in J. M. Winter (ed.), *War
and Economic Development*,
Cambridge, Cambridge University
Press, 1975, p. 241.

14 E. Wilson, *Only Half Way to
Paradise*, London, Tavistock, 1980.

15 See J. Lewis, *Women in Britain Since
1945*, Oxford, Blackwell, 1992.

16 C. Pateman, M. L. Shanley,
introduction, in M. L. Shanley,
C. Pateman (eds), *Feminist

Interpretations and Political Theory*,
Cambridge, Polity Press, 1991, p. 3.

17 J. B. Elshtain, *Public Man, Private
Woman*, Oxford, Martin Robertson,
1981, p. 141.

18 Ibid., p. 4.

19 R. M. Titmuss, 'The social division
of welfare', in *Essays on the Welfare
State*, London, Allen and Unwin,
1958.

20 H. Rose, 'Re-reading Titmuss: The
sexual division of welfare', *Journal of
Social Policy*, 10,4, 1981, pp. 477–
502, p. 497.

21 R. M. Titmuss, *The Gift Relationship*,
London, Allen and Unwin, 1970.

22 D. A. Riesman, *Richard Titmuss:
Welfare and Society*, London,
Heinemann, 1977, p. 178.

23 See U. O'Connor, *Biographers and
the Art of Biography*, London,
Quartet Books, 1991.

24 M. C. Bateson, *With a Daughter's
Eye*, New York, Pocket Books, 1984,
p. 288.

25 Christopher Isherwood's book about
his parents, *Kathleen and Frank*
(London, Minerva, 1971), is more
revealing about him in some ways
than his autobiography, *Christopher
and His Kind* (London, Eyre
Methuen, 1977).

26 Isherwood, *Kathleen and Frank*,
p. 2.

27 N. Nicolson, *Portrait of a Marriage*,
London, Weidenfeld and Nicolson,
1973.

28 J. Harris, *William Beveridge: a
biography*, Oxford, Clarendon Press,
1977, p. 457.

29 R. Manning, *A Corridor of Mirrors*,
London, Women's Press, 1987,
p. 69.

30 This is the recollection of Frank
Honigsbaum (letter to A. Oakley,
14.5.95).

31 E. Bagnold, *Enid Bagnold's
Autobiography*, London, Century,
1985, p. 44.

32 W. K. Hancock, *Country and
Calling*, London, Faber and Faber,
1954, pp. 189–90.

33 I. Smallwood, *A Childhood at Green Hedges*, London, Methuen, 1989.
34 Lord Beveridge, *India Called Them*, London, Allen and Unwin, 1947.
35 Harris, op. cit., p. 69.
36 S. de Beauvoir, *A Very Easy Death*, London, Penguin, 1969.
37 Ibid., p. 32.
38 Bateson, op. cit., p. 77.
39 Lord Horder, introduction, in J. Marchant (ed.), *Rebuilding Family Life in the Post-War World*, London, Odhams Press, 1945, p. 5.
40 Sir A. S. MacNalty, 'Health and the family', in J. Marchant (ed.), op. cit., p. 67.
41 S. Bok, *Alva Myrdal*, Reading, Mass., Addison-Wesley, 1991, p. 119.
42 S. J. Lee, *The European Dictatorships*, London, Routledge, 1987.
43 H. Rose, op. cit., p. 488.
44 L. F. Haber, *The Poisonous Cloud: Chemical warfare in the first world war*, Oxford, Clarendon Press, 1986.
45 D. J. Kevles, *In the Name of Eugenics: Genetics and the uses of human heredity*, New York, Alfred A. Knopf, 1985, p. 49.
46 Beveridge, op. cit., pp. 378–9.
47 'Science searches its soul for the devil within', *Observer*, 19.2.95.
48 S. Chitty, *Now to My Mother*, London, Weidenfeld and Nicolson, 1985.
49 L. P. Hopkinson, *Nothing to Forgive*, London, Chatto and Windus, 1988, p. 11.
50 Chitty, op. cit., p. 161.
51 Ibid., p. 165.
52 J. Lacan, *Images de Mon Père*, Paris, 1991.
53 S. Lacan, *Un Père Puzzle*, Paris, Diagraphe, 1994.
54 J. Myrdal, *Childhood*, Chicago, Lake View Press, 1991; J. Myrdal, *Another World*, Chicago, Ravenswood Books, 1984.
55 Bok, op. cit.
56 J. Myrdal, *Childhood*, p. v.
57 Ibid., p. 57.
58 Ibid., p. 59.
59 J. Myrdal, *Another World*, pp. 192–3.
60 Ibid, p. 133.
61 J. Myrdal, *Childhood*, p. 115.
62 Bok, op. cit., p. 13.
63 Obituary of Mrs Alva Myrdal, *The Times*, 3.2.86.
64 Bok, op. cit., pp. 70–1.
65 Obituary of Professor Gunnar Myrdal, *The Times*, 19.5.87.
66 Bok. op. cit., p. 90.
67 R. Dahrendorf, *A History of the London School of Economics and Political Science 1895–1995*, Oxford, Oxford University Press, 1995, p. 385.
68 Winter, op. cit.

INDEX